The drawings of Van Gogh

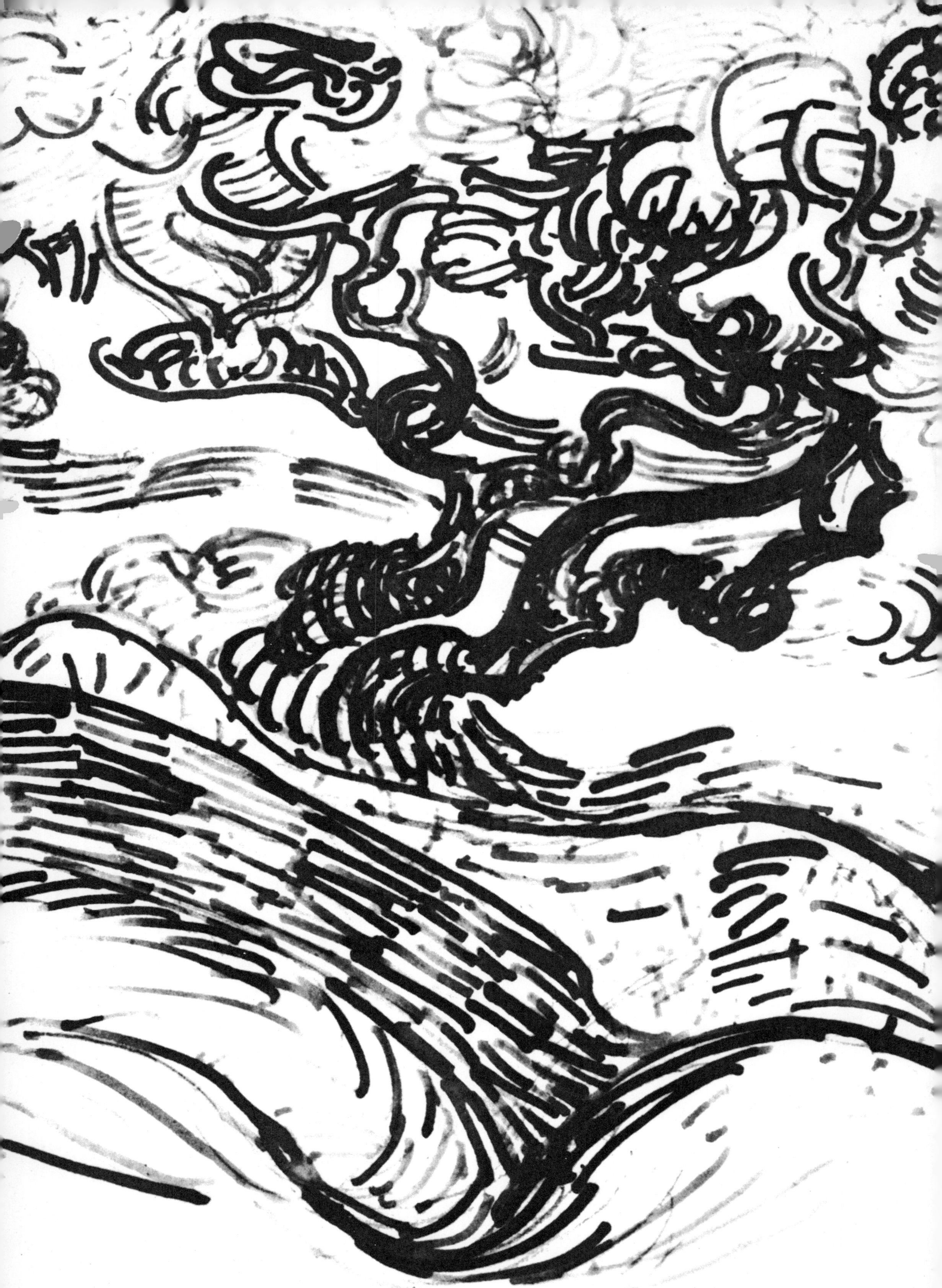

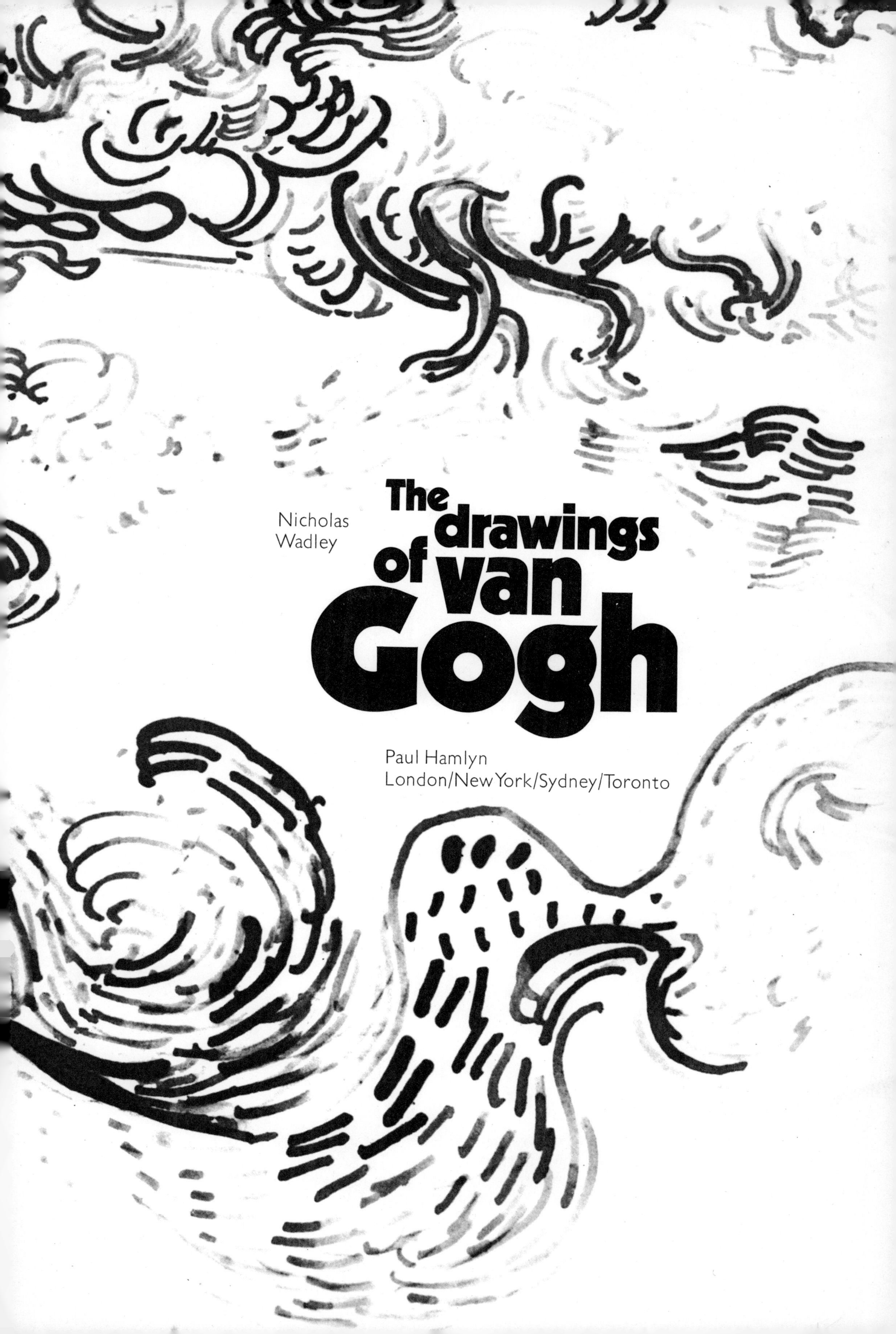

Nicholas
Wadley

The drawings of van Gogh

Paul Hamlyn
London/New York/Sydney/Toronto

Acknowledgements

The author wishes to express his thanks to Dr E. Meijer, Director of the Vincent van Gogh Foundation, Amsterdam and Mr Gilbert Lloyd of Marlborough Fine Art, London for their assistance in compiling this book. The drawings and paintings in this volume are reproduced by kind permission of the following collections and galleries to which they belong: Art Institute of Chicago. Bequest of Kate Brewster (Plate 128); Floris Bremmer Collection, The Hague (Plates 11, 28); Brooklyn Museum (Plate 106); E. G. Bührle Collection, Zürich (Plate 87a); Charles Clore Collection, London (Plate 65); Garman-Ryan Collection, London (Plate 32); Kunsthalle, Bremen (Plate 107); Kunstmuseum, Winterthur (Plate 97); Mr and Mrs Paul Mellon Collection (Plate 94); Musée du Louvre, Paris (Plate 86b); Museum Van Baaren, Utrecht (Plate 38); Museum of Fine Arts, Budapest (Plates 55, 90); Museum of Modern Art, New York. Abby Aldrich Rockefeller Bequest (Plate 88); Nasjonalgalleriet, Oslo (Plate 67); Mrs A. R. W. Nieuwenhuizen Segaar-Aarse Collection, The Hague (Plate 12); Philadelphia Museum of Art. The Samuel S. White III and Vera White Collection (Plate 91); Oskar Reinhart am Römerholz Collection, Winterthur (Plate 100); Georges Renand Collection, Paris (Plate 25); Rijksmuseum Kröller-Müller, Otterlo (Plates 1a, 1b, 4, 6, 7, 9, 13, 14, 15, 16, 17, 18, 19, 20, 21, 22, 24, 26, 27, 30, 31, 33, 34, 35, 37, 39, 41, 43, 44, 45, 46, 47, 48, 50, 51, 52, 54, 59, 63, 66, 68, 69, 76, 87b, 89, 98, 102, 132); Staatliche Graphische Sammlung, Munich (Plate 110); Staatliche Museen, Berlin (Plates 109, 111); Dr R. S. Steinmetz Collection. On loan to Haags Gemeentemuseum, The Hague (Plate 49); Thannhauser Foundation, New York (Plate 92); Vincent van Gogh Foundation, Amsterdam (Plates 2, 3, 5, 8, 10, 23, 29, 36, 40, 42, 53, 56, 57, 58, 60, 61, 62, 64, 70, 71, 72, 73, 74, 75, 77, 78, 79, 80, 81, 82, 83, 84, 85, 86a, 89, 93, 96, 99, 101, 103, 104, 105, 108, 112, 113, 114, 115, 116, 117, 118, 119, 120, 121, 122, 123, 124, 125, 126, 127, 129, 130, 131). Quotations from *The Complete Letters of Vincent van Gogh* are reproduced by kind permission of the New York Graphic Society, Greenwich, Connecticut, U.S.A. and Thames & Hudson Ltd., London.

Published by the Hamlyn Publishing Group Limited
London, New York, Sydney, Toronto
Hamlyn House, Feltham, Middlesex, England

Phototypeset by Yendall & Co Ltd, London
Printed by Continental Printing Company, Hong Kong

'I have bought myself a very beautiful book on anatomy,' Van Gogh wrote to his brother in the autumn of 1884. 'It was in fact very expensive, but it will be of use to me all my life, for it is very good. I have also what they use at the Ecole des Beaux-Arts, and what they use in Antwerp . . . The key to many things is the thorough knowledge of the human body, but it costs money to learn it. Besides, I am quite sure that colour, that chiaroscuro, that perspective, that tone and that drawing, in short, everything has fixed laws which one can and must study, and one who says, "Oh, one must know it all instinctively," takes it very easy indeed. If that were enough! But it isn't enough, for even if one knows it ever so much by instinct, that is just the reason to try ever so hard to pass from instinct to reason. That's what I think' (381)*. Vincent's brother Theo was the hapless recipient of all the painter's ideas, from the dogmatic pronouncement to the tentative suggestion. Very few of Theo's replies have survived, and yet the one-sided correspondence is remarkably complete. The replies were important more for keeping this channel of self-analysis alive than for their comment or criticism. In his letters Van Gogh spoke to himself, put his thoughts on paper. While he was living with Theo in Paris, from 1886-8, he wrote only five letters that survive: one to Theo on arrival, three to Theo while he was away in Holland and one to another painter. Living with Theo and in close contact with many other artists, he had ample outlets for his ideas. Nevertheless, the interesting suggestion that his painted self-portraits (which first appear in any quantity during these years in Paris) were a substitute means of self-investigation implies that what he needed and wanted as an artist, if unconsciously, was a relatively passive audience to be addressed from a position of isolation. His feelings of exhaustion at the end of the Paris period (his most strenuous in terms of direct personal contacts with artists) and the breakdown of his long-awaited 'partnership' with Gauguin less than a year later offer confirmation of this.

* Numbers given after quotations are reference numbers relating to *The Complete Letters of Vincent van Gogh*.

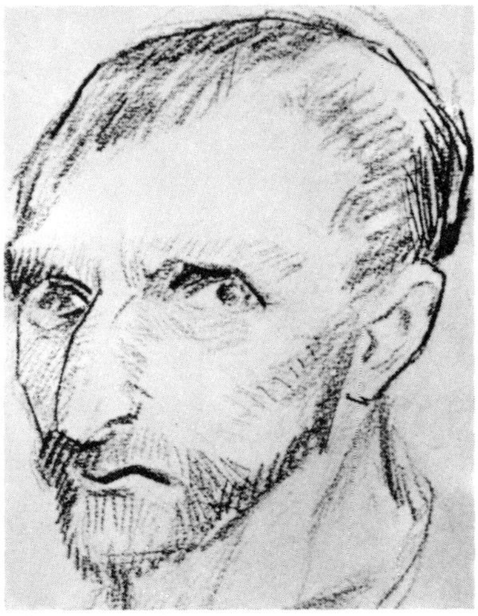

Detail of Plate 79

The tone of the 1884 letter is a stern corrective to those who might still subscribe to an 'uncontrolled genius' picture of Van Gogh, and his letters are full of such conviction. Until 1885-6 he was very much the thirsting novice, only too conscious of his own clumsy inadequacy and dedicated to the mastery of orthodox practices—the disciplines of anatomy, perspective and colour, the conventional techniques of the academies in Brussels, Antwerp and Paris. He felt uneducated and believed that with education his ideas would find full expression. Of the ideas to be expressed he never had any doubt: 'Poetry surrounds us everywhere but putting it on paper, is, alas, not as easy as looking at it.' His belief in drawing as the fundamental discipline of all art is absolute in the early years. Until his conversion to colour painting in Paris—in other words for half his short career as an artist—drawing is the whole basis of his art. His largely monochromatic painting of that period was an extension of his graphic ideas. Of the 800 or so drawings in the catalogue raisonné of his œuvre, over two thirds belong to the years up to 1885; of the 850 or so paintings over two thirds belong to the years 1888-90. After 1885, as this imbalance suggests, the relationship between his drawings and his paintings underwent a fundamental change.

Van Gogh's obsession with drawing media in the early years has a complex background. First of all—and this was particularly important because of his financial dependence on Theo—it was a lot cheaper in materials to draw than to paint. Secondly, his first ambition, founded on his admiration of English graphic artists, was to be an illustrator. Finally, a concern with drawing is a thoroughly conventional article of academic dogma, which, when one remembers his early awe of academic authority, probably influenced his attitude. He wrote to Theo in July 1882: 'When I see how several painters here whom I know, have problems with their watercolours and paintings, so that they cannot bring them off, I often think: friend, the fault lies in your drawing' (221). This verdict might well have been given by a graduate of the Ecole des Beaux-Arts. The comparative austerity of the graphic media seemed to him to offer a necessary technical discipline before exploring the complex luxuries of oil and colour. During an early excursion into painting, September 1882, he states this point clearly: 'You see I am absorbed with all my strength in painting . . . until now I have restrained myself, and I am not sorry for it. If I had not drawn so much, I would not be able to catch the impression of and get hold of a figure that looks like an unfinished clay figurine. But now I feel myself on the high sea . . .' (228). This buoyancy was premature and further periods of 'restraint' followed, but the principle remains.

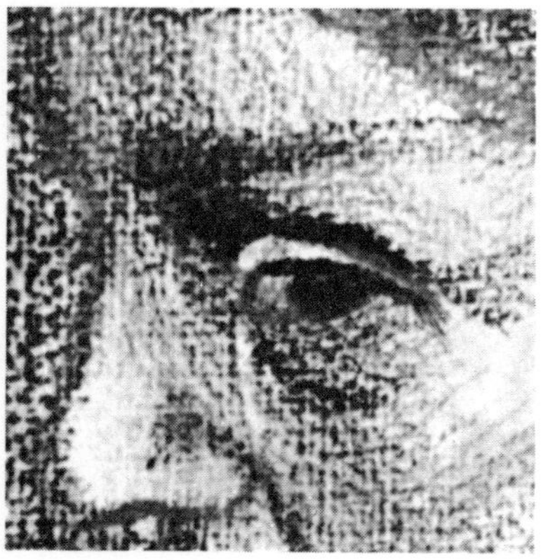

Detail of Plate 44

When one examines the range of his graphic media and realises his compulsive will to learn and experiment, 'restraint' seems the wrong word. He was meticulous about the papers he used for drawing. The inhibitions of his debt to Theo did not prevent him from stressing repeatedly in letters of 1882-3 the precise off-white colour ('no dead white, rather the colour of unbleached linen, no cold tones') and the weight of Ingres paper that he needed. He preferred to make up his own sketch-books from loose sheets of different papers and in general recognised the artist's obligation to know his materials intimately: 'You know that I am working on many different things, for I should so much like to know many different techniques . . . it stimulates one to work hard, and creates new ideas' (273). With other great draughtsmen of the late 19th century, Redon, Seurat and Degas, he shared a deep sympathy for the peculiar properties of his media. Listen to him selling the crayon to Theo: 'Will you do me a *very great* favour—send me a few pieces of that crayon by mail? There is a soul and life in that crayon—I think the conté pencil is dead. Two violins may look the same on the outside, but in playing them, one sometimes finds a beautiful tone in one, and not in the other. Now that crayon has a good deal of tone or depth. I could almost say that crayon knows what I want, it listens with intelligence and obeys; the conté pencil is indifferent and unwilling. The crayon has a real gypsy soul; if it isn't asking too much of you, send me some of it' (272). In the next letter he talks of combining it with sepia wash, of rubbing in breadcrumbs to achieve half-tones and of introducing lithographic crayon for the densest tones. His discovery of and experiments with a new medium are discussed not only in terms of technique, but also in terms of a whole new area of motifs that its properties suggest.

This marriage of technique to subject, of his expertise to his passion, demonstrates the homogeneity of Van Gogh as man and artist. His ambition was to make himself as complete an artist as possible without sacrificing any part of the faiths and beliefs that had prompted him to become an artist in the first place. This amounted to as great a discipline as any modern artist has imposed on himself. His drawings offer us the same sort of intimate testimony of this discipline as it evolved and was put into practice as do his letters. This is partly because such a large proportion of them belong to his tentative early years, but also because the personal immediate nature of drawing lets us come closer to the artist than the public face of a painting. Many of the drawings are illustrations to the letters, putting their ideas into visual terms for the benefit of Theo and sometimes of himself.

To Van Gogh art and literature were almost as one. He looked on them in the same light, discussed them in the same terminology. 'My God, how beautiful Shakespeare is!' he writes, 'Who is mysterious like him? His language and style can indeed be compared to an artist's brush, quivering with fever and emotion' (133). From the earliest letters he visualises situations in the novels he is reading in terms of paintings he knows. Later he also talks about his own paintings in terms of these novels, their moods, morals and images. In this sense his letters are a part of his art. They are often illuminated by the same lights of heightened perception and lyrical imagination.

Van Gogh's taste in literature ranged from embarrassingly sentimental trivia to the classics and the Bible. His central interest was probably his love of the great 19th-century novelists, both French and English. He was an avid reader. Dickens's Christmas stories were 'so profound that one must read them over and over again' and he read and re-read all of Balzac. He also singles out for repeated praise Zola, Hugo, de Maupassant ('to Zola as Vermeer is to Rembrandt'), Daudet, Loti and Michelet. This literary taste, in both its incongruous range and its specialisation, is directly comparable to his taste in art. 'The love of books is as sacred as the love of Rembrandt, and I even think the two complete each other.' He could compare a little-known Victorian illustrator favourably with his idol Rembrandt, although he fully recognised the different scale and quality of the artists. His yardstick was the degree of 'human sentiment'. His lack of prejudice and sophistication led him to appreciate the ideals he stood for at all levels of creativity or conduct. Reputation, style and fashion meant little to him in face of these values: art for art's sake and manners for society's sake were irrelevant trappings. For most of his life he could see himself at a low ebb in creative achievement and in social significance without losing faith in his values. It is in this light that we can best understand his sympathetic devotion to a prostitute. She represented life. Vincent measured art and literature by their credibility as reality (from the beautiful to the ugly), by their moral explanation of life, by their sympathy with human suffering. Craftsmanship was irrelevant when not geared to the expression of these values: he sometimes went out of his way to recognise such values in a work in order to justify its craftsmanship.

The roots of all the ideas discussed so far are to be found in Van Gogh's life story up to 1880, the year in which he resolved to become an artist. Son of a pastor and nephew of three art dealers, he was born in North Brabant in 1853. Accounts of his early childhood in a country parsonage vary. His own recollections range from the comment to Theo that 'My youth was sombre and cold and sterile under the influence of the *rayon noir*. And, brother, your youth really too' (347) to idyllic descriptions of the rural surroundings. Theo's wife Jo has written of a friendly, sociable and devoted atmosphere in the Van Gogh family in the early years, presumably describing Theo's own memories. Vincent is described as devoted to his father. He was, all agree, physically the strongest of six children and temperamentally the most difficult and moody. His early years in The Hague working for the firm of art dealers Goupil, in which his uncle was a partner, were an apparent success. In 1873 he moved to the London branch with a glowing testimonial. Within three years the picture was dramatically different. He had become withdrawn and melancholy and after several clashes with employers and clients at the Paris branch, 1875-6, he was dismissed in April 1876. The only outside event that seems to have had any bearing on his state of mind was his confession of love to Ursula Loyer, daughter of his London landlady, which was rejected absolutely. In Paris he became fanatically religious—his letters of the time are full of Biblical texts—and almost anti-social in his isolated way of life.

During the next four years Van Gogh made many frustrated attempts to establish personal relationships and to some extent the whole of his life was punctuated with similar failures—with women, with society, with artists. After dismissal from Goupil's, he became successively an assistant lay preacher at schools in England, bookshop assistant in Dordrecht, student of theology in Amsterdam, pupil at an Evangelical school in Brussels and finally lay preacher and missionary in the Borinage mining district of Belgium. Each phase of these disrupted years was characterised by determined ambition, an unorthodoxy that conflicted with established convention and an urgency that antagonised the authorities. Each ended in failure. In the Borinage he tried to submerge his social and personal identity into the workers' community. His passionate involvement made a deep impression on some of those around him and witnesses have recalled his extreme self-denial and his dramatic religious conversion of non-believers. The ecclesiastical authorities in Brussels considered his zeal 'excessive' and his way of life—he had abandoned his respectable lodgings and given away most of his clothes—as unfit to represent the church. In July 1879 he was dismissed from the position for which he considered himself most fit and to which he had given himself completely. At this stage his self-denial reached such an extreme that he felt he must sever connections even with his family.

In July 1880 he wrote to Theo from Cuesmes in Belgium: 'Involuntarily, I have become more or less a kind of impossible or suspect personage in the family, at least somebody whom they do not trust, so how could I in any way be of any use to anybody? Therefore, above all, I think the best and most reasonable thing for me to do is to go away and keep at a convenient distance, so that I cease to exist for you all.

'As moulting time—when they change their feathers—is for birds, so adversity or misfortune is the difficult time for us human beings. One can stay in it—in that time of moulting—one can also emerge renewed; but anyhow it must not be done in public and it is not at all amusing, therefore the only thing to do is to hide oneself. Well, so be it' (133). Later in the same letter, very long and self-questioning, he analyses his recent past, his present situation and his possible future. Among all his letters it must rank as a major soliloquy: it expresses the state of mind in which his career as an artist began. He confesses his love of art and literature, justifying them as related expressions of God. ('There is something of Rembrandt in Shakespeare, and of Correggio in Michelet, and of Delacroix in Victor Hugo, and then there is something of Rembrandt in the Gospel, or something of the Gospel in Rembrandt, as you like it—it comes to the same.') The contemplation that they promote, he tells Theo, 'unconsciously raises your thoughts above the ordinary level'. His own failure and inactivity he tries to explain as a period of contemplation from which he might rise to something worthwhile.

His situation at the time was that of 'the idle man who is idle in spite of himself, who is inwardly consumed by a great longing for action but does nothing, because it is impossible for him to do anything, because he seems to be imprisoned in some cage, because he does not possess what he needs to become productive, because circumstances bring him inevitably to that point. Such a man does not always know what he could do, but instinctively he feels, I am good for something, my life has a purpose after all, I know that I could be quite a different man! How can I be useful, of what service can I be? There is something inside of me, what can it be? . . . A caged bird in spring knows quite well that he might serve some end; he is well aware that there is something for him to do, but he cannot do it. What is it? He does not quite remember. Then some vague ideas occur to him, and he says to himself, "The others build their nests and lay their eggs and bring up their little ones"; and he knocks his head against the bars of the cage. But the cage remains, and the bird is maddened by anguish. "Look at that lazy animal," says another bird in passing, "He seems to be living at ease." Yes, the prisoner lives, he does not die; there are no outward signs of what passes within him—his health is good, he is more or less gay when the sun shines. But the season of migration comes, and attacks of melancholia—"But he has everything he wants," say the children that tend him in his cage. He looks through the bars at the overcast sky where a thunderstorm is gathering, and inwardly he rebels against his fate. "I am caged, I am caged, and you tell me I do not want anything, fools! You think I have everything I need! Oh! I beseech you liberty, that I may be a bird like other birds!" A certain idle man resembles this idle bird' (133).

Van Gogh the evangelist concentrates his energies on his own condition, with Theo involved as a witness: here the character of the letters is epitomised. At the same time his repeated recognition of the artist as a spiritually enlightened thinker is the foundation of his decision to devote his life to art: '. . . it is with evangelists as with artists'. He compares the development of a mission to the passage from rough draft, to sketch, to picture. He turned to art *as* an evangelist. The orthodox channels of evangelism had been tried and found closed or overgrown with unacceptable inhibitions. 'Why I have been out of employment for years is simply that I have other ideas than the gentlemen who give places to men who

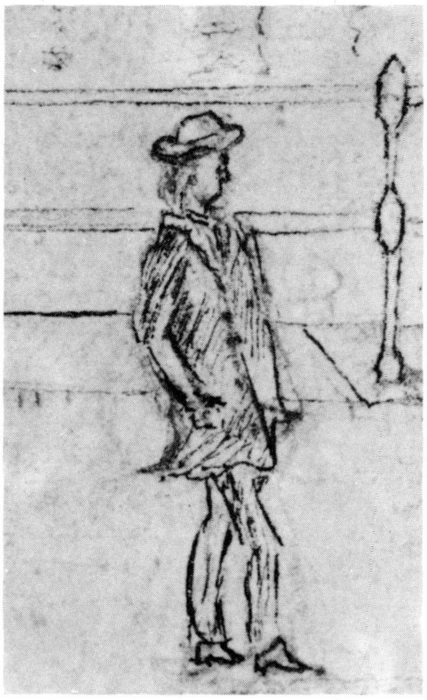

Detail of Plate 2

think like they do. It is not merely a question of the dress over which they have hypocritically reproached me, it is a much more serious question, I assure you.' His enrolment for classes in anatomy and perspective in Brussels (October 1880) was a necessary alternative to his intended enrolment in the Amsterdam Theological Seminary three years earlier. His first ambition was to be a draughtsman of the people: the next five years were spent in equipping himself for that role.

The earliest of Van Gogh's drawings to survive—from the age of eight—are conventionally accomplished. They are mostly copies (Plates 1a and 1b) and show a natural and precocious facility for assimilation and execution. The next phase of drawings is more complex. It embraces some studies from nature that retain the technical sensitivity of the *Bridge* study and others in which there is a painful groping to record his observations. The awkward figure walking past a pond in The Hague (Plate 2)—possibly his first self-portrait—might almost have come from the artless pages of the Grossmiths' *Diary of a Nobody*. Nevertheless the difficult and graceless passage of the branches overhead from straight line to looping curve has a naïve integrity. In the Ramsgate drawings (Plate 4) this freedom from convention has acquired the uninhibited assurance of the true primitive—a reliance on emphatic contours and an equal disposition of focus and detail throughout the motif. After this there is a break in his drawings. The reduction of this absorbing and habitual activity was just one aspect of the depressed withdrawal of the mid-70s. It was one of the self-indulgences of life that he felt obliged to live without. 'He has even stopped drawing', his parents wrote.

The number of modern artists who have expressed or demonstrated the desire to be 'as a newborn' or 'a savage', to 'unlearn', to 'see as if for the first time', and so on, must run into several figures. In 1876 Van Gogh *had* this immediacy of vision; he had even unlearnt his few adolescent tricks. In practice he always retained his heightened perception. He always believed in forceful expression as a primary objective and quoted Millet's words: 'I would rather say nothing than express myself feebly.' But Van Gogh's case is a remarkable inversion of the modern envy of a primitive state. In 1880, when he took up drawing seriously, he lamented his lack of sophistication in an acute envy of the conventionally trained. It took him all of five years to be grateful for his freedom, to relax and realise fully that 'I should be desperate if my figures were correct'. And what price his beautiful anatomy book then?

For all the frustration of his inability, drawing did very quickly offer him a sense of release from his cage of inactivity and he no longer saw life as 'the great university of misery'. Earlier drawing had seemed a potential distraction from his true vocation, but in December 1881 he writes 'Just think how I have been struggling along for years in a kind of false position. And now—now comes a dawn of real light' (164). Through his drawing he felt at least that he could realise his role as 'a friend of the poor'. The essential difference between this activity and any of his previous occupations was, paradoxically, that he could now express himself in a vacuum. While he was drawing he was responsible to no one but himself, and the chief beneficiary of his artistic activity was undoubtedly himself. Up to a point this remains true for most of his career. Admittedly he unsealed the vacuum for contact with other artists—van Rappard, Mauve, the Impressionists and others in Paris, Gauguin, Bernard—but in each case gratefully withdrew into the world of his own ideas again afterwards. It is true too that he was open to Theo. But then Theo was so closely committed to Vincent financially, emotionally and ideologically, that their personalities almost merge. The deliberate use of his Christian name as a signature, which Vincent explained as being more easily remembered than 'Van Gogh', lends a final seal of intimacy to his activity as an artist.

Van Gogh's decision to use art as a means of serving humanity at large presupposed that his art would have an audience. His defence of his own work was at its most passionate when its suitability for public exhibition was challenged. But, particularly in the early years, actual contact with his audience seems to belong to a distant future. The 'message' quality of his early art and its powerful comment on social injustice and so on, is mingled with a strong autobiographical element, an enclosed and intimate self-documentation. The extreme self-sacrifice that his career as an artist involved—and which he accepted more or less unquestioningly from the outset—was undertaken with a long-term mission for society in mind. Later he talks principally of creating a long-term investment on behalf of succeeding generations of painters.

On the other hand he *was* interested in the mass-circulation of graphic media and more than once became excited about the possible function of the reproduction as a means of reaching a wide, popular audience. The only really practical proposition that he discussed with Theo in the early years was in the field of illustration. Theo appears to have told him of the demand from illustrated papers for drawings of 'current events'. Optimistic that the editors would share his interpretation of the term, Vincent envisaged himself supplying 'scenes from the daily life of people'. While in England he had developed an admiration for the Victorian illustrators of topical social scenes—pictorial journalists whose realistic images were overlaid with a moralising pathos. Around 1882 he was busy collecting their lithographs and woodcuts: Fyldes, Millais, Holl and Herkomer he singles out for frequent mention. He found the same interest and inspiration in his national school—particularly Israëls—and it is the same monumental sympathetic statement of the working man that drew him to Millet. Millet's vision of the worker as the true celebration of nature, life and God was probably the most important single influence on Van Gogh. Not only did he draw many subjects and motifs from the vast library of prints by and after Millet that he collected during his life, but Millet's work embodied in a remarkably complete form Van Gogh's own instincts about art and life. Quotations from Sensier's biography of Millet acquire in the letters the authority of a Biblical text, particularly in the later years.

This sort of art represented not so much the greatest achievement as the most right-minded achievement by artists of any period—and his knowledge of earlier periods was not negligible. 'For me one of the highest and noblest expressions is always that of the English, for instance Millais and Herkomer and Frank Holl. What I mean in regard to the difference between the old masters and the modern ones is—perhaps the modern ones are deeper thinkers . . . Ruysdael and Rembrandt are sublime . . . but there is something in the modern painters that appeals to us more personally and intimately' (218). And again, in November 1882: 'Up to Millet and Jules Breton, however, there was always in my opinion progress; but to surpass these two—don't even mention it . . . Israëls, for instance, may equal Millet, but among genii superiority or inferiority is out of the question. Now in the realm of art a summit has been reached . . . Since Millet we have greatly deteriorated' (241). At this stage he extended his own feeling of inadequacy to his whole generation. He even talks of his fear that 'perhaps in a few years there will be a kind of panic in this regard.' He saw no real alternative to the sort of art he was committed to. The comparative lack of direction he felt in his own time lent urgency to his later ambitions for 'the new art' and his talk of 'a renaissance'. What is more the foundations of this 'new art' were certainly to be sought among the older generation: the sentiments of Millet and Israëls, the techniques of Delacroix and Monticelli.

This was the theoretical and philosophical background to the drawings of 1880-5. His working environment during these years was for the most part among 'scenes from the daily life of the people' and this by choice. After a few months at the Brussels Academy, where he met the painter Ridder van Rappard, he spent most of 1881 with his family in Etten. Here he still made copies from old master drawings (Plate 11) and after Millet and his other figure studies include transcriptions of family photographs. They preserve his early competence to achieve a likeness without much technical difficulty. The quality and technique of his landscape studies is more varied: working without a ready-formulated two-dimensional form of the motif, he naturally experienced more complex problems. His style vacillates between a primitive toughness and a more orthodox refinement (see Plates 13, 14 and 15). This stylistic ambivalence increased considerably during the last four months at Etten. Late in August 1881 he spent four days in The Hague and made his first contact with the painter Anton Mauve, a relative of his mother.

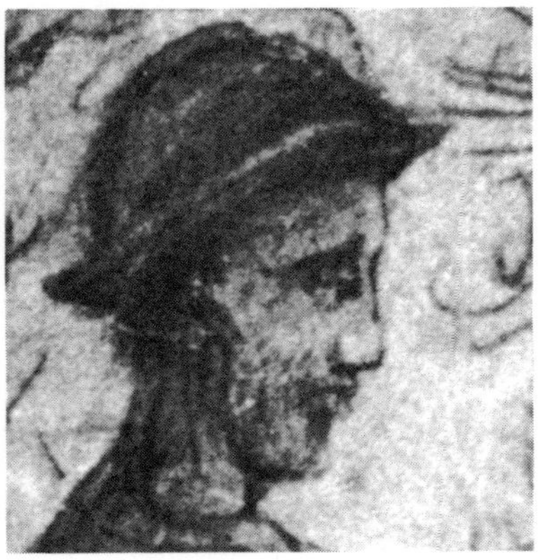

Detail of Plate 6

Mauve and Van Rappard (with whom Vincent corresponded until 1885) were the two artists whose personal advice and criticism made most impact on him in the pre-Paris years. Mauve on this occasion advised him to concentrate more on drawing the figure from life. He writes to Theo in September: 'My drawing has changed, the technique as well as the results. Also, as a result of some things Mauve told me, I have begun to work from the live model . . . Studying the *Exercices au Fusain* by Bargue [*Exercises with Charcoal*, a drawing textbook] carefully and copying them over and over again have given me a better insight into drawing the figure. I have learned to measure and to observe and to seek for broad lines' (150). His faith in elementary primers was unshakeable: he copies not a few but all of the plates, not once but repeatedly.

In the first ambitious series of figure studies started in September 1881, the range of techniques and of mastery is wide. Compared with the moving compositions of *Miners* and *Miners' Wives* of 1880 (Plates 6 and 7)—naïve perhaps, but consistent in vision and technique—the Etten studies betray the strain of education. The stiff movement, odd proportion and self-conscious attention to irrelevant detail are attributes not so much of the true *naïf* draughtsman as of the *naïf* struggling to be conventional. The unequivocal central placing of the figure, as well as being a mark of the primitive, also suggests the house-training of teach-yourself books. Within these inhibitions and the unpredictable variety of the execution, there are considerable strengths. Such moments as the complete understanding with which he saw and drew the active hands of an old woman sewing (Plate 18) stand out. So do a few sharp characterisations. But for the most part the poses are passive and formal, and when active, clearly contrived. Typical examples are the carpenter (Plate 17) and the man planting (Plate 19) with their tendency towards profile and the model's frozen attention to the occupation in hand.

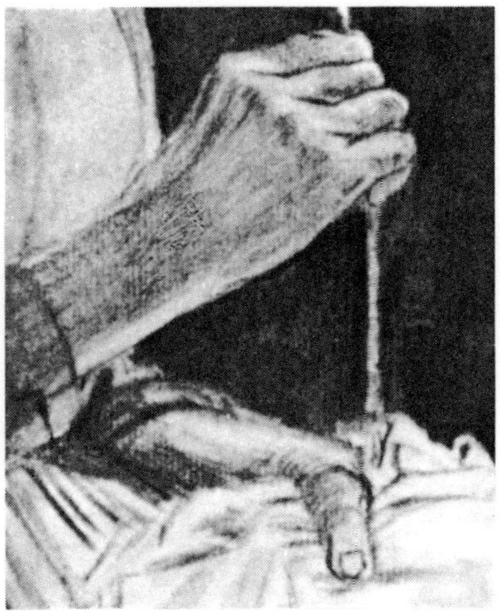

Detail of Plate 18

The stay in Etten ended after another disastrously unreciprocated love of Van Gogh's, this time for his young widowed cousin Kee Vos. This was family embarrassment enough, but heated arguments with his father about religion brought even intimate family relationships to their lowest ebb. In December 1881 he was asked to leave the house. The disagreement with his father was almost predictable. It was probably Vincent's humble and total respect for his father's contented devotion to the priesthood that had directed his own ambition towards the Church as a vocation. Vincent's bitter experience at the hands of the clergy as employers and administrators necessarily compromised his feelings about his father's position. Frequently, in post-Etten letters to Theo, he sees their father's contentment more as an unquestioning lack of ambition and finds difficulty in reconciling it with his own experience of Church authority. '. . . In the Bible I see quite different things than Father does, and what Father draws from it in his academic way I cannot find at all.' Nevertheless, after two years in The Hague, Vincent went back to live with the family in his father's new parish at Nuenen.

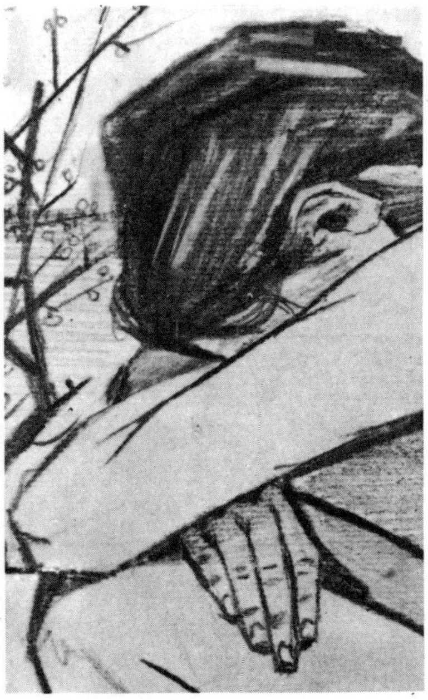

Detail of Plate 32

In The Hague Van Gogh tackled the problem of perspective with characteristic determination (Plates 24-29); but above all this period saw the rapid maturity of his drawing from the figure. His technique gained self-possession and an individual positiveness. The drawings of pensioners —great black monuments in charcoal—prefigure the colossal peasants of Nuenen and are just as animated with character-study. In *Sorrow* (Plate 32) he produced one of the greatest nude drawings of his century.

Without knowing its immediate context or its place in his œuvre, even the casual observer of the drawings must realise that there is something particularly significant about *Sorrow*. Its drawn frame, the English title (a homage to Victorian illustrators), the text from Michelet below and the contrived landscape setting all suggest a symbolic set-piece. The drawing of the figure, taut and angular like the branches, has an expressive strength that is scarcely credible in a drawing made only a few months after the Etten studies. The tight contour, as economic and as powerful as Brueghel's, is the touch of a master draughtsman. Vincent spoke of its 'rather dry technique'. The control of the line and the absence of shading are perfectly geared to the subject, with a maturity not predicted in his earlier work and unparalleled at this period. In none of his other studies of the same sitter does he use quite the same technique or achieve the same power of expression.

The model was a prostitute known as Christine or Sien, with whom Vincent lived for most of his stay in The Hague. This relationship, although as hopeless in the long run as the others, held great meaning for him. Of all his drawings of her, *Sorrow* epitomises his quest for homogeneity between art and life. He wrote to Van Rappard: 'I never had such a good assistant as this ugly (???), faded woman. In my eyes she is beautiful, and I find in her exactly what I want; her life has been rough, and sorrow and adversity have left their marks upon her—now I can get something from her' (R8). In his lengthy justifications of the liaison to Theo (who thoroughly disapproved) it is also clear that both his anti-clericalism and his wounded feelings about Kee Vos's rejection of him ('I had not forgotten another woman for whom my heart was beating, but she was far away and refused to see me') lent fuel to his enthusiasm for Christine. Thus 'When you wake up in the morning and find yourself not alone, but see there in the morning twilight a fellow creature beside you, it makes the world look so much more friendly. Much more friendly than religious diaries and white-washed church walls, with which clergymen are in love . . .' and '. . . she [Kee] never realises, I fear, that God perhaps really begins when we say the word with which Multatuli finishes his Prayer of an Unbeliever: "O God, there is no God!" For me that God of the clergymen is as dead as a doornail. But am I an atheist for all that? The clergymen consider me so—so be it—but I love, and how could I feel love if I did not live and others did not live; and then if we live, there is something mysterious in that . . . that is God, or as good as God' (164).

His wish to identify with the most unfortunate levels of life—already demonstrated in the Borinage—and his talk of prostitutes as 'my sisters, in circumstance and experience' is strongly reminiscent of the 19th-century English view of fallen women, pitiable victims of life but potentially (through neighbourly salvation) life's richest expression. The following could almost be the text to a Pre-Raphaelite painting: 'a woman must not be alone in society and at a time like that in which we live, which does not spare the weak but treads them under foot, and drives over a weak woman because she has fallen down. Therefore, because I see so many weak ones trodden down, I greatly doubt the sincerity of much that is called progress and civilisation. I do believe in civilisation, even in a time like this, but only in the kind that is founded on real humanity' (197).

This humanitarian sense of self-sacrifice which replaced his earlier religious feelings—completely orthodox except in their intensity—remained the motive force behind his art until he reached Paris. At The Hague he drew the inmates of almshouses and soup kitchens. In these studies and in the more ambitious compositions of 1882—the *State Lottery* (Plate 40), *Women Carrying Coal* (Plate 41)—there is implicit comment on social injustice. *The Church* (Plate 34), a strange montage of assorted heads, has a touch of Hogarthian satire. Of the impressive landscape drawing *Roots* (Plate 33) he wrote: 'I tried to put the same sentiment into the landscape as I put into the figure [Sorrow]: the convulsive, passionate clinging to the earth, and yet being half torn up by the storm. I wanted to express

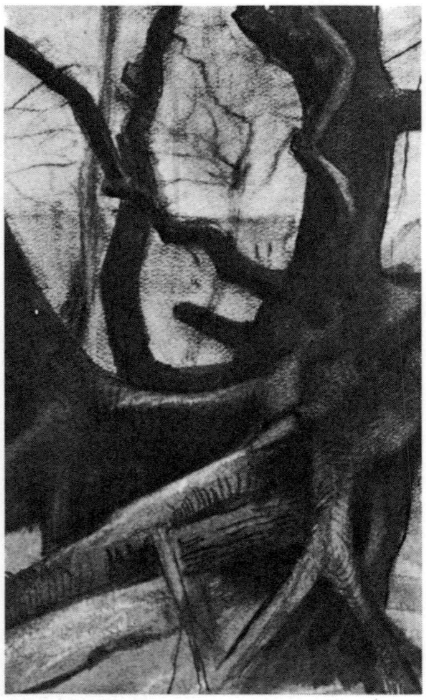

Detail of Plate 33

something of the struggle for life in that pale, slender woman's body, as well as in the black, gnarled and knotty roots. Or rather, because I tried to be faithful to nature as I saw it, without philosophising about it, involuntarily in both cases something of that great struggle is shown' (195). This last sentiment, that the artist's recognition of truth involved involuntary feelings as much as objective vision, he could only accept with some difficulty in the early years. It was to become the essential philosophy behind his mature art.

If there were few landscapes from The Hague period, the three months at Drenthe (September-December 1883) were spent on little else. Although his first comments include delight that 'the men here wear short breeches, which show the shape of the leg and make the movements more expressive', his overriding absorption was with the poetic melancholy of vast stretches of heathland. The optimism of his letters and their sometimes rapturous descriptions are clouded only by his self-reproach about leaving Christine and her children in The Hague. What is significant about his descriptions of the Drenthe landscape is their increasing preoccupation with colour as an expression of mood. In a number of the Hague drawings he used colour in a more spirited manner, independently of the tonal composition. In Drenthe he began to state clearly for the first time: 'I am drawing, but you know quite well that painting must be the main thing, as much as possible.' His charcoal drawings of the peat bogs and moss-covered cottages (Plates 50, 51) are painterly and atmospheric: line plays a minimal role. Soft passages of dense tone evoke the slow sadness of the heathland. This technique was only used to this effect in Drenthe and in a few urban studies in Antwerp and Paris. It offers a total contrast to the jagged pen drawings of the Nuenen landscape two years later. After this renewed preoccupation with the concerns of painting—and he even suggested that Theo might resolve his own problems by taking up painting at this point—it was at Nuenen (December 1883 to November 1885) that Van Gogh realised his first ambition to be a 'draughtsman of the people'.

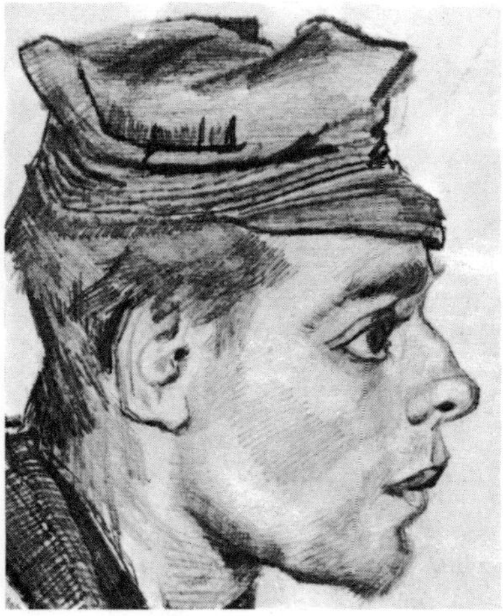

Detail of Plate 58

The great *Weavers* series of 1884 and the heroic *Gleaners* of 1885 reconciled evangelical passion with art with the maturity that brought his Dutch period to its climax. The figures have a more timeless monumentality than the pensioners of The Hague. There are some remarkable portrait-like heads (Plate 58). These are part of his project for a series of painted 'Heads of the People'. He talks of plans for more than fifty heads in his letters, but in the event he only painted about thirty-five and his idea of reproducing them as a series never materialised. The Nuenen studies are a complete pictorial embodiment of his ideals rather than self-conscious illustrations of them. A liking for the quaint and picturesque that softens earlier figure drawings is gone: no extraneous detail dilutes his single-minded intention. What is more, the strength of his draughtsmanship could now carry it consistently: dense areas of tonal hatching are completely reconciled to his tough linear drawing. His sense of structure is confident and expressive. But the individuality of the sitters is relatively insignificant. This is true of the figure's place in all of Van Gogh's art. Man's occupation and social position are important attributes, but his pictorial role is that of a symbolic emblem. Gesture and facial expression are seldom used: when they do appear (Plates 62 and 64) they surprise us. Portrait faces are passive or, if articulate, enigmatic. The most expressive poses (*Sorrow*, Plate 32) are intensely pathetic by virtue of their enclosed and inert condition. There is little facial expression, no extrovert gesture. He had little sympathy with Baroque rhetoric: 'Nothing touches me less than Rubens expressing human sorrow' (444). The early miners, the Nuenen weavers and the sowers and reapers of all periods are, as figures, undramatic transcriptions of men going about their various occupations. Their real significance only derives from the context of Van Gogh's romantic idealism, and later from the context of his colour symbolism.

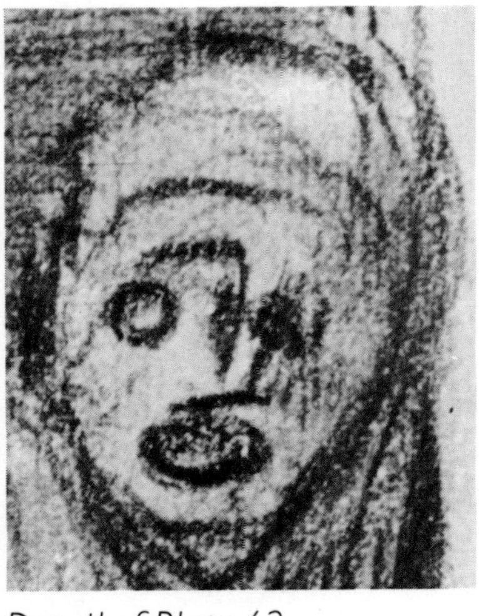

Detail of Plate 62

Although its final statement was made in a painting—*The Potato Eaters* of 1885 (Plate 63)—this first career was essentially that of a draughtsman.

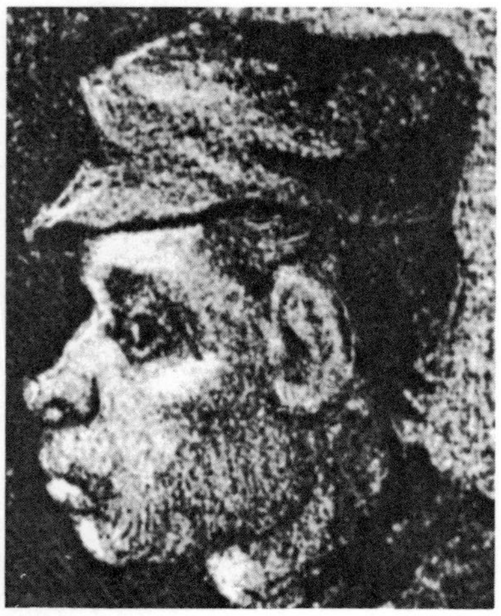

Detail of Plate 63

The context of this painting is a consummation of his early drawings. 'I have tried to emphasise that those people, eating their potatoes in the lamplight, have dug the earth with those very hands they put in the dish, and so it speaks of manual labour, and how they have honestly earned their food. I have wanted to give the impression of a way of life quite different from that of us civilised people. Therefore I am not at all anxious for everyone to like it or admire it at once. All winter long I have had the threads of this tissue in my hands, and have searched for the ultimate pattern . . . it might prove to be a real peasant picture . . . such pictures may teach [city] people something' (404).

The Potato Eaters was then a composite tissue, its threads being the great charcoal drawings of Nuenen peasants. As a painting it marks the painful start to his second career. After the incisiveness of the studies, themselves unconventional enough, the clumsy brushwork has a gauche quality absent from the drawings since Etten (Plate 86a). It was in response to a criticism of this painting that he delivered an impassioned defence of 'imperfection' and 'distortion' in art. After comparing the correctness of academic life drawing to the arbitrary proportions by which Daumier made his figures 'live', he concludes: 'Tell Serret that *I should be desperate if my figures were correct,* tell him that if one photographs a digger *he would certainly not be digging then.* Tell him that I adore the figures by Michelangelo though the legs are undoubtedly too long, the hips and the backsides too large. Tell him that, for me, Millet and Lhermitte are the real artists, for the very reason that they do not paint things as they are, traced in a dry analytical way, but as *they*—Millet, Lhermitte, Michelangelo—feel them. Tell him that my great longing is to learn to make those very incorrectnesses, those deviations, remodellings, changes of reality, so that they may become, yes, untruth if you like—but more true than the literal truth' (418).

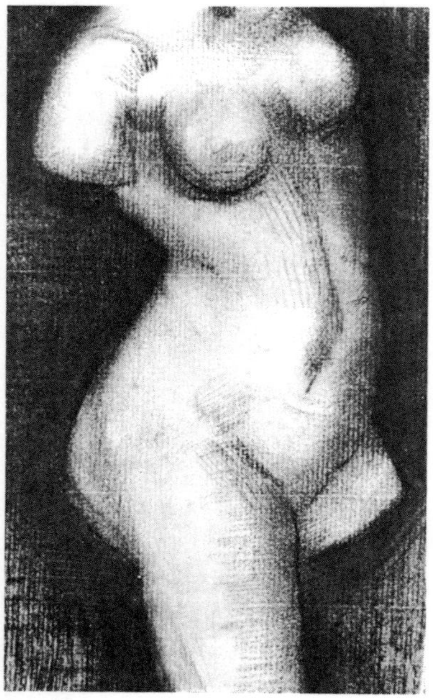

Detail of Plate 70

Like Degas and Seurat, Van Gogh was a traditionalist. Like them he proposed the principles for a vital modern academy. His great longing to learn took him next to Antwerp, 1885-6, and in February 1886 to Paris. In Antwerp he attended painting and drawing classes at the Academy; in Paris he studied at the Ecole des Beaux-Arts. The figure studies of these years embrace the most bizarre range of styles of his whole career (Plate 70ff). His highly formed personal technique was bastardised this time by studio tricks of hatching and shading. The grotesque confrontation of the 'draughtsman of the people' and an antique cast is epitomised in his reported comment on the Venus de Milo—'fine female, nice hips'. One of Mauve's tips to him in 1881 had been to stand further back from the motif. In all of these drawings there is something of his urgent, 'on-top-of-the-model' aggression, both intimate and attacking. A fellow student in Antwerp recalls him rounding on a critical tutor, enraged, 'So you don't know what a young woman is like, God damn you! A woman must have hips and buttocks and a pelvis in which she can hold a child.'

The two years in Paris were a turning point in his career. Exposure to city life, the Louvre, the dealers' galleries, Japanese art and the talk of painters inspired exhilaration and conflict in his mind. When he escaped to seclusion in Arles in February 1888, he experienced a sense of relief that he could return to his earlier ideas. But by that time he was a very different artist.

In Paris he was infected by the city's art-for-art's-sake mood. In his drawings in Antwerp and Paris the decline of his 'evangelism through art' is explicit. Some of his street scenes evoke a Seurat-like vision of metropolitan melancholy (Plate 72) and there are a few Zola-like comments on urban life (Plate 75). But for the most part the figure is a completely objective device, no longer the embodiment of a philosophical ideal. A study after Michelangelo nudges shoulders with a café interior (Plate 77). In his paintings he responded to the sophisticated techniques of Seurat and the Japanese; in his pastels he toyed with the snapshot composition and broken colour of the Impressionists. He emerged as a painter and a colourist. In the works of 1888-90, the vast output on which his reputation as a painter stands, colour became his principal vehicle of expression. His feelings for the figure and the landscape were expressed through the deliberate means of his mastery of painting. His philosophical ideals were expressed by his use of analogy and symbol—very self-conscious at first but becoming increasingly intuitive—more than by the passionately immediate transcription of his peasant drawings.

With this change drawing took on a new dual role in his art. Previously it had provided the vision and the structure of his painting. Now his vision was coloured, and colour-structure was the foundation of his painting. In a letter of 1883 he had envisaged a type of painting without drawing, when describing two oil sketches '. . . . a kind of life is in the figure, though it is nothing but a few patches of colour—it's not summoned by the correctness of the drawing, for there is practically no drawing. What I mean to suggest is that in these studies I believe there is something of that mysteriousness one gets by looking at nature through the eyelashes, so that the outlines are simplified to blots of colour' (309). This hesitant suggestion was given strength by the painting he saw in Paris. His own mature paintings are built out of a post-Impressionist fabric of colour-marks. In these last years his drawing becomes an almost separate, self-sufficient activity. But there is a remarkable conversation between the two media, a mutual feeding of technique and devices to be absorbed and transformed from one to the other.

The influence of Japanese prints made a major contribution to his second career. In Antwerp he had decorated his room with 'a lot of little Japanese prints on the wall, which amuse me very much. You know those little women's figures in gardens, or on the beach, horsemen, flowers, knotty thorn branches' (437). At this stage his interest was identifiable with the contemporary usage of the term *Japonaiserie*. He used the word repeatedly to describe the bizarre silhouettes and sky-lines of the Antwerp docks, the eccentric characters, things picturesque, things in constant movement ('the queerest surroundings, everything fantastic, and at all instants interesting contrasts present themselves'). In Paris and Arles his interest became more than a diversion. In Paris he painted copies of several Japanese prints (Plate 84). The prints he showed most interest in were those by Hokusai and Hiroshige, more luxuriant in colour and pattern than the austerely disciplined works of Utamaro that appealed to Manet and others. In Arles, where they also hung on his wall, he used the phrase 'it was pure Hokusai' as his highest expression of praise in describing the landscape or the people. Their exotic colour scale was obviously important to him and so was the fact that these prints were a form of popular art, made by the artist-craftsmen and available in some quantity. Above all he admired the economy and precision of their draughtsmanship: 'Their work is as simple as breathing and they do a figure in a few sure strokes. . . . I must manage to do a figure in a few strokes' (542).

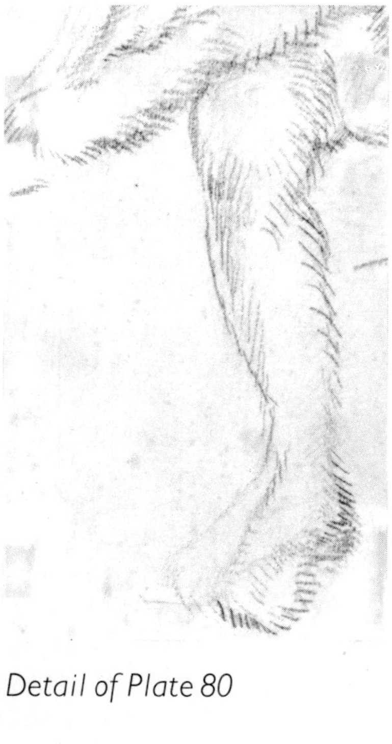

Detail of Plate 80

Clearly, Japanese influence contributed to his painting style, in which saturated colour areas replaced a structural use of tonal drawing. More significantly, it was a main source for the highly refined calligraphic style of drawing that he developed in Arles in the spring and summer of 1888. The dramatic diagonal and vertical types of composition (Plates 88 and 98) that he used extensively in Arles are a direct reflection. So too is their ornamental diversity of mark. Another source for his Arles drawing style lies in his own Impressionist-influenced paintings of 1886-7. In several of the Paris figure drawings (Plates 78, 80 and 81) he articulated the figure not so much by the strong contour of The Hague or the vigorous structure of Nuenen as by a series of short, light strokes laid side by side, more or less at right angles to the contour. This jerky hatching is a direct borrowing from Parisian painting techniques, the pencil behaving like a brush. This idea of a drawing compiled of separate, discontinuous strokes—and many Paris sketches are drawn entirely in this angular shorthand—anticipates the early Arles drawings.

In Arles he used the reed pen extensively, in a characteristically thorough emulation of the Japanese draughtsmen. The first few months there demonstrated his extraordinary ability to assess a medium's potential and then extend it to new extremes. In the early stages he obviously relished the varying breadths of line he could now obtain with a reed pen and its capacity for flourish. Unfamiliarity also produced unresolved marks. The famous Saintes-Maries study (Plate 88) demonstrates this. The aggressive calligraphy of the foreground suddenly weakens into the out-of-character desultoriness of the smoke spirals and uppermost foliage. He rapidly found ways to maintain the pitch of expressive animation throughout the surface without losing its range of contrast. Sometimes he combined the reed pen with a fine nib or with pencil to extend the scale of the line's tone and width. Very often he used more than one size of reed pen in the same drawing.

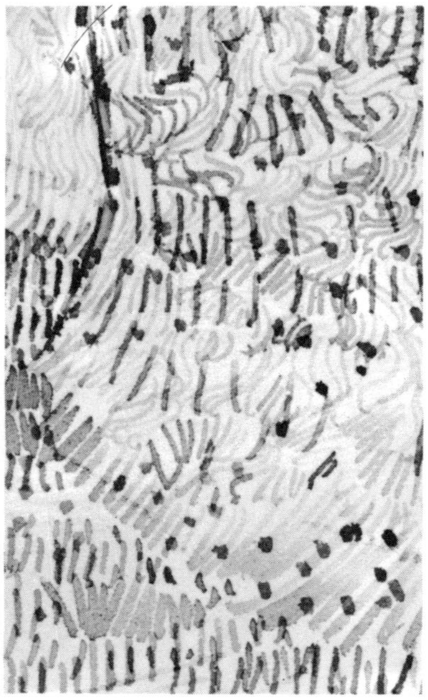

Detail of Plate 91

In the *Haystacks* drawings (Plates 90 and 91) and in the elaborate studies of the landscape around Montmajour that he made in July 1888 (Plates 93-95), the style reached its full development. Intricately schematic, it exploits a wide scale of marks as powerful as the painter's palette. The detail is exquisitely worked and the whole technique is clearly as consciously evolved as his developed colour theory. Of the palette he had written 'I retain from nature a certain sequence . . . however I don't mind so much whether my colour corresponds exactly, as long as it looks . . . as beautiful as it looks in nature.' So here the nature of each mark does not necessarily bear a precise correspondence to the motif in shape, scale or direction. But the whole formal harmony corresponds to a vision of the motif. The whole surface is articulated. There is no clear-cut distinction between positives and negatives and very often the sky is knit into the composition by finely graded stippling. Nevertheless, as well as being richly decorative façades, these studies evoke strong sensations of luminosity and atmosphere and sometimes even of colour. They also convey something of that exotic and savage presence that Van Gogh recognised in the Mediterranean landscape, the exotic South in which 'I feel as though I were in Japan'.

The spectacular invention of his repertoire of spikes, dots, plumes, arabesques and brutal hatching was at its height in the Arles months. The evolution of this rich sign language coincided exactly with the dazzling extension of his palette. The two media were alternative vehicles, equally original. The subtle relationship of colour sequences that holds his paintings together is paralleled in the drawings by a complex network of contrasts and analogies of form and texture. 1888 was the year of his greatest achievement. The scope of his art had been enormously widened by the influences of Paris. Now he was able to digest them and reconcile them to his basic ideas. In Arles the renewed solitude and the stimulating new environment combined to lift his painting and drawing on to a different level of activity.

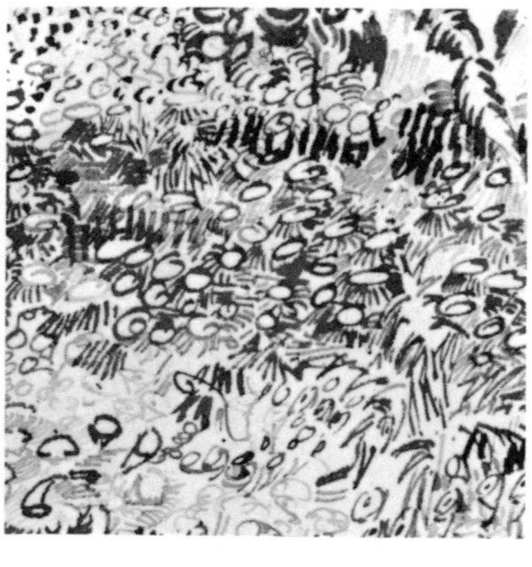

Detail of Plate 100

At this peak in his œuvre he and Theo at last succeeded in persuading Gauguin to join him in Arles. This was to be the start of an artists' colony of the South, some sort of self-supporting community. As far as art was concerned Vincent was prepared to sit at Gauguin's feet: 'Gauguin and not I will be head of the studio'. This role would have suited the arrogant and empirical Gauguin perfectly. In the event it did not suit Van Gogh and the whole episode, from October to Christmas, brought little benefit to anybody. Their temperamental incompatibility reached its climax in Van Gogh's self-mutilation late in December. In practice it became clear to both of them that they stood for opposed artistic ideas. 'Our arguments are terribly electric, we come out of them sometimes with our heads as exhausted as discharged batteries.' To us there are some remarkable parallels in their interests; their preoccupation with symbolism and their common talk of painting 'as if in a dream'. But for Van Gogh 'dreaming' was a way of describing the intoxication of passionate looking; Gauguin was interested in dreaming *as opposed to* looking. As far as technique was concerned, they were totally at odds. Gauguin was committed to flat, evenly applied coloured areas in painting and to a very simple linear graphic style. Van Gogh had only just perfected his refined harmonies of broken colour, his rich handling of paint and his elaborately textural style of drawing. For him the two months of Gauguin's stay were a serious distraction and after Gauguin had left and he had come out of hospital, January 1889, he once more withdrew to his own ideas. His painting was more affected by Gauguin's influence than his drawing: The enclosed, compartmentalised character of paintings like *La Berçeuse* is a deferential gesture to Gauguin's art.

When he reasserted his individuality, his painting was influenced by his drawing style. The Arles paintings of the spring of 1889 and particularly those painted at the St-Rémy asylum (May 1889-May 1890) owe a great deal to the calligraphic technique of 1888. In his developed paintings of 1888, the significance of each separate brushmark was as the carrier of a colour. The painting's structure lay in the intricate colour-harmonics of these marks. In the later paintings the colour-marks are also lines: they acquire almost as much significance from their length, shape and direction as from their colour. The pulsing, rhythmic articulation of surface that typifies the St-Rémy canvases was born out of his drawing. Back in Nuenen in 1885 he had marvelled at the weavers' irridescent colour mixtures in their tweeds, almost comparing them as colourists with Delacroix. In St-Rémy his paintings began to look like embroideries, curvilinear patterns of looping, coloured stitches. In this painting style the range of textures is considerably reduced: the rhythms change their speed and their colour but not their basic formal character.

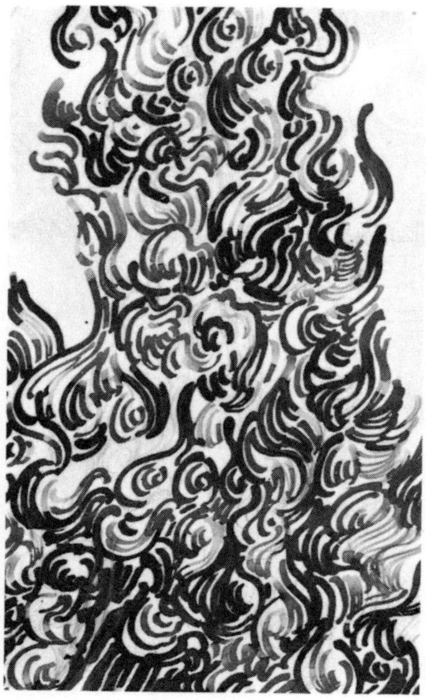

Detail of Plate 106

The later drawings correspond more closely to these paintings: several of them include colour notes. Their construction is more open, and the more limited variety of mark in any one study relates directly to the paintings. Each drawing evolves around a certain rhythmic theme rather than on the complex interaction of many textures. Trees, figures and houses are graphically fixed with the same obsessive repetition of curving lines, from time to time concentrating into the screwed-up vortex motif he used particularly for cypress trees (Plate 106).

One device of technique peculiar to the drawings is a curious type of hatching in which swollen sheaves of short parallel lines succeed one another along a tree trunk or a limb, rather like an anatomical diagram of muscles (Plates 112 and 121). Even a chair leg acquires this strange animation (Plate 114). The series of tree studies in which this mannerism first matures are among the most original of the St-Rémy drawings (Plate 118ff). Aggressively economical in execution, their dramatic use of asymmetry and silhouette is another striking expression of his *Japonaiserie*. The calligraphic rhythms are bare and exposed against open fields of white paper. The 'open-work' quality of their construction is rare in his graphic œuvre. The series forms a distinct stylistic period.

The only earlier drawings with a comparable feeling are to be found among the rapid sketches in letters to Theo, or in studies—altogether more brutal—like the *Potato Eaters* scribble (Plate 62). In the last St-Rémy drawings and at Auvers he either returned to the heavily covered surfaces or he used a very elegant vignette form. In the latter (Plate 126) the whole tense arabesque is contained between foreground and skyline contours rather like an 1880s Cézanne landscape.

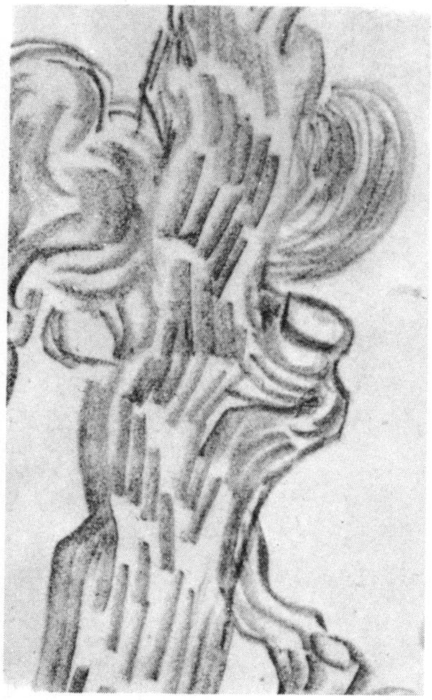

Detail of Plate 121

After the year in the asylum at St-Rémy, he left of his own accord and the comment 'cured' was entered in the records against his name. He tried to convince himself that his illness was a 'disease of the South' and longed to return to the North. With Pissarro's help Theo arranged for him to stay in Auvers, not far from Paris, under the care of Dr Gachet. Vincent soon found stimulation from Gachet's educated and interested companionship and generally felt that recovery was a possibility.

The obsessive elaboration of his Arles drawings and the organic instability of his St-Rémy work have been likened to the drawings of psychopaths. The compulsive repetition of certain convoluted forms

(Plate 106), which recurs in many later drawings, even worried Theo who wrote: 'The last drawings give the impression of having been made in a fury, and are a bit further removed from nature' (T12). On more than one occasion Vincent described himself as 'working like a man possessed' and 'hardly conscious of myself'. But it seems just as hazardous to propose a precise relationship between Van Gogh's mental illness and the character of his art as it does at this stage to reconstruct the exact nature of that illness. It is fairly clear that between the series of severe breakdowns that he suffered during 1889-90, he was capable, articulate and self-possessed. The technique and vision of his later work is reasonably consistent. In all the drawings he appears very conscious of the composition's relationship to the field. The outstanding change in his painting style during the St-Rémy months—the lowering of his colour scale for most of 1889—was just as consciously articulated in letters to Theo as earlier developments and this new palette was quite as rich in its subtle complexity as the more radiant scale of Arles. On the other hand it is also clear that his art was his life in an extreme sense: losing himself in his painting and drawing was a means of fending off the terrible depressions that followed each attack. 'I can do very well without God both in my life and in my painting, but I cannot, ill as I am, do without something which is greater than I, which is my life—the power to create' (531).

Early in 1889 he had written to Theo that drawing 'costs less and distracts my mind just as much [as painting].' The final collapse of confidence that led to his suicide in Auvers in July 1890 was certainly intensified by the fear that 'a more violent attack may destroy forever my ability to paint'. In one of his last letters he wrote: 'once back here I set to work again—though the brush almost slipped from my fingers, and knowing exactly what I wanted, I have since painted three big canvases already. They are vast stretches of corn under troubled skies, and I did not need to go out of my way to express sadness and the extreme of loneliness' (649). In 1884 he had lectured Theo and himself about passing 'from instinct to reason'. Now, clearly, they were as one.

The subjective autobiography of his art, an expression of his state of mind, is constant throughout his œuvre. Yet at the same time he was a highly educated artist, consciously devoted to technical experiment and highly critical in his objective study of the motif. What made this paradox possible was the homogeneity of his philosophy, his vision and his technique. They were totally interdependent. In the early years his vision was articulated by his religious ideology. He wrote that he 'saw drawings and pictures' in the dirtiest corners and the poorest huts—'all reality is symbolic'. His initial struggle for mastery of drawing techniques was to give adequate expression to this inspired evangelical vision. Similarly the objective act of looking at the landscapes of Arles, St-Rémy and Auvers was rarefied both by his highly refined colour analysis and by a passionate nature-mysticism. In the early months in Arles he toyed with the idea of a specific colour-symbolism: certain colour harmonies to express a preconceived mood. This rather literary use of symbolic colour gave way to a more abstract symbolism based on the whole dazzling orchestration of his palette (or the full scale of his calligraphy). His written descriptions of the landscape offer evidence that he actually *saw* the landscape in these intensified terms. His perception was heightened by his technical learning and his spiritual ideals, sharpened to such a degree that it was recognised by contemporaries as abnormal.

The critic Albert Aurier, whose brilliant article was the first to be published on Van Gogh, expressed it perfectly: '. . . he is a hyperaesthete with obvious symptoms who perceives with abnormal and possibly even painful intensity the imperceptible and secret character of lines and forms, and even more of colours, of light, of the magic irridescence of shadows, of nuances which are invisible to healthy eyes. . . . He is no doubt conscious of the pigment, of its importance and beauty, but also, and most frequently, he considers this enchanting pigment only as a marvellous language destined to express the Idea. Almost always he is a symbolist . . . ' (*Mercure de France*, Paris, January 1890). Vincent's reaction to this penetration of the hermit-like world of his art fused pleasure and anxiety. In his letters he characteristically regretted that he was given too much credit for the ideas of others (with particular mention of Monticelli) and expressed marked concern at the implication of abstract values in his art. 'Aurier's article might have encouraged me if I had dared to have let myself, to venture further away from reality and to make colour something like a music of tones. But the truth is so dear to me and the search for being truthful as well. Well I think I still prefer being a cobbler to being a musician who works with colours' (626). Against Gauguin's advice to a painter 'don't copy nature too much . . . art is an abstraction', Vincent firmly moralised: 'Abstraction in art is an enchanted path'.

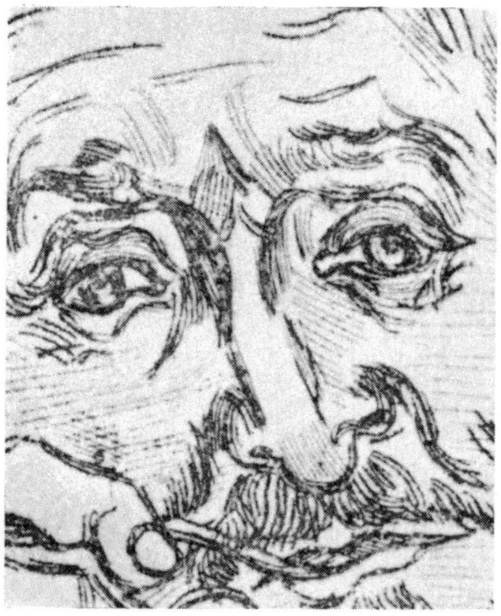
Detail of Plate 132

His symbolism was nature-based. Just as his inspired colour and calligraphy were rooted in visual experience, so his symbolic images were based on the 'search for being truthful'. The sower and the reaper stand at the two poles of his symbolic imagery, the creation-death extremes of a natural cycle. With the sower belong the sun, stars, sunflowers, the colour yellow and expansive linear rhythms: with the reaper, night, cypress trees, crows, the colours black and dark blue and a more convulsive and restrictive effect of line and space. Several interesting parallels exist between this and the sort of late 19th-century theories of expression by colour and line that Seurat and Kandinsky explored. But apart from Delacroix's colour theory Van Gogh was largely unaware of such ideas and his use of this sort of symbolism was personal, empirical and intuitive. The contrast between the melancholic resignation of his figures and the pantheistic radiance of his landscapes is symbolic of his whole experience of life. One of his very late figure studies, the portrait etching of Dr Gachet (Plate 132), he wrote to Gauguin, showed 'the heart-broken expression of our time'.

In all of these contexts, Van Gogh's drawings belong with his paintings. The influence of his unique late drawing style is difficult to isolate from his total influence, because so much of its character fed back into his painting. The drawing media were for him an adaptable and virile part of the artist's repertoire, no part of which should be discarded before exhaustive exploration. In his eyes drawing was neither subsidiary to painting nor isolated from painting. For all his adoption of the spectral palette of the Impressionists he never lost his respect for black and white. Their opposition features largely in his discussions of complementary colours and he once compared the power of their contrast to that of red and green.

He certainly extended the limits of graphic art both in terms of its formal vocabulary and the expressive potential of that vocabulary. His major contribution to the history of drawing lies in the style he invented in Arles. Most proto-Expressionist draughtsmen of the late 19th and early 20th centuries achieved an expressiveness of mark by artless laxity or by wilful aggression. Obviously Van Gogh's drawings of 1888 have a strength of attack about them, but they also have a high degree of artistic sophistication that prefigures some of the more decorative calligraphic styles, also oriental-inspired, of modern painters and draughtsmen. Some writers have been at pains to dissociate the Arles drawings from the idea of 'decoration'. Certainly they are far removed from decoration as an amusing diversion such as Van Gogh had recognised in Japanese prints in Antwerp. Certainly they have nothing in common with the exquisite narcissistic ornament of so much near-Art Nouveau painting of the 1890s. But the early 20th-century concept that grew out of Post-Impressionism and Art Nouveau and that prompted Matisse's comment that 'decoration is at the same time expression', puts quite a different light on the usage of the word. It is a meaning that is fundamental to the decorative surface treatment of so much 20th-century art, whether figurative or not. Presumably what Matisse recognised in the *Haystacks* drawing (Plate 91), which he owned, was precisely this aspect of decoration as structure and expression. The elaborate animation of Van Gogh's drawing surface, bearing increasingly less relationship to scale, perspective or particularities of observed shape, is nothing if not decorative. Its distinction is that it became the vehicle both for his exalted experience of reality and for the full realisation of his maturity as an artist.

Van Gogh's final attitude towards art as communication was related more to artists than to society at large. His talk of an artists' colony in his own time is transformed into a concern for future generations of colourists, portrait and figure painters and artists 'of the South'. 'A link in a chain' is a characteristic self-description. Previously it was the chain of humanity, now it was more exclusively the chain of art. But he laments the discontinuity of art history. 'Why doesn't one hold on to what one has, like the doctors and engineers? Once a thing is discovered and invented, they retain the knowledge, in these wretched fine arts everything is forgotten, nothing is kept' (519). The free history-consciousness of the modern artist might have allayed his despair. The revelation of a historical rediscovery has often served as a creative stimulus far more powerful than the pseudo-science of academic traditionalism. Van Gogh added to the formal and theoretical repertoire of 'past art'. His prolific short career also lends intensity to the faculties of memory, vision and discovery.

Notes on the plates

The plates are grouped into the main periods of Van Gogh's artistic activity. Each period is preceded by a short biographical note and the drawings within each period are arranged more or less chronologically. The F references at the end of certain headings refer to de La Faille, 1928. Vol III (see Bibliography).

The Early Years (until April 1881)
This period was spent in a succession of jobs and places:
1869-76. With Goupil & Co., art dealers at The Hague (1869-73), London (1873-5), and Paris (1875-6).
1876. Teaching in England (Ramsgate and Isleworth), then at home in Etten.
1877-8. Theological College, Amsterdam and Evangelical School in Brussels.
1878-90. Working and preaching in the Borinage mining district of South Belgium at Pâturages, Wasmes and Cuesmes.
1880-81. Brussels. Took lessons in anatomy and perspective. Met the painter Van Rappard.
The drawings range from childhood copies of 1862 to the first fruits of his resolve to become an artist in the late summer of 1880.

Plate 1a — Bridge. Signed and dated 11th January 1862. Pencil. $4\frac{3}{4} \times 14\frac{1}{2}$ in. ($12 \times 36{\cdot}5$ cm.). Rijksmuseum Kröller-Müller, Otterlo.
The majority of Van Gogh's early drawings were copies (see also Plates 1b, 8, 9, 11). The choice of artists to copy was at first arbitrary and varied. As copies they are not the work of a child-genius, but their execution is remarkably accomplished for a boy of 8 or 9. The contour is firm but not inflexible, the shading schematic but sensitive. Either we believe that each casual mark was painstakingly reproduced or that, as seems more likely, there is here a remarkable fluency of assimilation. His mother wrote: 'It's a remarkable gift he has and he may get much from it.'

Plate 1b — Dog. Signed and dated 28th December 1862. Pencil. $7 \times 11\frac{1}{4}$ in. ($18 \times 28{\cdot}5$ cm.). Rijksmuseum Kröller-Müller, Otterlo.
Copy after a lithograph by Victor Adam (1801-66), whose many series of prints enjoyed wide currency at the time. See note to Plate 1a.

Plate 2 — The Lange Vijverberg in The Hague. 1869-73. Pen and pencil. $8\frac{3}{4} \times 6\frac{3}{4}$ in. ($22{\cdot}5 \times 18{\cdot}5$ cm.). Vincent van Gogh Foundation, Amsterdam. (F837).
One of four drawings (F836-839) assigned by Van Gelder to Van Gogh's first stay in The Hague. It has been suggested that they were not made *in situ*, but based on earlier studies. Some of the easy formulations (lamp-post, railings) and the contrived nature of the figure might seem to confirm this. We know that working from rough sketches became his common practice. At the same time there is a painful searching in the drawing of the branches, which suggests that all the complex problems of the motif were in front of him.

Plate 3 — Vicarage and church at Etten. April 1876. Pencil. $3\frac{1}{2} \times 7$ in. ($9 \times 17{\cdot}5$ cm.). Vincent van Gogh Foundation, Amsterdam.
Presumably drawn shortly before his departure for Ramsgate, this strong primitive drawing is comparable to the sketches he made there and in London. Naïvely topographical, they share an assertive independence from the conventions so faithfully copied in the '60s (Plates 1a and b). This style is remarkably close to that with which he took up drawing again around 1878-9 (Plate 5).

Plate 4

Square at Ramsgate. May 1876. Pen and pencil. $2\frac{1}{4} \times 2\frac{1}{4}$ in. (5·5 × 5·5 cm.). Vincent van Gogh Foundation, Amsterdam.
A sketch enclosed in a letter (67) to Theo, 31st May 1876, showing the view from the school where he taught. His lodgings were in another house in the same square. In the letter, with typical sentiment, he identifies the view as 'that through which the boys wave good-bye to their parents . . . None of us will ever forget the view from the window' (67).

Plate 5

Au Charbonnage. November 1878. Pencil, pen and ink. $5\frac{1}{2} \times 5\frac{1}{2}$ in. (14 × 14 cm.). Vincent van Gogh Foundation, Amsterdam.
A study of an inn at Laeken in the Borinage, where the local miners ate their lunch, sent to Theo on November 15th 1878 (letter 126). In describing the locals he refers to the peculiar religious humility of 'those who walk in the darkness, in the centre of the earth' and in support quotes from a sentimentally loaded geography primer. This is one of the last and most impressive of his early, naïve line drawings; its instinct for textural elaboration, shortly abandoned, anticipates the Arles style.

Plate 6

Miners. August 1880. Pencil, lightly coloured. $17\frac{1}{2} \times 22$ in. (44·5 × 56 cm.). Rijksmuseum Kröller-Müller, Otterlo. (F831).
The first independent figure drawings that he began after his dismissal as an evangelist assert the essential character of his art for the next five years. Deeply rooted in his observation, they give vivid information about appearances—of the miners and the landscape of trees, mineshafts and slagheaps. But more significant is the strong evocation of mood: the pathetic lot of the people and their solitary resignation to it.

Plate 7

Miners' wives carrying sacks. ('The Bearers of the Burden'). Probably April 1881. Pen, pencil, brush. $17 \times 23\frac{1}{2}$ in. (43 × 60 cm.). Rijksmuseum Kröller-Müller, Otterlo. (F832).
Vincent worked on subjects like this in Van Rappard's studio with a view to publication in illustrated journals. The leading inscription reflects this idea.

Plate 8

The Sower (after Millet). August/September 1880. Pen and wash, heightened with green and white. $19 \times 14\frac{1}{2}$ in. (48 × 36·5 cm.). Vincent van Gogh Foundation, Amsterdam. (F830).
Van Gogh's admiration of Millet dates from the early 1870s and found expression in his art and his thinking for the rest of his life. 'I have already drawn "The Sower" five times . . . I am so entirely absorbed in that figure' (August 1880, 135). This motif and *The Angelus* (Plate 9) were copied from photographs (see letter 138), but most of his copies were after engravings that Theo collected for him. Millet was a major influence on him in Belgium and at Etten, both for the attitude to the figure, objective but expressive, and for the softer tonal treatment that slowly replaced his early linear style.

Plate 9

The Angelus (after Millet). October 1880. Pencil, red chalk and wash, heightened with white. $18\frac{1}{2} \times 24\frac{1}{2}$ in. (47 × 62 cm.). Rijksmuseum Kröller-Müller, Otterlo. (F824).
Inscribed bottom left 'd'après J. F. Millet, l'Angélus du Soir'.
See note to Plate 8.

Plate 10

En Route. January 1881. Pencil and pen. $3\frac{3}{4} \times 2\frac{1}{4}$ in. (9·5 × 6 cm.). Vincent van Gogh Foundation, Amsterdam.
One of two small figure studies sent to Theo from Brussels with the comment 'I can see perfectly well that they are not good, but they are beginning to look like something' (140). At a time when he was ostensibly absorbed in the impersonal disciplines of technique, perspective and anatomy, many sketches remained subjective and intimate, like personal texts.

Etten (April to December 1881)
Living in his parents' house. Family relationships were seriously strained by the repercussions of his frustrated passion for his young widowed cousin, Kee Vos-Stricker. In December, after an argument about religion, his father asked him to leave the house (see letter 169). The drawings show a struggle between his latent expressionism and his early obligations towards orthodoxy.

Plate 11 — The daughter of Jacob Meyer (after Holbein). 1880-81. Pencil. 17 × 12 in. (43 × 30·5 cm.). Floris Bremmer Collection, The Hague. (F847).
It is known that Vincent made copies after Holbein both in Brussels (letters 137, 138) and Etten (147). The style is close to some Etten figure studies but not conclusively so, and anyway the second-hand nature of the drawing makes stylistic dating hazardous. At the time he was copying almost anything and everything from drawing text books: the Holbeins he describes as 'splendid. Now that I am drawing them I feel it even more strongly than before. But I assure you they aren't easy' (138). The contours are laboriously deliberate and some of the folds, copied for their own sake, become strange hieroglyphs.

Plate 12 — Portrait of the artist's father. 1881. Pencil and washed chinese ink. 13 × 9¾ in. (33 × 25 cm.). Collection Mrs A. R. W. Nieuwenhuizen Segaar-Aarse, The Hague. (F876).
Not mentioned in the letters, this is Vincent's only likeness of his father, a gentle, well-liked priest. Other family likenesses were made from photographs during the Etten months; comparing the assurance of features and structure in this face with contemporary studies from life, this was possibly so here as well.

Plate 13 — View of a wood. 1881 (Summer ?). Charcoal heightened with white. 16½ × 21¾ in. (42 × 55 cm.). Rijksmuseum Kröller-Müller, Otterlo. (F903).
This softer, diffused style of landscape drawing with charcoal appears at several stages of Van Gogh's early work and finds its fullest realisation in the atmospheric Drenthe landscapes (Plates 52, 53). Vanbeselaere's specific dating of June/July for this drawing is based on an insubstantial reference in letter 147.

Plate 14 — Windmills at Dordrecht. August 1881. Pencil, watercolour, black and green chalk, heightened with white. 10¼ × 23½ in. (26 × 60 cm.). Rijksmuseum Kröller-Müller, Otterlo. (F850).
Made on an excursion to Dordrecht during Vincent's trip to see Mauve at The Hague. He had seen the motif from the train and returned especially to record it (letter 149). Considering the frequent occurrence of mills in the Dutch landscape, their rare appearance in Vincent's œuvre is a reminder of the very personal and immediate environment of his subject-matter.

Plate 15 — The linekeeper's house. October 1881. Charcoal heightened with white. 17¼ × 23½ in. (44 × 59·5 cm.). Rijksmuseum Kröller-Müller, Otterlo. (F900).
Vincent enthused to Van Rappard about the beauty of this row of pollard willows (R1). From the drawing the nature of his commitment is clear. The contrast of the robust, simple trunks and the sudden dramatic animosity of the branches is intensely seen. Compare this with Plates 2, 3 or 6 for his developed grasp of organic structure.

Plate 16 Sower. September/December 1881. Charcoal. $22\frac{3}{4} \times 13\frac{1}{2}$ in. (57·5 × 34 cm.). Rijksmuseum Kröller-Müller, Otterlo. (F856).
The inspiration for these Etten studies of single figures at work (see also Plates 17-21) was four-fold: Millet's precedent, Mauve's advice, text-book exercises and observation. The poses are self-consciously contrived (Vincent conceded Van Rappard's comment that 'he is not a man who is sowing, but one who is posing as a sower', R2) and the forms are defined with a lip-biting determination. The fruits of this intense struggle were to come in The Hague and Nuenen. At Etten he relied on local acquaintances for models and had great difficulty in explaining that he did *not* want them 'in their Sunday best, with impossible folds in which neither knees, elbows, shoulder blades, nor any other part of the body have left characteristic dents or bumps' (148). Nevertheless he tackled his work with vigour and a growing sense of achievement. 'I have drawn five times over a man with a spade, a digger, in different positions, a sower twice, a girl with a broom twice. Then a woman in a white cap peeling potatoes; a shepherd leaning on his staff; and, finally, an old, sick farmer sitting on a chair near the hearth, his head in his hands and his elbows on his knees. And of course I shall not stop here. . . . I no longer stand helpless before nature, as I used to' (150).

Plate 17 Carpenter. September/December 1881. Charcoal. $22\frac{3}{4} \times 16$ in. (57·5 × 40·5 cm.). Rijksmuseum Kröller-Müller, Otterlo. (F878).
See note to Plate 16.

Plate 18 Woman mending. September/December 1881. Charcoal, black chalk, watercolour, heightened with white. $24\frac{1}{2} \times 18\frac{3}{4}$ in. (62 × 47·5 cm.). Rijksmuseum Kröller-Müller, Otterlo. (F1221).
This drawing has sometimes been assigned to The Hague period; stylistically the drawing of face and drapery seems closest to other Etten studies.

Plate 19 Man with a basket sowing. September 1881. Black chalk, watercolour, heightened with white. $24\frac{1}{2} \times 18\frac{3}{4}$ in. (62 × 47·5 cm.). Rijksmuseum Kröller-Müller, Otterlo. (F865).
See note to Plate 16.

Plate 20 Boy with a sickle squatting. October 1881. Black chalk, watercolour. $18\frac{1}{2} \times 24$ in. (47 × 61 cm.). Rijksmuseum Kröller-Müller, Otterlo. (F851).
The model was possibly a gardener, Piet Kaufman (see letters 150 and R3).

Plate 21 Man reading by the fire. October 1881. Charcoal, watercolour, heightened with white. $17\frac{3}{4} \times 22$ in. (45 × 56 cm.). Rijksmuseum Kröller-Müller, Otterlo. (F897).
A Millet-like motif, which recurs in variants throughout the Dutch period (e.g. Plates 31, 42).

The Hague (December 1881 to September 1883)
After the split with his father, Vincent went to work in The Hague under the instruction of the painter Mauve, a relative of his mother whom he had met in August. Under Mauve's influence he developed his lifelong principle, seldom broken, never to work from memory. The disadvantages of life in The Hague (loneliness and expense) were partly compensated by commissions from an uncle, C.M. (Cornelius Marinus van Gogh, an Amsterdam art dealer), for views of The Hague (Plate 24ff). In February 1882 he befriended a prostitute, Christine (Sien), mother of one child and pregnant with a second, and she posed for him (Plates 30-32, 45). After her confinement in July, they set up house together and his pride in this domestic responsibility is reflected in letters and drawings. But the relationship put paid to his friendship with Mauve, C. M. and others. Much of his working time, particularly in the winter, was spent in local almshouses and soup kitchens where he drew the pensioners (Plates 36-39, 42, 43). There were a few more ambitious compositions in watercolour (Plates 40, 41). His drawing matured rapidly in the confident sense of structure and in the sympathetic and experimental use of media. It is clear from letters that he was preparing himself for a career as an illustrator (see notes to Plates 36, 40, 41).

Plate 22 The forge. 1882/4. Pen and ink, pencil, heightened with white. $14\frac{1}{2} \times 10\frac{1}{4}$ in. (37 × 26 cm.). Rijksmuseum Kröller-Müller, Otterlo. (F1084).
This problematic drawing has been variously assigned to the Etten, Hague and Nuenen periods. The Kröller-Müller catalogue suggests June 1881 on the strength of the perspective drawing of a forge mentioned in letter 149. Although this evidence seems convincing (no other drawing of a forge is known) the stylistic evidence offers little support for it. The competent perspective is clearly in advance of any other drawing of that date. The insistent parallel hatching of the drawing otherwise first appears in drawings at The Hague (Plate 24 and F1073, 1085) and is only this fully developed in the early Nuenen landscapes (Plates 54, 55). On these grounds a date between 1882 and early 1884 seems more likely than summer 1881. We know that he went to a blacksmith for help with his perspective frame in August 1881 (see Plate 29).

Plate 23 Peasant digging. January 1882. $19\frac{1}{4} \times 11\frac{1}{4}$ in. (49 × 28·5 cm.). Pen, pencil. Vincent van Gogh Foundation, Amsterdam. (F908).
Probably one of the series of men digging in a potato field made soon after his arrival in The Hague (letter 169); most of his motifs at this time were of a more obviously urban nature. There already seems to be a stronger grasp of a whole body committed to one action than at Etten.

Plate 24 A corner of the old town (Paddemoes). March 1882. Pen, pencil. $9\frac{3}{4} \times 12\frac{1}{4}$ in. (25 × 31 cm.). Rijksmuseum Kröller-Müller, Otterlo. (F918).
This drawing, made on the spot in pencil and reworked the next day in ink, was what inspired Van Gogh's uncle C.M. to commission twelve views of The Hague; these were to include this study and two others that were already made (see letters 180, 181). His uncle promised a further commission for twelve views of Amsterdam if the project was successful. In April this was replaced by a request for 'six special detailed views of the town' (184) and in June, Vincent mentions having sent off seven more views of The Hague to his uncle (205). Plates 25-27 are probably from or related to the second series; the problem is complicated by there being different versions of the same motif. Many of the studies were made from his window: 'I have tried to draw the things as naïvely as possible, exactly as I saw them in front of me' (205). He obviously went out of his way to incorporate a lot of detail, but in terms of exactitude, his main preoccupation was with the perspective construction of the composition (see Plate 29).

Plate 25 Rooftops. July 1882. Watercolour heightened with white. $15\frac{1}{4} \times 21\frac{3}{4}$ in. (39 × 55 cm.). Georges Renand Collection, Paris. (F943).
See note to Plate 24. 'Just imagine me sitting at my attic window as early as four o'clock in the morning studying with my perspective frame the meadows and the yard when they are lighting the fires to make coffee in the little cottages. . . . Over the red tile roofs a flock of white pigeons comes soaring between the black smokey chimneys. Behind it all, a wide stretch of soft, tender green, miles and miles of flat meadow; and over it a grey sky, as calm, as peaceful as Corot or Van Goyen' (219).

Plate 26 Behind the Schenkweg. May 1882. Pen and brush, pencil, heightened with white. $11\frac{1}{4} \times 18\frac{1}{2}$ in. (28·5 × 47 cm.). Rijksmuseum Kröller-Müller, Otterlo. (F939).
See note to Plate 24.

Plate 27 Fish-drying barn. May 1882. Pencil, pen and brush, heightened with white. $11 \times 17\frac{1}{4}$ in. (28 × 44 cm.). Rijksmuseum Kröller-Müller, Otterlo. (F938).
See note to Plate 24. This subject is often mentioned in the letters. Two other versions are known.

Plate 28 Melting snow. March 1883. Watercolour heightened with white. $15\frac{1}{4} \times 23$ in. (39 × 55 cm.). Floris Bremmer Collection, The Hague. (F1022).
In the winter of 1882-3, Vincent returned to some of the same motifs. This is virtually the same view as that in Plates 25 and 26.

Plate 29 A perspective frame. August 1882. Pen and ink. Vincent van Gogh Foundation, Amsterdam.
A sketch included in letter 223. Vincent was already preoccupied with the problems of perspective in Etten (149) and during 1882, after reading a translation of Dürer's treatise on perspective, designed a portable frame for his own use. The frame illustrated is apparently his second, more sophisticated version; it was constructed for him by a local carpenter and blacksmith, with pointed adjustable legs to stand on uneven ground. His discussion of the frame's use implies that he saw it not only as a technical aid in measuring proportions but also as a means to some sort of emotional stability and security in front of the landscape. 'I think you can imagine how delightful it is to turn this "spy-hole" frame on the sea, on the green meadows, or on the snowy fields in winter . . .' (223).

Plate 30 A woman mourning. April 1882. Pencil, pen and brush (sepia). $22\frac{3}{4} \times 16\frac{1}{2}$ in. (58 × 42 cm.). Rijksmuseum Kröller-Müller, Otterlo. (F935).
See note to Plate 32.

Plate 31 Woman with a cigar sitting near a stove. April 1882. Black chalk, pencil and brush (sepia), washed and heightened with white. 18 × 22 in. (45·5 × 56 cm.). Rijksmuseum Kröller-Müller, Otterlo. (F898).
See note to Plate 32.

Plate 32 Sorrow. April 1882. Black crayon. $17\frac{1}{2} \times 10\frac{1}{2}$ in. (44·5 × 26·7 cm.). Garman-Ryan Collection, London. (F929 bis).
'My very best drawing' (219). Inscribed beneath with this text from Michelet: 'How can there be on this earth a woman who is lonely and desperate?' Its implications are part evangelism, part autobiography, and part an epitaph for Sien, the ex-prostitute who first posed for him in the spring of 1882 (Plates 31-33) and later lived with him. His relationship with Sien was prompted principally by his desolation after Kee Vos's rejection of him, but also by his missionary spirit. In 1876 he had enthused over an English short story called *Janet's Repentance* about a selfless clergyman, devoted to the poor: 'During his long illness he was nursed by a woman who had been a drunkard, but by his teaching, and leaning as it were on him, had conquered her weakness and found rest for her soul' (55). His own feelings in The Hague were comparable: 'I can only marry once and how can I do better than marry her? It is the only way to help her; otherwise misery would force her back into her old ways, which end in a precipice' (192).
Vincent discussed the drawing in terms of the importance of linear contours (182, 221) and of his desire to 'make drawings that *touch* some people. *Sorrow* is a small beginning' (218).

Plate 33 Roots. April 1882. Black chalk, pencil, watercolour. $19\frac{1}{4} \times 27$ in. (49 × 68·5 cm.). Rijksmuseum Kröller-Müller, Otterlo. (F933).
At several stages of his career Vincent was fascinated by eccentric tree structures, 'twisted and gnarled stumps and tree roots, fantastical like those Albert Dürer etched in "Knight Death and the Devil"' (126). Vincent compares *Roots* to *Sorrow* for expressive content and discusses its execution—'I have brushed it in with lead pencil and scraped it off again as if it were a painting'—in a long dismissal of easy techniques (195).

Plate 34 The church. October 1882. Pencil, pen and watercolour. 11 × 15 in. (28 × 38 cm.). Rijksmuseum Kröller-Müller, Otterlo. (F967).
'I am also making one of a church bench which I saw in a little church in the Geest, where people from the workhouse go' (235). It is a patchwork drawing of separate, near-caricature studies with more than a hint of anti-clericalism.

Plate 35 Woman walking to the left. 1882/3? Pencil. $12\frac{1}{2} \times 6$ in. (32 × 15·5 cm.). Rijksmuseum Kröller-Müller, Otterlo. (F1050).
Stylistically there is some link between this drawing and the pensioner studies (Plate 36ff), but the shorthand hatching seems more deft, brisk and confident and the rather more fashionable dress seems peculiarly out of context for the period. The profile resembles Sien: if it is her, she must be wearing the 'warm woman's coat' sent with a parcel of clothes from Vincent's parents in October 1882 (236).

Plate 36 Pensioner, back view. October 1882. Pencil. $18 \times 9\frac{3}{4}$ in. (46 × 25 cm.). Vincent van Gogh Foundation, Amsterdam. (F960).
After *Sorrow*, the series of pensioner drawings (Vincent preferred the local term 'orphan-men') is the most interesting part of his Hague period. Their mood ranges from the pathetic to the anecdotal and picturesque. He laid great importance on 'characteristic figures' both as the means to a major, definitive statement in painting (235) and as a series of lithographs of 'workman types' to be sold in folios.
Models were relatively accessible for a small fee and at one stage the foreman of a nearby works agreed to send on to Vincent any men who had been laid off work (238). This model, described by Vincent as having 'a queer bald head, large deaf ears and white whiskers' (235), appears in several drawings. In his letters of the period he talks a lot of Daumier and of English graphic artists, in both cases with clear reference to the sort of motif and the sort of sentiment with which he himself was working.

Plate 37 Pensioner drinking coffee. October 1882. Pencil, black chalk. $19\frac{1}{4} \times 11$ in. (49×29 cm.). Rijksmuseum Kröller-Müller, Otterlo. (F976).
See note to Plate 36.

Plate 38 Pensioner with a stick. October 1882. $21\frac{3}{4} \times 11\frac{3}{4}$ in. (55×30 cm.). Black crayon. Museum Van Baaren, Utrecht. (F963).
See note to Plate 36.

Plate 39 Man and woman talking. October 1882. Pencil, black chalk. $18 \times 10\frac{1}{4}$ in. 45·5 × 26 cm.). Rijksmuseum Kröller-Müller, Otterlo. (F989).
See note to Plate 36.

Plate 40 The state lottery. October 1882. Watercolour. $15 \times 22\frac{1}{2}$ in. (38×57 cm.). Vincent van Gogh Foundation, Amsterdam. (F970).
For Vincent the subject was 'the contrast of misery and that kind of forlorn effort of the poor wretches to try to save themselves by buying a lottery ticket, paid for with their last pennies, which should have gone for food' (235). This watercolour and *Women carrying coal* (Plate 41) are the nearest he reached to a major statement in painting at The Hague (cf. note to Plate 36). In them colour begins to make a positive contribution, independent of the drawing.

Plate 41 Women carrying coal. November 1882. Watercolour heightened with white. $12\frac{1}{2} \times 19\frac{3}{4}$ in. (32×50 cm.). Rijksmuseum Kröller-Müller, Otterlo. (F994).
A return to the subject of his earliest independent works (Plates 6, 7). 'In reality it is something like *The Reapers* by Millet, severe, so you understand that one mustn't make a snow effect of it. . . . It would really be right for the *Vie Moderne*' (241).

Plate 42 Old man in sorrow. November 1882. Black chalk, pencil. $19\frac{3}{4} \times 12\frac{1}{4}$ in. (50×31 cm.). Vincent van Gogh Foundation, Amsterdam. (F997).
In a letter Vincent recalled his earlier drawing of this motif (F863, see note to Plate 16) and thought of making a lithograph from it (247). This he did, titling one print *'At Eternity's Gate'* (in English); the same title was used for a painted copy of this drawing (F702) made at St-Rémy in May 1890. Its whole concept is clearly related to *Sorrow* (Plate 32).

Plate 43 Old fisherman with a pipe. January 1883. Pen, pencil, black chalk (washed), heightened with white. $18 \times 10\frac{1}{4}$ in. (46×26 cm.). Rijksmuseum Kröller-Müller, Otterlo. (F1010).
One of several studies on this theme. The fisherman's hat was a studio prop which Vincent had bought—'an old one over which many storms and seas have passed' (261).

Plate 44 Girl with a shawl. December 1882/February 1883. Pencil, black crayon (washed), heightened with white. $14 \times 23\frac{3}{4}$ in. (35·6 × 60·5 cm.). Rijksmuseum Kröller-Müller, Otterlo. (F1007).
The outstanding portrait study of The Hague years, this drawing of Sien's daughter is also remarkable for its technique. 'I finished my drawings pretty well in pencil, indeed as much as possible. Then I fixed them and dulled them with milk. And then I worked it up again with lithographic crayon where the deepest tones were, retouched them here and there with a brush or pen, with lampblack, and worked in the lighter parts with white body colour' (256). Later in the same letter he compares the subtlety of 'black and white' to painting with colour.

Plate 45 Mother breast-feeding her child. Spring 1883. Pencil. $17\frac{1}{4} \times 10\frac{3}{4}$ in. ($43{\cdot}3 \times 27$ cm.). Rijksmuseum Kröller-Müller, Otterlo. (F1062).
Sien with her baby, one of a series of this subject (F1061-71), several of which show the coarse grain of the drawing board or whatever, pressing through the paper. On many occasions Vincent warned against easy, seductive materials; he believed a hard, carpenter's pencil was the artist's proper discipline. This austere dogmatism contrasts with his compulsion to experiment and improvise.

Plate 46 Woman by the willows. 1883? Pencil (rubbed). $14 \times 22\frac{3}{4}$ in. ($35{\cdot}5 \times 60{\cdot}5$ cm.). Rijksmuseum Kröller-Müller, Otterlo. (F1092).
A rare study for The Hague of a figure in the landscape. As in Plate 44, the pencil drawing is partially erased to soften the tones and merge the composition's main areas. He used various methods for this—brushing with water, ink or milk, scraping with a pencil stump or rubbing with breadcrumbs.

Plate 47 Man sowing. March-April. Black chalk, pencil, brush and printer's ink, oil?, heightened with white. $24\frac{1}{2} \times 16\frac{1}{4}$ in. ($62{\cdot}5 \times 41{\cdot}5$ cm.). Rijksmuseum Kröller-Müller, Otterlo. (F882).
One of several Hague drawings made in an extraordinary mongrel technique invented by Van Gogh for its chiaroscuro effects. The main tones were achieved with black printer's ink diluted with turpentine, and mixed with either Chinese white oil paint or powdered zinc white to effect a scale of greys. He was delighted by the deep tone of the black, drew into the washes with black chalk or pencil and then heightened some passages with white (278, 279).

Plate 48 Woman on her deathbed. April 1883. $13\frac{3}{4} \times 24\frac{1}{2}$ in. (35×62 cm.). Rijksmuseum Kröller-Müller, Otterlo. (F841).
For medium and technique, see note to Plate 47. An unusual motif in Van Gogh's œuvre, usually identified with his mention of 'a few reclining figures; some time I shall need figures of corpses or of sick people' (280).

Plate 49 The white horse. November 1882 or May 1883. Black crayon and charcoal. $16\frac{1}{2} \times 23\frac{1}{4}$ in. (42×59 cm.). Dr R. S. Steinmetz Collection (on loan to Haags Gemeentemuseum, The Hague). (F1032).
This study was probably made in connection with a projected series on dustmen (289), but the symbolic image of horses and peculiarly of white horses had long held significance for him. In 1878 he had written of old horses as particularly potent symbols of tragic old age (126) and in November 1882, he complained of the hard bargain driven by the owner of 'an old white horse, just the poorest nag imaginable, at the gasworks' that he wanted to draw (241). Later he compared the over-criticised avant-garde painters of Paris to broken-down old cab horses.

Drenthe (September to November 1883)

In September 1883 with much self-questioning, self-reproach and self-defence, Vincent left Sien and her children and went to work at Drenthe for three months, influenced in his choice of environment by the examples of Mauve, Liebermann and Van Rappard, who had all worked there. Living in great poverty, he identified with the meagre life of the peat-workers, while his response to the landscape prefigures his late painting. The Drenthe episode was forecast in another of his naïve self-identifications in August 1883. 'Recently I often think of a story I read in an English magazine, a tale about a painter . . . who went to a lonely place in the peat fields, and there, in that melancholy setting, found himself again and began to paint nature as he saw it' (309).

Plate 50 Cottage in the heather. November 1883. Pen and ink (washed). $8\frac{3}{4} \times 11\frac{1}{2}$ in. ($22{\cdot}5 \times 29$ cm.). Rijksmuseum Kröller-Müller, Otterlo. (F1097).
'I found this cottage on a muddy evening after the rain; seen on the spot it is splendid' (335).

Plate 51 Cottages in the heather. September/November 1883. Black chalk heightened with white. $18 \times 23\frac{3}{4}$ in. ($46 \times 60{\cdot}5$ cm.). Rijksmuseum Kröller-Müller, Otterlo. (F1248).

Plate 52 Ploughman and three women. October 1883. Pencil. $8\frac{1}{4} \times 13\frac{1}{2}$ in. (21×34 cm.). Rijksmuseum Kröller-Müller, Otterlo. (F1096).
An almost identical sketch is enclosed in letter 333.

Nuenen (December 1883 to November 1885)
Spent with a grudging gratitude in his parents' house at his father's new parish at Nuenen, these two years saw the culmination of Van Gogh's Dutch period. The great series of Weavers, Gleaners and 'Heads of the People' and the first major oil painting, The Potato Eaters, *were all made at Nuenen. It was a period of confident and expansive achievement more than self-conscious struggle and experiment. Although he still used a wide range of media, he now seemed able to concentrate his energies on content and expression. Much of his technical effort was being given to painting.*
In January 1884 his mother broke her thigh and Vincent nursed her with extraordinary care. His father died in March 1885, but the event is scarcely mentioned in the letters (see 397, 398). From May 1885 onwards, he went to live in his own rented studio. The period was punctuated by troubled relations with the local residents; at one time the pastor forbade them to pose for him. Most of his drawings were sent straight to Theo; he speaks of them as Theo's property, for which his allowance is payment in advance. He spent a few days in Amsterdam in October 1885 and then, increasingly restless, left Nuenen for Antwerp.

Plate 53 The timber auction. January 1884. Watercolour heightened with white. $13\frac{1}{4} \times 17\frac{1}{4}$ in. ($33{\cdot}5 \times 44$ cm.). Vincent van Gogh Foundation, Amsterdam. (F1113).
'I have also made a drawing, just an impression of a lumber auction' (351), but although it is more spirited in colour than usual it is scarcely an objective impression. There is the same depressive melancholy in the faceless resignation of the figures as at The Hague (cf. Plate 40).

Plate 54 Chapel between the trees. January 1884. Pen and ink. $6\frac{1}{2} \times 5\frac{1}{4}$ in. ($16{\cdot}5 \times 13{\cdot}5$ cm.). Rijksmuseum Kröller-Müller, Otterlo. (F1117).
Probably a study for the painting of the same motif (F25) made for his mother when she was bedridden after her accident (355).
See following note.

Plate 55 The presbytery garden in winter. March/April 1884. Pen and ink. $21\frac{1}{4} \times 15$ in. (54×38 cm.). Museum of Fine Arts, Budapest. (F1130).
One of at least three studies of this motif which he sent to Van Rappard for criticism and—in the event—enthusiastic approval (363a, 364, 366, R43-44). This vigorous hatched style of pen drawing, often used for sketches in the letters, reached its fullest development in the spring of 1884. The tragic angularity of the branches seems to anticipate Mondrian's early studies of the Dutch landscape.

Plate 56 The weaver. February 1884. Pencil, pen and ink. $10\frac{1}{2} \times 15\frac{3}{4}$ in. (27×40 cm.). Vincent van Gogh Foundation, Amsterdam. (F1121).
This subject was one of his major preoccupations in 1884; around 30 versions survive in different media (F24-37, 1107-24). He was fascinated by the complexity of the loom, but foreseeably concluded that machines, like books or clothes, were really an expression of their users. ('The thing is made of oak grimed by sweated hands' R44.) Weavers he rated with miners as 'a race apart'. He sought to identify himself—and by implication all worthwhile artists—with the working classes; witness his delight when a doctor judged him to be a steel worker from the condition of his hands.

Plate 57 The weaver. January 1884. Water colour. $13\frac{1}{2} \times 17\frac{1}{2}$ in. (34×44 cm.). Vincent van Gogh Foundation, Amsterdam. (F1107).
See note to Plate 56.

Plate 58 Head of a peasant. Winter 1884-5. Pencil $13\frac{3}{4} \times 8\frac{1}{2}$ in. ($35 \times 21{\cdot}5$ cm.). Vincent van Gogh Foundation, Amsterdam. (F1146).
Still convinced that his career lay in the field of illustration, Van Gogh embarked on a series of 'Heads of the People' (389-398). In the winter he could get models easily and he worked furiously at the series, satisfied if one in twenty was worth keeping. The contrast between the best of the drawings—eloquent and assured like this head—and the crude sketches in the letters 'scratched in a hurry and from memory' is remarkable. The determining factor—having the model in front of him—is also what distinguishes the sensitive power of these studies from *The Potato Eaters*, the composite painting that concludes the series.

Plate 59 Peasant. 1885. Black chalk. $13\frac{3}{4} \times 8\frac{1}{4}$ in. (35×21 cm.). Rijksmuseum Kröller-Müller, Otterlo. (F1328).
Compare the loose, improvised technique of this rapid sketch with the refined execution of the posed studies.

Plate 60 Seated peasant woman. Early 1885. Pencil, pen and ink. $13\frac{3}{4} \times 8\frac{1}{4}$ in. (35×21 cm.). Vincent van Gogh Foundation, Amsterdam. (F1190).
See note to Plate 58.

Plate 61 Peasant woman, front view. Early 1885. $13\frac{1}{2} \times 8\frac{1}{2}$ in. ($34{\cdot}5 \times 21{\cdot}5$ cm.). Black crayon. Vincent van Gogh Foundation, Amsterdam. (F1224).
See note to Plate 58.

Plate 62 The potato eaters, sketch. April 1885. Black crayon. $8\frac{1}{4} \times 13\frac{3}{4}$ in. (21×35 cm.). Vincent van Gogh Foundation, Amsterdam. (F1227).
An early sketch of the composition showing only four figures; it contains the essence of the final composition's lighting and action in a very dramatic and spontaneous form.

Plate 63 The potato eaters. April 1885. Lithograph. $10\frac{1}{2} \times 12$ in. ($26{\cdot}5 \times 30{\cdot}5$ cm.). Rijksmuseum Kröller-Müller, Otterlo. (F1661).
One of nine lithographs made during the Dutch period, this drawing was copied from the second painted version of the subject (F78, Rijksmuseum Kröller-Müller). There was a heated interchange with Van Rappard about this print lasting several months (R51-56). He also sent Theo some prints (401) saying that he intended to make 'a definite picture of the sketch'. The final version (F82, Vincent van Gogh Foundation, Amsterdam, see Plate 86) incorporated and elaborated all the earlier ideas, including the awkward device of the foreground figure. The subject was of great significance to him and in a sense it demonstrates his whole early philosophy and his ambitions for an 'art of the people'. (See letter 404.)

Plate 64 Gravedigger. 1885. Black crayon. $13\frac{1}{2} \times 8\frac{1}{4}$ in. (34·5 × 21 cm.). Vincent van Gogh Foundation, Amsterdam. (F1331).
One of two studies of this model, which are extremely rare in Van Gogh's œuvre for their dramatic expression and gesture. Nowhere else except in copies does such a dramatic relationship confront the spectator. The motif is not mentioned in the letters.

Plate 65 Gleaner. Summer 1885. Black crayon. $20\frac{1}{2} \times 15$ in. (52 × 38 cm.). Charles Clore Collection, London (F1265 bis).
After the interior studies of the winter, Van Gogh launched into a campaign of drawing peasants in the fields (Plates 65-69), among which the gleaners stand out in quantity and quality. Compared with the posed interiors, they are physically dynamic and assertive. The fleeting peculiarities of shape and movement are fixed in a form that is both accurate reportage and monumental composition. The drawing media are submitted to this dual discipline and in the struggle, Van Gogh's feelings for the nobility of the peasant found an expression worthy of succession to Millet.

Plate 66 Binding of corn sheaves. Summer 1885. Black chalk. $17\frac{1}{2} \times 23$ in. (44·5 × 58·5 cm.). Rijksmuseum Kröller-Müller, Otterlo. (F1262).
See note to Plate 65.

Plate 67 Gleaner. Summer 1885. Black chalk. $16\frac{3}{4} \times 20\frac{3}{4}$ in. (42·5 × 51·5 cm.). Nasjonalgalleriet, Oslo. (F1280).
See note to Plate 65.

Plate 68 Peasant reaping. Summer 1885. Black chalk. $16\frac{1}{4} \times 22\frac{3}{4}$ in. (41·5 × 58 cm.). Rijksmuseum Kröller-Müller, Otterlo. (F1322).
See note to Plate 65.

Plate 69 Peasant reaping. Summer 1885. Black chalk. (F1322 verso).
See note to Plate 65.

Antwerp (November 1885 to February 1886)
Three months of great stimulation, anticipating the changes to come in Paris. The vital urban environment offered a new and disturbing way of life. His letters contain excited discussion of the city's experiences: the docks, the dance halls and pubs, museums and exhibitions. His discovery of Japanese prints and his admiration of Rubens precipitated a new attitude to colour. He attended life classes and painting classes at the Academy; his mood there varied from an earnest submission to disciplines to a slightly cynical independence. His relations with tutors were often heated. He had thoughts of returning to Nuenen before joining Theo (440, 452), but on February 27th suddenly left for Paris (459).

Plate 70 Study from an antique cast. 1885/6.
Vincent van Gogh Foundation, Amsterdam. (F1363c).
One of fifteen sheets of such studies which de La Faille dates as Paris. Vincent drew from the antique in Antwerp and Paris and believed it was valuable to him (447), but most of his comments about academic practice in Antwerp were scathing: 'They go so far as to say that "Colour and modelling are trivial and easily picked up, it's the contour that is the essential and the most difficult". You see one can learn some new things at the Academy. I never knew before that colour and modelling came so easily' (452). His sensualisation of the plaster original is typical. Nevertheless the facile background hatching of this drawing is one of several studio mannerisms that Vincent picked up there.

Plate 71 Seated nude child. Winter 1885/6. Black crayon.
Vincent van Gogh Foundation, Amsterdam. (F1366 verso, detail).
Detail of a sheet showing other studies of the same child. This is one of the most impressive of the Antwerp and Paris nude drawings—opinions on the date fluctuate between the Paris and Antwerp periods. The great variations of his drawing techniques under new and conflicting influences makes dating on stylistic grounds difficult (see note to Plate 80).

Plate 72 Square in Antwerp. Winter 1885-6. Black crayon. $4\frac{1}{4} \times 3\frac{3}{4}$ in. ($11 \times 9{\cdot}5$ cm.).
Vincent van Gogh Foundation, Amsterdam. (F1354).
The mood and technique of this small sketch are remarkably close to Seurat's conté studies of melancholy Parisian suburbs.

Plate 73 Market at night. Winter 1885-6. Pencil. $8\frac{1}{4} \times 11\frac{3}{4}$ in. (21×30 cm.).
Vincent van Gogh Foundation, Amsterdam. (F1355A).

Plate 74 Het Steen. December 1885. Pen, ink, coloured chalks.
$5 \times 8\frac{1}{4}$ in. (13×21 cm.). Vincent van Gogh Foundation, Amsterdam. (F1351).
One of several more or less topographical views of the city. 'It is just the thing for foreigners who want a souvenir of Antwerp and for that reason I shall make still more city views of that kind' (441). A number of the Antwerp studies show a more adventurous use of bright colour areas.

Paris (February 1884 to February 1888)
His stated reasons for coming to Paris were to continue study of the nude and the antique at Cormon's studio and to study in the Louvre. As well as this he discovered in himself a real dedication to Japanese art and in contemporary Parisian painting (Impressionist and Post-Impressionist) revelations of colour and technique. Under these influences he was transformed from a draughtsman to a painter. He met Lautrec, Gauguin and Bernard (with all of whom he later corresponded), Pissarro and the dealer Père Tanguy. He praised Degas' nudes and Monet's landscapes (459a) and was lastingly impressed by Cézanne and Seurat as well. The experience of Paris completely disrupted the developed state of his art at Nuenen. It also distracted him from the mission for a socially conscious art. Although in Arles he tried to reconcile these new ideas to the old, he never wholly returned to his earlier ambitions. He lived in Theo's apartment the whole two years.

Plate 75 Woman and dog. 1886/8. Pen and ink, coloured crayon. $6\frac{1}{2} \times 4$ in. ($16{\cdot}5 \times 10$ cm.). Vincent van Gogh Foundation, Amsterdam.
This strange illustration-like drawing is out of keeping with the general character of the Parisian townscapes he drew. The literary characterisation of the heroine is completed by the accompanying couplet at the bottom:
'De son métier elle ne faisait rien
Le soir elle baladait son chien,
La Vilette.'

Plate 76 La Fosse Commune. 1886. Brush, pen and ink, coloured chalk, heightened with white. $14\frac{1}{2} \times 19$ in. ($36{\cdot}5 \times 48$ cm.). Rijksmuseum Kröller-Müller, Otterlo.
An almost identical pen drawing exists (F1399). Of the Paris drawings this is the closest to the Dutch period in subject and mood. The similarity of the left hand digger's pose to a Hague drawing (Plate 23) may not be coincidence.

Plate 77 Study after Michelangelo and figures in a café. 1886/8. Pen and ink, pencil. $13\frac{3}{4} \times 10\frac{1}{4}$ in. (35×26 cm.). Vincent van Gogh Foundation, Amsterdam. (F.1365).
It has apparently gone unnoticed by previous writers that the nude drawing is a copy after Michelangelo's *Dying Captive* in the Louvre or from a cast of it. Van Gogh had already cited Michelangelo in defence of his own distortions of anatomy back in Nuenen. The transformation of the original proportions here makes the outrage of his Antwerp tutors comprehensible.

Plate 78 Violinist and pianist. 1887/8. Green crayon $10\frac{1}{4} \times 13\frac{3}{4}$ in. (26×35 cm.). Vincent van Gogh Foundation, Amsterdam.
One of a series of fairly recently published drawings of café-concert motifs (Tralbaut, 1955, see bibliography). This is a drawing technique derived very closely from the means and vision of Impressionism. This brilliant shorthand graphic style, in which a figure is compiled of loosely related strokes, marks a turning point between the monumentally structural Dutch drawings and his late drawings. See also Plates 80-83; Plate 77 shows an intermediate state.

Plate 79 Self-Portrait. Summer 1886. Pencil. $8\frac{1}{4} \times 7\frac{1}{2}$ in. (21×19 cm.). Vincent van Gogh Foundation, Amsterdam. (F1379).
Sent with letter 460 to Theo, who was away in Holland. There are over 20 painted self-portraits from the Paris period but only two extant drawings; in fact, apart from two other sketches sent from Antwerp (448), there are no further self-portraits among the drawings.

Plate 80 Seated female nude. 1887/8. Pencil. $11\frac{3}{4} \times 9$ in. (30×23 cm.). Vincent van Gogh Foundation, Amsterdam.
In Antwerp Van Gogh had tried to approach the nude through various forms of academic technique: in adapting this Impressionist technique (see Plate 78) to life drawing, he turned his back on the academic principle of drawing by contour. In replacing the contour with separate marks, he was unconsciously opening the way to a textural style of drawing without shading.

Plate 81 Reclining nude. 1887/8. Pencil. $9\frac{1}{2} \times 12\frac{1}{4}$ in. (24×31 cm.). Vincent van Gogh Foundation, Amsterdam. (F1404).
See note to Plate 80. There is a painting of this pose.

Plate 82 La Fenêtre Chez Bataille. 1887 (dated). Pen and ink, coloured chalks. $21 \times 15\frac{1}{2}$ in. ($53{\cdot}5 \times 39{\cdot}5$ cm.). Vincent van Gogh Foundation, Amsterdam. (F1392).
Inscribed with the title. A good example of the transformation of his art under Parisian influence. The drawing is coloured, concentration is on light effect and the picture is devoid of explicit symbolic allusions to all but the psychoanalytical.

Plate 83 Boulevard de Clichy. *c.* 1887. Pen and ink, coloured chalks. $15 \times 20\frac{3}{4}$ in. ($38 \times 52{\cdot}5$ cm.). Vincent van Gogh Foundation, Amsterdam. (F1393).
One of several atmospheric impressions of Paris, looser and less topographical than the Antwerp views. The asymmetry of composition and the cutting of two close-up figures are Impressionist devices most dramatically employed by Degas, whom Vincent admired.

Plate 84 Copy after Hiroshige's woodcut *Ohashi Bridge in the Rain*. 1887/8. Oil on canvas. $28\frac{3}{4} \times 21\frac{1}{4}$ in. (73 × 54 cm.). Vincent van Gogh Foundation, Amsterdam. (F372).

Vincent's new-found reverence for Japan was the other formative source for his Arles style of drawing, bringing a new sense of decoration and the exotic. The prints he chose to copy and collect were strong in colour, dramatic in design and elaborate in texture. His copies carry all the same implications of the best academic copying of European old masters—homage, submission, education.

Plate 85 Le Père Tanguy. 1887. Pencil. $8\frac{1}{2} \times 5\frac{1}{4}$ in. (21·5 × 13·5 cm.). Vincent van Gogh Foundation, Amsterdam. (F1412).

There are several painted portraits of Tanguy; the most conventional of them is dated 1887. Most are painted with a stylisation that merges into the backdrop of Japanese prints as here. Tanguy dealt in artists' materials and often took paintings in exchange for paint and canvas, to the dismay of his apparently unpleasant wife (461, 506). Tanguy—already accepting paintings from Cézanne, Pissarro, Gauguin, Seurat and others—offered Van Gogh the same terms, despite the unlikelihood of selling.

Van Gogh's painting technique 1885-90.

The development of Van Gogh's painting technique in the later 1880s was closely related to his contemporary drawings. As these details show, his mature painting became increasingly concerned with the manipulation of linear brushmarks. In 1885 (Plate 86a), there was no particular system to his application of paint. At this stage his painting was disorganised and undisciplined by comparison with his accomplished drawings; he was more interested in tone than colour and, in this particular painting at least, was more concerned with content than technique.

Close contact in Paris with current French art and with Japanese prints (1886-88) opened new possibilities in the articulation of surfaces and an absorbing concern with the concept of style. His paintings and drawings were highly experimental. He called his flower paintings 'gymnastics' and they display a rich range of improvised hatchings, stipplings and calligraphy (Plate 86b).

In Arles he resolved the chaos and by the autumn of 1888 (Plate 87a) his painting style was an ordered post-Impressionist system of small brush-marks, fairly even in size and direction. Their subtlety and complexity lay in the colour harmonies within this structure. At the same time in Arles, he was elaborating his formally complex calligraphic drawing style (Plate 88ff). In St-Rémy this calligraphy fed into his painting and the painted surfaces became massive, rhythmic orchestrations of coloured curvilinear units (Plate 87b). This extraordinary marriage of painting and drawing techniques constitutes the basis of Van Gogh's mature art.

Plate 86a Detail of *The Potato Eaters*. 1885. Nuenen. Vincent van Gogh Foundation, Amsterdam. (F82).

Plate 86b Detail of *Fritillaries in a Vase*. 1886. Paris. Musée du Louvre, Paris. (F213).

Plate 87a Detail of *The Sower*. 1888. Arles. E. G. Bührle Collection, Zürich. (F450).

Plate 87b Detail of *Road with Cypresses*. 1890. St-Rémy. Rijksmuseum Kröller-Müller, Otterlo. (F683).

Arles (February 1888 to May 1889)

Arles was first an escape from the exhausting excitement of Paris, but more particularly it was a 'gateway to the South', to Africa and the dreamworld of the Orient, in an aura of snow-capped mountains, brilliant sunlight, dazzling blossoms and patchwork landscapes. Uplifted by the environment, Van Gogh's painting matured with extraordinary rapidity during the summer and autumn. In his drawings he extended certain aspects of Impressionist and oriental techniques to a point that opened a new field of European graphic art, an expressive and decorative calligraphy, original and incessantly inventive.
In June he worked at the nearby coastal village of Saintes-Maries-sur-Mer and from May to July on the plains around Montmajour. A series of portraits, painted and drawn, of local people runs right through the period. He lived in furnished rooms at first but by October, when Gauguin arrived, he had his own house and studio ('The Yellow House'), simply furnished and decorated with prints and his own paintings.
Gauguin's stay of two and a half months brought excited optimism, distraction and disaster. On December 23rd, after one of many heated arguments, Van Gogh suffered his first mental crisis. He severed part of his ear and delivered it wrapped in newspaper to a girl in the local brothel. Gauguin returned later to find the police at the house and Vincent unconscious; he telegraphed Theo and left.
Vincent was discharged from hospital in January and befriended by the Roulin family, but was forced to return to hospital in February after a petition to the mayor signed by 80 Arles citizens. In May he decided to enter the asylum at St-Rémy nearby.

Plate 88 Cottages at Saintes-Maries. June 1888. Reed pen, pen and ink. $9\frac{1}{2} \times 12\frac{1}{2}$ in. ($24 \times 31{\cdot}5$ cm.). Museum of Modern Art, New York. Abby Aldrich Rockefeller Bequest. (F1435).
Van Gogh first mentioned using a reed pen at Etten, 1881 (146), but possibly that was not the authentic oriental reed used at Arles. Here he achieved quite new effects with it, in an expansive style which generates both an extraordinary sense of organic energy and a resolved stability of design. The uncertainty of this early example was quickly refined without losing its raw vitality.

Plate 89 Street at Saintes-Maries. June 1888. Reed pen and ink $12 \times 14\frac{1}{2}$ in. ($30{\cdot}5 \times 47$ cm.). Vincent van Gogh Foundation, Amsterdam. (F1437).
The dominant role of the sun in Van Gogh's symbolic view of nature is repeatedly reflected in his drawings (see also Plates 87b, 96, 97, 110, 111, etc.).

Plate 90 Haystacks. June 1888. Reed pen, pen and ink. $9\frac{1}{2} \times 12\frac{1}{2}$ in. ($24 \times 31{\cdot}5$ cm.). Museum of Fine Arts, Budapest. (F1426).
One of several studies of haystacks. This is probably a copy that he made for Theo of the more elaborate version (Plate 91): 'You will think the one with the ricks in a farmyard too bizarre, but it was done in a great hurry as a cartoon for a picture and it is to show you the idea' (498). The drawings he made in situ at this time were highly detailed; the paintings of this motif have none of the drawings' complexity.

Plate 91 Haystacks. June 1888. Reed pen, pen and ink. $9\frac{1}{2} \times 12\frac{1}{2}$ in. ($24 \times 31{\cdot}5$ cm.). Philadelphia Museum of Art, Samuel S. White III and Vera White Collection. (F1427).
See preceding note. This outstanding example of his Arles style was previously owned by the American painter John Russell, whom he had met in Paris and later wrote to. It later belonged to Matisse.

Plate 92 The Zouave Milliet. June 1888. Reed pen. $12\frac{3}{4} \times 9\frac{1}{2}$ in. ($32{\cdot}5 \times 24$ cm.). J. K. Thannhauser Collection, New York.
Milliet, a Zouave lieutenant, was one of Vincent's few friends in Arles and sat for several portraits. Milliet had served in Indo-China, which fed Van Gogh's taste for the exotic (and Gauguin's too).

Plate 93 Le Crau, view from Montmajour. May ?/July 1888. Reed pen, pencil. $18\frac{3}{4} \times 23\frac{1}{2}$ in. (48×60 cm.). Vincent van Gogh Foundation, Amsterdam. (F1420). He first worked at Montmajour in May 1888 (490), the date usually given to this study, and then more extensively in July (509). A drawing described to Bernard, in July, 'It doesn't look Japanese, but actually it is the most Japanese thing I have done' (B10) has also been identified with this study.

Plate 94 Vegetable gardens, the plain of Le Crau. June 1888. Reed pen and chinese ink. $9\frac{1}{2} \times 12\frac{3}{4}$ in. ($24 \times 32{\cdot}5$ cm.). Mr and Mrs Paul Mellon Collection. (F1486).
This is possibly the *Harvest* drawing referred to as 'rather more serious' in letter 498. It carries a strong sense of receding space in the diminishing scale of the marks, from the stabbed nib-ends in the foreground to the finely peppered stippling of the sky. There is a strong sense of light too, and in the rich variety of marks an equivalent of colour. 'I spend my time in painting and drawing landscapes or rather studies of colour' (501a).

Plate 95 Montmajour. July 1888. Reed pen, pen and chinese ink. $18\frac{3}{4} \times 23\frac{1}{4}$ in. ($47{\cdot}5 \times 59$ cm.). Rijksmuseum, Amsterdam. (F1446).
This raw, undomesticated landscape with strange outcrops of rock breaking across the atmospheric, distant plain, compares interestingly with the motifs of Cézanne (at Aix), Seurat (at Grandcamp) and Monet (at Etretat) of roughly the same date, all of them moving away from the more intimate motifs of Impressionism.

Plate 96 The Sower. June 1888. Reed pen and ink. $9\frac{1}{2} \times 12\frac{1}{2}$ in. ($24 \times 31{\cdot}5$ cm.). Vincent van Gogh Foundation, Amsterdam. (F1441).
This motif held the obsessiveness of an icon for Van Gogh: even at this date the pose still derives closely from Millet (cf. Plate 8). The textural variation of the drawing is within a limited scale of dots and lines, which are simultaneously vehicles for space, information and decoration.

Plate 97 View of Arles. Summer 1888. Reed pen, pen and ink. $9\frac{1}{2} \times 12\frac{1}{2}$ in. ($24 \times 31{\cdot}5$ cm.). Kunstmuseum, Winterthur. (F1514).
The high horizon and clear separation of texture areas—common devices in his 1888 drawings—create a Japanese sense of design.

Plate 98 The washerwomen. July 1888. Pen and ink. $12\frac{1}{2} \times 9\frac{1}{2}$ in. ($31{\cdot}5 \times 24$ cm.). Rijksmuseum Kröller-Müller, Otterlo. (F1444).
The dramatic perspective emphasises Van Gogh's remarkable blending of movements through space and across the surface.

Plate 99 Corner of a public park. July 1888. Reed pen and chinese ink. $12\frac{1}{2} \times 9\frac{1}{2}$ in. ($31{\cdot}5 \times 24$ cm.). Vincent van Gogh Foundation, Amsterdam. (F1477).
The emblematic nature of Van Gogh's use of textures can be seen here in an extreme form. The whole surface is divided into areas of distinct but analogous graphic devices.

Plate 100 Garden. July 1888. Pen, reed pen and ink. $19\frac{1}{2} \times 24$ in. ($49{\cdot}5 \times 61$ cm.). Oskar Reinhart am Römerholz Collection, Winterthur. (F1455).
Almost despite the profusion of different marks, there is a very powerful sense of space, depth and light.

Plate 101 Hospital garden in Arles. May 1889. Pen and ink (sepia). $18 \times 23\frac{1}{4}$ in. ($45{\cdot}5 \times 59$ cm.). Vincent van Gogh Foundation, Amsterdam. (F1467). One of few drawings made during his spell in the hospital at Arles. Compared with his Arles drawings in general, it is rather insensitive, comparable to quick copies (Plate 93), and possibly referred to in his comment 'the others are hasty studies made in the garden' (595).

Plate 102 Orchard with a low fence. May 1889? Brush and ink. $18 \times 23\frac{3}{4}$ in. ($45{\cdot}5 \times 60{\cdot}5$ cm.). Rijksmuseum Kröller-Müller, Otterlo. (F1505). The sombre mood anticipates the *sous-bois* motifs of St-Rémy. The dating given above was suggested by Cooper on the basis of Vincent's description of an otherwise unidentified drawing—'very dark and melancholy for one of spring'—in his last letter from Arles (590).

St-Rémy (May 1889 to May 1890)

Van Gogh spent exactly a year at the St-Paul de Mausole asylum at St-Rémy with no personal contacts of any intimacy. He suffered four more breakdowns or seizures, three of them immediately preceded by short visits to Arles (July, January, February), the other, late in December, was probably precipitated by news of the imminent birth of Theo's child and consequent feelings of guilt over his dependence on Theo. The child, a son named Vincent, was born on January 31st. After the fourth and most severe seizure he attempted suicide by poison. His output between seizures remained prolific. He worked in the surrounding landscape and in the asylum grounds. When he was confined to his room he either drew from his window or made copies after his own works or those of other artists (Delacroix, Doré, Daumier, Millet). His style of drawing became freer: the range of textures was reduced but the rhythms took on a new compulsive and organic vitality.

During this year he also had his first public successes. Albert Aurier published his article on Van Gogh in Paris in January and later in the same month he was represented by invitation at Les XX *in Brussels. Here he sold his first painting,* The Red Vineyard, *painted in Arles, November 1888.*

In March, 10 paintings were exhibited at the Salon des Indépendants, Paris, and well received in artists' circles. He determined to leave St-Rémy and did so on May 16th, spending three days with Theo and his wife in Paris on his way to Auvers.

Plate 103 Stone bench in the hospital garden, St-Rémy. May 1889. Reed pen and ink. $24\frac{1}{2} \times 19$ in. ($62{\cdot}5 \times 47$ cm.). Vincent van Gogh Foundation, Amsterdam. (F1522). The claustrophobic composition, airless and with no horizon, is typical of many St-Rémy drawings and paintings. So is the preoccupation with diseased and parasitic growths. Some have analysed both of these elements as an expression of Van Gogh's mental condition. He describes the surroundings at St-Rémy with great precision and objectivity—see letter 592, for example.

Plate 104 A lobby in the asylum. Summer 1889. Gouache and watercolour. 24×19 in. ($62 \times 47{\cdot}5$ cm.). Vincent van Gogh Foundation, Amsterdam. (F1530). Most of the early interiors of the period are in this brutally simplified technique, washed in with simple areas of watercolour and heightened with gouache.

Plate 105 Fountain in the hospital garden. Summer 1889. Reed pen and chinese ink. $19 \times 17\frac{3}{4}$ in. (48×45 cm.). Vincent van Gogh Foundation, Amsterdam. (F1531). The most impressive example of the style of angular hatching that he used at first in St-Rémy. The motif is well suited to it and the whole structure coalesces into a concrete massiveness absent from his drawing since Nuenen.

Plate 106 Cypresses. June 1889. Reed pen and ink. $24\frac{1}{2} \times 18\frac{1}{2}$ in. (62·5 × 47 cm.). Brooklyn Museum. (F1525).
There is a painted version of this motif (F613) and a sketch of it is included in letter 596, June 25th. The cypress had a particular symbolic significance for him ('an Egyptian obelisk . . . a splash of black in a sunny landscape'). The intricate spirals of 1888 (cf. Plate 91) took on an aggressive contortion in St-Rémy.

Plate 107 Starry night. June 1889. Reed pen, pen and chinese ink. $18\frac{1}{2} \times 24\frac{1}{2}$ in. (47 × 62·5 cm.). Kunsthalle, Bremen. (F1540).
The *chef d'œuvre* of his St-Rémy drawings and the study for one of the major paintings of the period (F612). In this and other works he was undisguisedly working from his imagination rather than from nature, in a spirit that he recognised was akin to the current work of Gauguin and Bernard (595). When Theo criticised this new 'style consciousness' as 'prejudicial to the true sentiment of things' (T19), Vincent admitted that 'the studies . . . drawn with such great shadowy lines, were not what they ought to have been', but he goes on: 'in landscape I am going on trying to mass things by means of a drawing style which tries to express the interlocking of masses' (613). Again his high degree of critical self-awareness warns us against over-interpretation in the face of the drawings most likely to invite it.

Plate 108 Cornfield with cypresses. Summer 1889. Pen, pencil. $18\frac{1}{2} \times 24\frac{1}{2}$ in. (47 × 62·5 cm.). Vincent van Gogh Foundation, Amsterdam. (F1538).
A study for the painting F615 (Tate Gallery, London). See note to Plate 109.

Plate 109 L'Olivette, les Beaux. Summer 1889. Pencil, reed pen and ink. $18\frac{1}{2} \times 24\frac{1}{2}$ in. (47 × 62·5 cm.). Staatliche Museum, Berlin. (F1544).
This beautiful drawing is the nearest equivalent at St-Rémy to the refined complexity of the great Arles landscapes. It is a study for the painting F712 (J. H. Whitney, New York). Although many of these drawings are 'studies' for paintings in the sense that they resolve the painting's composition, they are also self-sufficient entities: the drawing and the painting are two distinct realisations of the theme, each with its own scale of expression. The hallucinatory formal distortions of these landscapes do in fact bear some reference to the strange shapes of gnarled olive trees, and to the peculiar rock structure of the local mountains, les Alpilles. But as Van Gogh himself said, they are, 'exaggerations from the point of view of arrangement, their lines are warped as in old wood'. They give 'the effect of the whole' (607).

Plate 110 The enclosed field. Summer 1899. Black chalk. $18\frac{1}{2} \times 24\frac{1}{2}$ in. (47 × 62 cm.). Staatliche Graphische Sammlung, Munich. (F1552).
The view from Vincent's window at the asylum, which provided a motif in itself and a background for many paintings and drawings (Plates 111, 112).

Plate 111 The reaper. June 1889. Reed pen, pen and ink. $18\frac{1}{2} \times 24\frac{1}{2}$ in. (47 × 62 cm.) Staatliche Museum, Berlin. (F1546).
He worked on this subject from June to September as a project of particular importance (see letters 597, 604). The finished painting (F618) —'the image of death . . . the opposite of that sower I had tried before' —relates closely to this drawing.

Plate 112 Sower in the rain. 1889/90. Pencil. $9\frac{1}{2} \times 10\frac{3}{4}$ in. (24 × 27·5 cm.). Vincent van Gogh Foundation, Amsterdam. (F1551).
The setting is the same as that of the last two drawings, but the style is moving towards the looser open technique of Auvers. De la Faille originally assigned it to the Auvers period, but there are a large number of St-Rémy drawings that anticipate his last manner.

Plate 113 Plant study. 1889/90. Reed pen and ink. $16\frac{1}{4} \times 12\frac{1}{4}$ in. (41×31 cm.). Vincent van Gogh Foundation, Amsterdam. (F1612).
There are a few examples running right through the French years of this sort of direct, concentrated study of small motifs (crickets, butterflies, etc.). There is a simple, lucid clarity of transcription here that contrasts totally with contemporary landscapes, in which form and space are amalgamated into a strange continuum of movement.

Plate 114 Studies of a hand and a chair. 1890. Pencil. $12\frac{1}{2} \times 9\frac{1}{4}$ in. ($32 \times 23{\cdot}5$ cm.). Vincent van Gogh Foundation, Amsterdam. (F1549 verso).
On the reverse is a charcoal drawing of the enclosed field with colour notes. The strange pulsating hatching of the chair anticipates the St-Rémy landscapes of 1890 (Plate 118ff).

Plate 115 Peasants at the table. Winter 1889/90. Pencil. $9\frac{1}{2} \times 12\frac{1}{2}$ in. (24×32 cm.). Vincent van Gogh Foundation, Amsterdam. (F1594 verso).
During the winter Vincent asked Theo to send him some of his Dutch drawings to work from. Several times he spoke of reworking old themes, including *The Potato Eaters* and views of Nuenen, in a general mood of nostalgia for the North and for what seemed to him now the stability and security of his life in Holland. His original optimism about 'the South' now turned to mistrust of living there; he even tried to attribute his illness to it.

Plate 116 Studies of hands, heads, and figures. 1890. Black crayon. $9\frac{1}{2} \times 12\frac{1}{2}$ in. (24×32 cm.). Vincent van Gogh Foundation, Amsterdam. (F1603 verso).

Plate 117 Studies of hands and for the sower. 1890. Black crayon. (F1603).
Two pages of sketches. The first includes some experiment with technique apparently for its own sake—the head and hand overlaid with hatching—but it was probably inconsequential doodling. It has been suggested (Tralbaut) that the hands on the second sheet at least were drawn in Antwerp and the *Sower* studies added to it later. His argument is on the basis of style, but there is more than a little stylistic argument in favour of St-Rémy (cf. Plate 114).

Plate 118 The tree. 1890. Pencil and charcoal. $11\frac{3}{4} \times 8$ in. ($30 \times 20{\cdot}5$ cm.). Vincent van Gogh Foundation, Amsterdam. (F1580).
In a series of landscape drawings, some with figures, that were probably executed early in 1890, Van Gogh developed the technique of the *Starry Night* in another way. There is a stronger sense of positive/negative distinction in his greater use of blank areas. But at the same time, the hatching within the positive forms retains an organic and vital animation of the old decorative, two-dimensional nature. The tension between the two qualities lends an extraordinary power and originality to this lesser-known series of spontaneous and economical drawings. Plates 118 to 124 represent the range of technique.

Plate 119 Landscape with row of pines. 1890. Black crayon. $9\frac{1}{4} \times 12$ in. ($23{\cdot}5 \times 30{\cdot}5$ cm.). Vincent van Gogh Foundation, Amsterdam. (F1578).

Plate 120 Four pines. 1890. Pencil. $11\frac{3}{4} \times 7$ in. (30×18 cm.). Vincent van Gogh Foundation, Amsterdam. (F1572).

Plate 121 Two pines. 1890. Pencil. $11\frac{3}{4} \times 8$ in. ($30 \times 20{\cdot}5$ cm.). Vincent van Gogh Foundation, Amsterdam. (F1591).

Plate 122 Figures in the snow. 1890. Pencil. $9 \times 12\frac{1}{4}$ in. (23×31 cm.). Vincent van Gogh Foundation, Amsterdam. (F1581).

Plate 123 Four men on the road. 1890. Black crayon. 9¾ × 12¾ in. (25 × 32·5 cm.). Vincent van Gogh Foundation, Amsterdam. (F1590).
The prominent role of the figures in Plates 122 and 123 may be seen as part of Van Gogh's return to his Dutch themes (see note to Plate 118).

Plate 124 Landscape study with a pine. 1890. Pencil. 9¼ × 12½ in. (25 × 32 cm.). Vincent van Gogh Foundation, Amsterdam. (F1583).
Although, from the colour notes, one may assume it was made with painting in mind, this slight sketch is one of the most dramatic of the St-Rémy landscape drawings and epitomises their poise between flatness and depth.

Auvers-sur-Oise (May to July 1890)
Van Gogh arrived in Auvers on May 21st and spent his last two months there. Theo had arranged that Dr Paul Gachet should care for Vincent and almost immediately a meaningful relationship based on sympathy and respect developed between them. He lived in a local inn, Chez Ravoux, but was a frequent visitor to Gachet's house. With his life and effects in some disorder (he talks of furniture that never arrives from Arles and of a heap of paintings lying under Theo's bed in Paris 'that I can touch up') Vincent felt the need for new progress and was grateful for Gachet's reassurances. Incredibly but typically at this stage, he once more starts asking Theo for the elementary drawing primers he had used in 1880: 'When you can you might send me Bargue's Exercises au Fusain *for a while. I need it urgently. . . .' (636) and 'I am terribly anxious to copy once more all the charcoal studies by Bargue, you know, the nude figures' (638).*
The moderate optimism of the first letters from Auvers, in which Vincent draws strength from Gachet's vulnerability—'he is as discouraged about his job as a doctor as I am about my painting' (637) and 'he certainly seems as ill or distraught as you or me' (638)—rapidly dissolved in July. He visited Theo in Paris on July 1st and soon after wrote in a very different vein: 'We must not count on Dr Gachet at all . . . he is sicker than I am' (648). His comment at the end of the same letter, '. . . the prospect grows darker. I see no happy future at all' is principally an expression of his anxiety about the future of Theo and his family and the extra burden he represented.
His last letter, found on him when he died, speaks of Theo's part in making his paintings. He shot himself on July 27th and died two days later.

Plate 125 Street in Auvers (la maison du Père Pilon). May 1890. Charcoal, pen and violet ink. 17½ × 21¾ in. (44·5 × 55 cm.). Vincent van Gogh Foundation, Amsterdam. (F1638).
Many of the Auvers landscapes incorporate coloured media—water-colours, gouache, ink or crayon. The quality of the drawing is very comparable to the later St-Rémy studies at first, but the organisation becomes looser and again covers the whole surface. The patterned areas are reduced to simple coarse textures of dots or circles and the rhythmic, linear passages lose something of their innate organic strength (e.g. the foreground in Plates 128, 130). *Houses behind the trees* (Plate 131) is probably the most compulsively expressionist drawing of his whole œuvre and makes the early St-Rémy studies that had disturbed Theo (Plate 106) seem almost serene. In terms of achievement it was a very mixed swansong. The mysterious Redon-like *Wooded River* (Plate 129) is a highpoint, but there is also the thoroughly out-of-character unevenness within one study like *Women working in the fields* (Plate 130), which ranges from the tough Gauguin-like frieze of silhouettes in the foreground to the desultory, throw-away treatment of the distant hills.

Plate 126 The house of Dr Gachet. May/June 1890. Black crayon. 17½ × 10¾ in. (44·5 × 27·5 cm.). Vincent van Gogh Foundation, Amsterdam. (F1636).
See note to Plate 125.

Plate 127 Houses and gardens with vines. June/July 1890. Charcoal, watercolour and oil. $17\frac{1}{4} \times 21\frac{1}{4}$ in. (43·5 × 54 cm.). Vincent van Gogh Foundation, Amsterdam. (F1624).
See note to Plate 125 and letter 648.

Plate 128 The farm. June/July 1890. Reed pen and ink, heightened with blue, grey and white. $17\frac{3}{4} \times 23\frac{1}{2}$ in. (45 × 60 cm.). Art Institute of Chicago, Bequest of Kate Brewster. (F1642).
See note to Plate 126.

Plate 129 Wooded river. June/July 1890. Black crayon, charcoal. $9\frac{3}{4} \times 12$ in. (23·5 × 30·5 cm.). Vincent van Gogh Foundation, Amsterdam. (F1627).
See note to Plate 125.

Plate 130 Women working in the fields. June/July 1890. Pencil.
9 × 12 in. (23 × 30·5 cm.). Vincent van Gogh Foundation, Amsterdam.
See note to Plate 125.

Plate 131 Houses behind the trees. June/July 1890. Black crayon, pen and violet ink, blue crayon. $9\frac{1}{2} \times 12\frac{1}{4}$ in. (24 × 31 cm.). Vincent van Gogh Foundation, Amsterdam. (F1637).
See note to Plate 125.

Plate 132 Portrait of Dr Gachet. May 1890 (dated). Etching.
$7 \times 5\frac{3}{4}$ in. (17·5 × 14·5 cm.). Cabinet d'Estampes, Amsterdam. (F1664).
Van Gogh's only etching; he was taught the technique by Gachet shortly after his arrival in Auvers. He described the etching in an unfinished letter to Gauguin: 'the heart-broken expression of our time. If you like, something like what you said of your "Garden of Olives", not meant to be understood' (643).

Bibliography

Cooper, Douglas
Drawings and Watercolours by Vincent van Gogh. New York, 1955 (Macmillan). 32 colour plates with notes.

de la Faille, J. B.
L'Œuvre de Vincent van Gogh, catalogue raisonné. Paris, 1928 (Editions G. van Oest). Volumes III and IV, drawings, watercolours and lithographs. (A new edition of the complete catalogue is now in preparation in which, although additions will be made, the original numbers will remain unchanged.)

Hammacher, A. M.
Van Gogh. Milan, 1953 (Martello). A selection of 33 drawings with introduction.

Marlborough Fine Art, London
Catalogue of the exhibition *Van Gogh's Life in his Drawings,* 1962. Drawings and documents with introduction and notes by A. M. Hammacher.

Muensterberger, W.
Vincent van Gogh, Drawings, Pastels, Studies. London, 1947 (Falcon Press). 114 works from the V.W. van Gogh collection, Laren. 8 colour plates.

Rewald, John
Post-Impressionism from Van Gogh to Gauguin. Museum of Modern Art, New York, 1956.

Rijksmuseum Kröller-Müller, Otterlo
Catalogue of 272 works by Vincent van Gogh in the museum's collection, 1959. Includes many of the early drawings, with detailed notes and documentation. Comprehensive bibliography.

Tralbaut, Marc
Vincent van Gogh in het caf' conc of het raakpunt met Raffaelli. Amsterdam, 1955.

Vanbeselaere, W.
De hollandsche Periode in het Werk van Vincent van Gogh. Antwerp, 1937; French edition 1938.

The Complete Letters of Vincent van Gogh. Greenwich, Conn., U.S.A. (New York Graphic Society) and London (Thames and Hudson), 1958. Three volumes, with illustrations of the drawings from the letters.

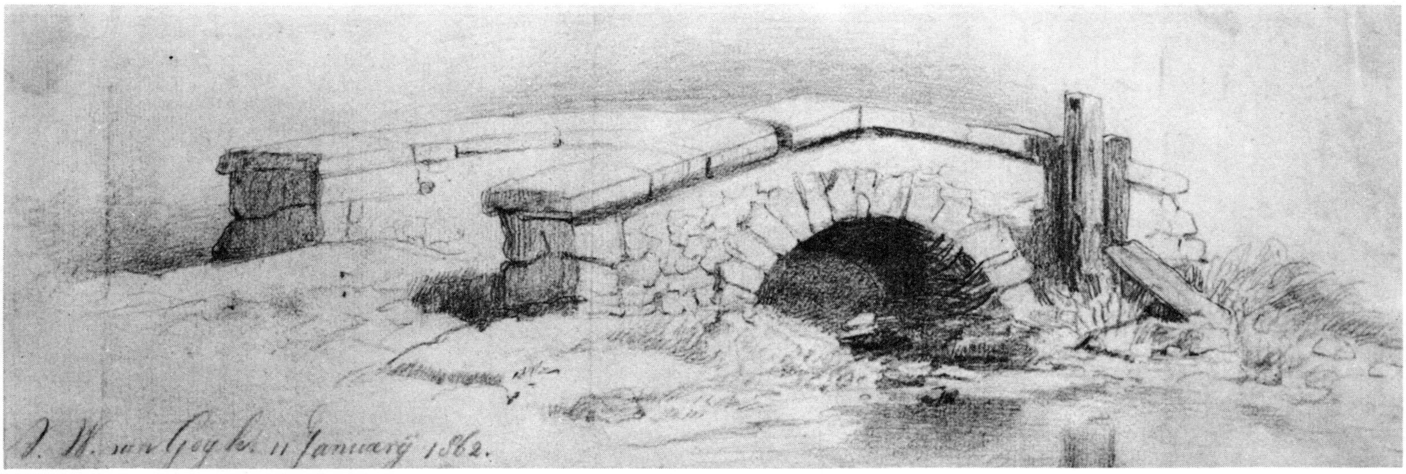

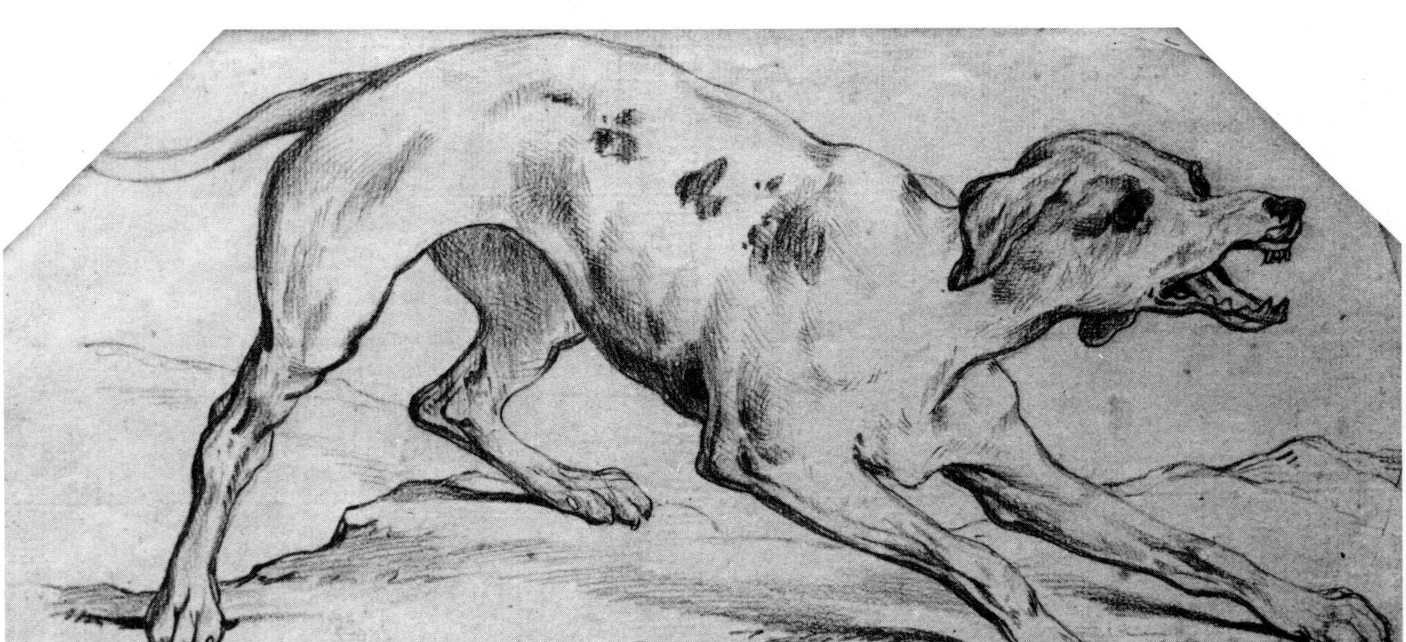

Plate Ia, Plate Ib

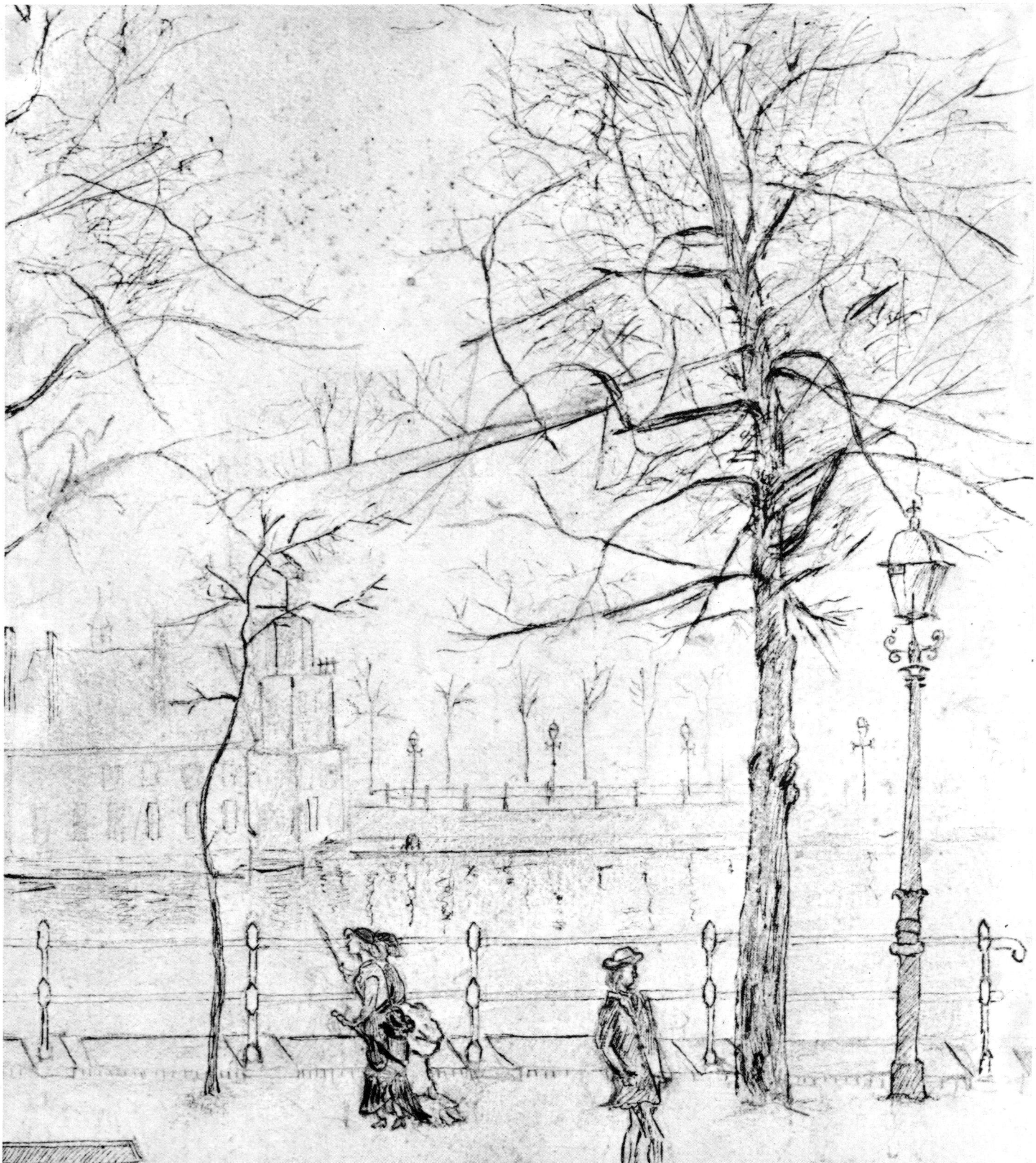

Plate 2

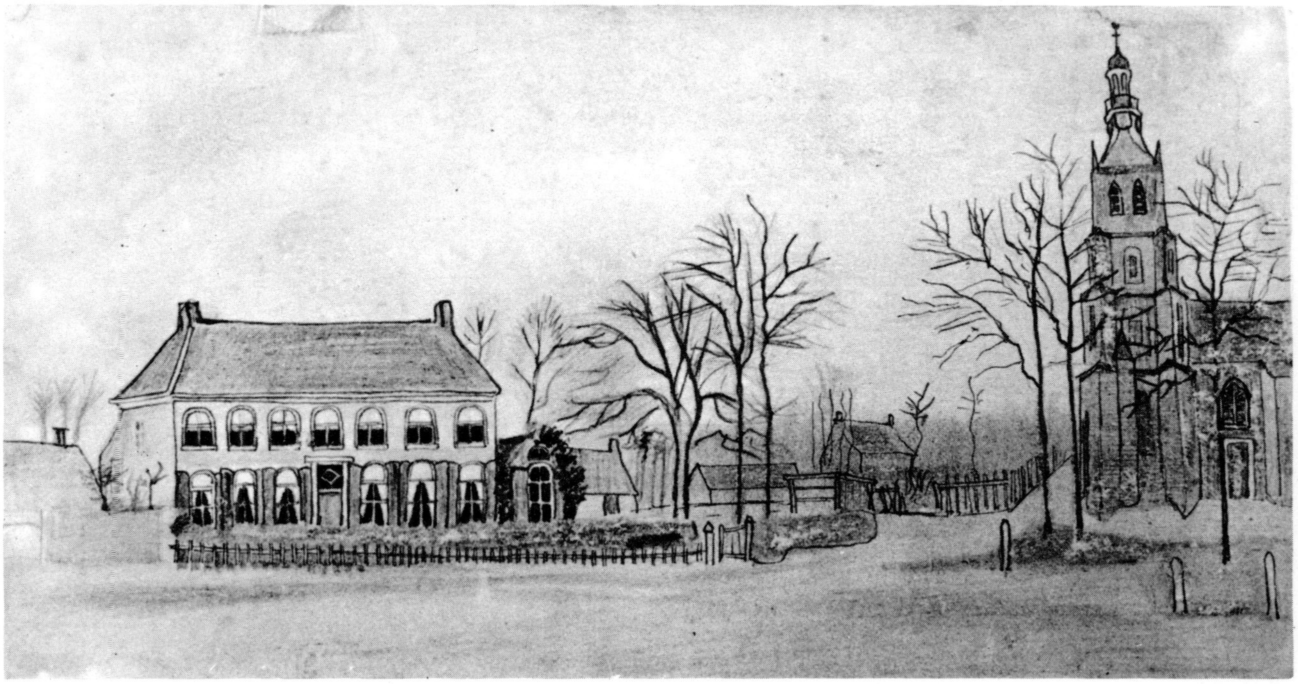

Plate 3

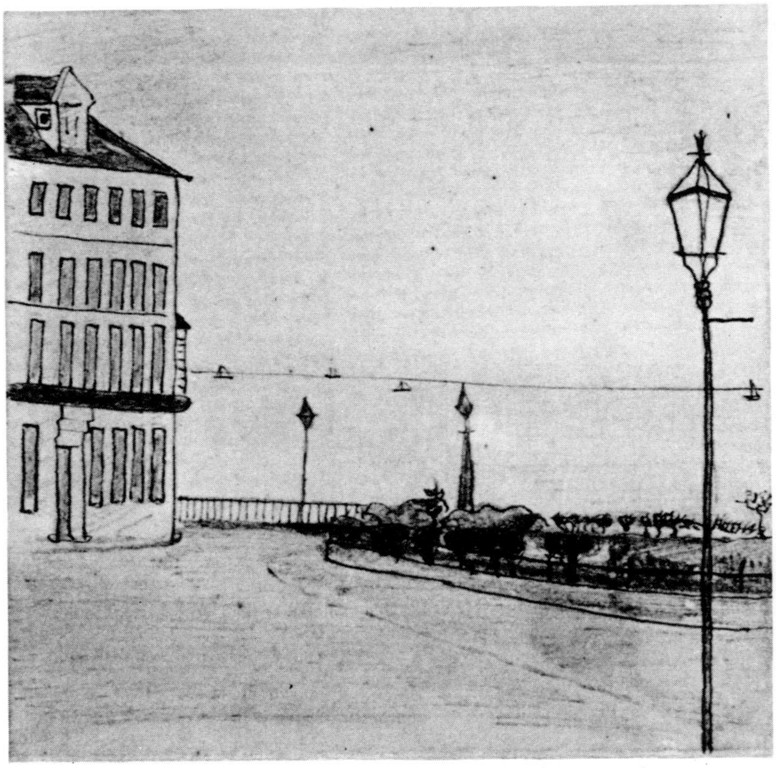

Plate 4

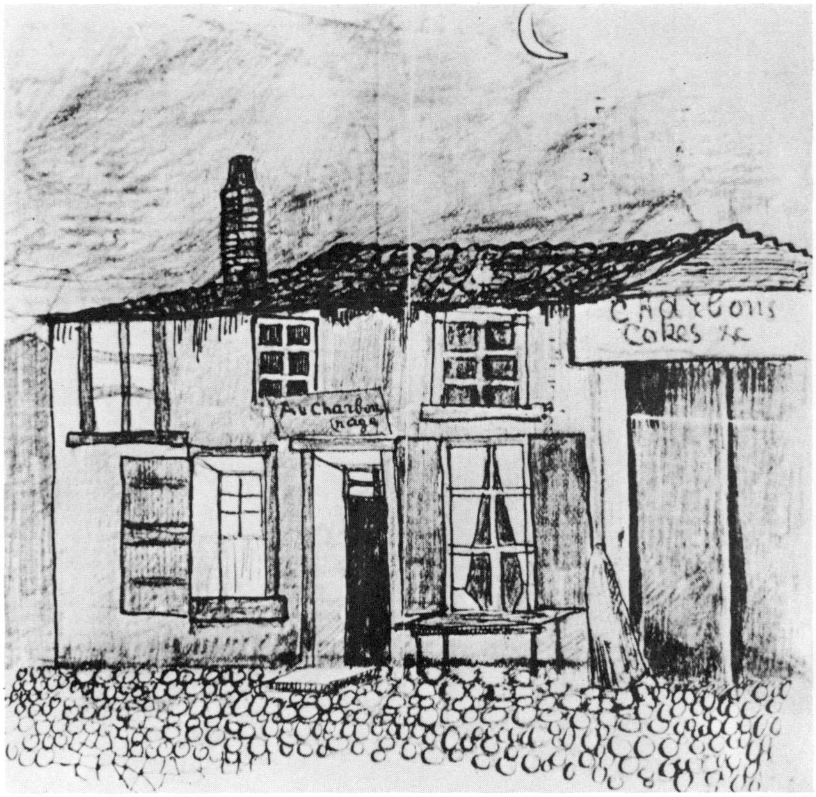
Au Charbon
Charbons
Cokes

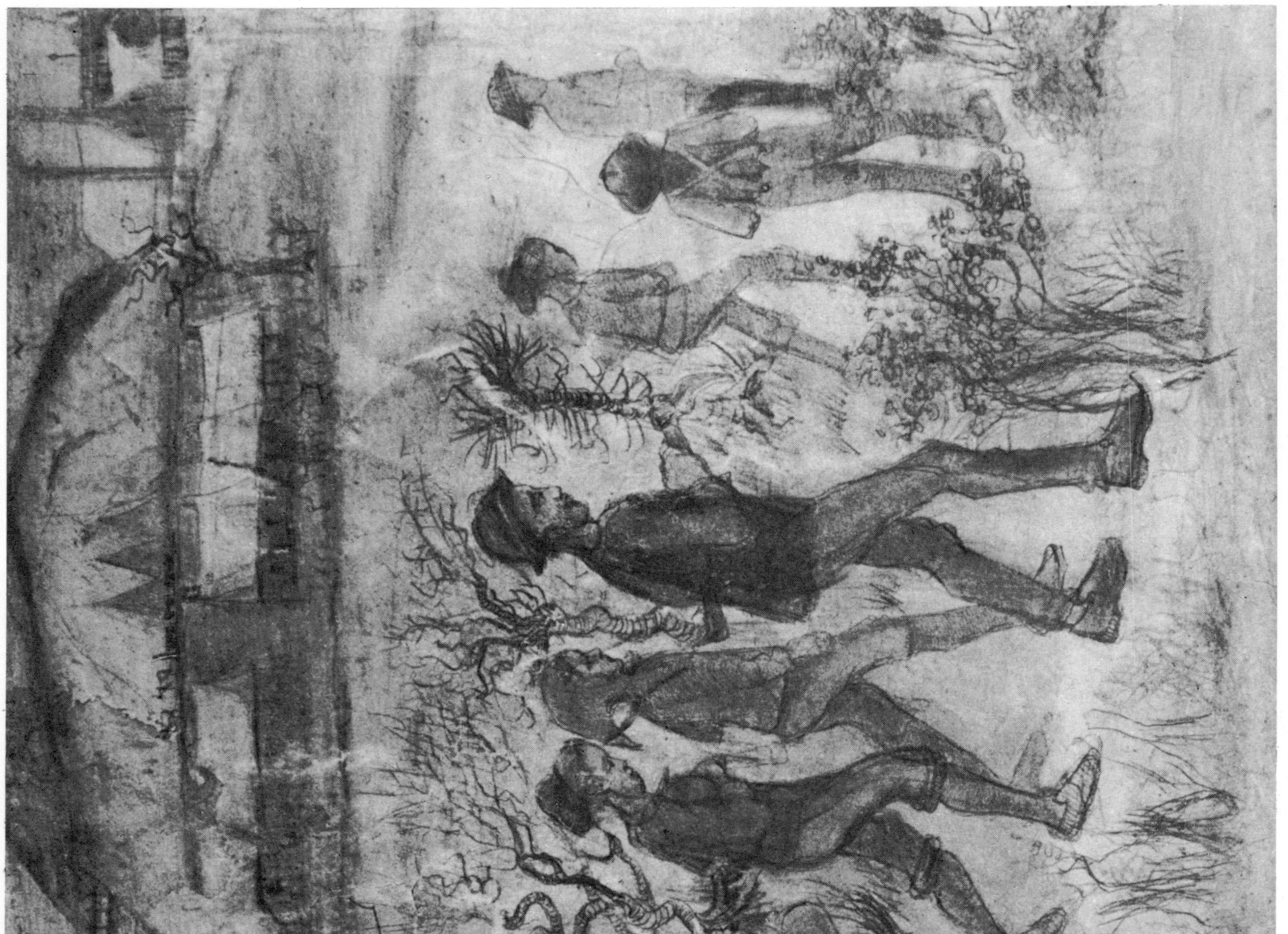

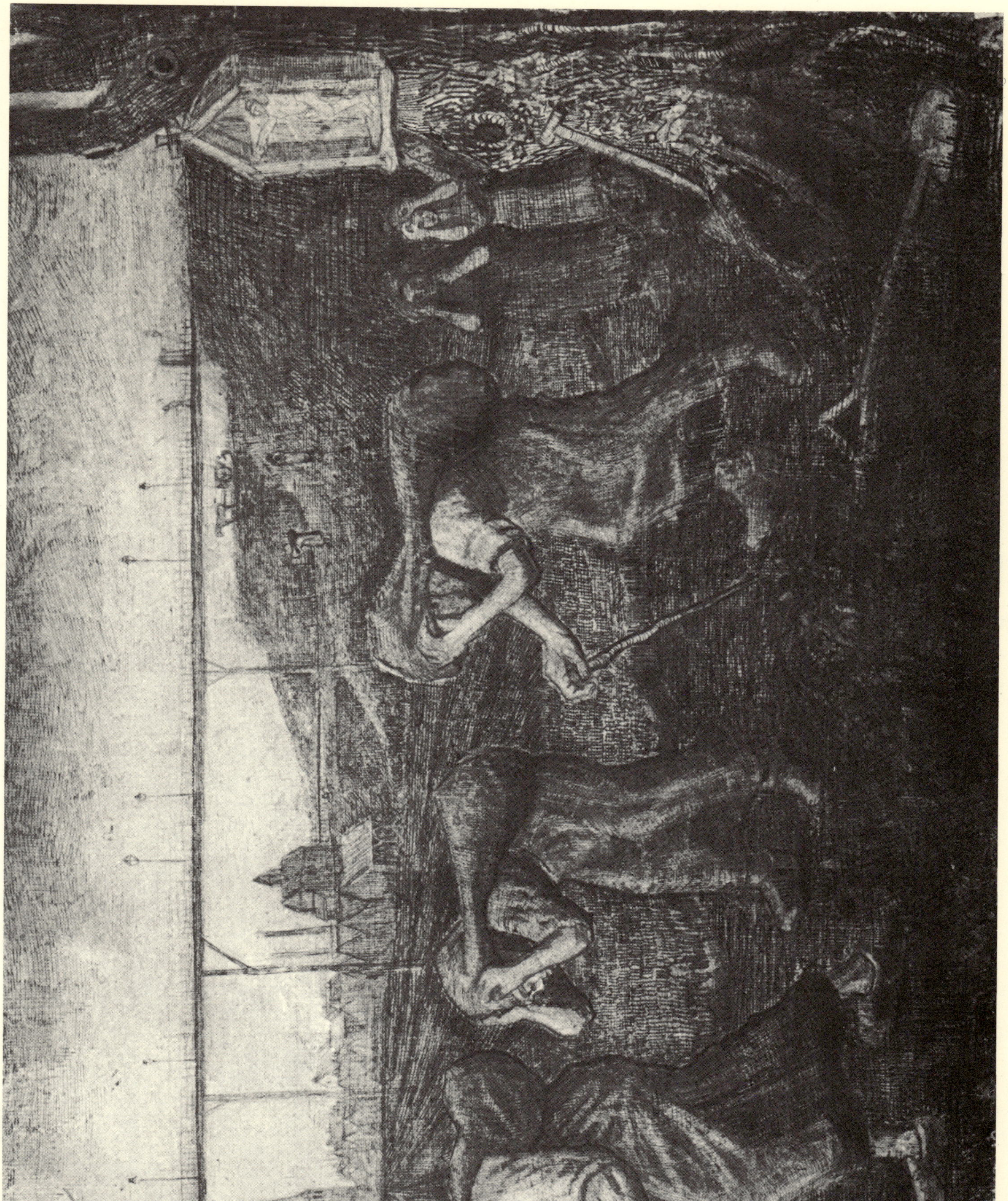

Plate 7

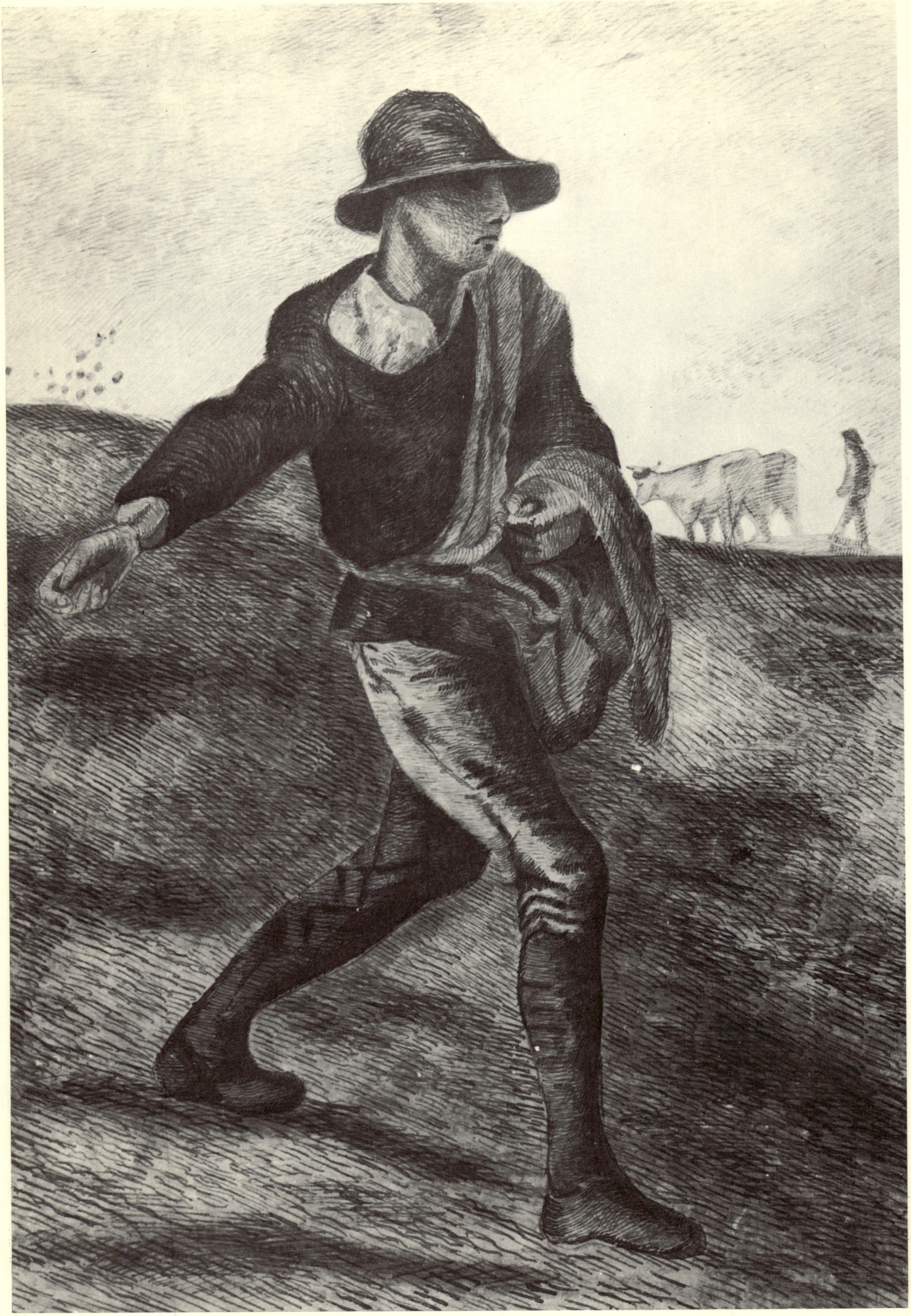

Plate 8

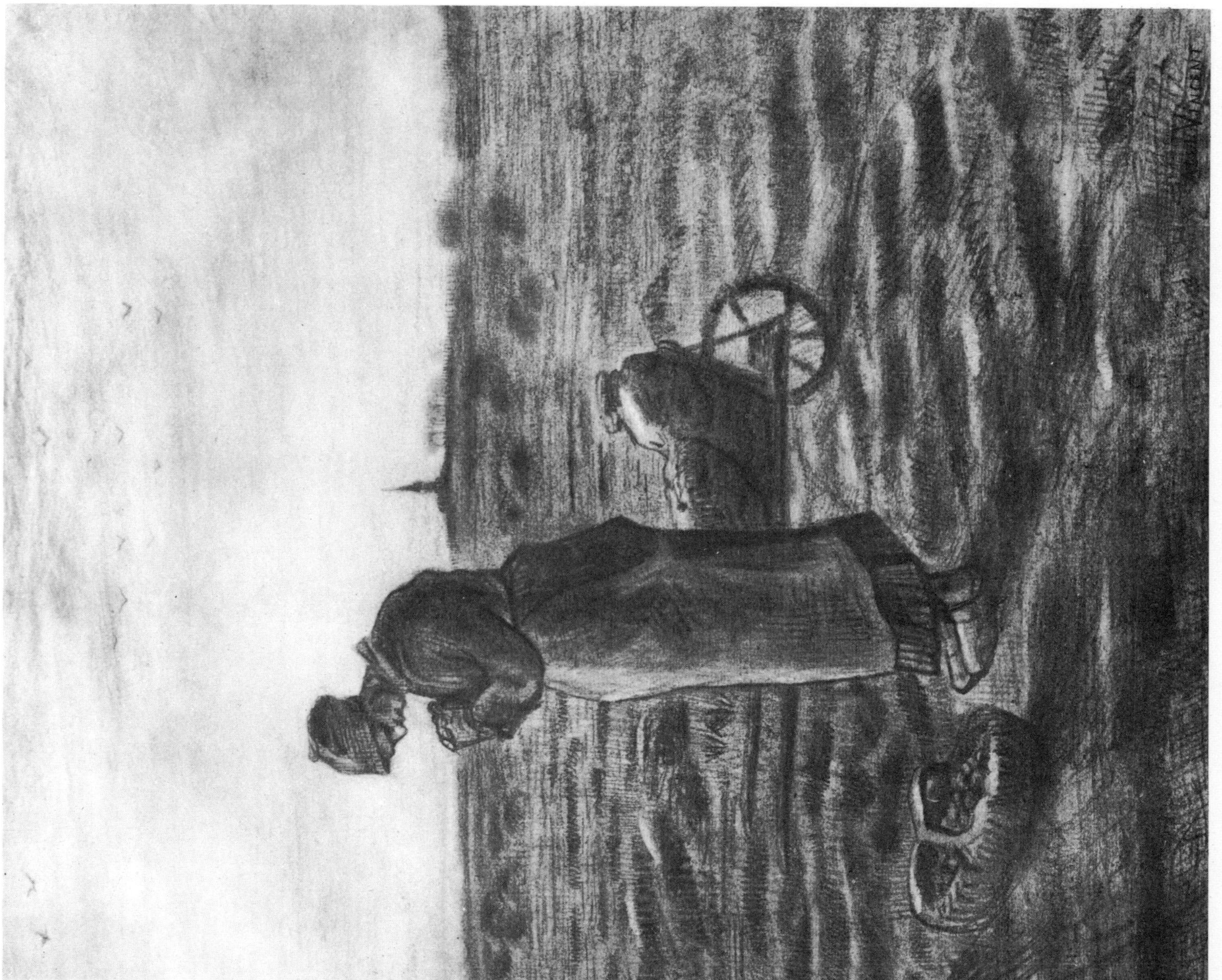

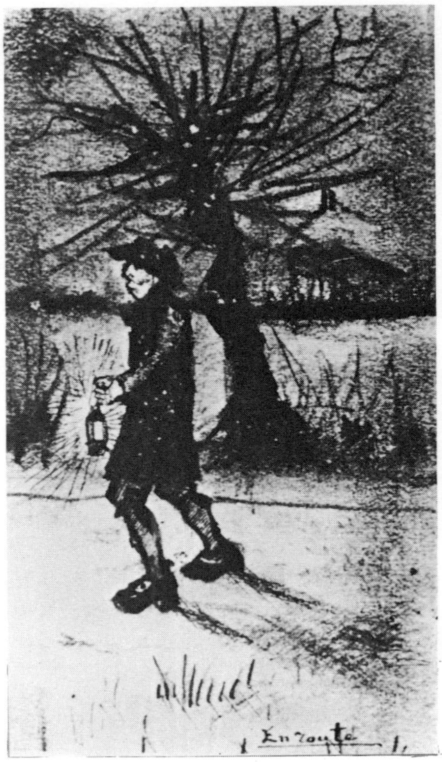

Plate 10

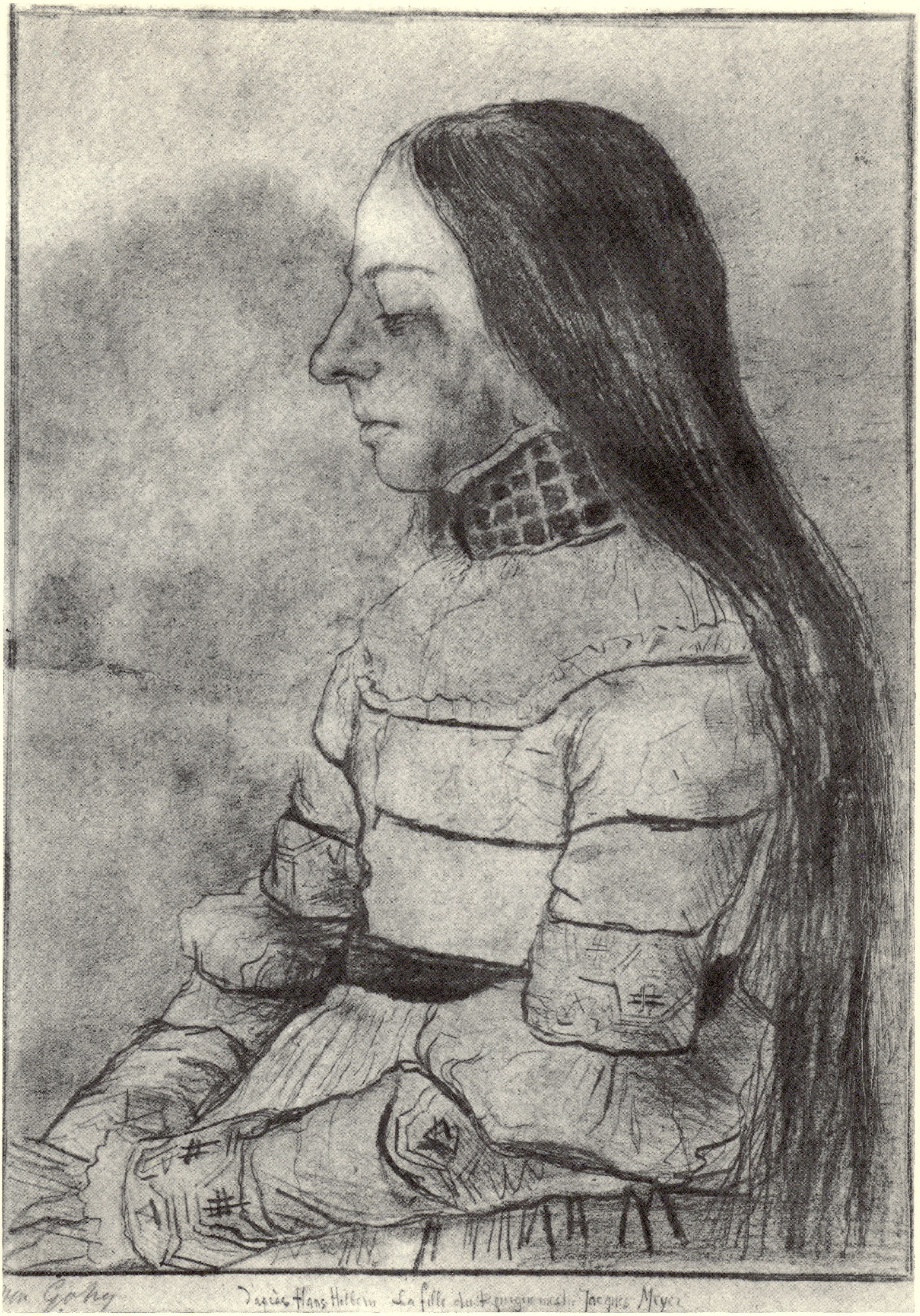
Gogh
D'après Hans Holbein La fille du Bourgmestre Jacques Meyer

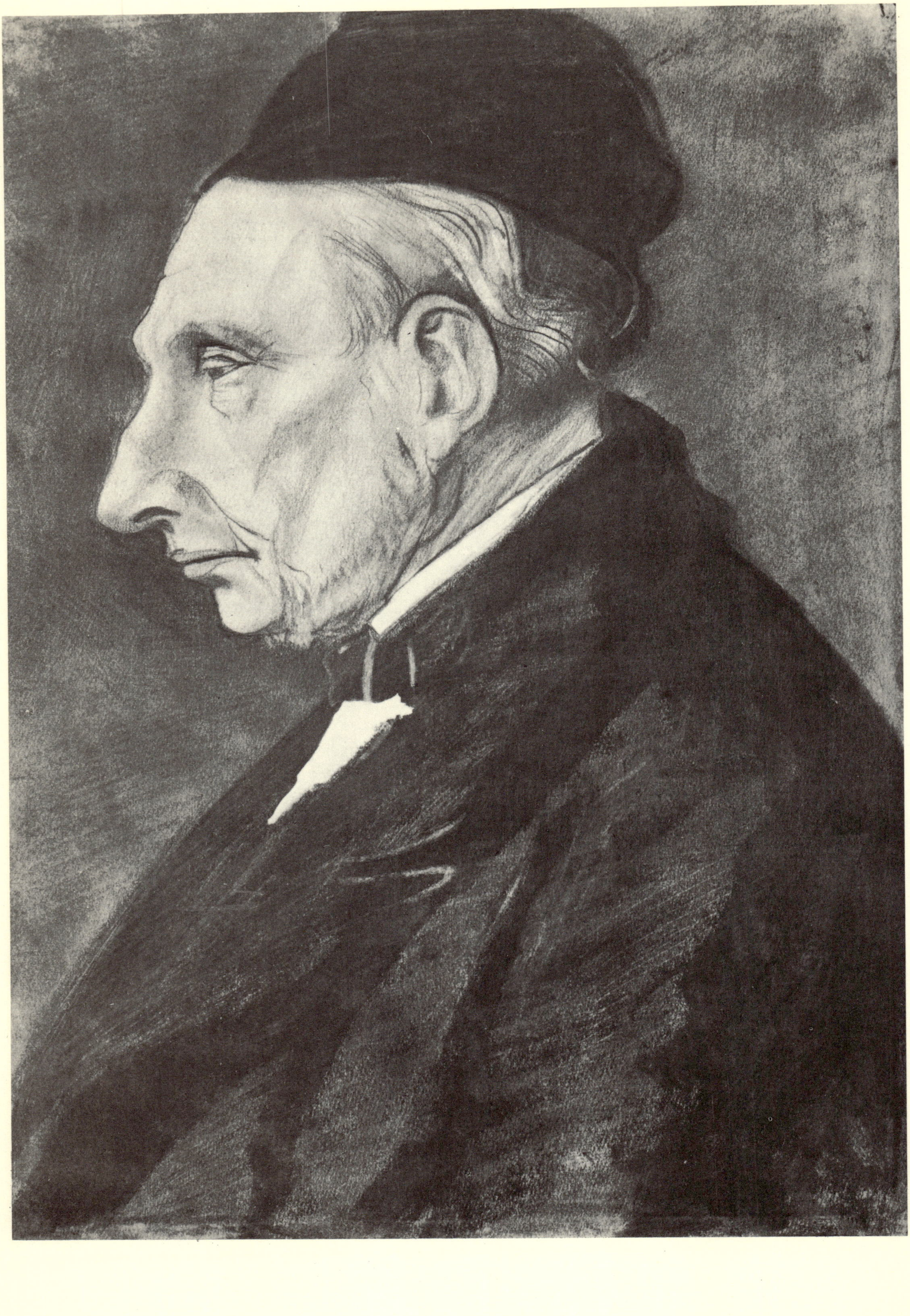

Plate 12

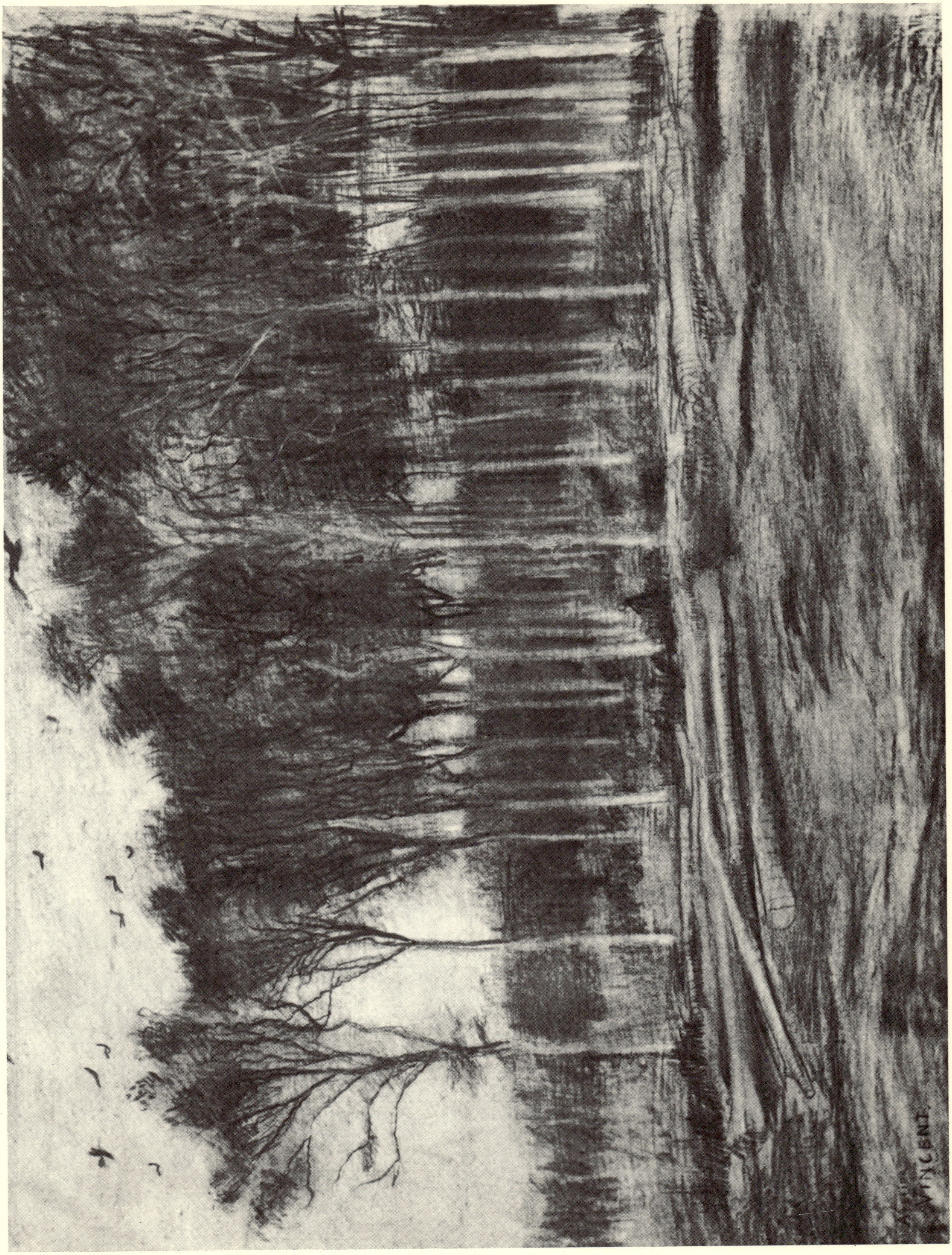
VINCENT

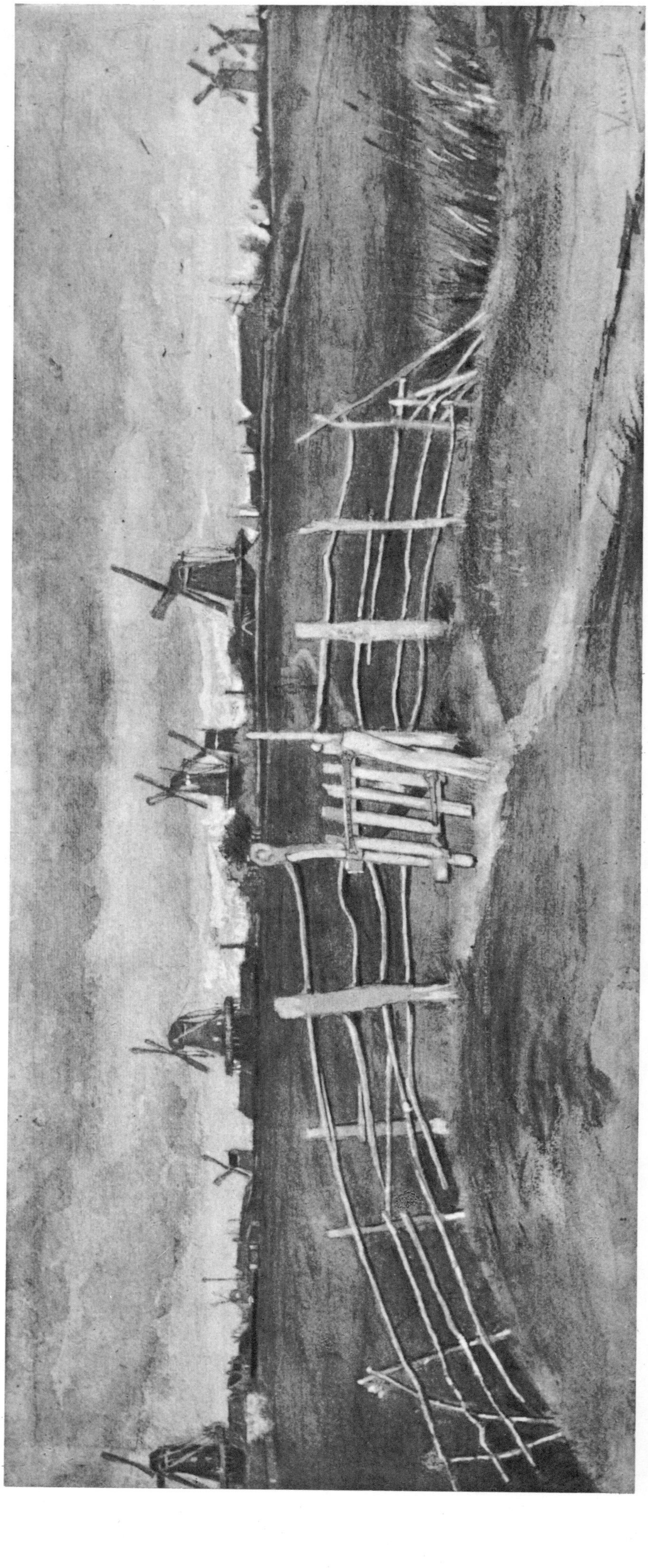

Plate 14

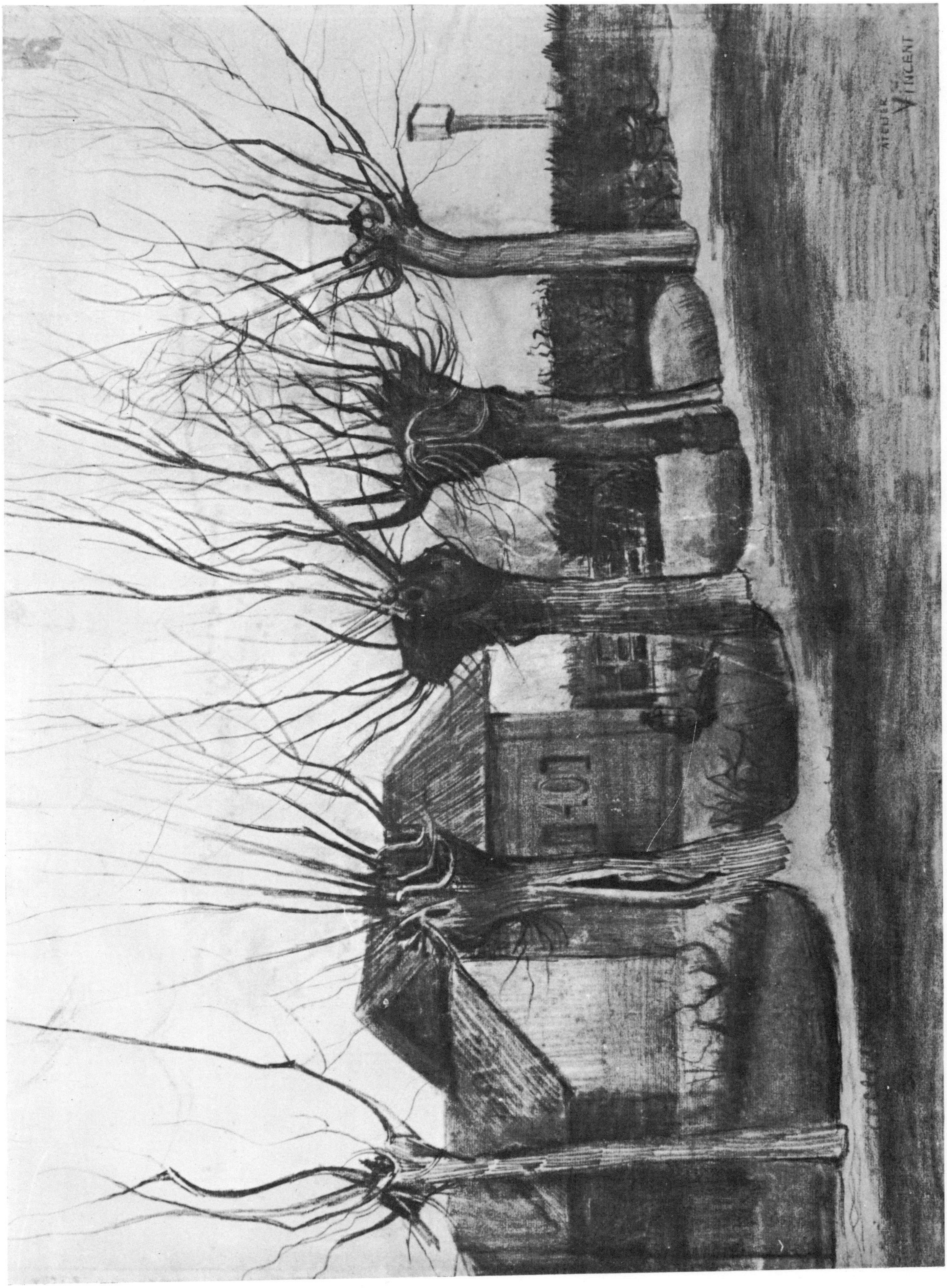

Plate 15

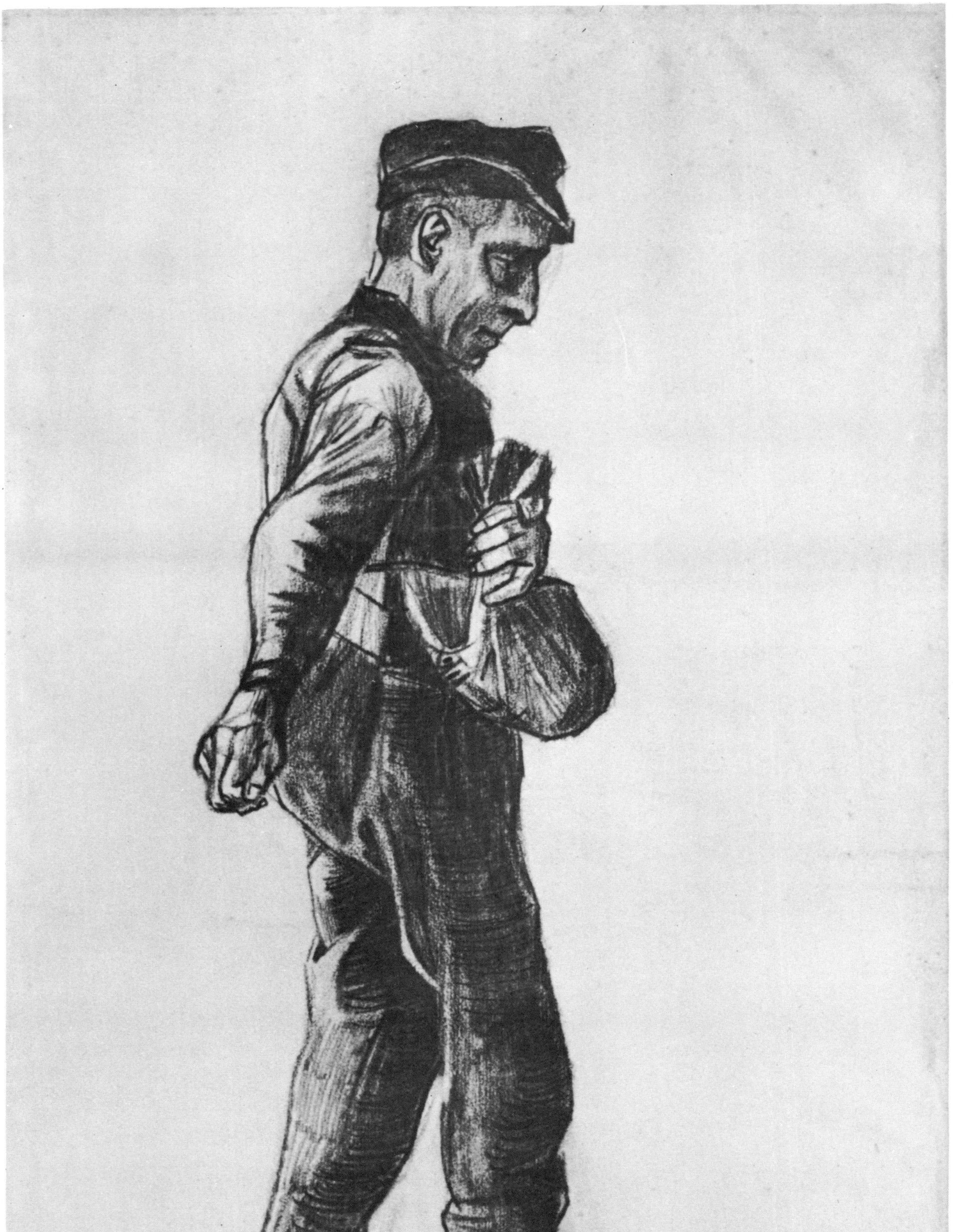

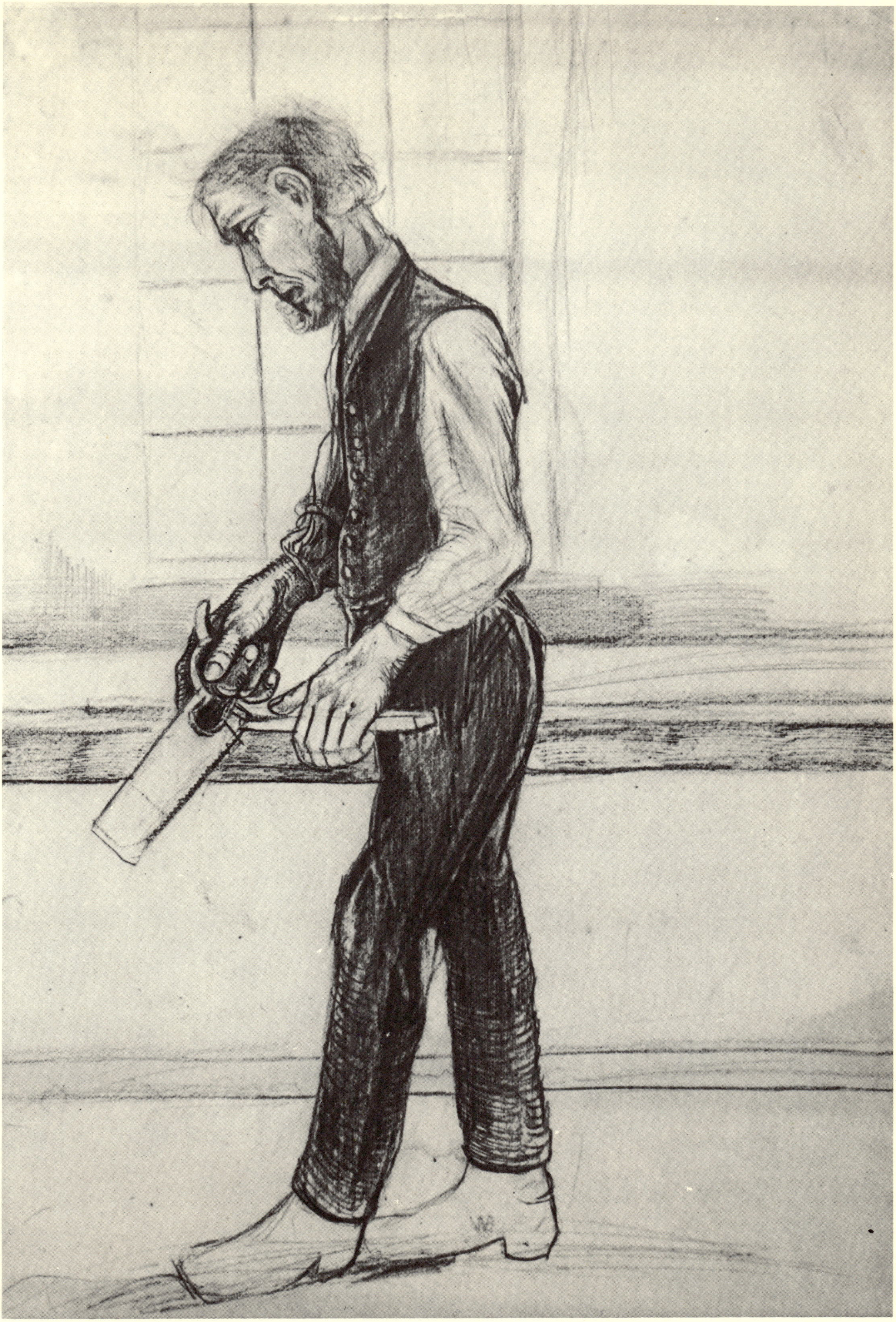

Plate 17

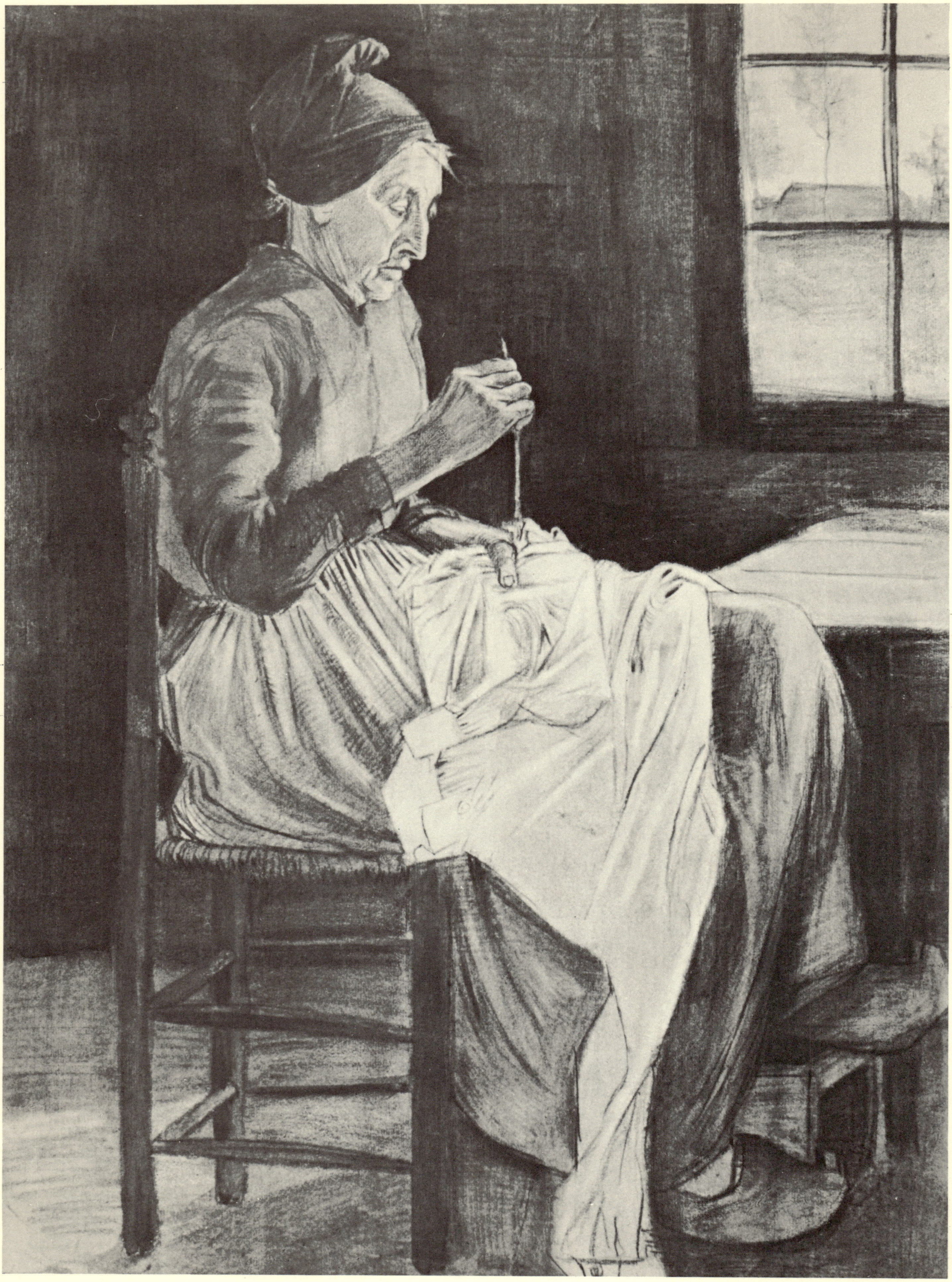

Plate 18

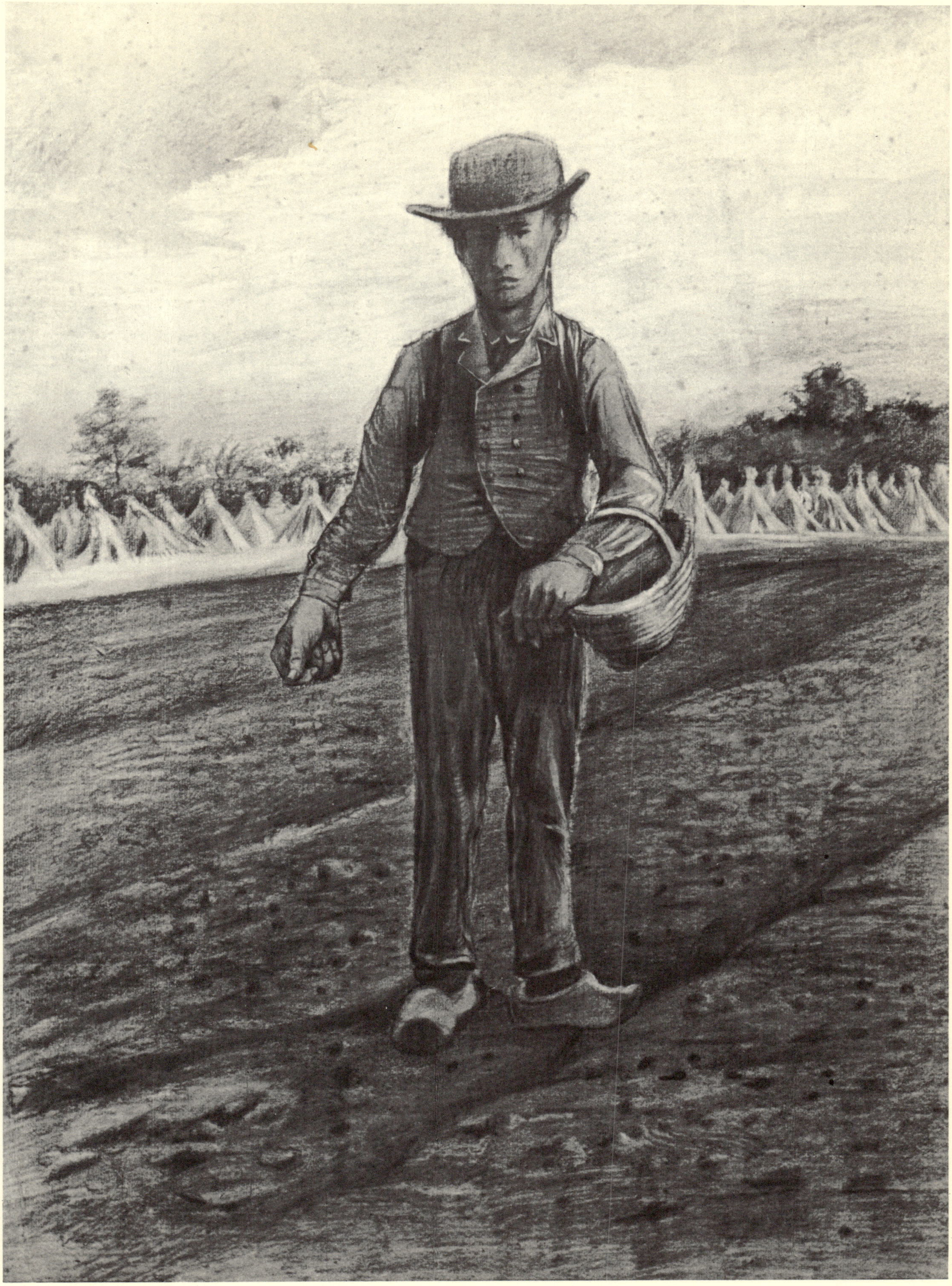

Plate 19

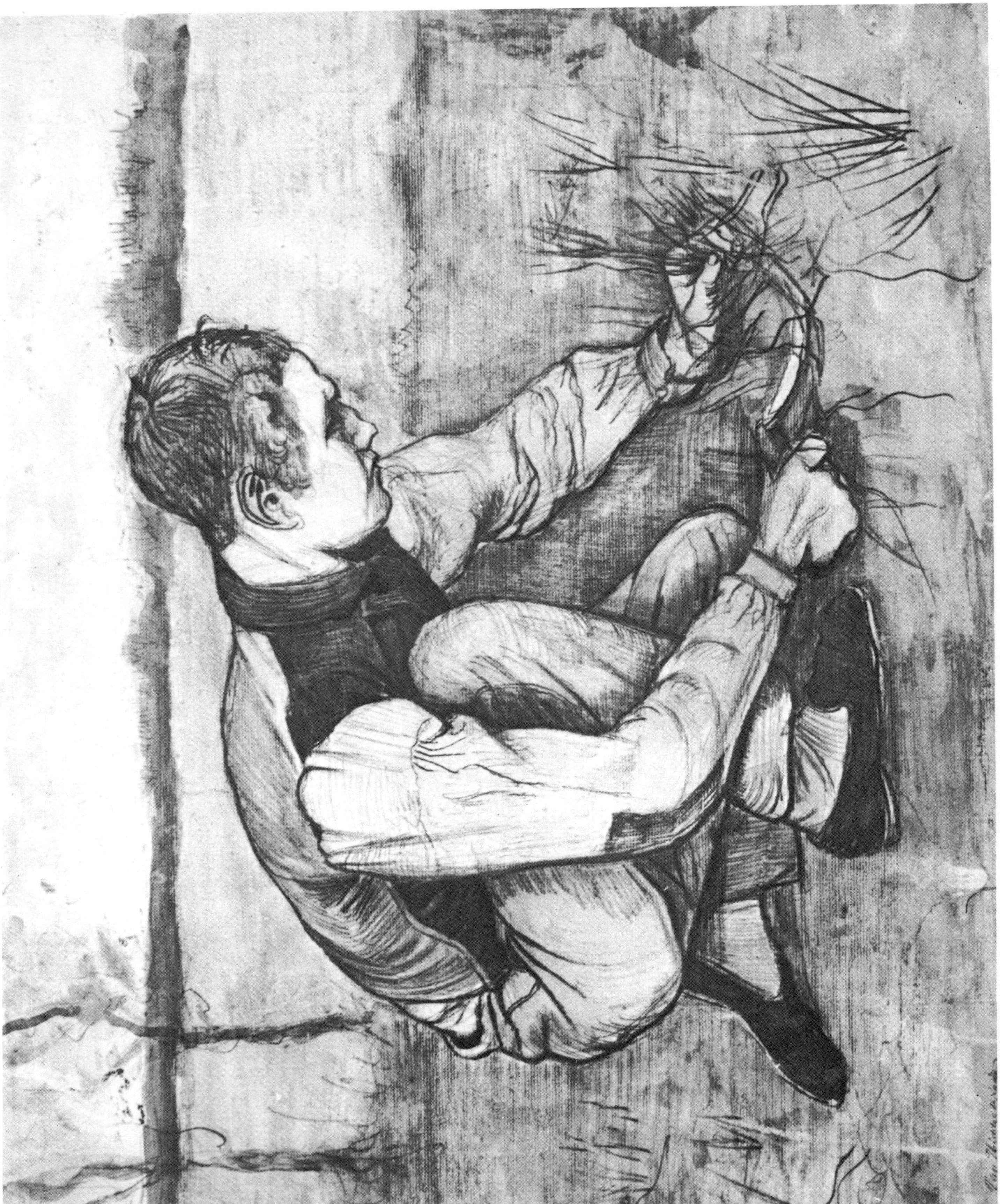

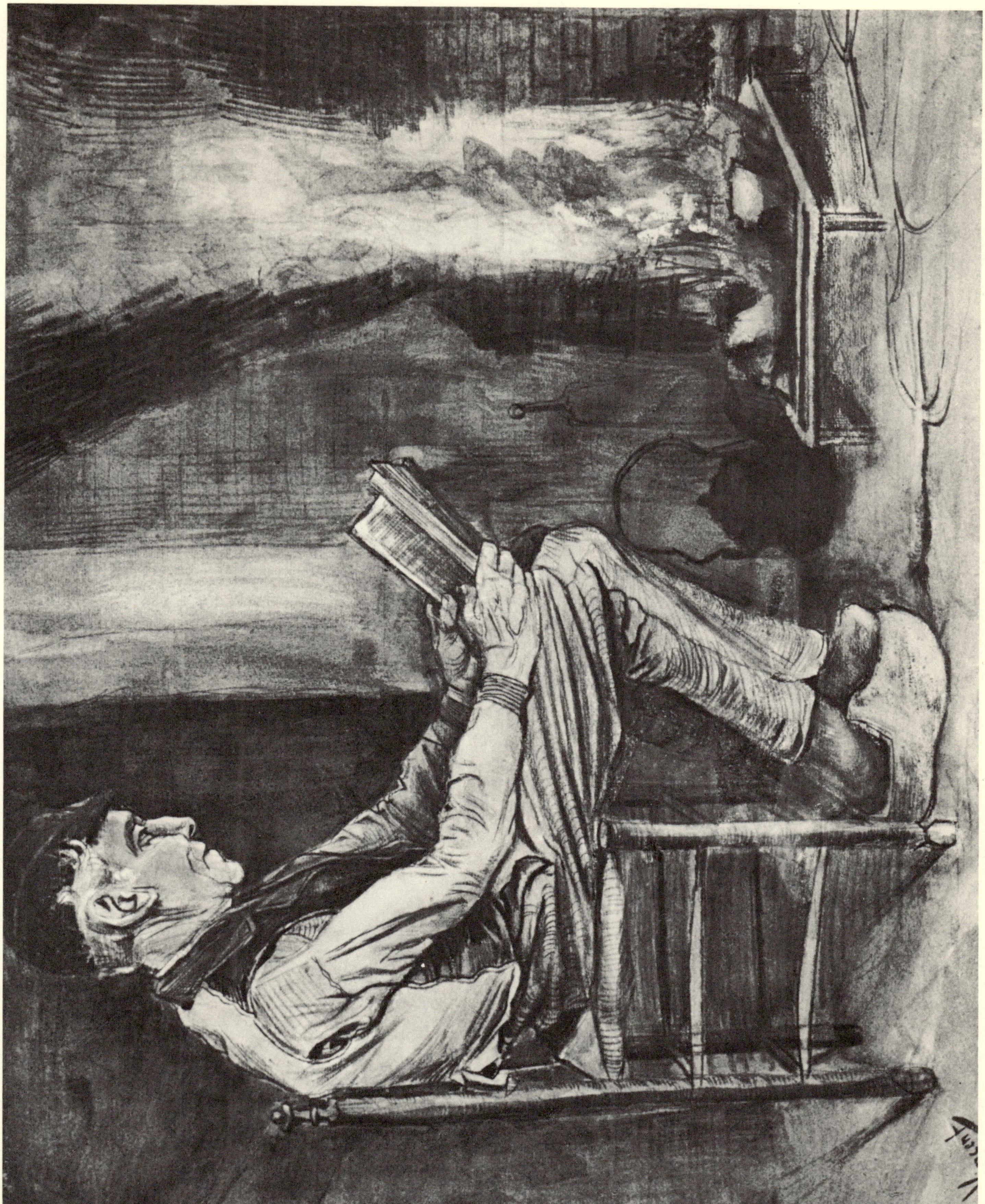

Plate 21

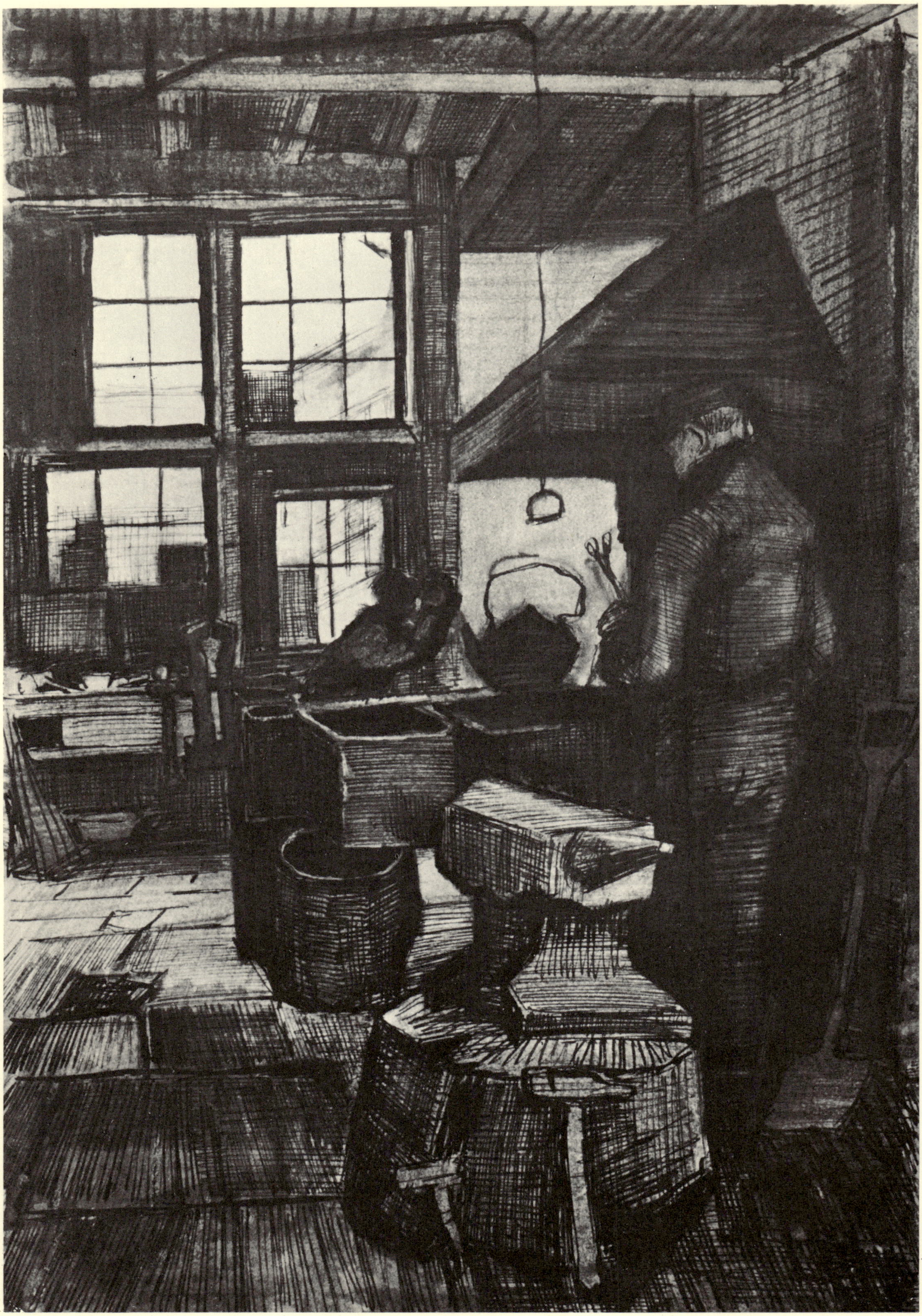

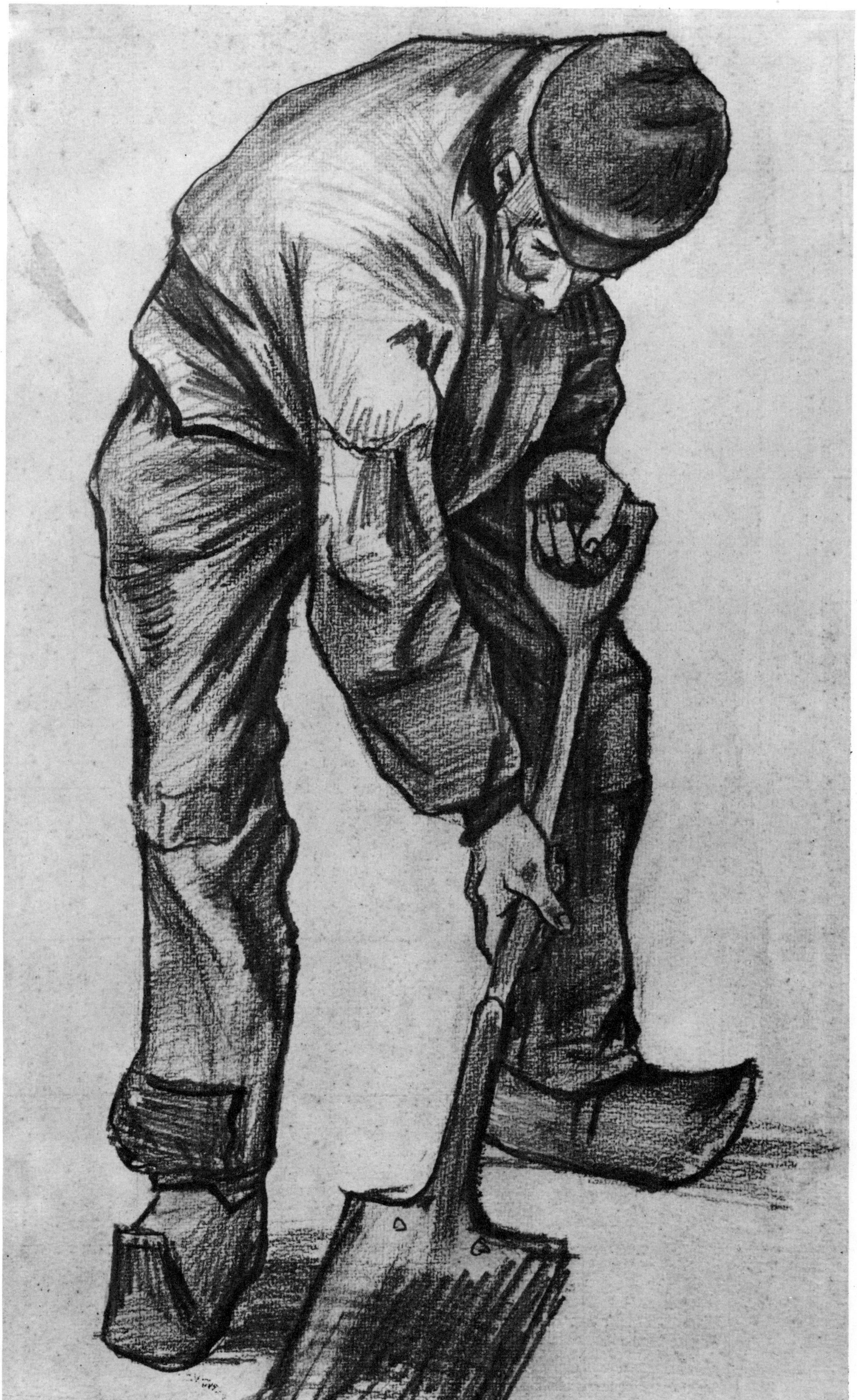

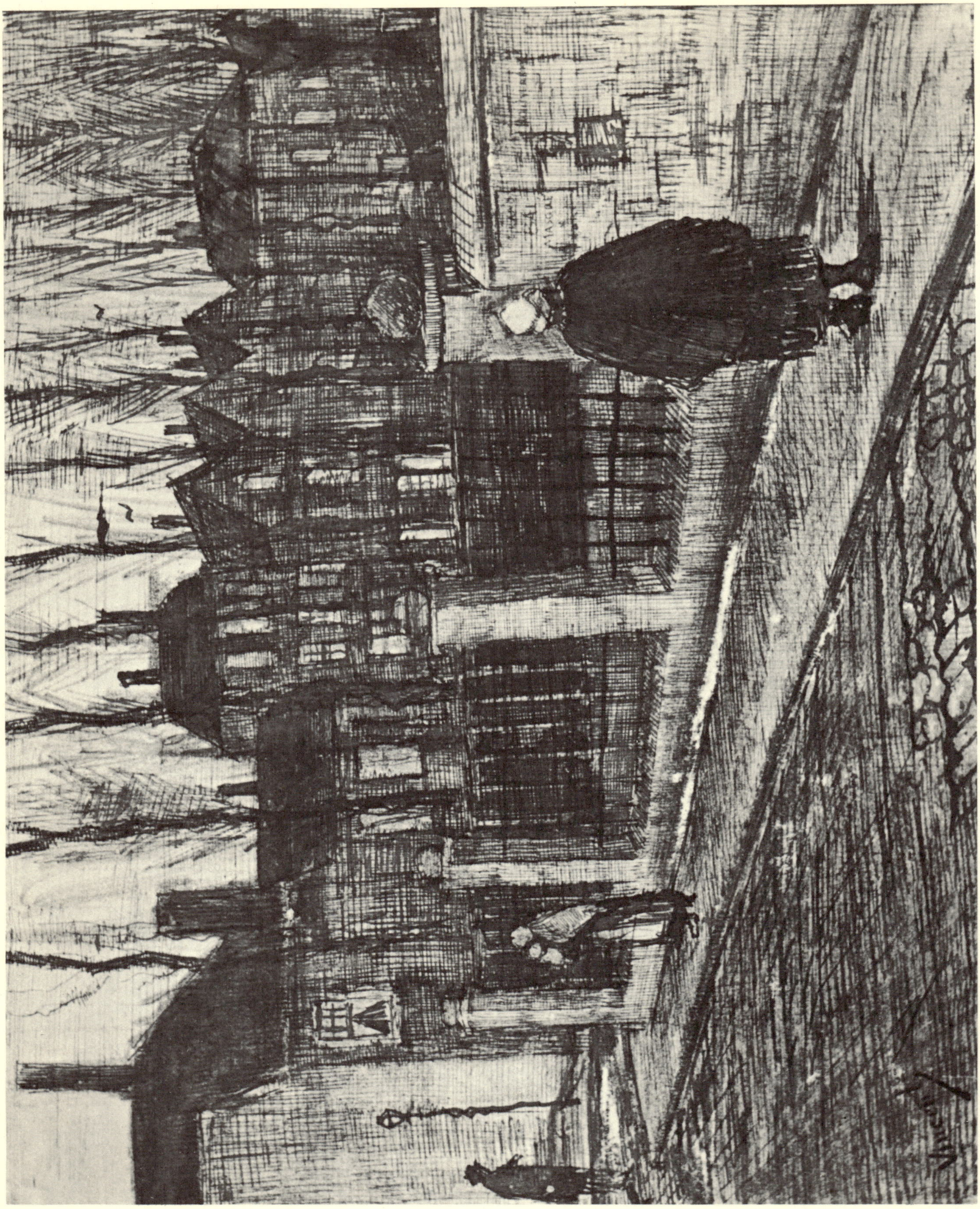

Plate 24

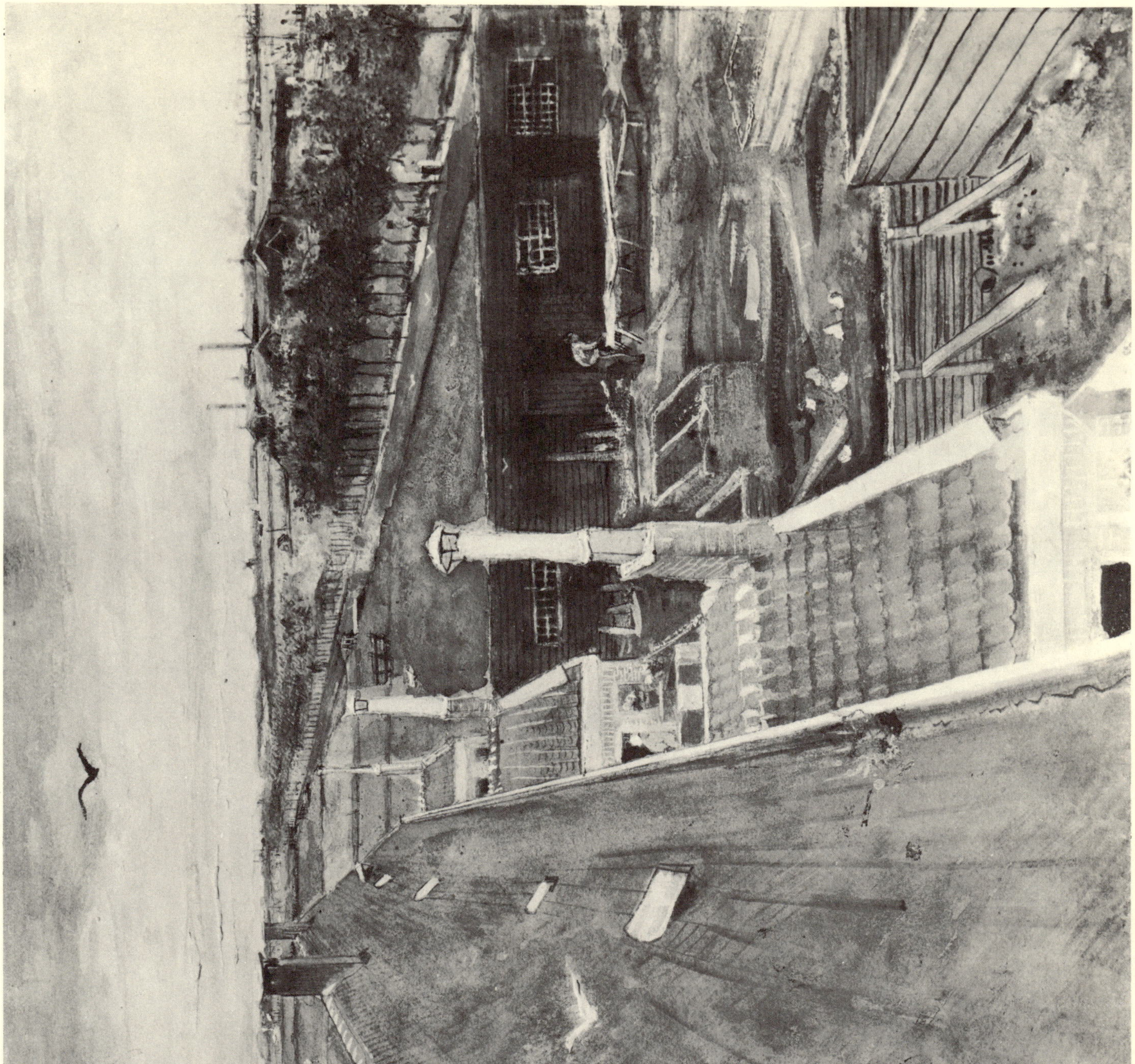

Plate 25

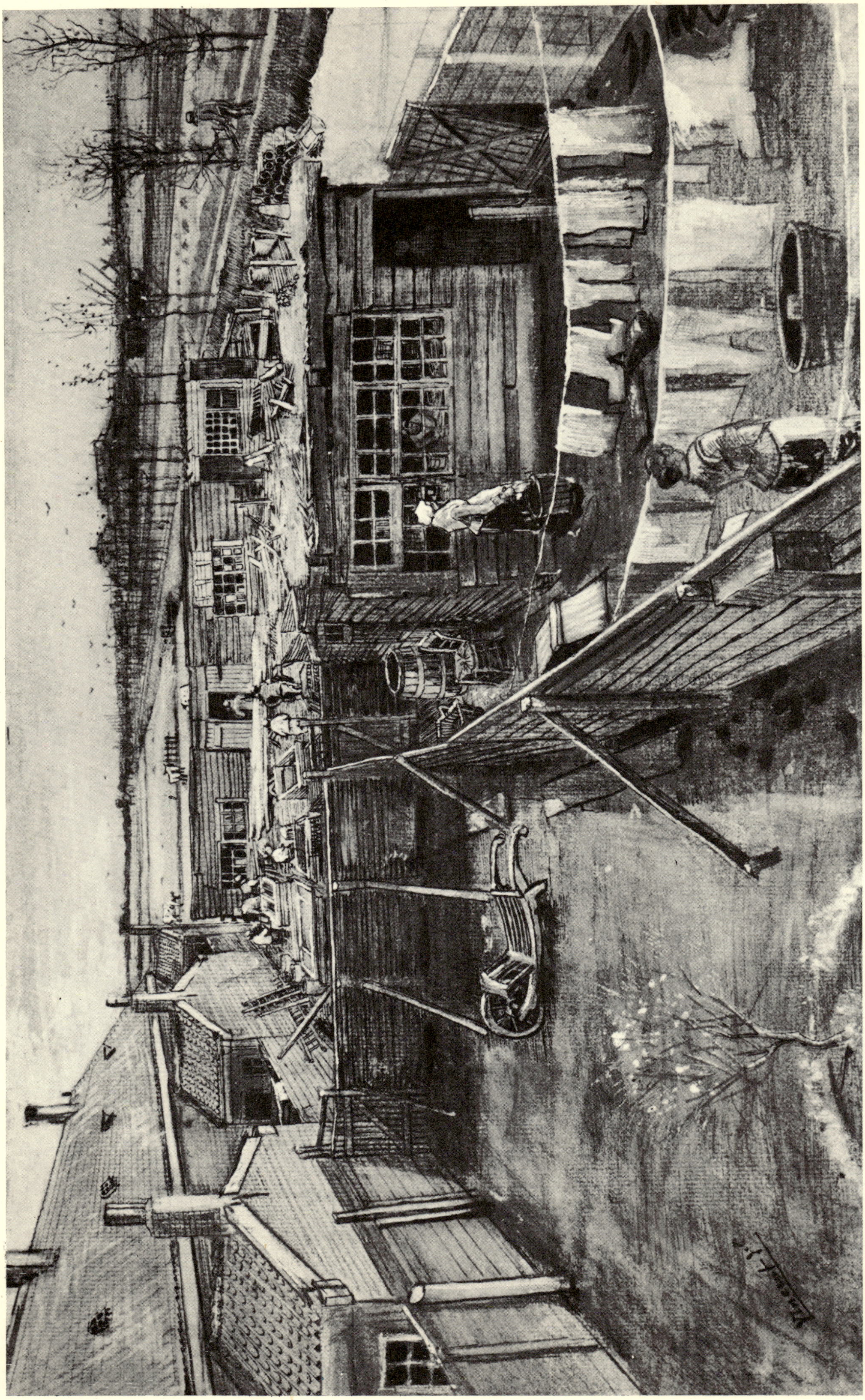

Plate 26

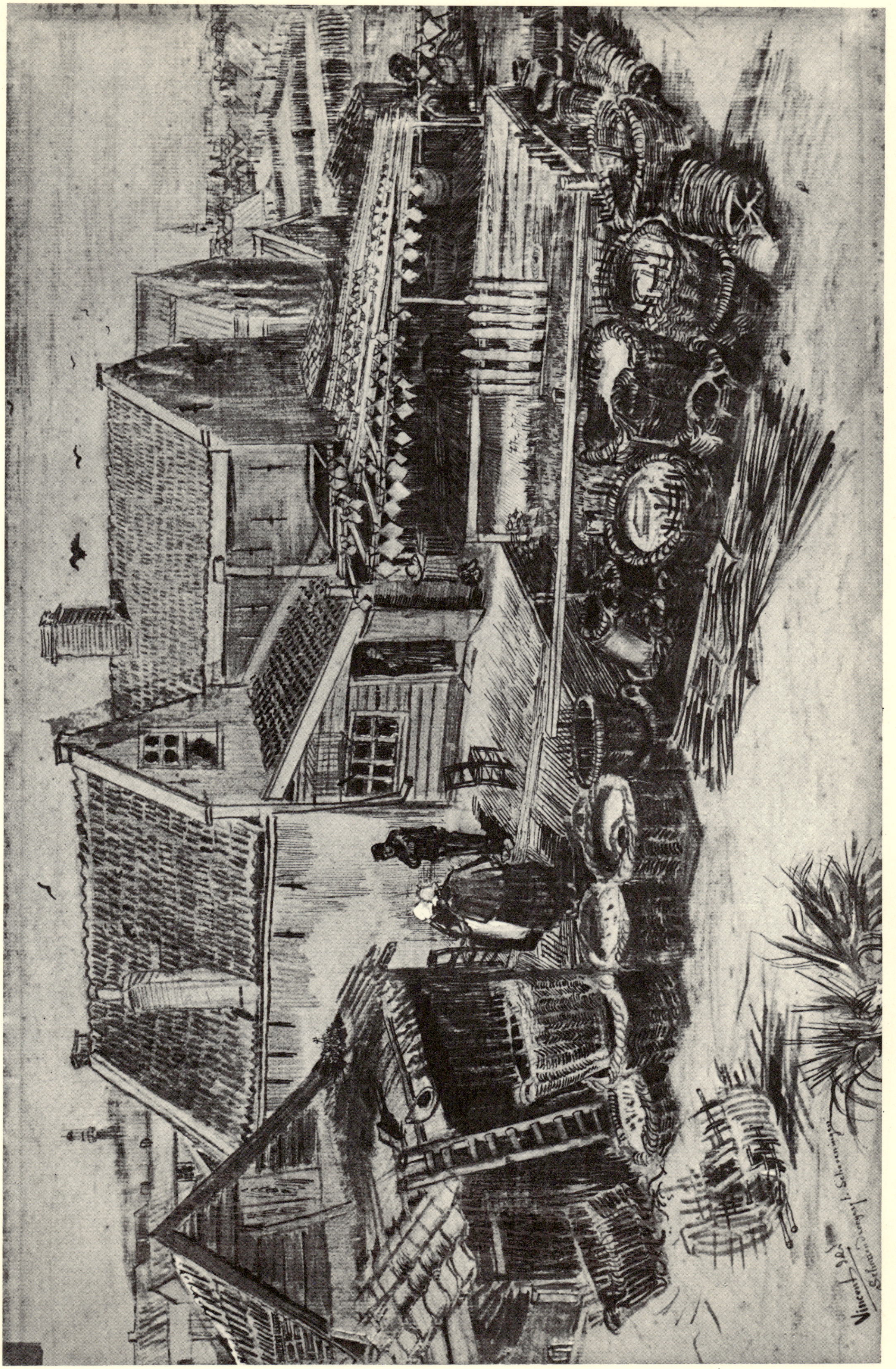

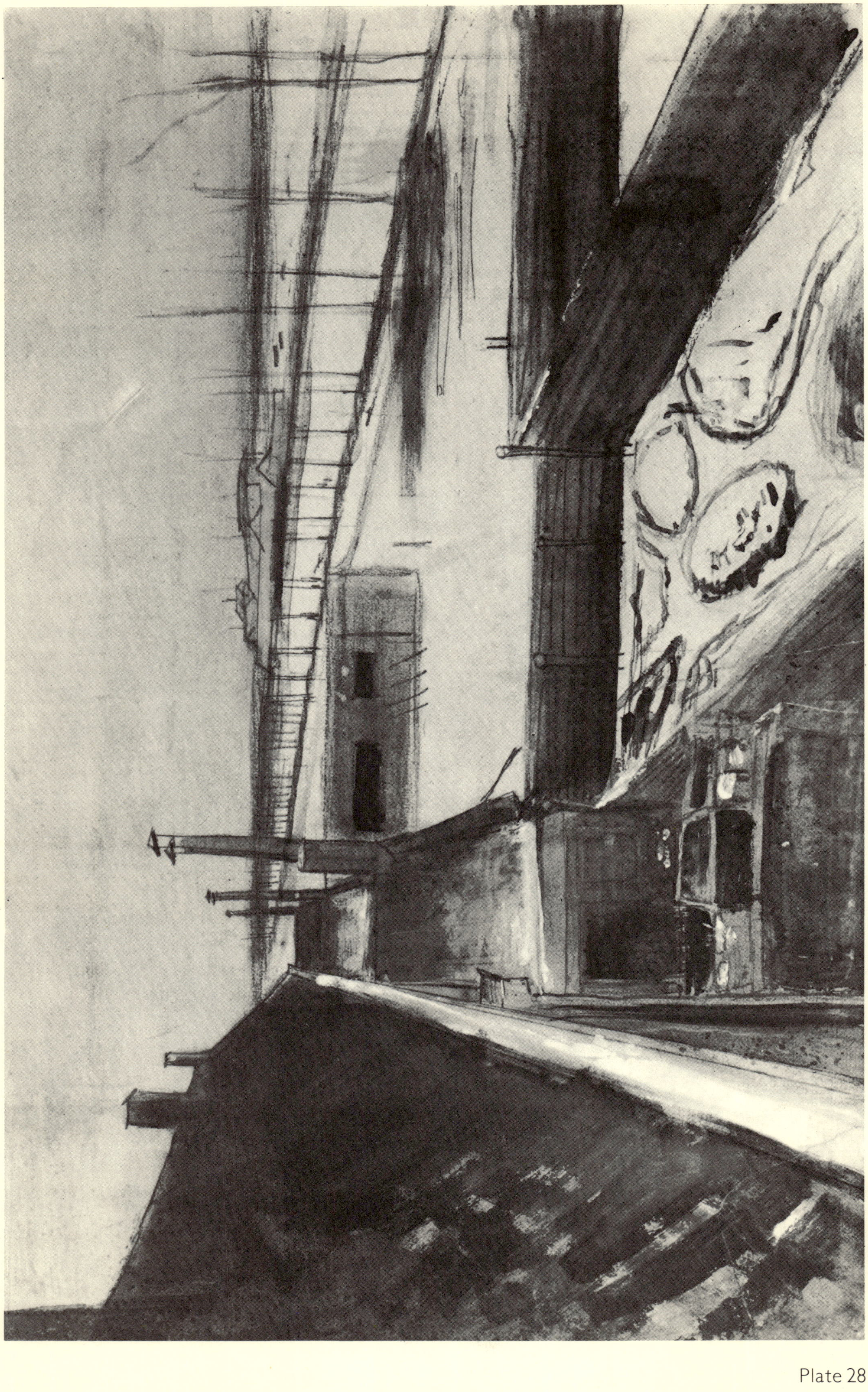

Plate 28

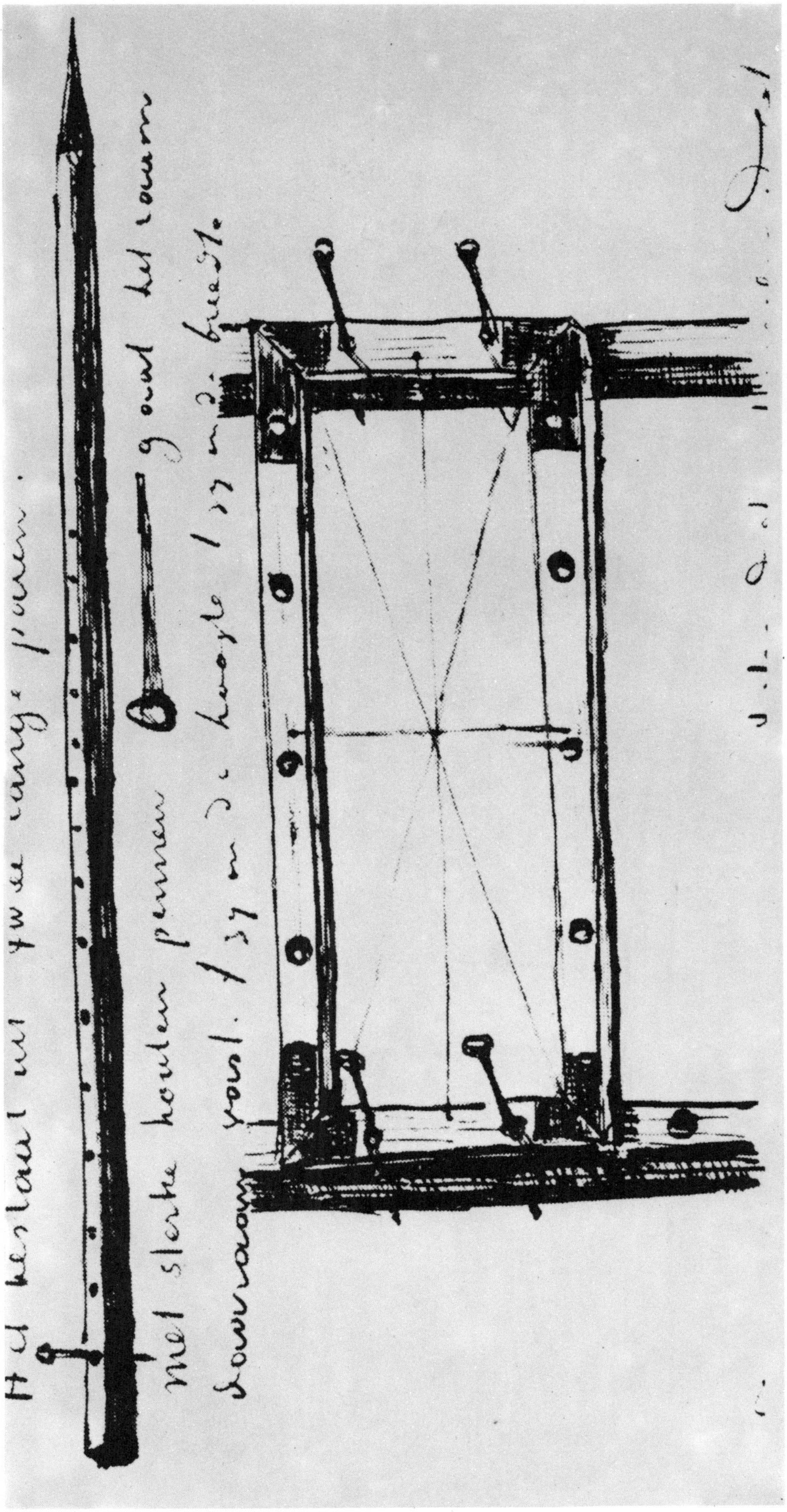
Het bestaat uit twee lange palen.
met sterke houten pennen gaat het raam

Plate 29

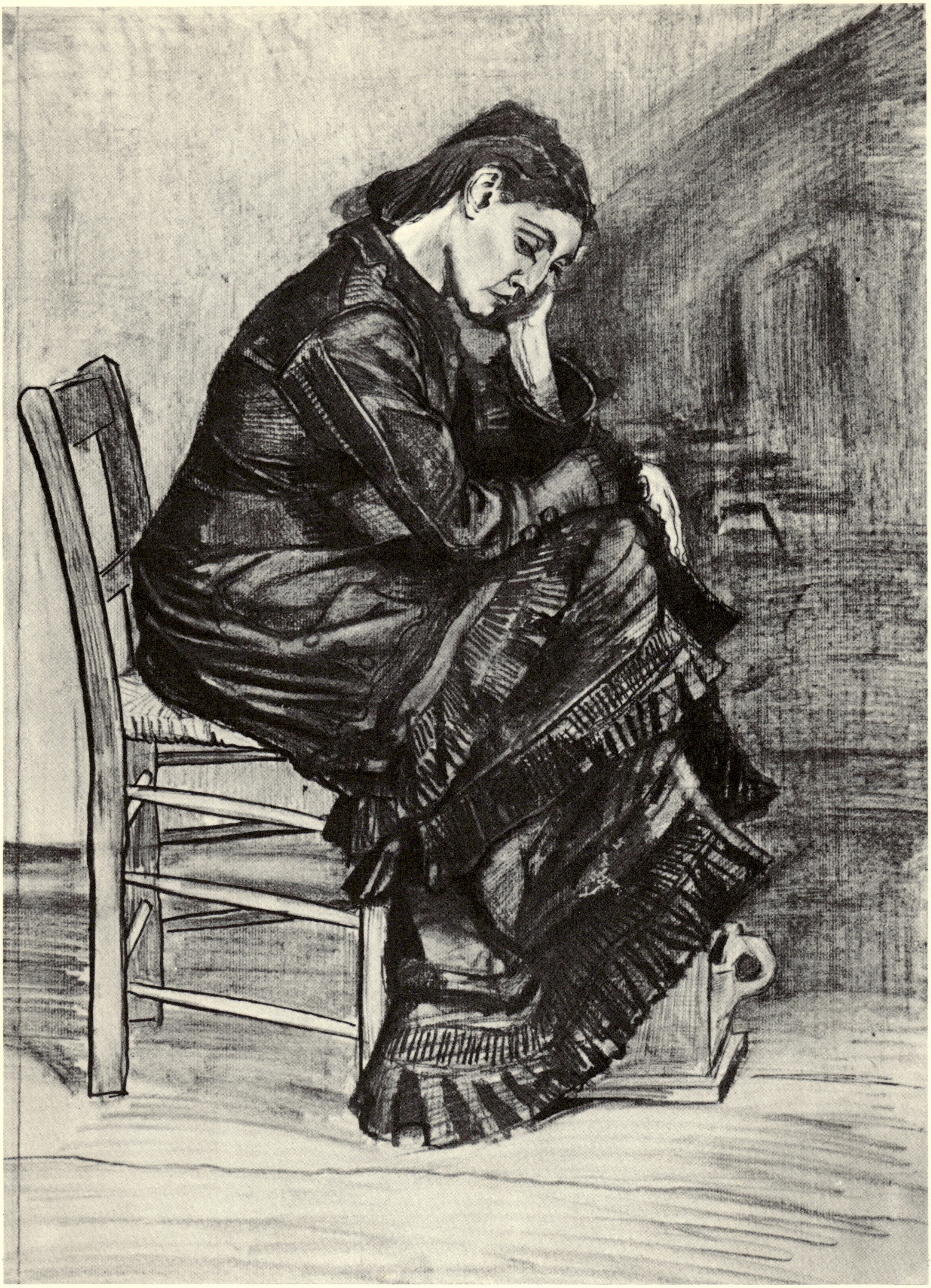

Plate 30

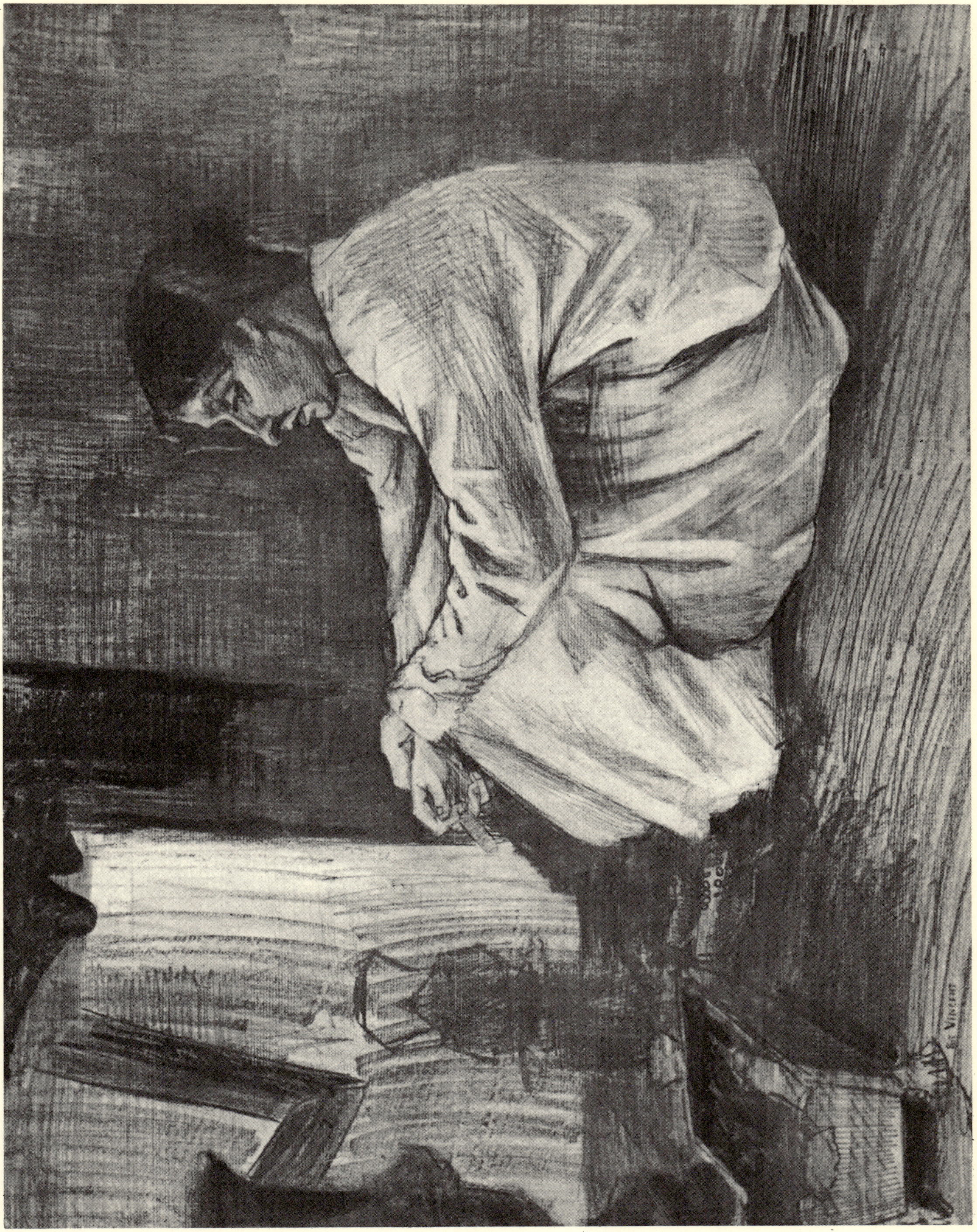

Plate 31

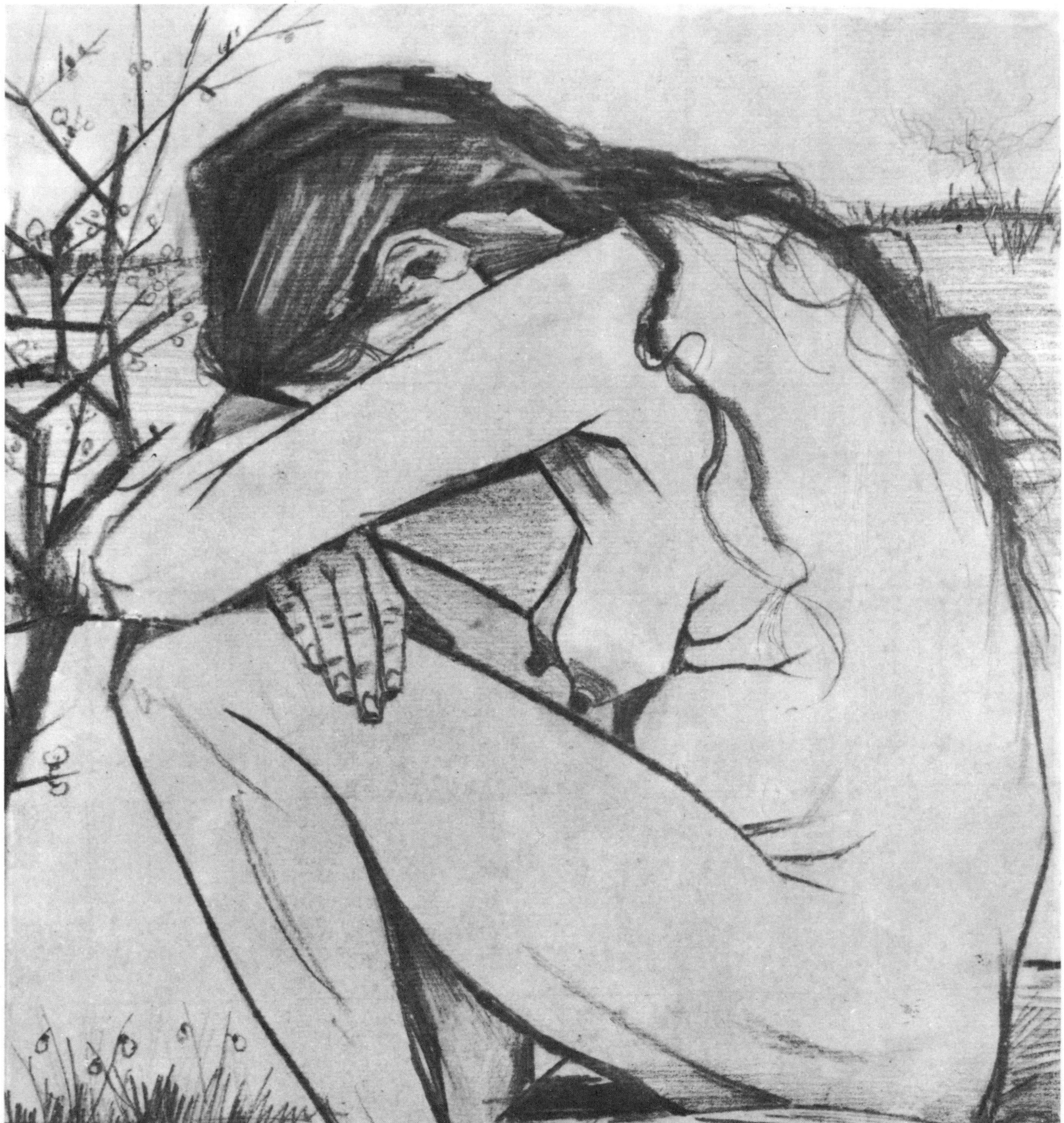
Sorrow
Comment se fait-il qu'il y ait sur la terre une femme seule
Michelet

Plate 32

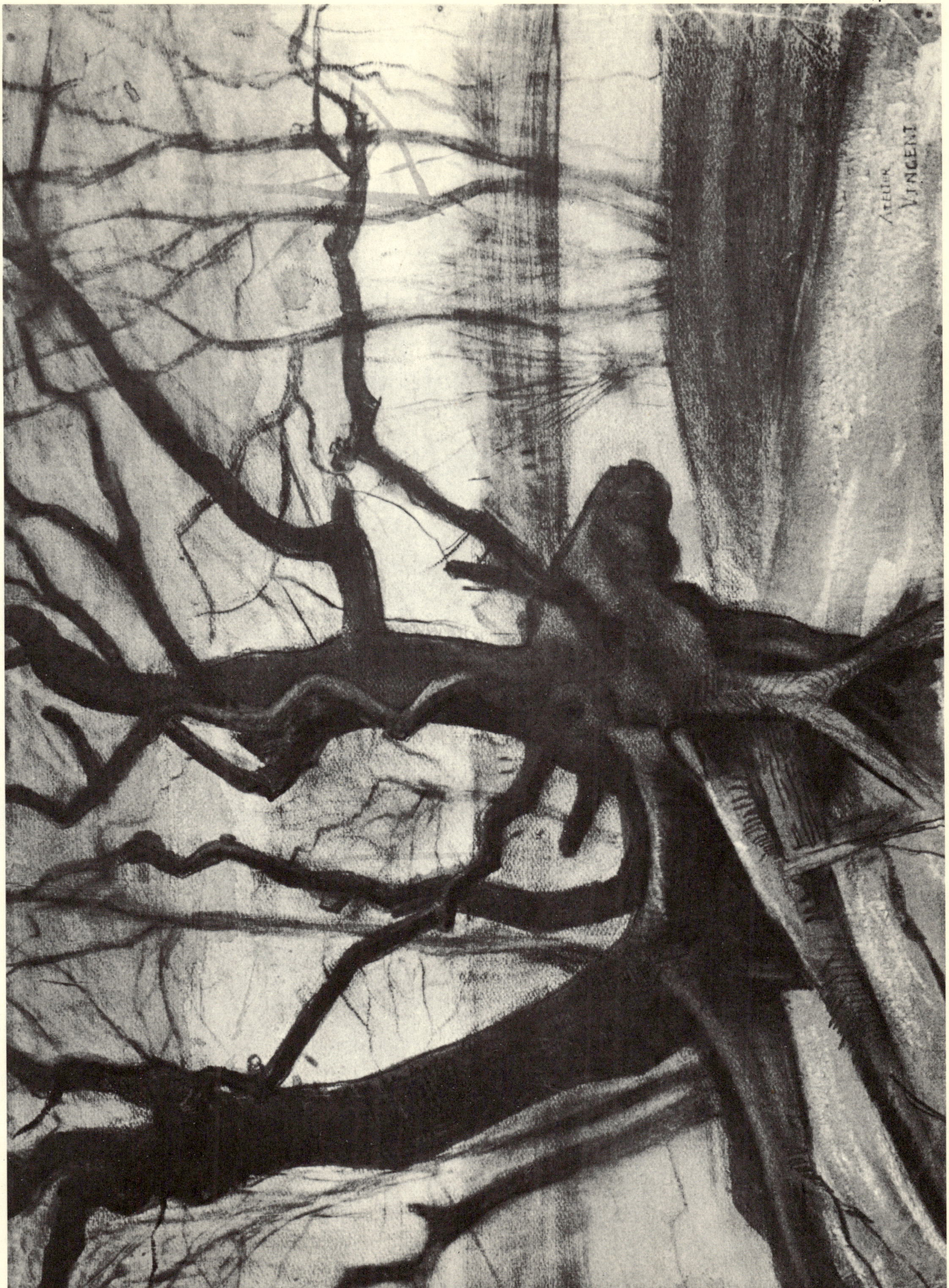

Plate 33

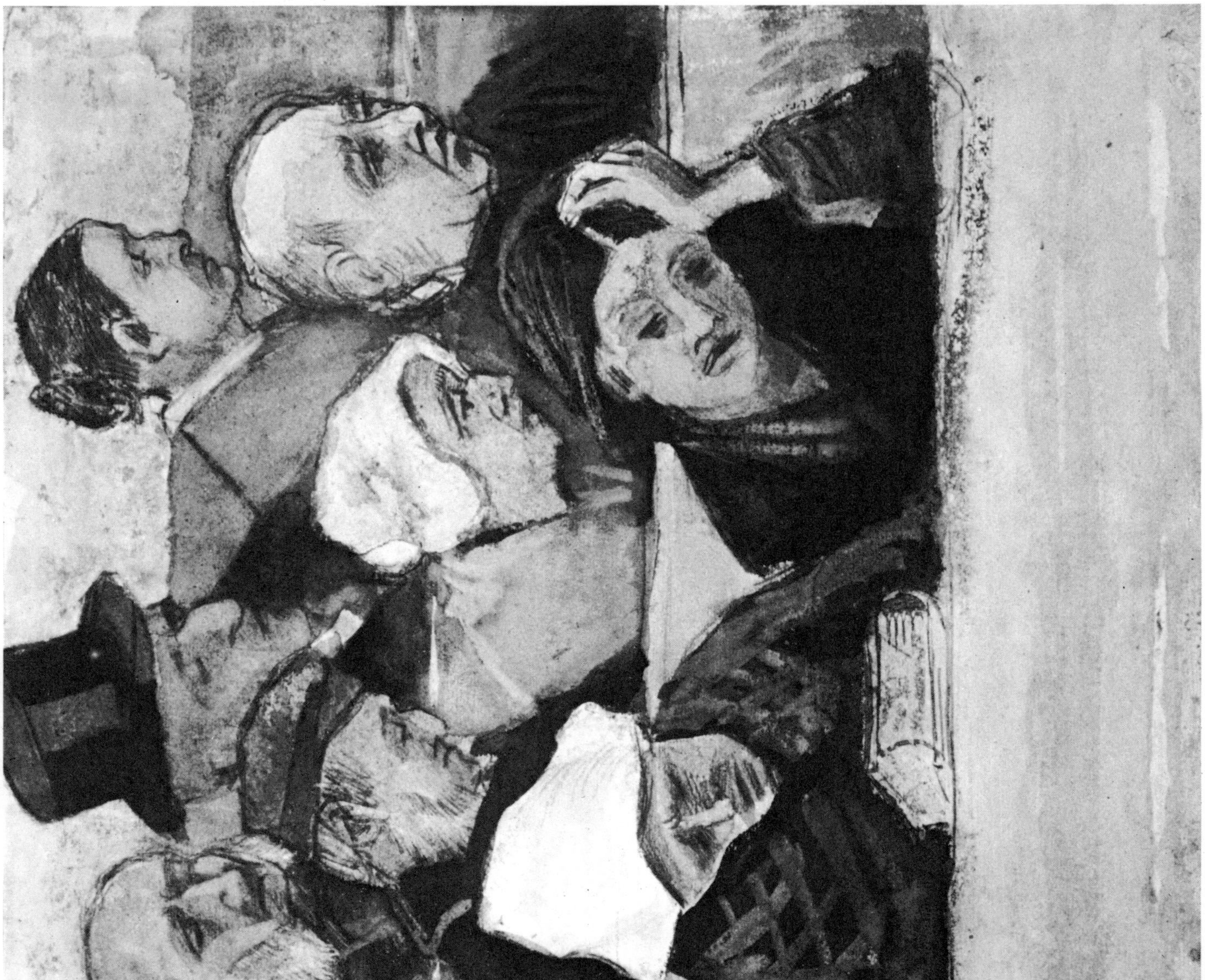

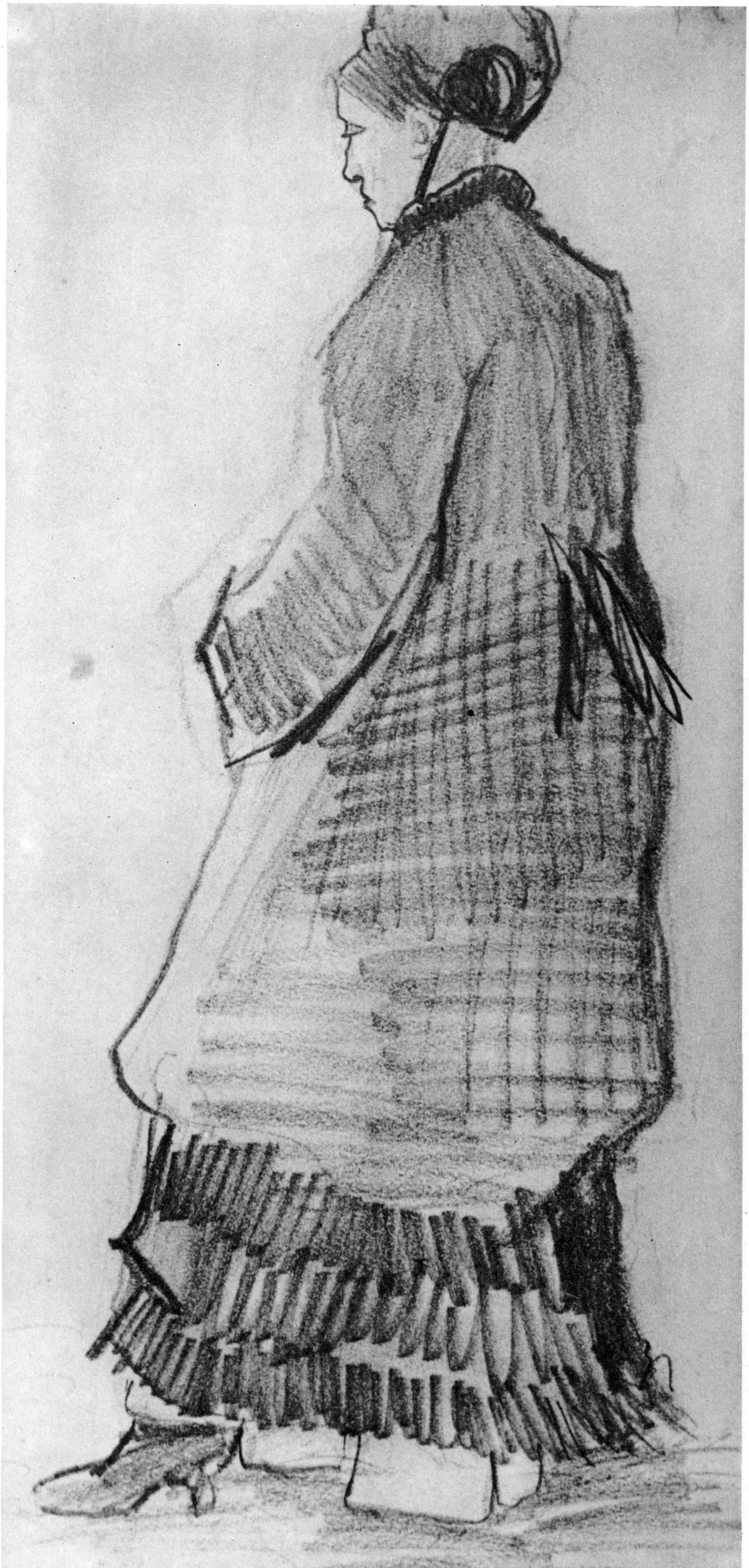

Plate 35

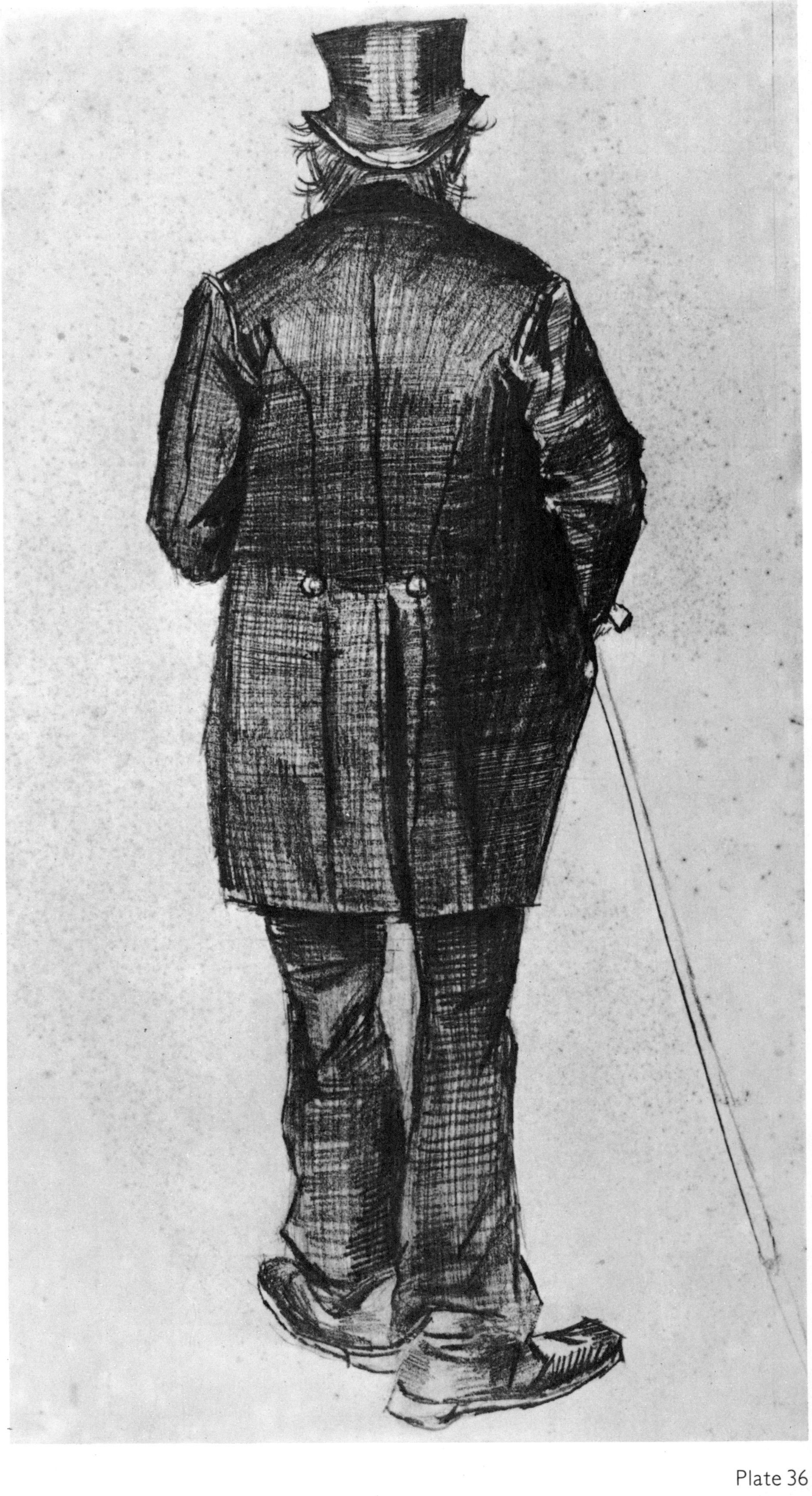

Plate 36

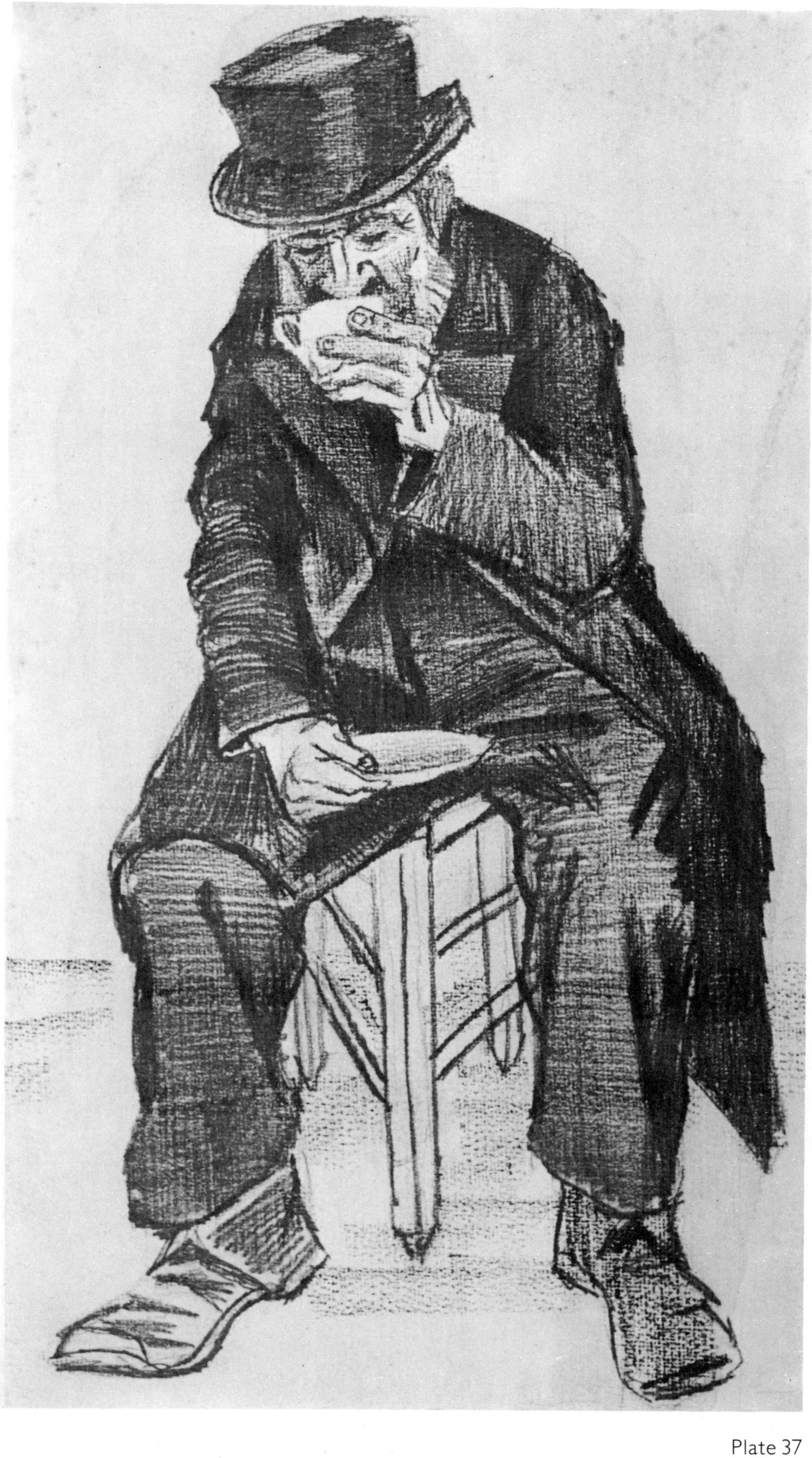

Plate 37

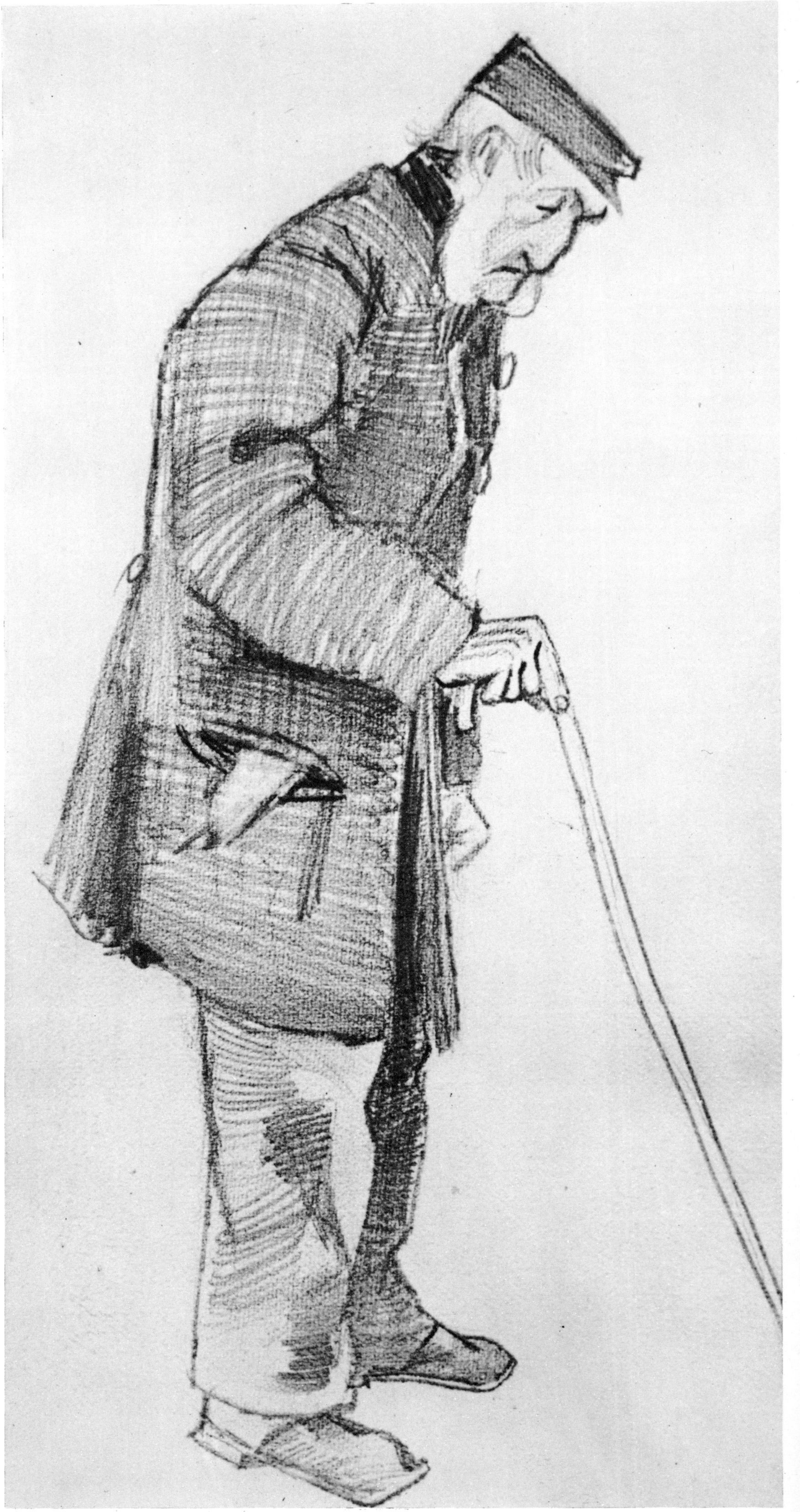

Plate 38

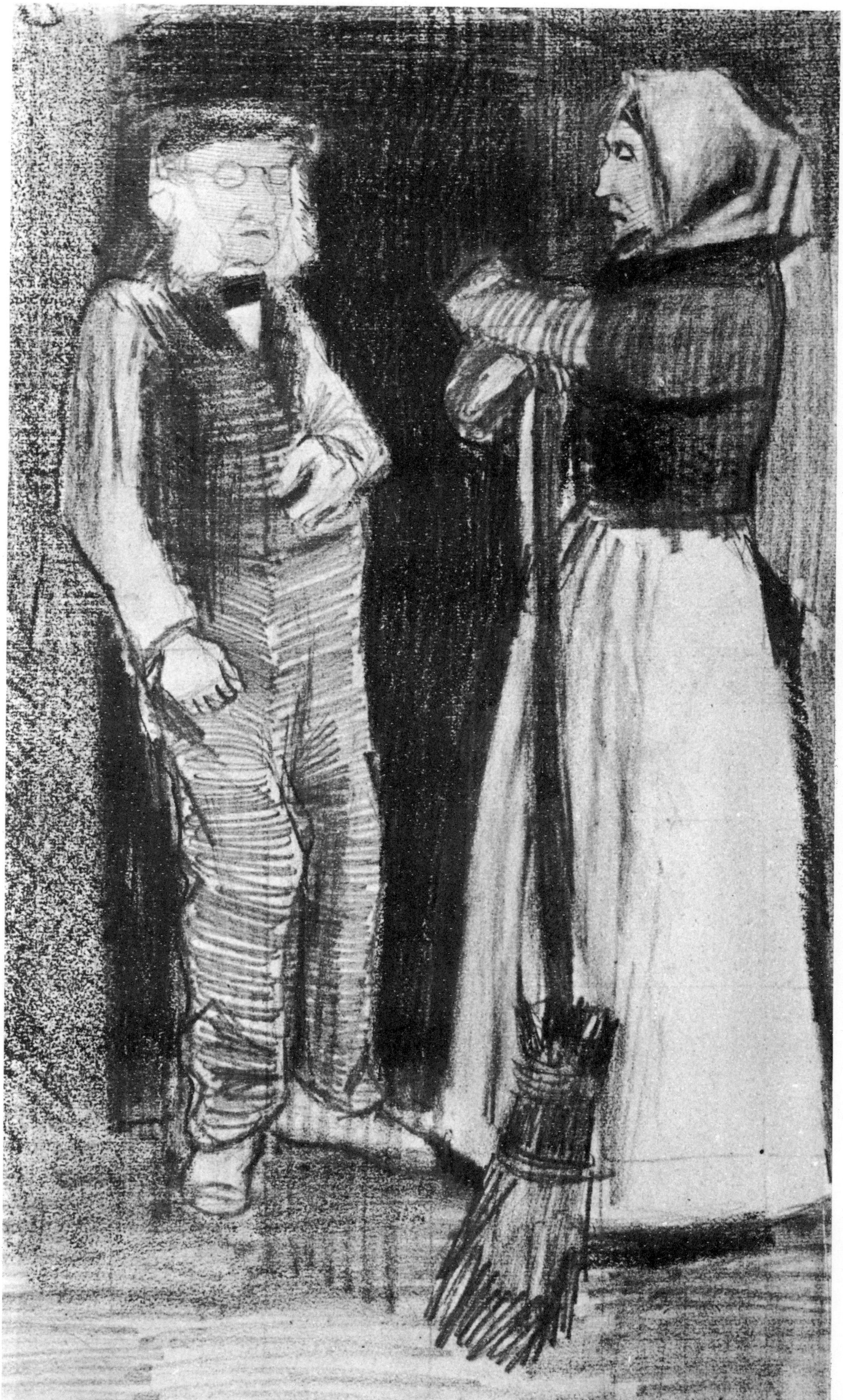

Plate 39

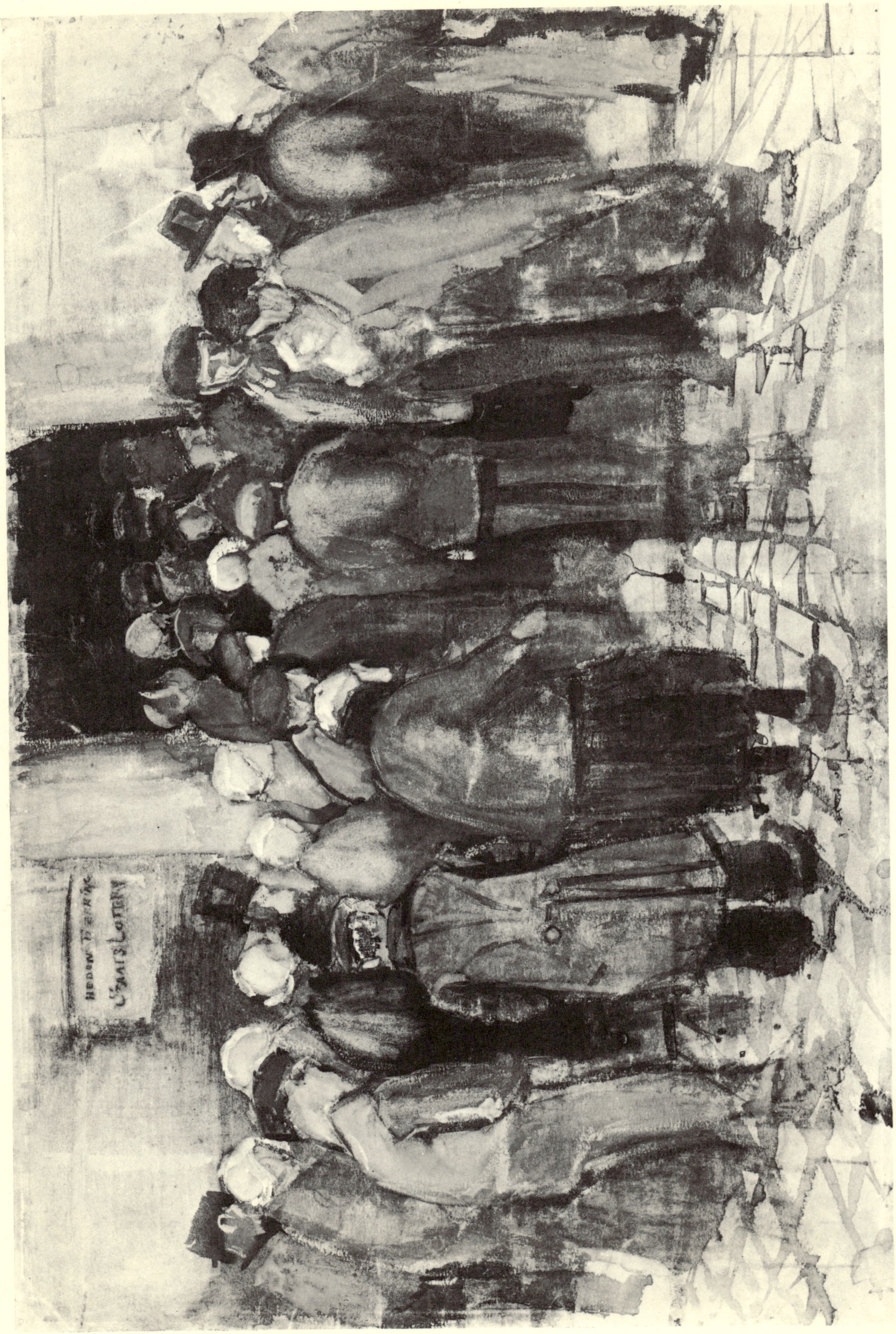

Plate 40

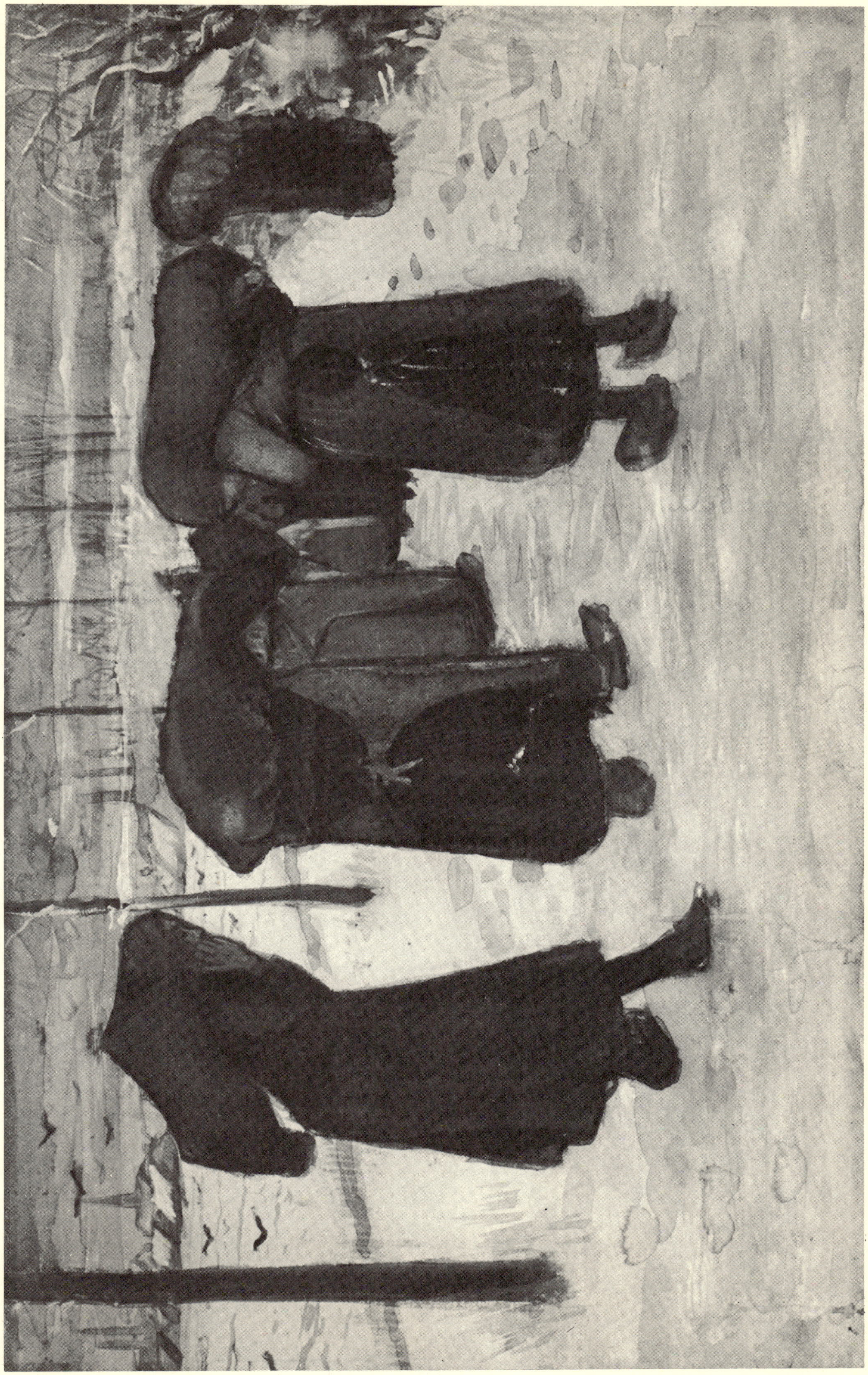

Plate 41

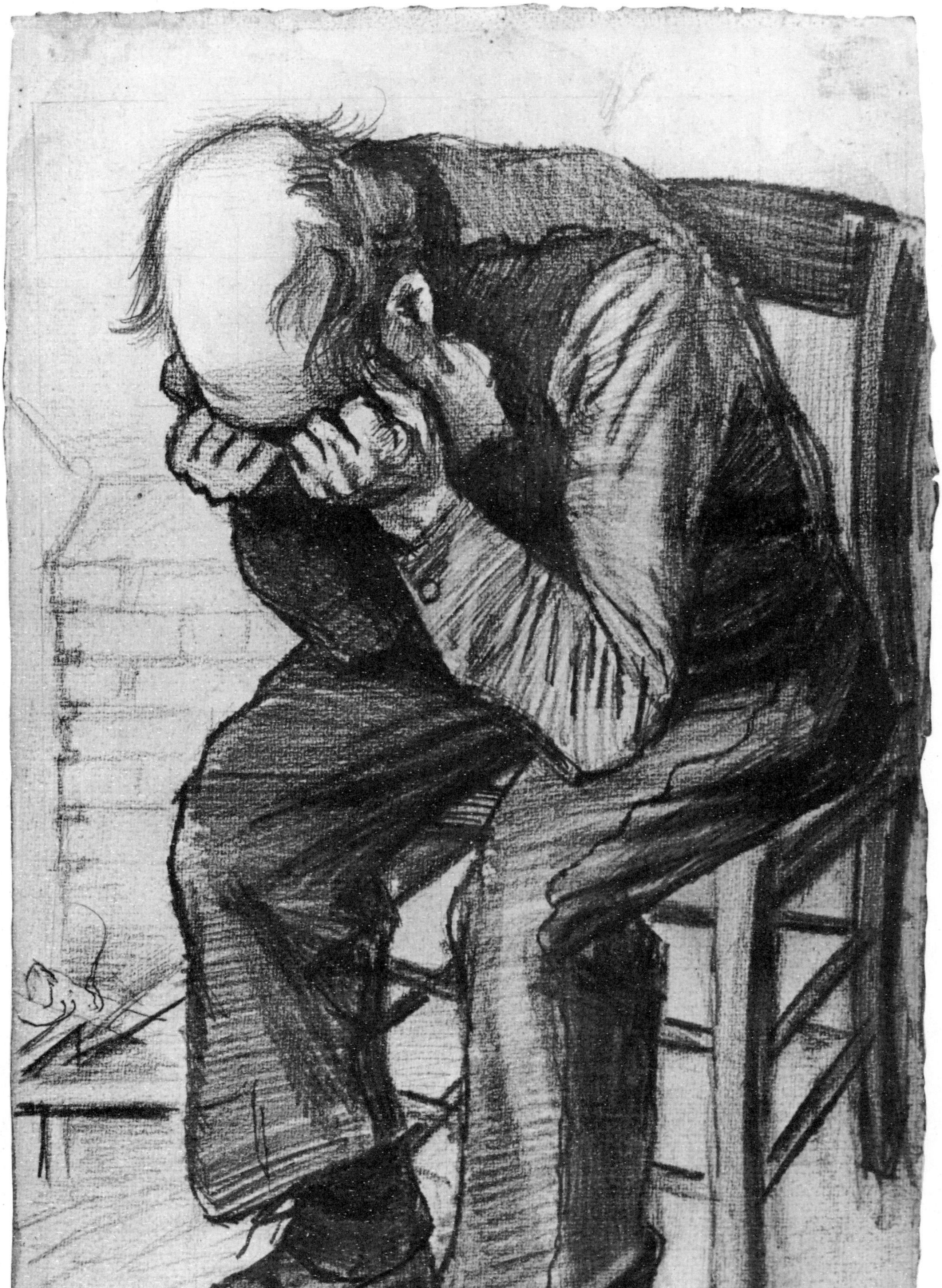

Plate 42

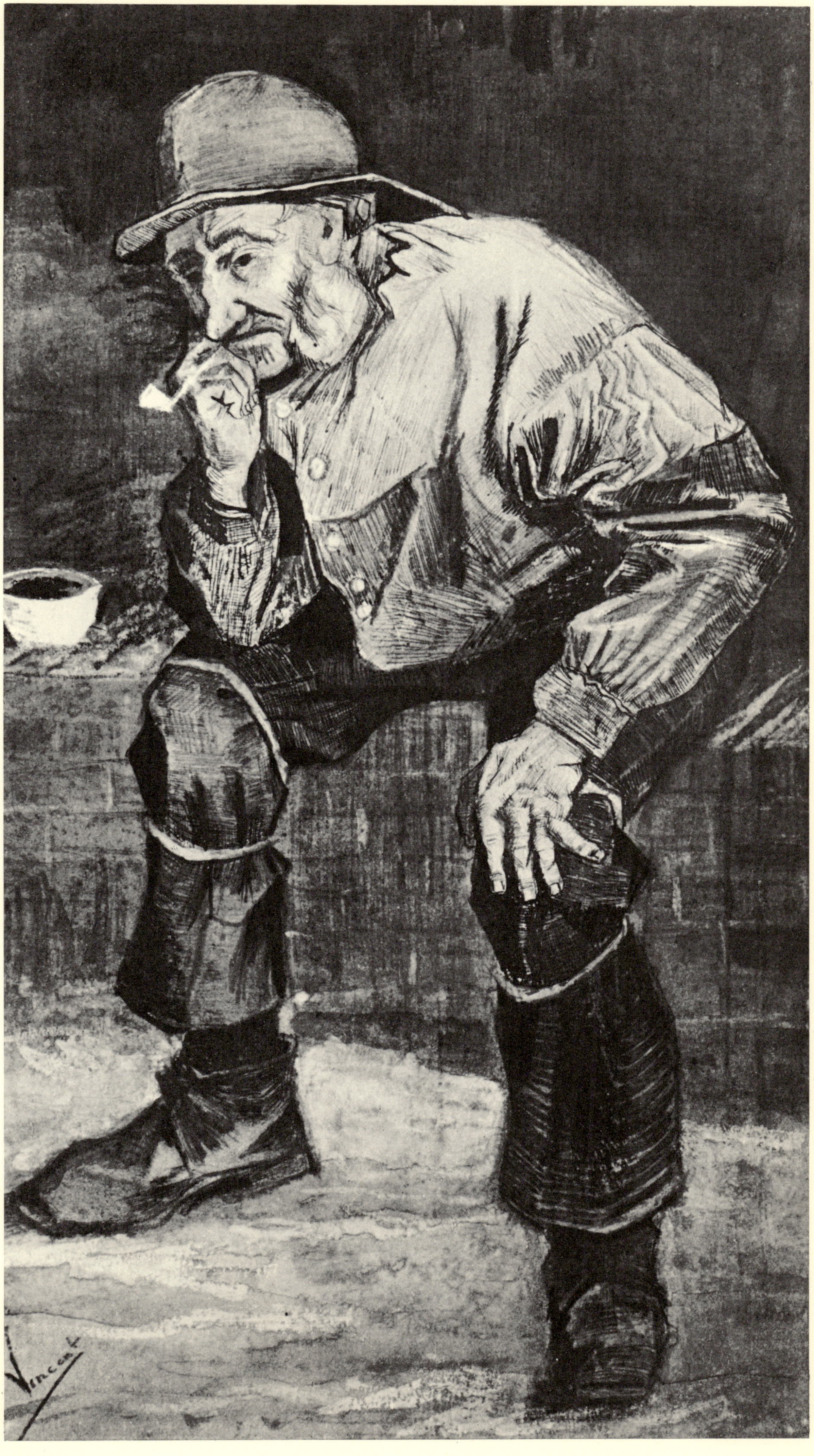

Plate 43

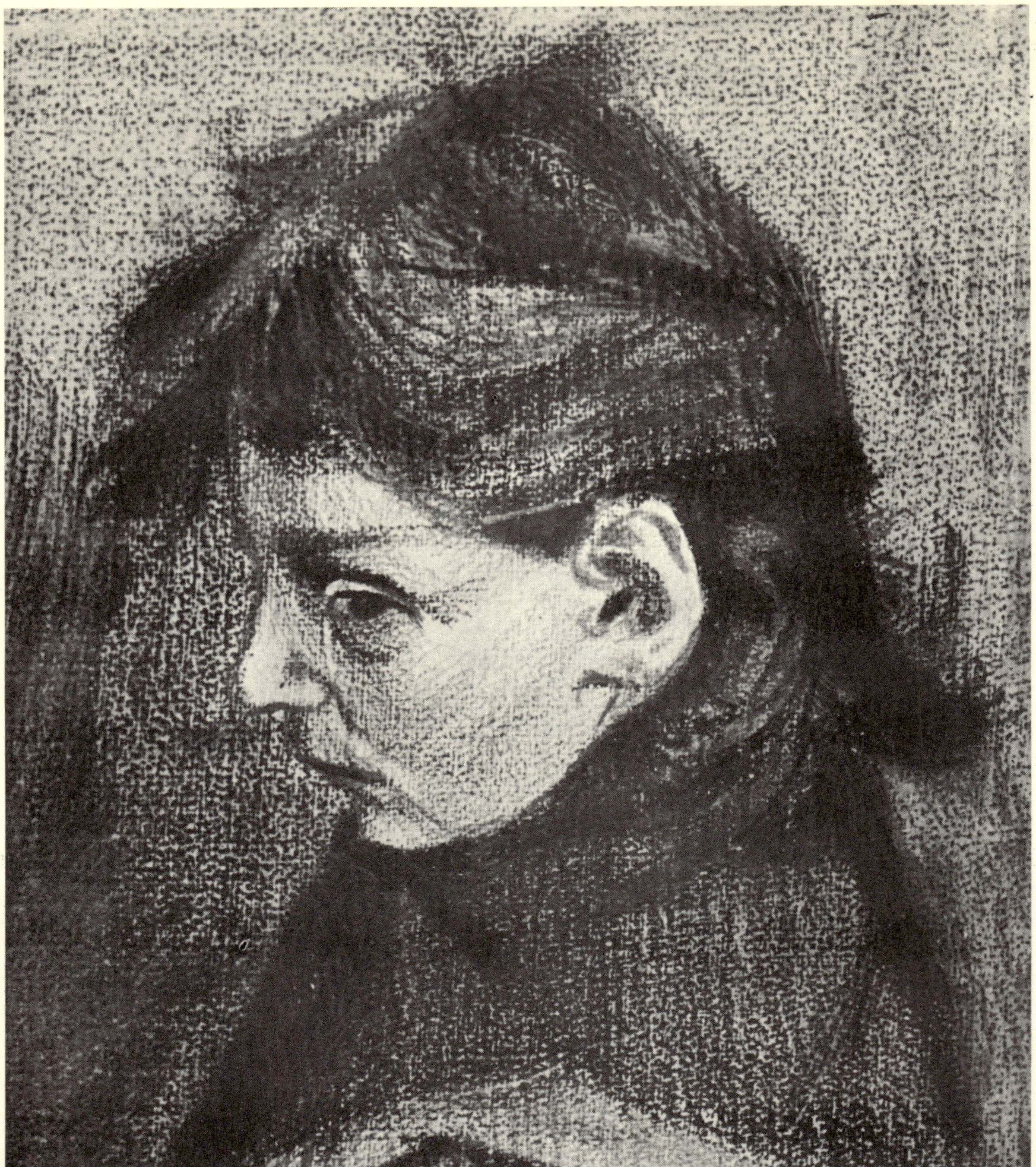

Plate 44

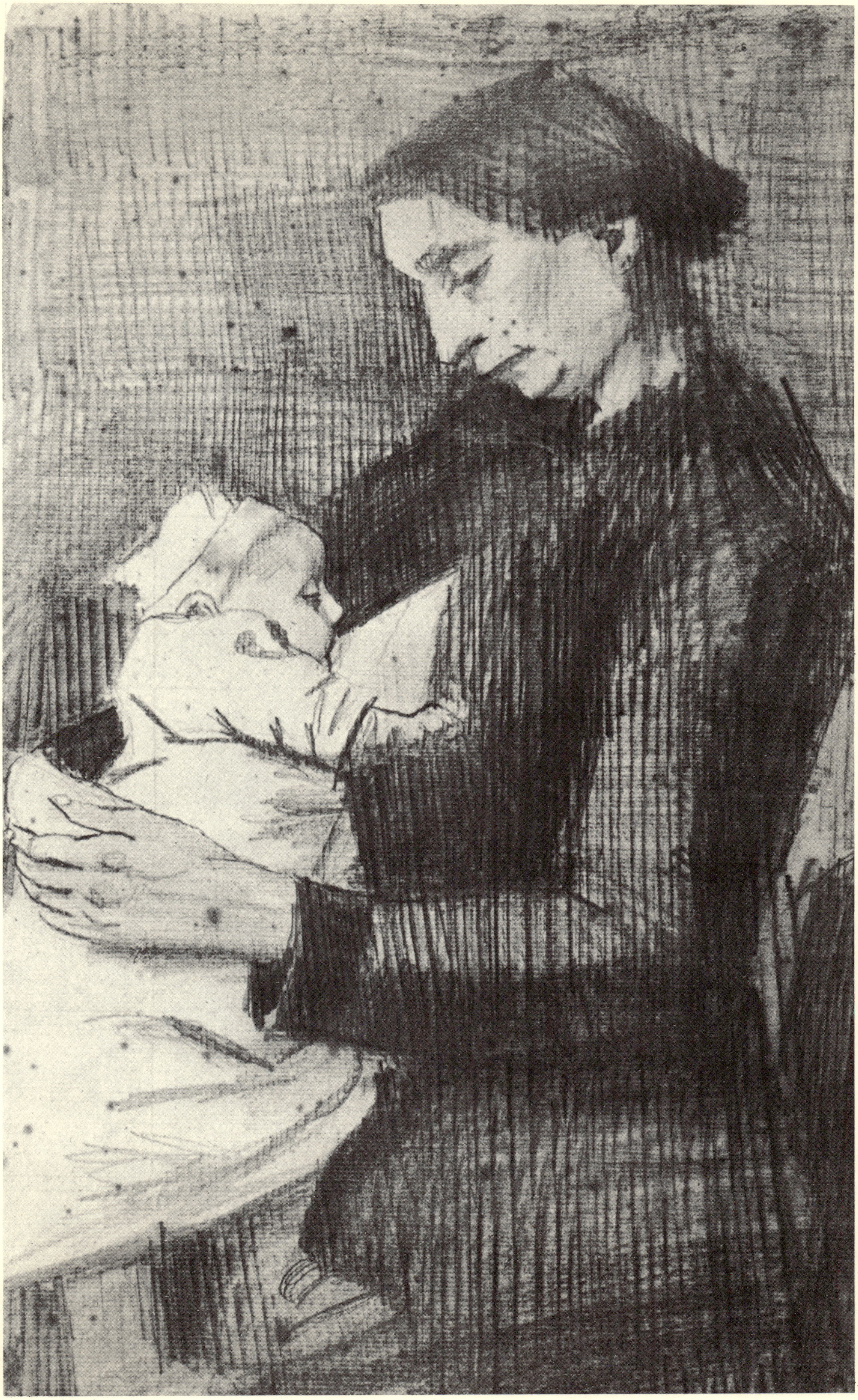

Plate 45

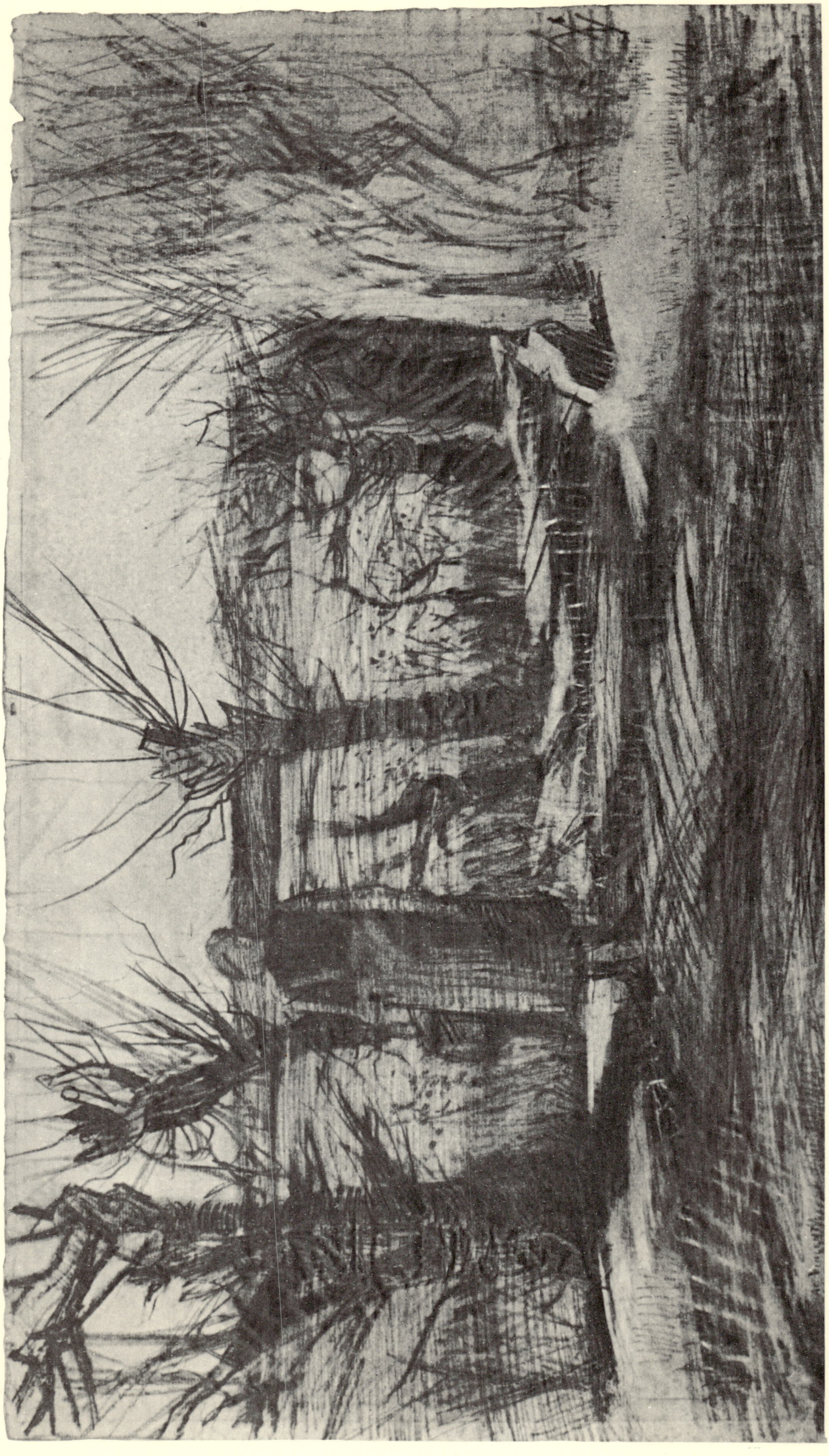

Plate 46

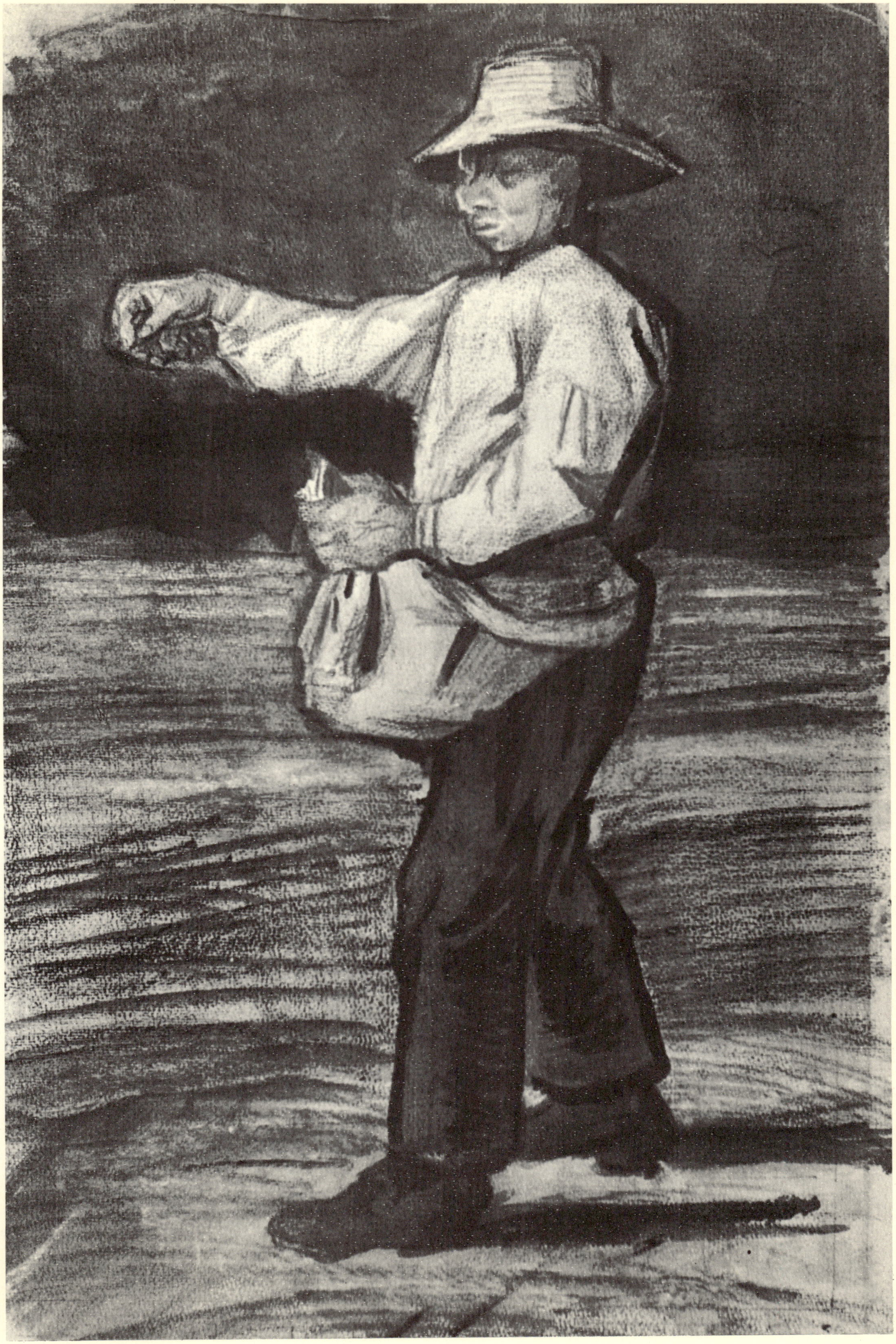

Plate 47

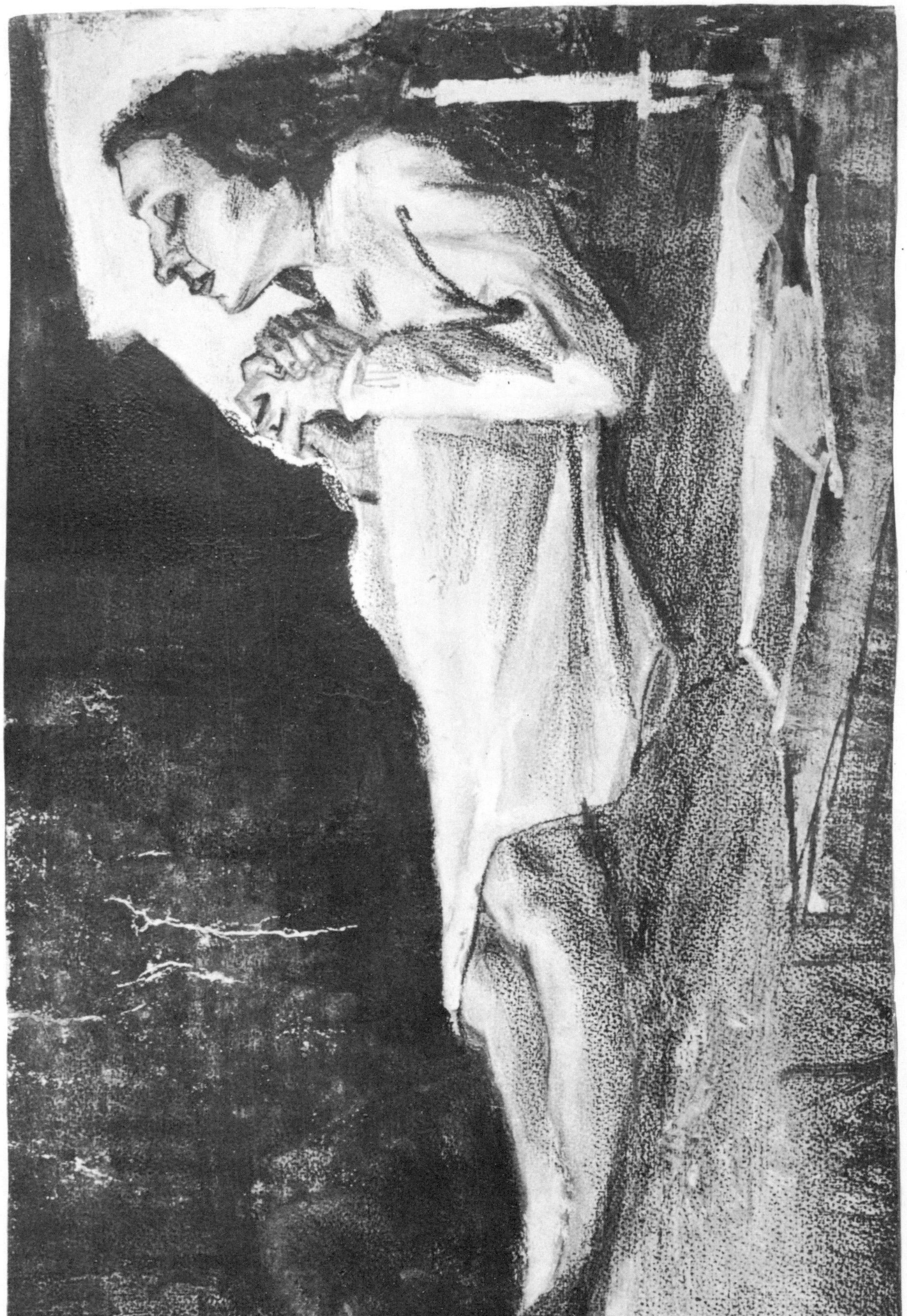

Plate 48

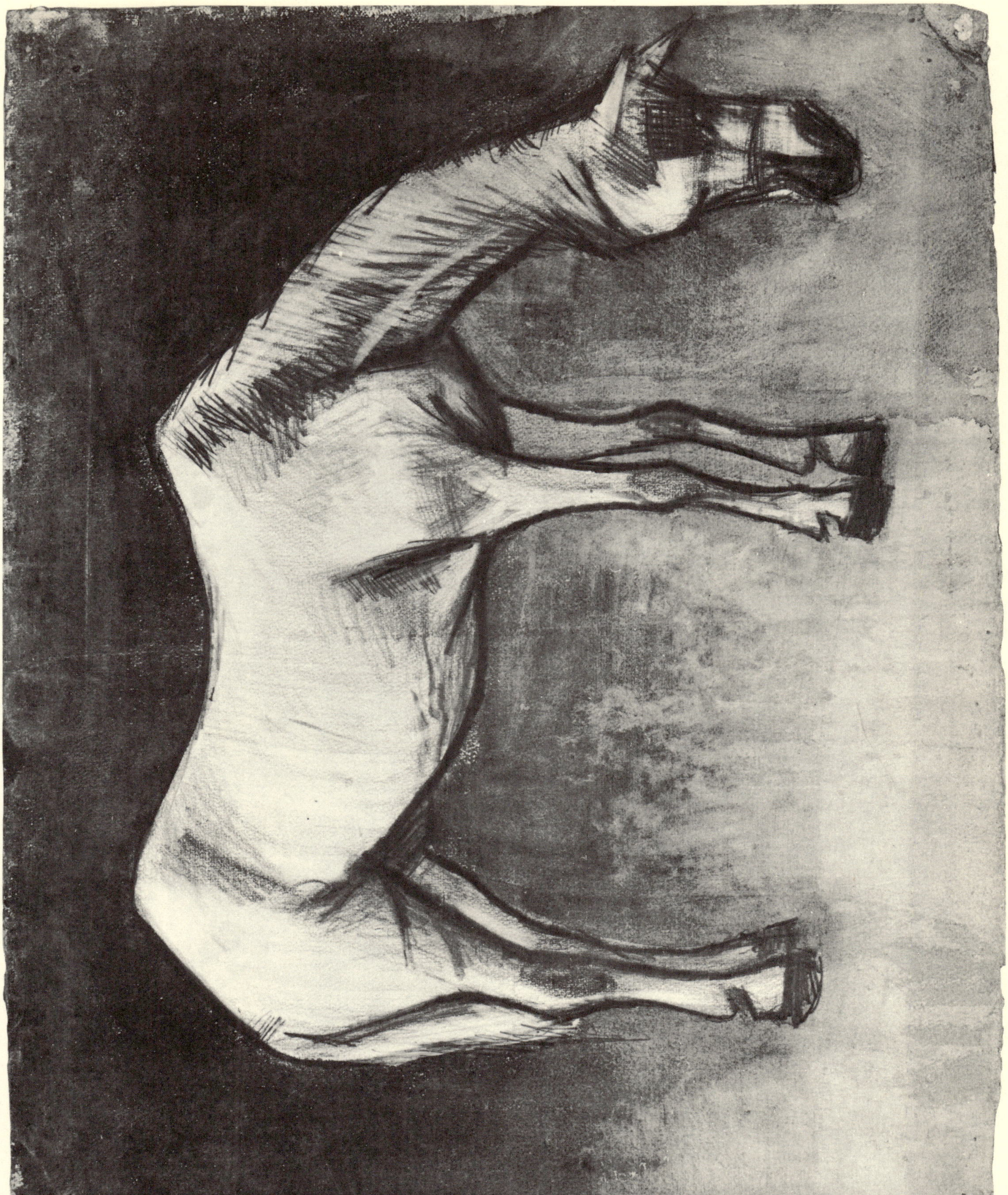

Plate 49

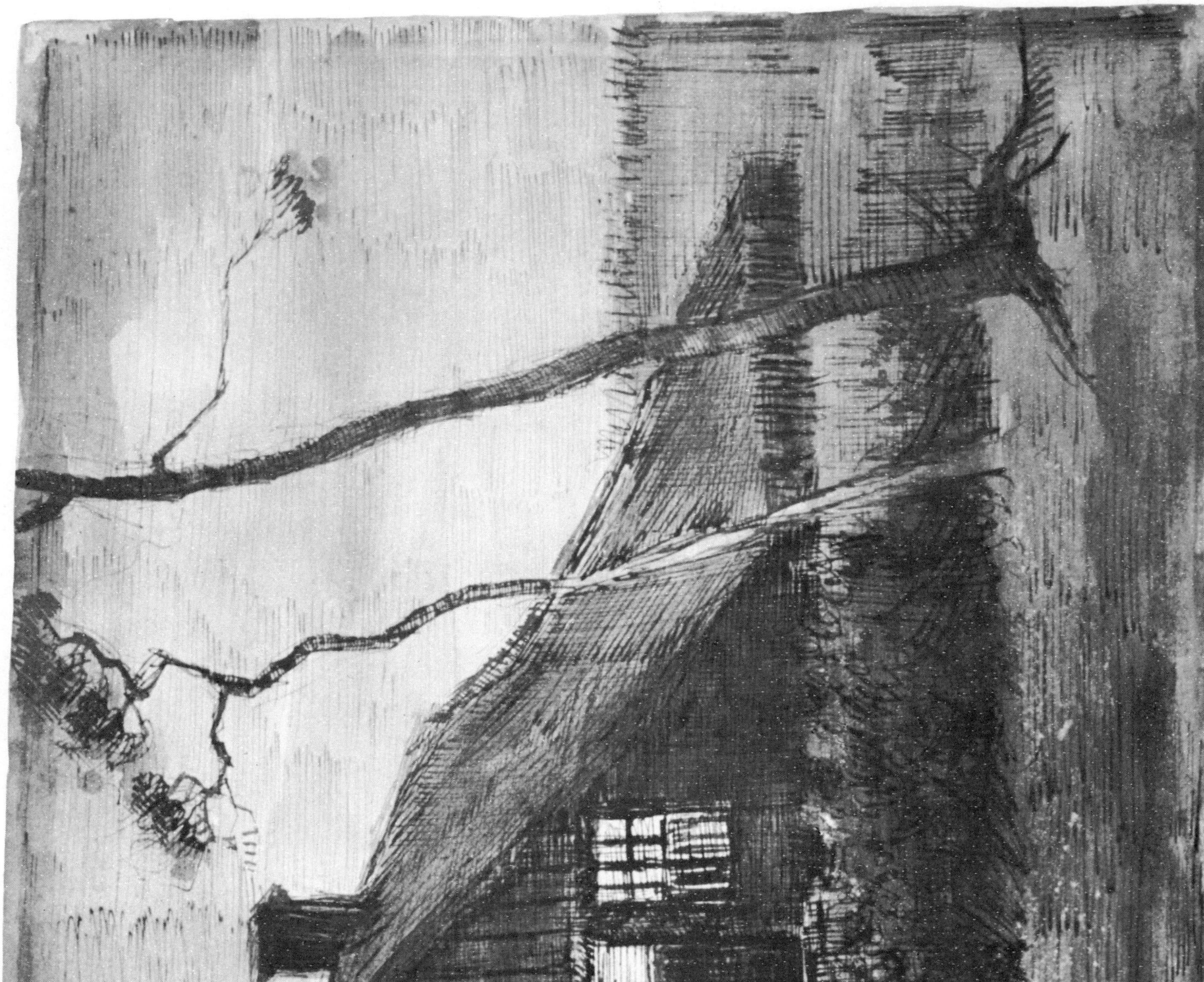

Plate 50

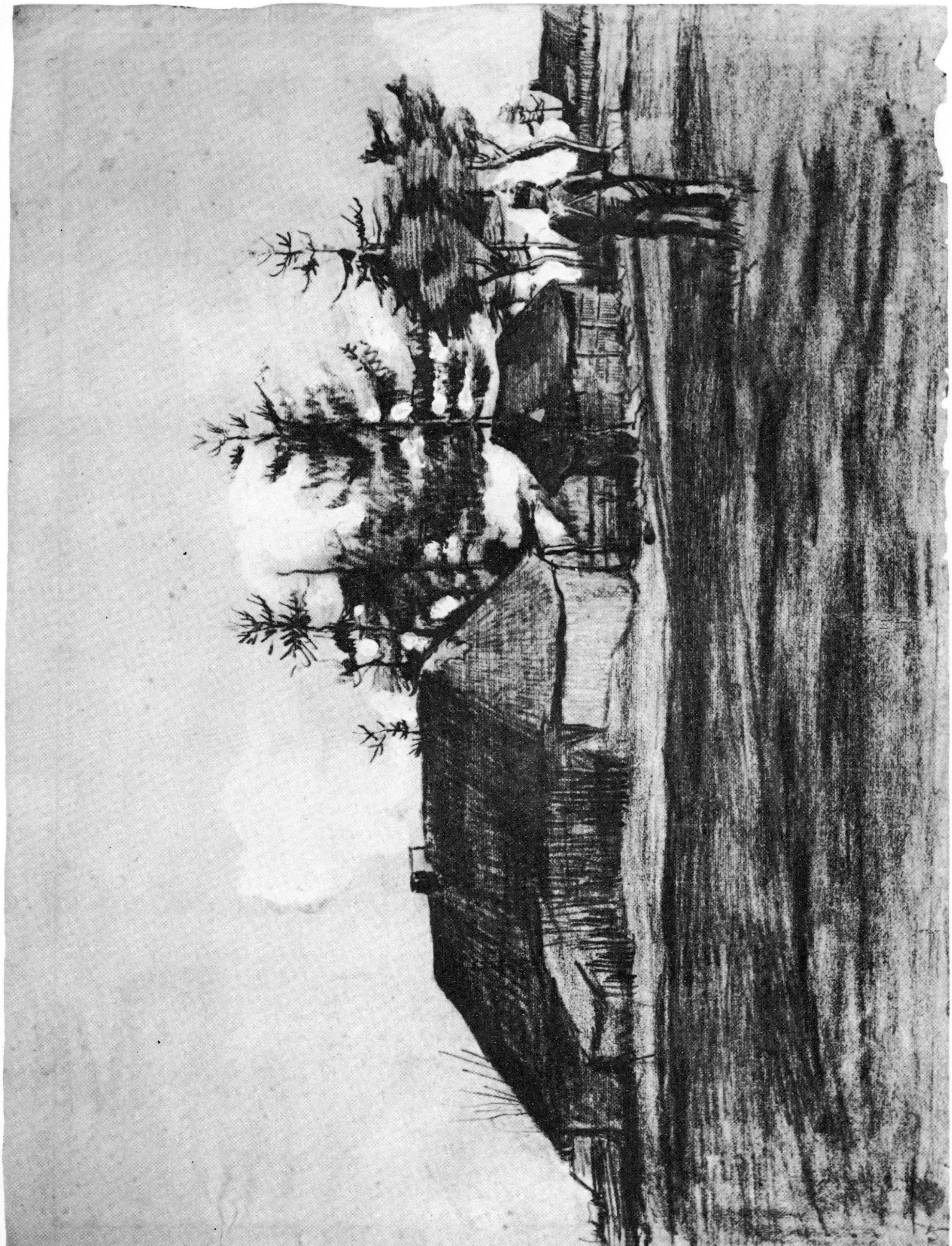

Plate 51

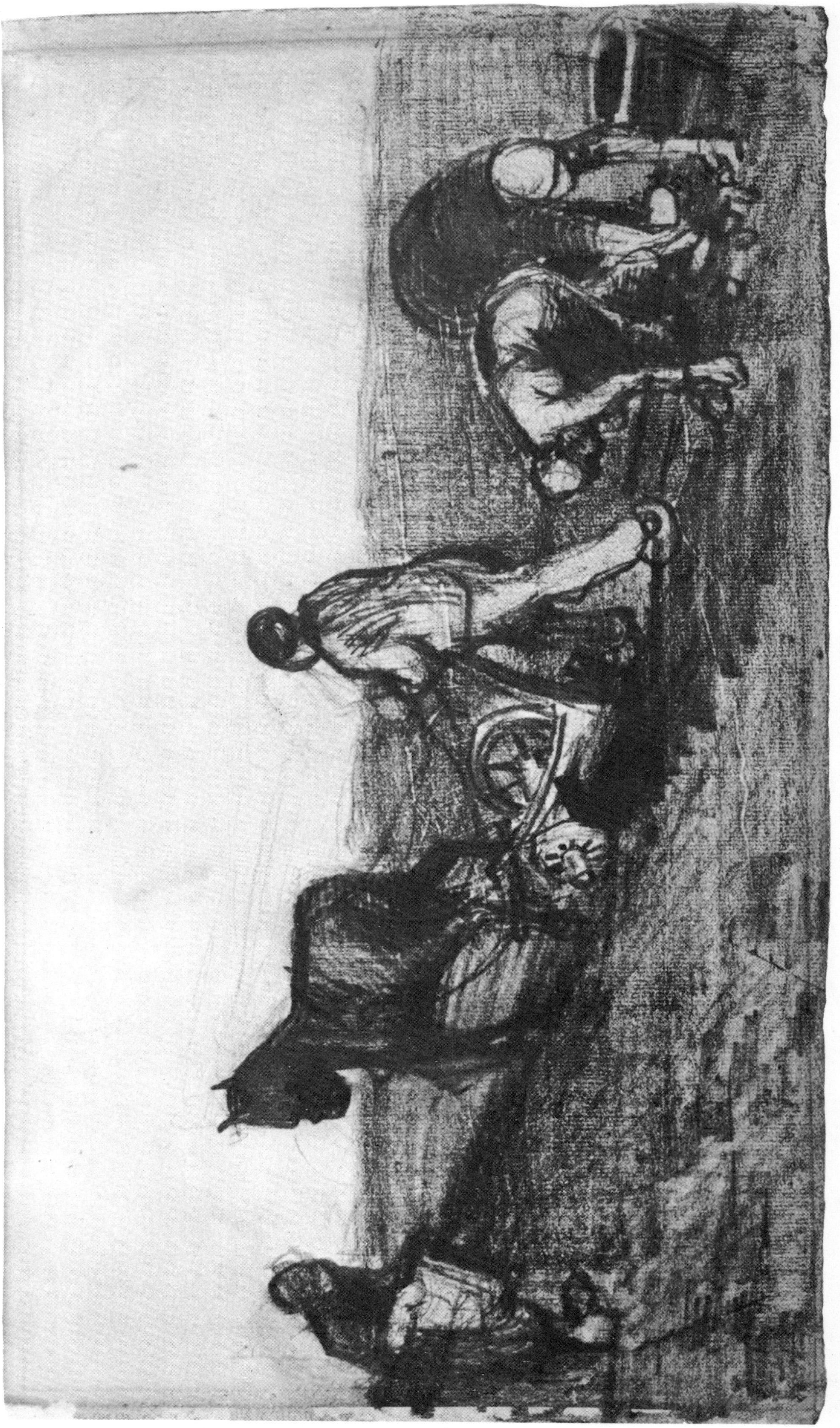

Plate 52

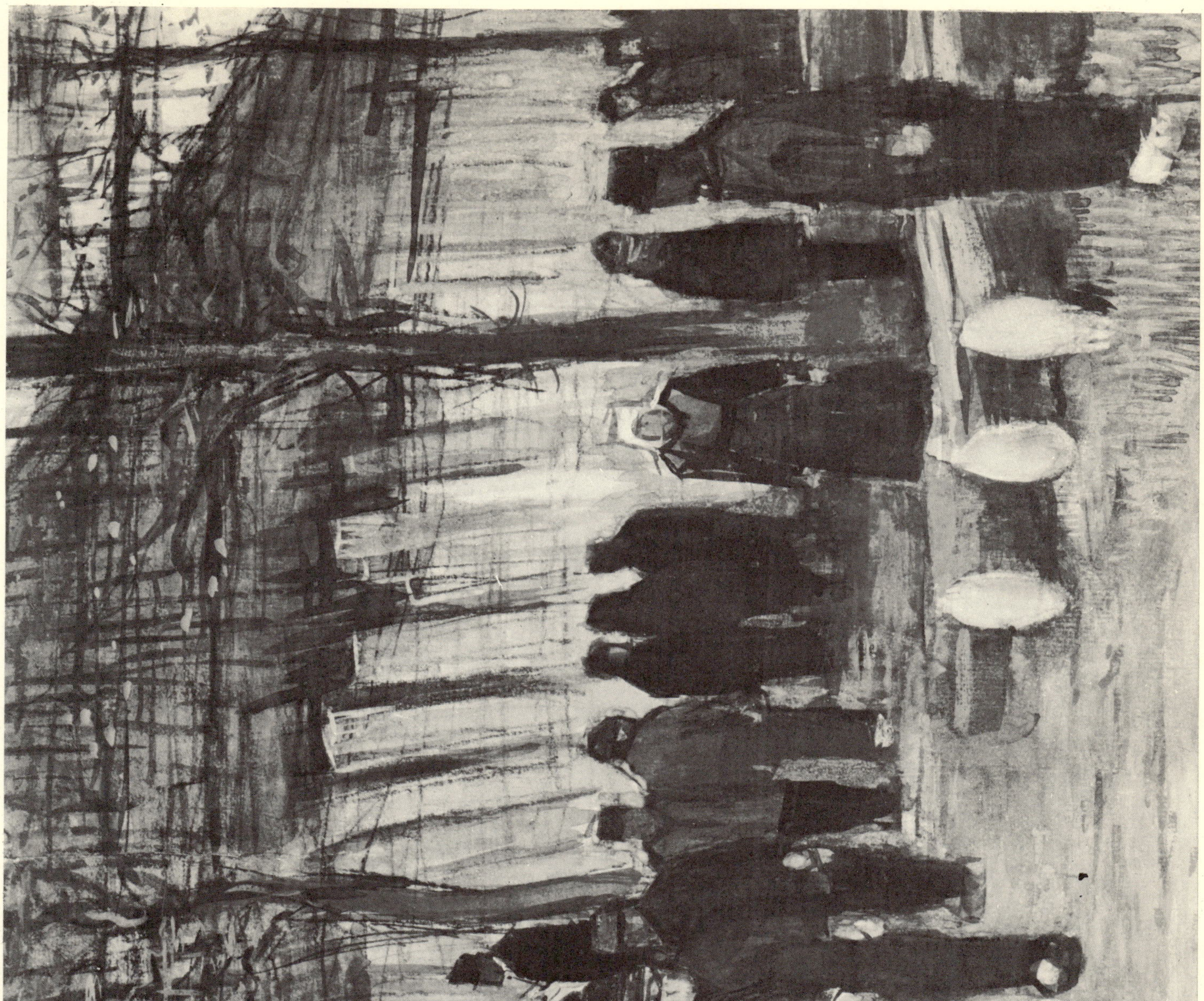

Plate 53

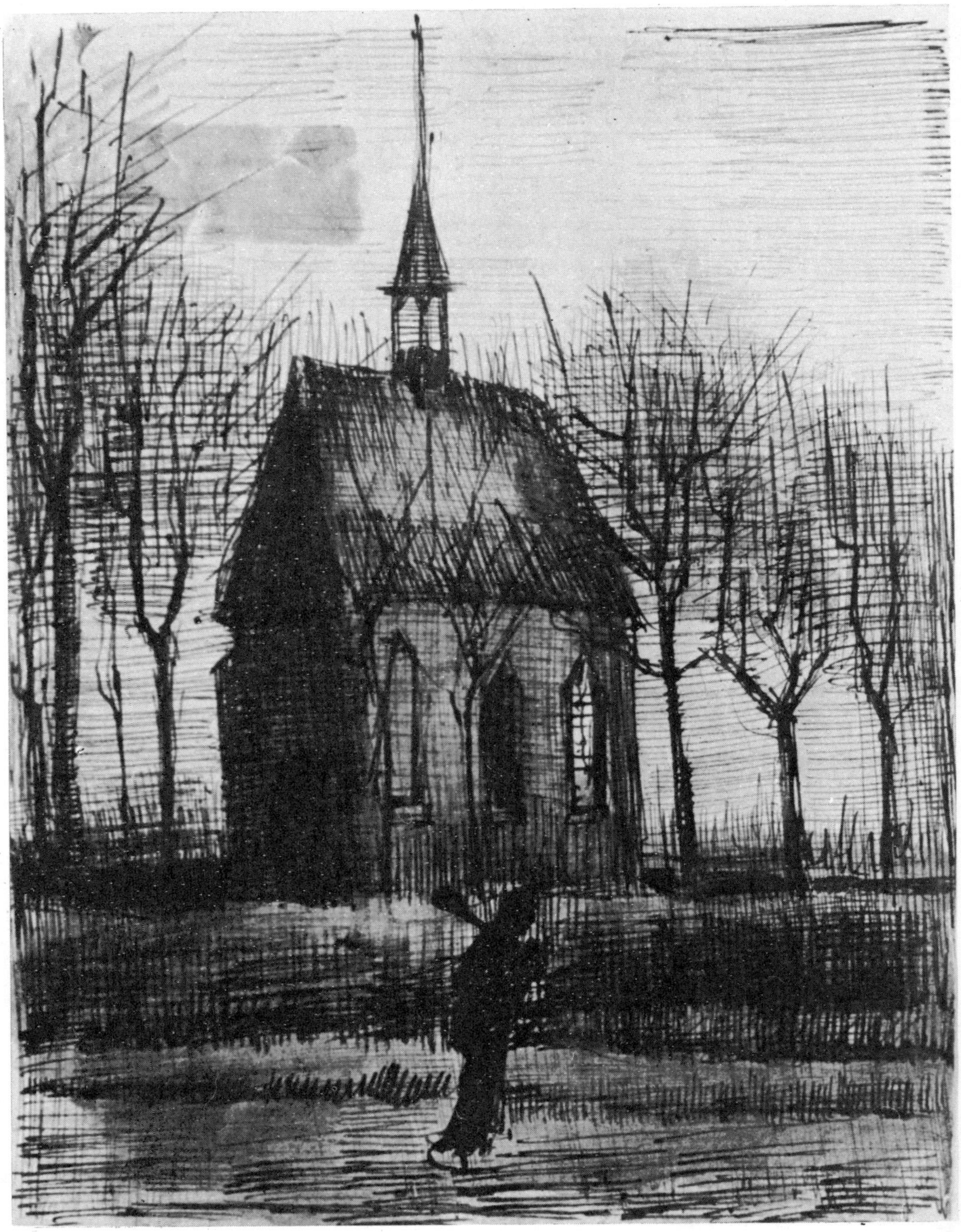

Plate 54

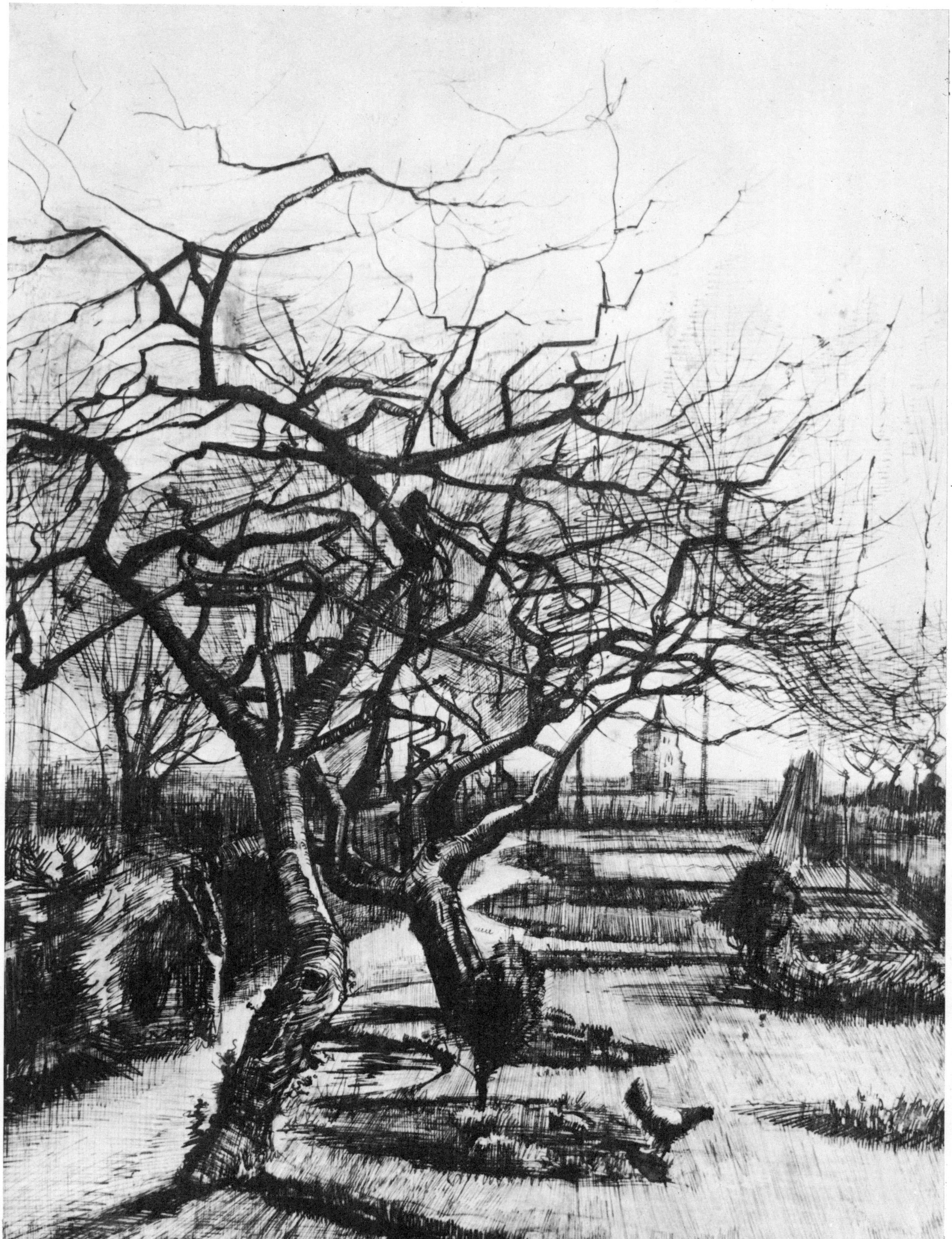

Plate 55

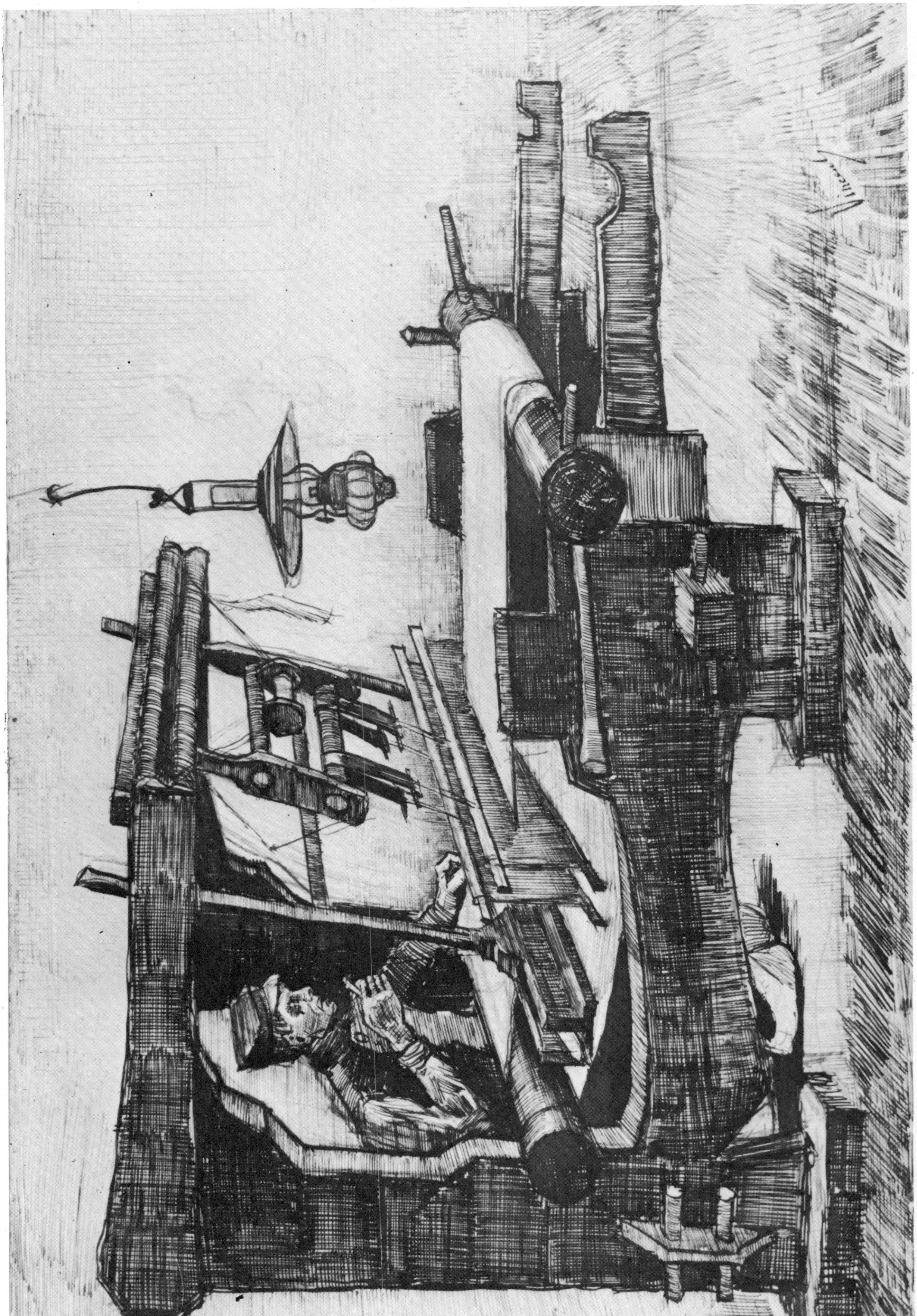

Plate 56

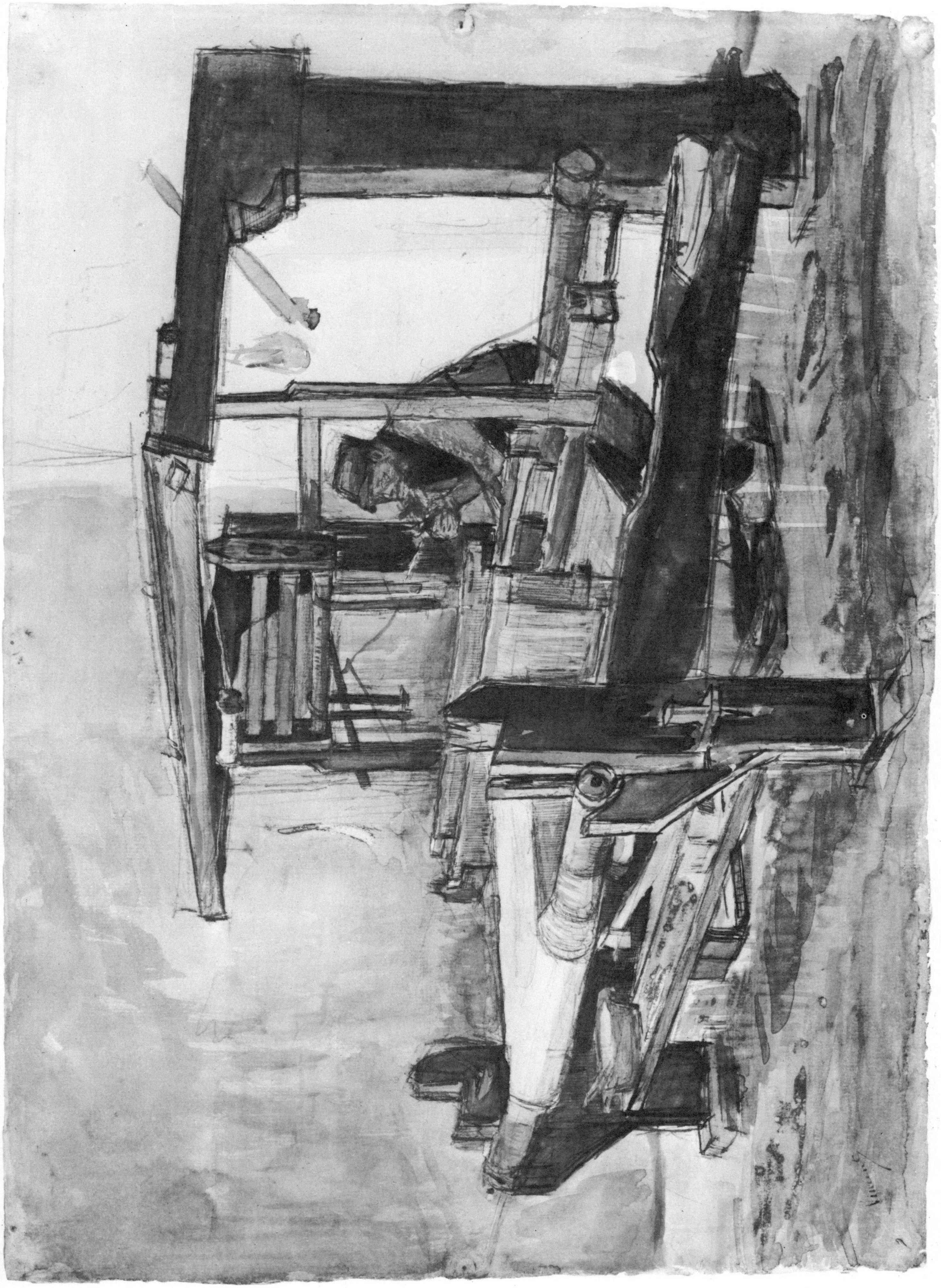

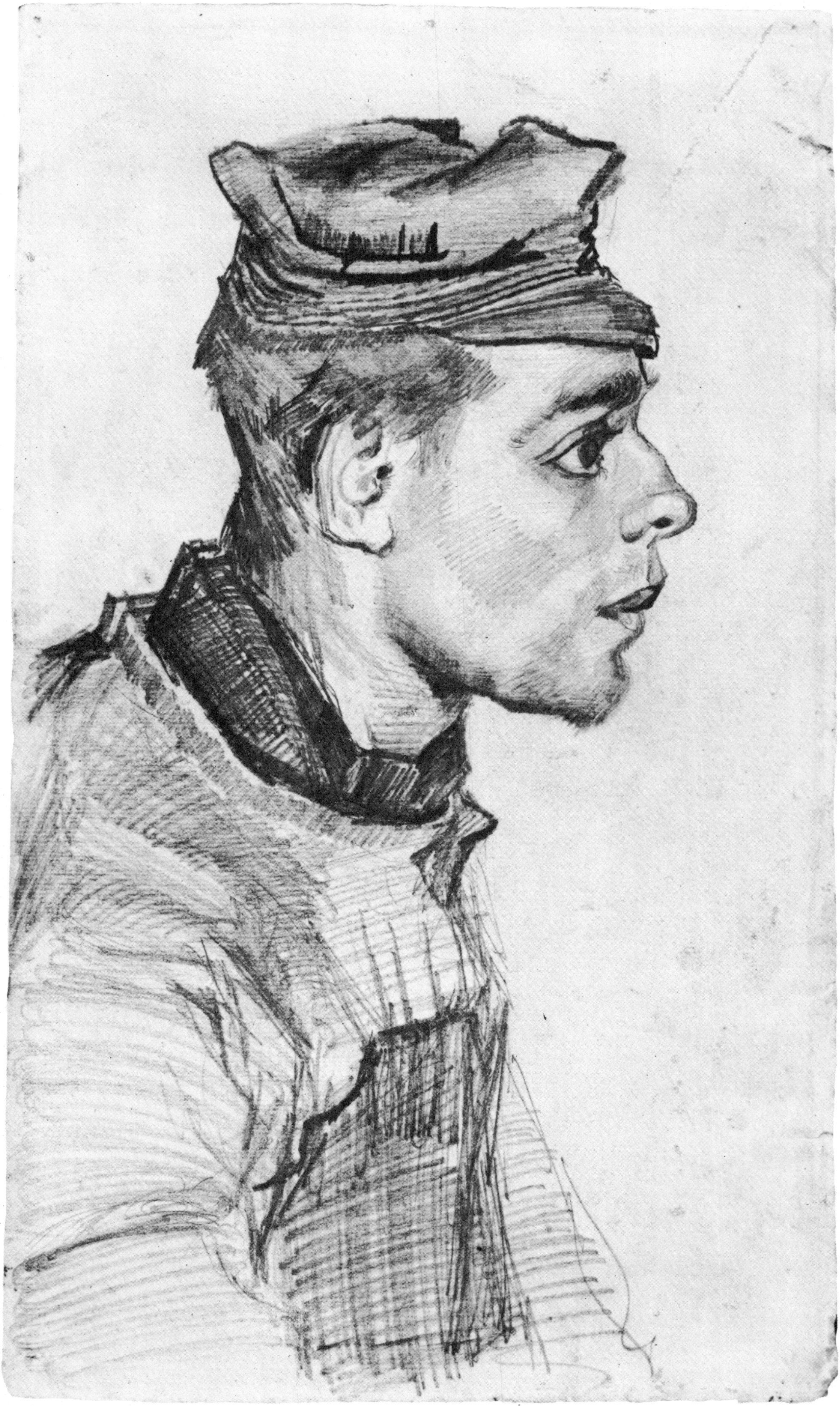

Plate 58

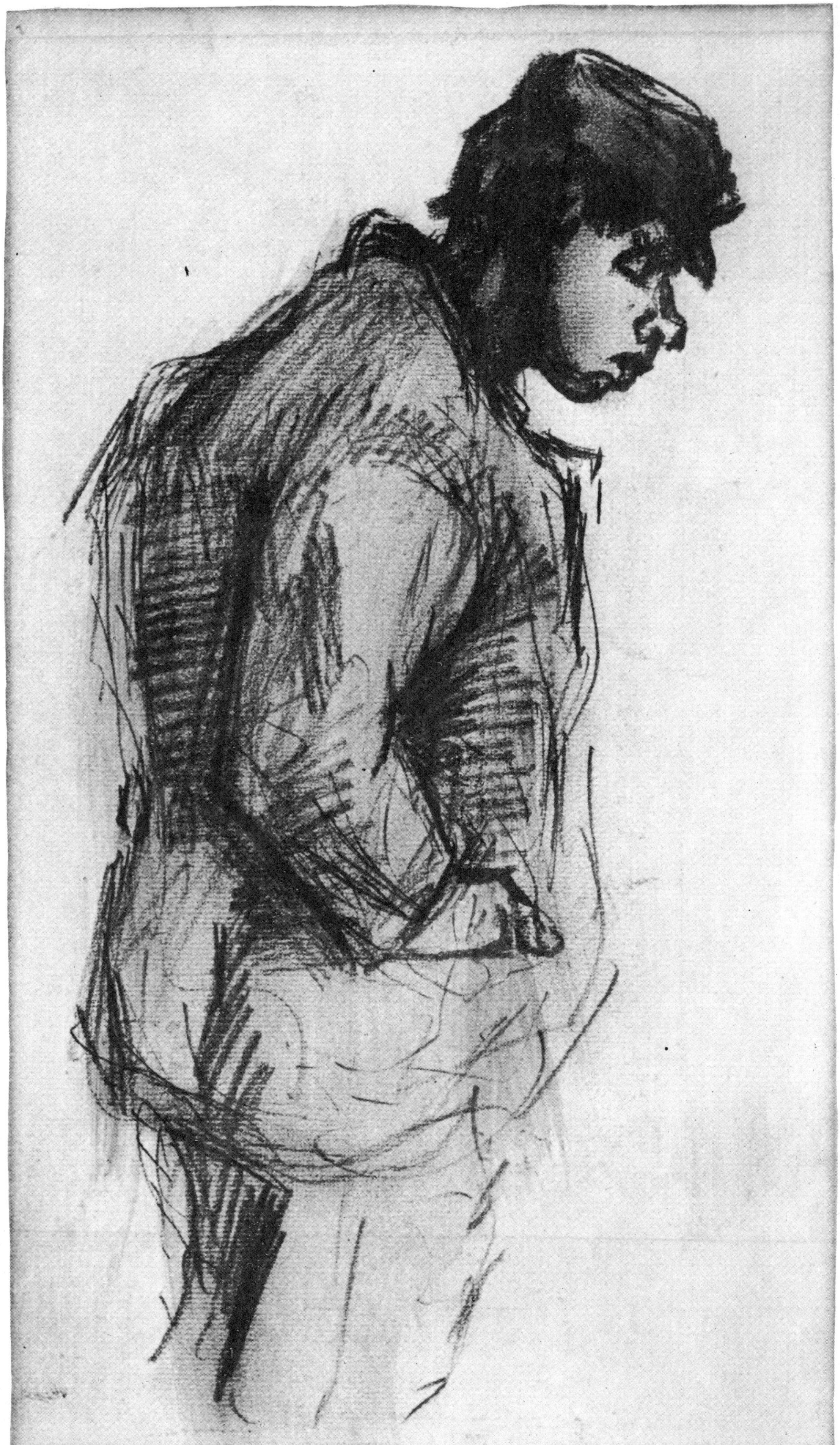

Plate 59

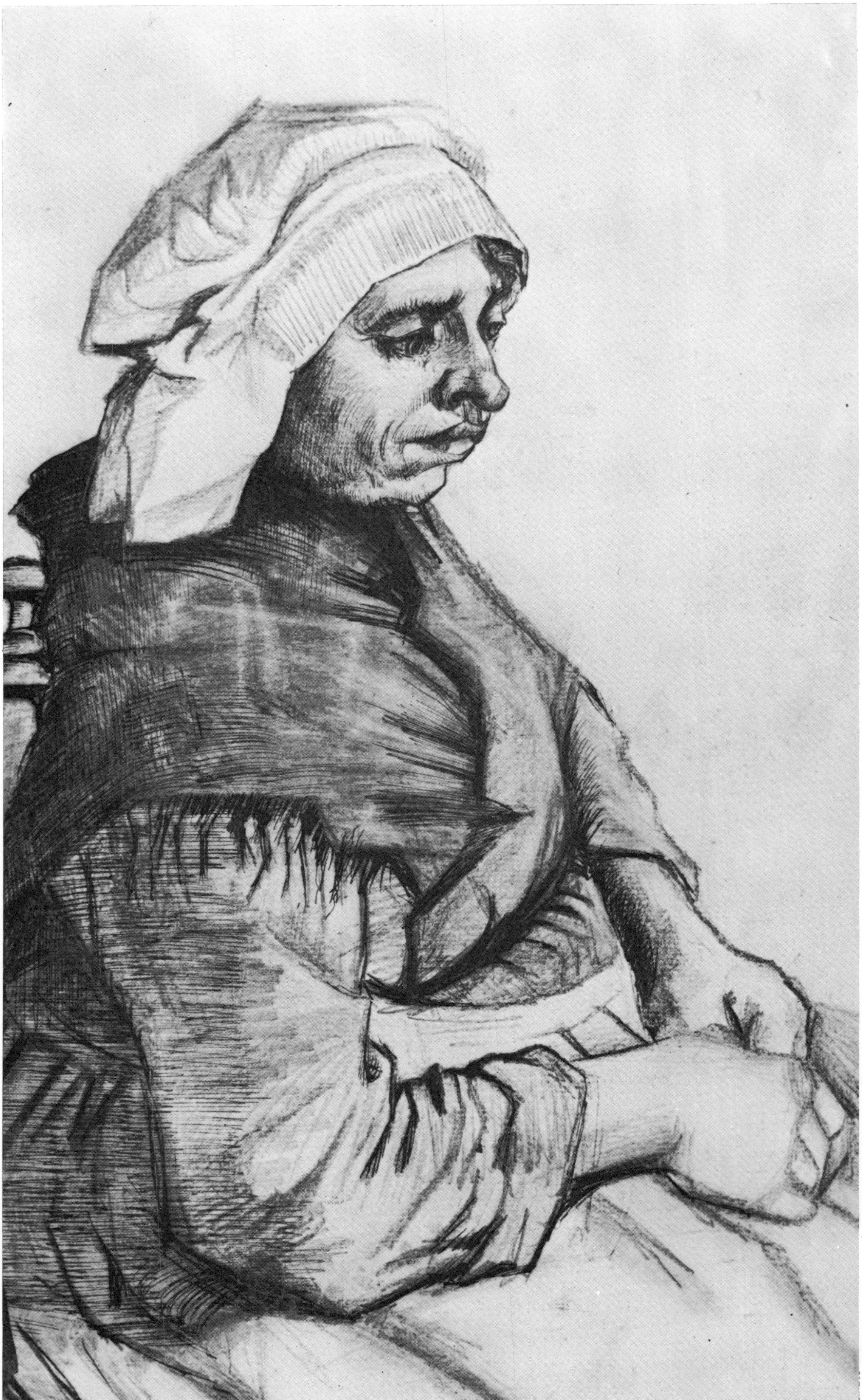

Plate 60

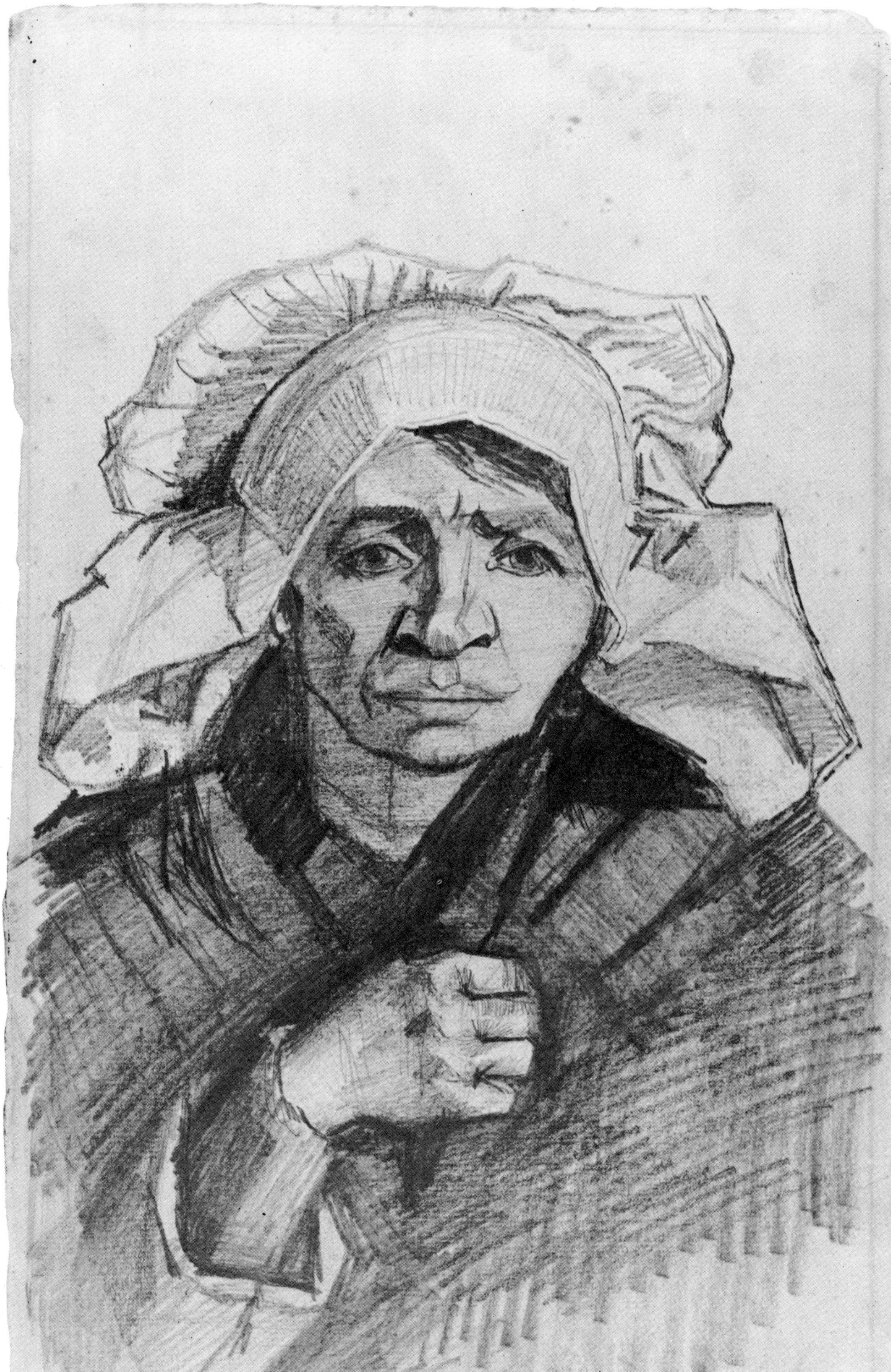

Plate 61

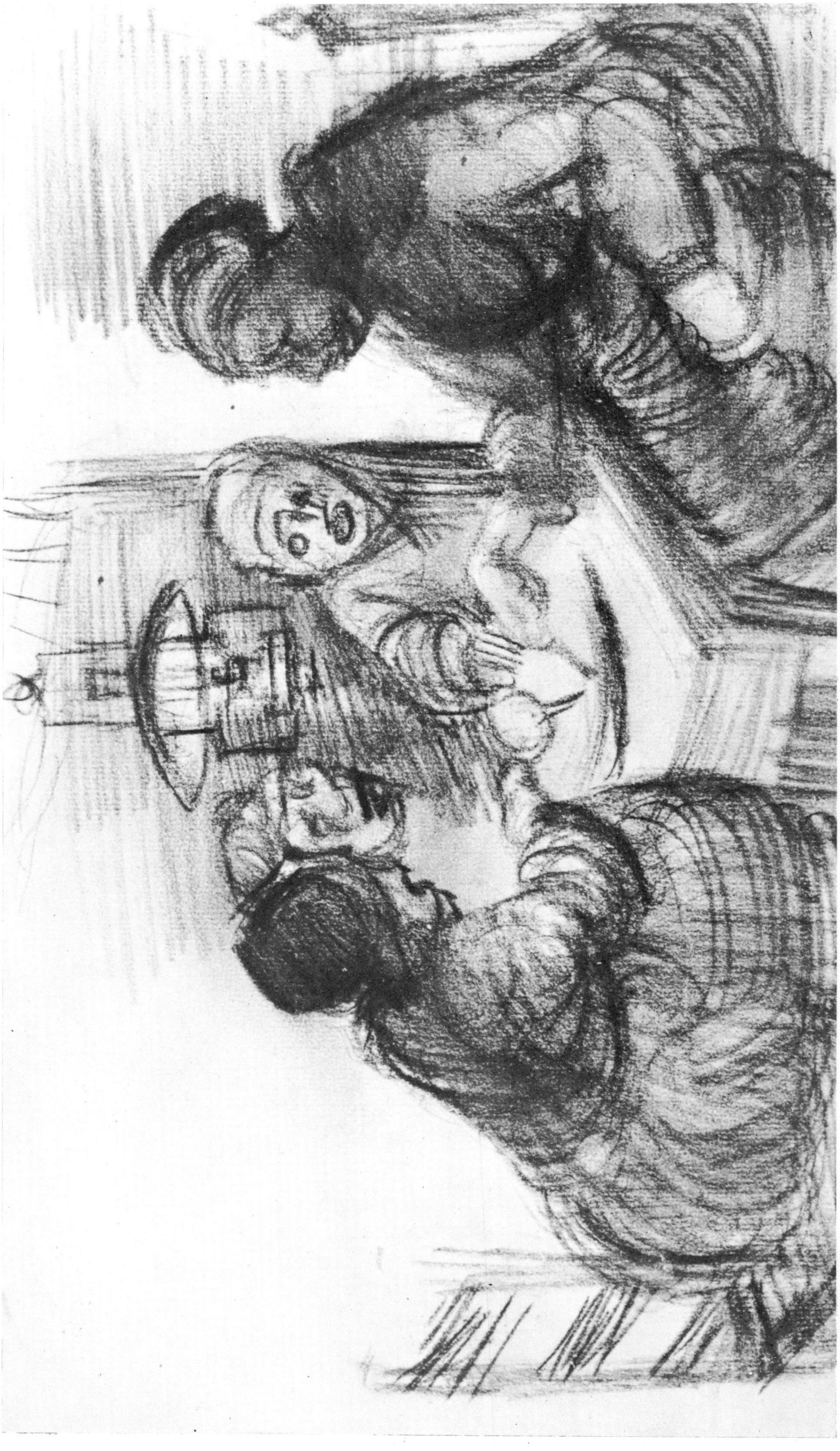

Plate 62

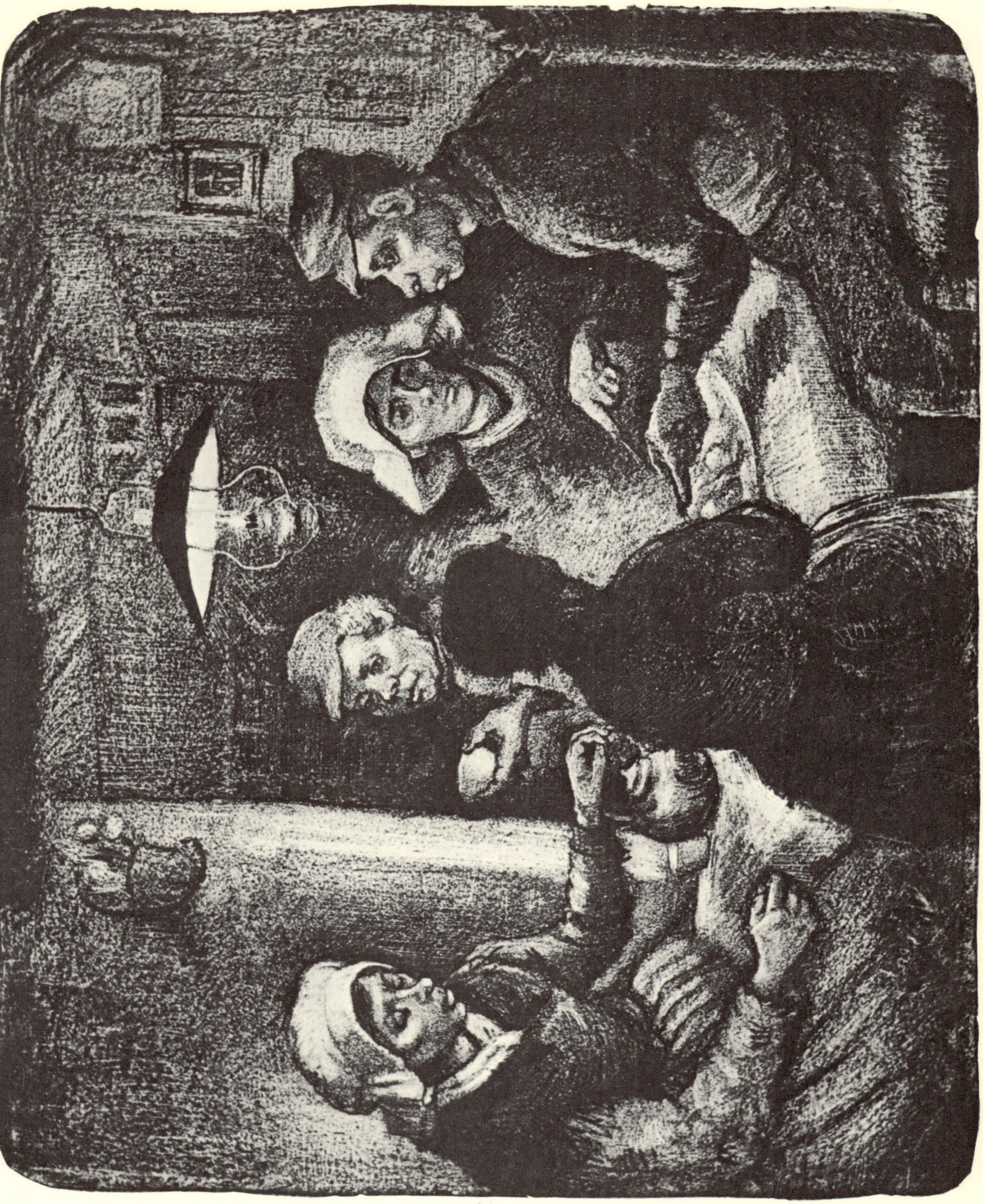

Plate 63

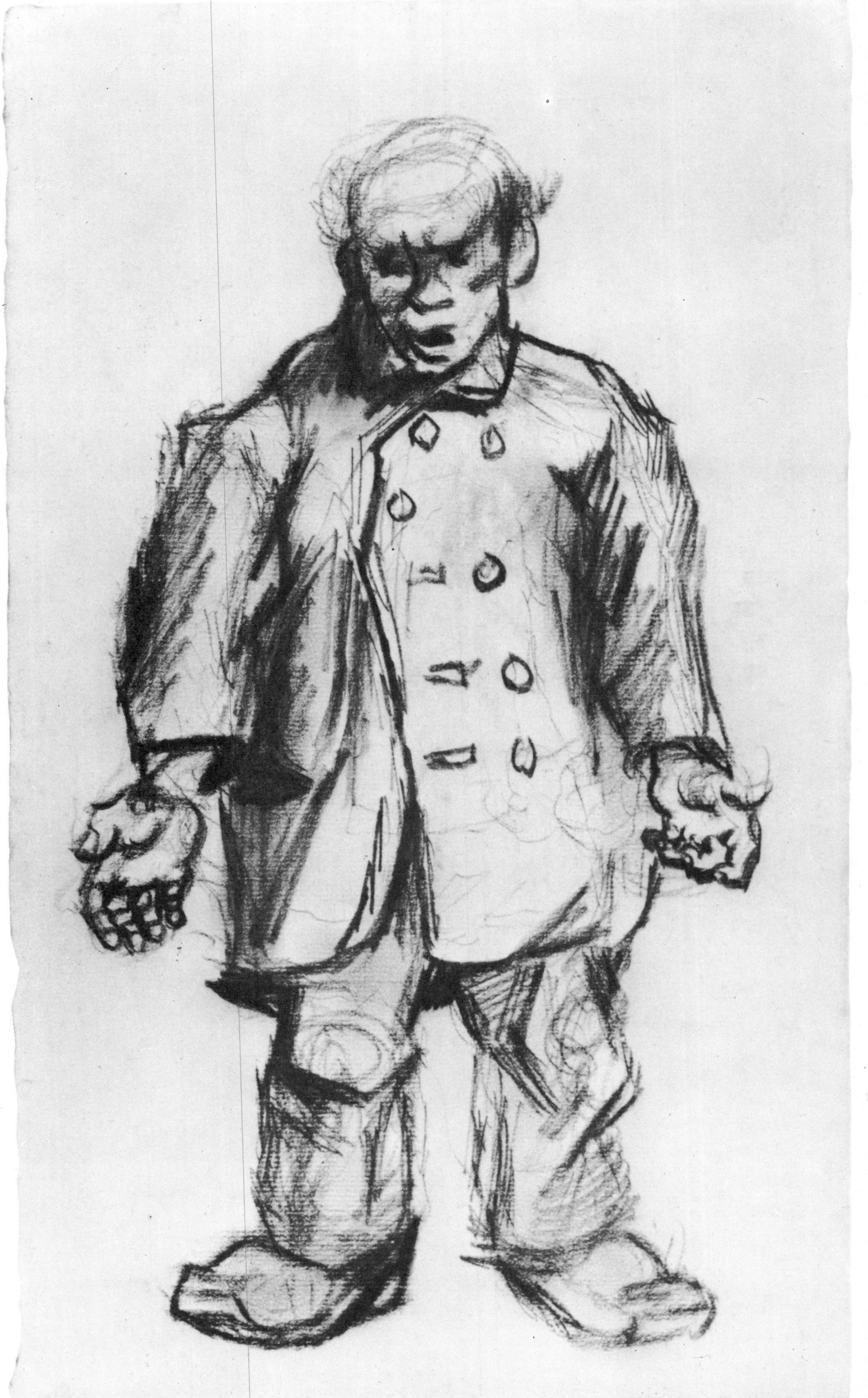

Plate 64

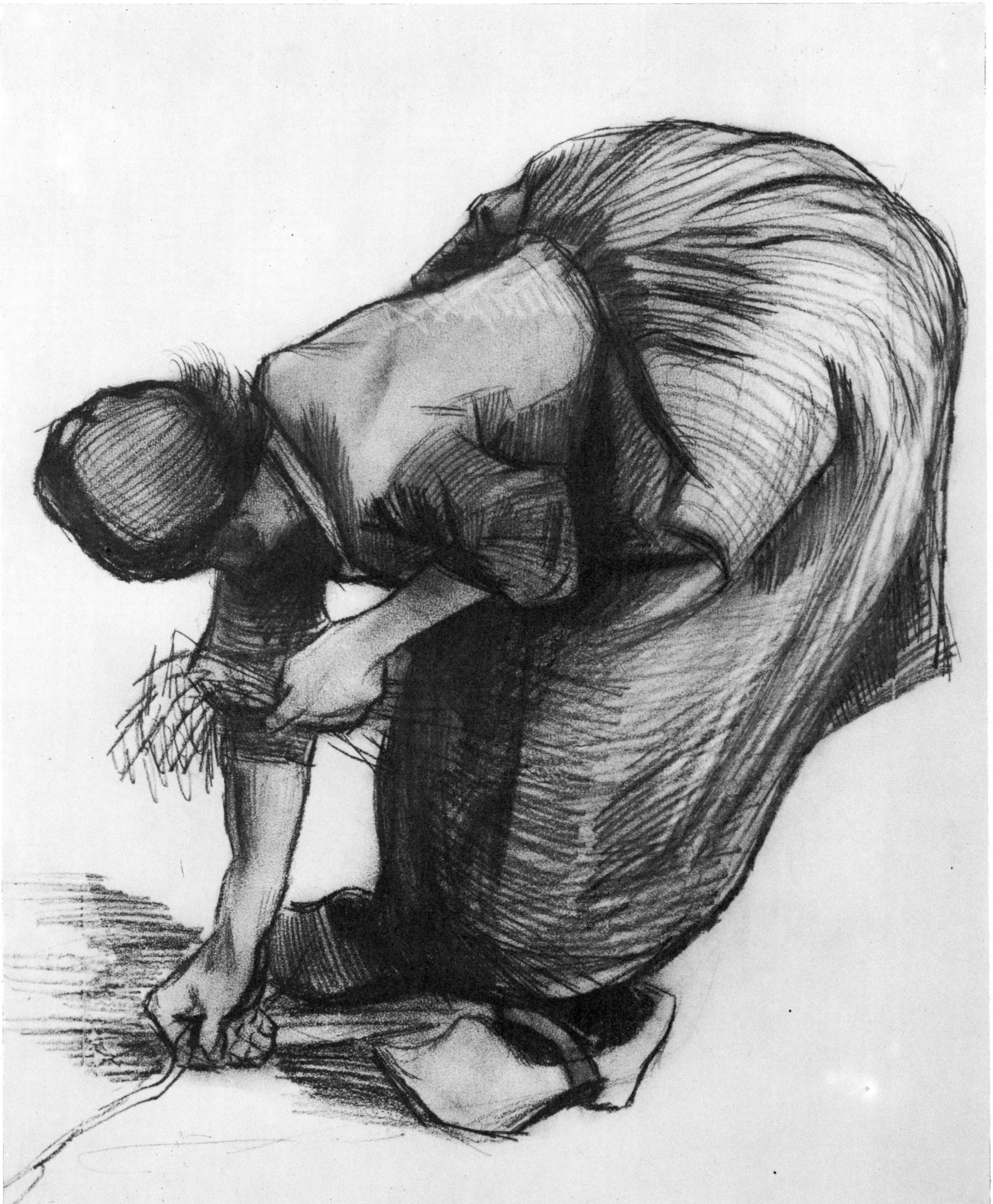

Plate 65

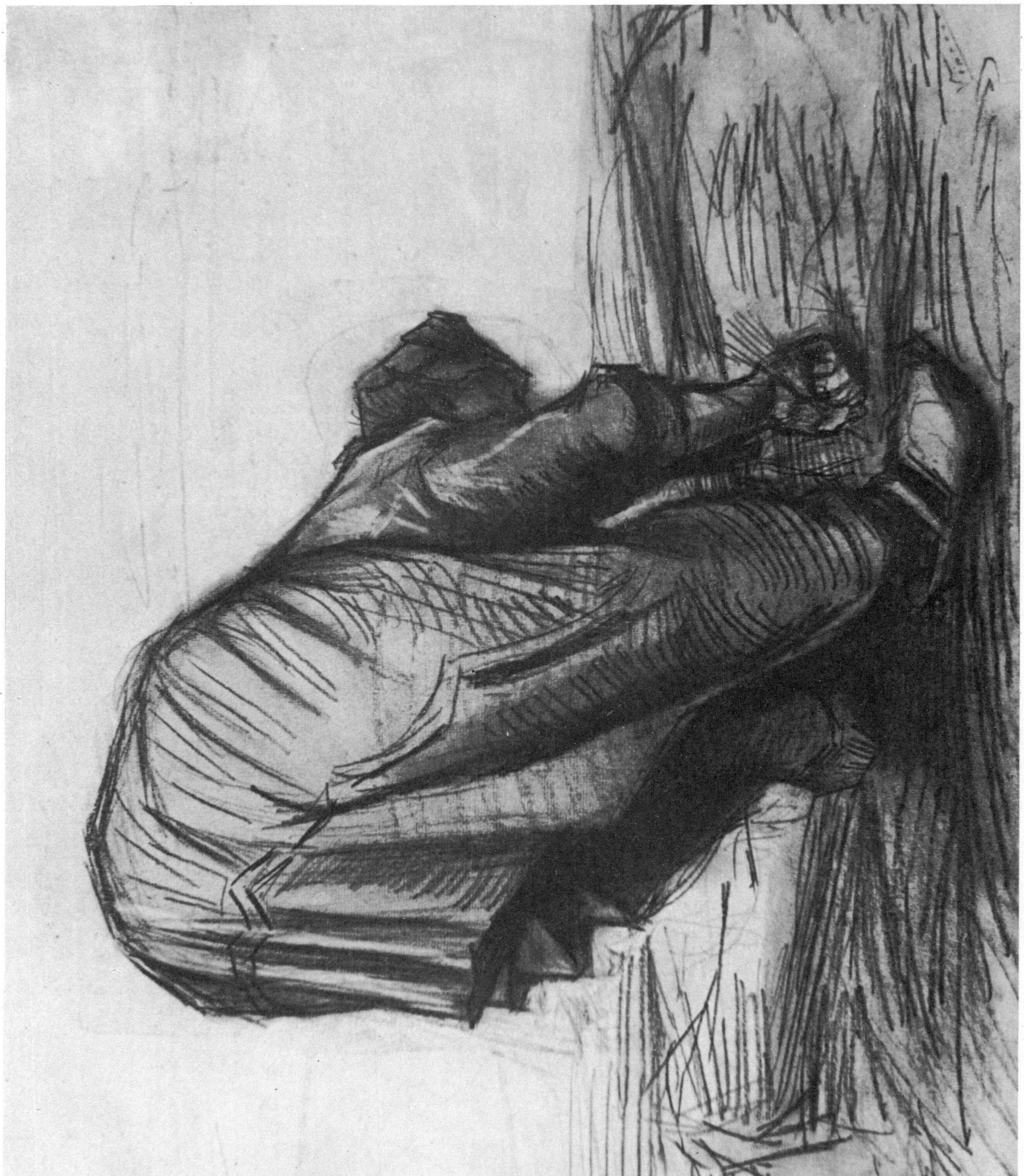

Plate 66

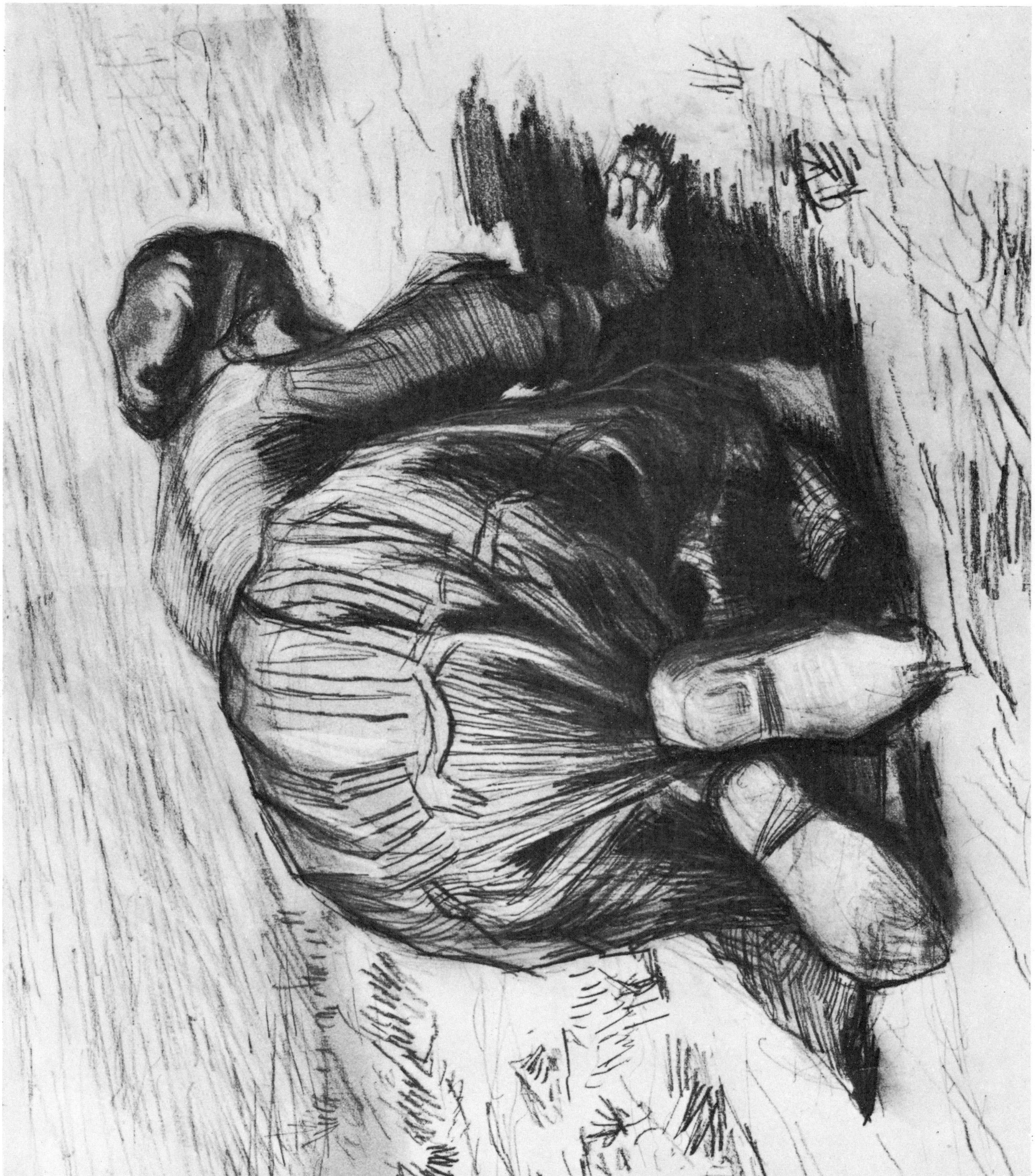

Plate 67

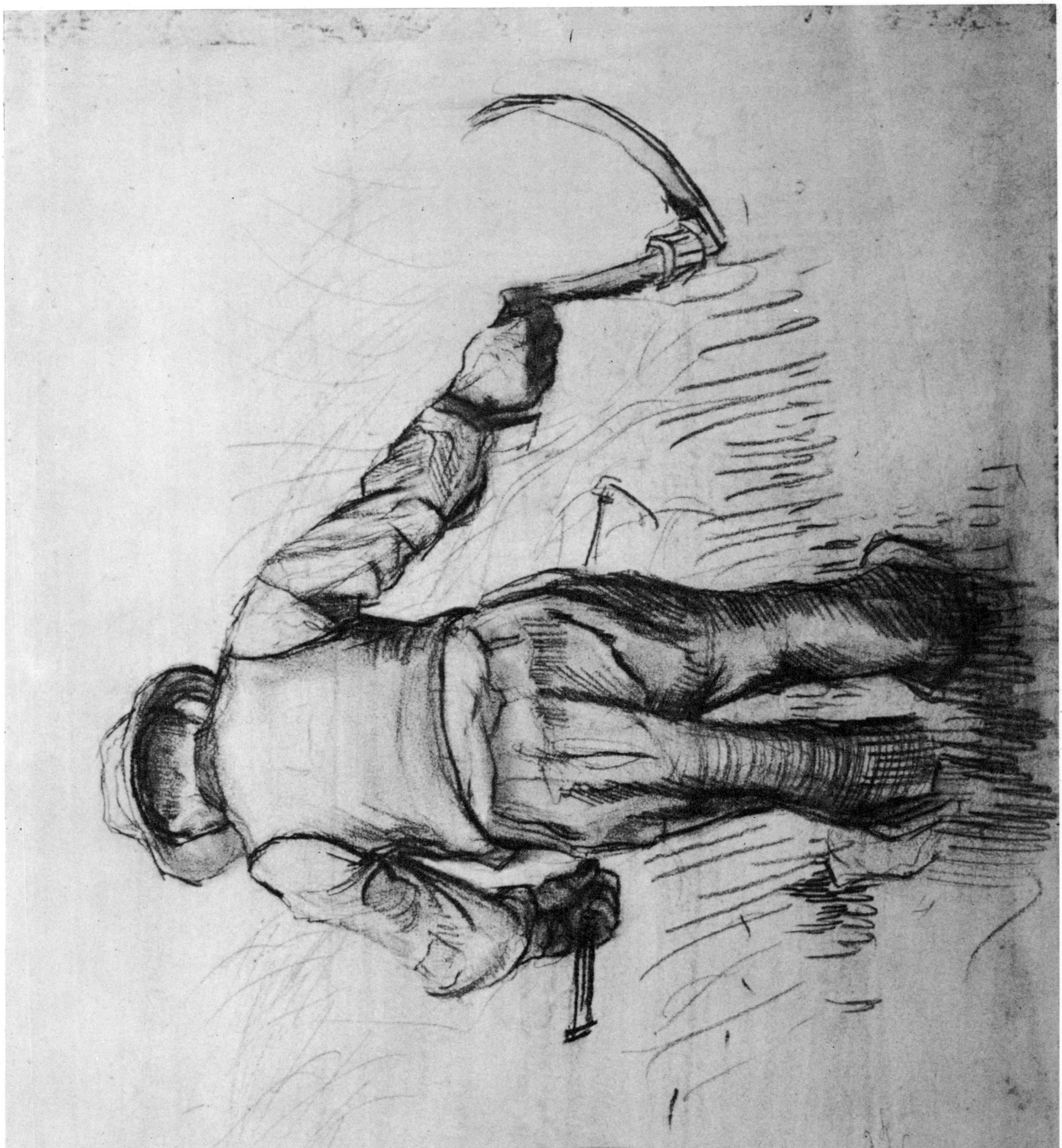

Plate 68

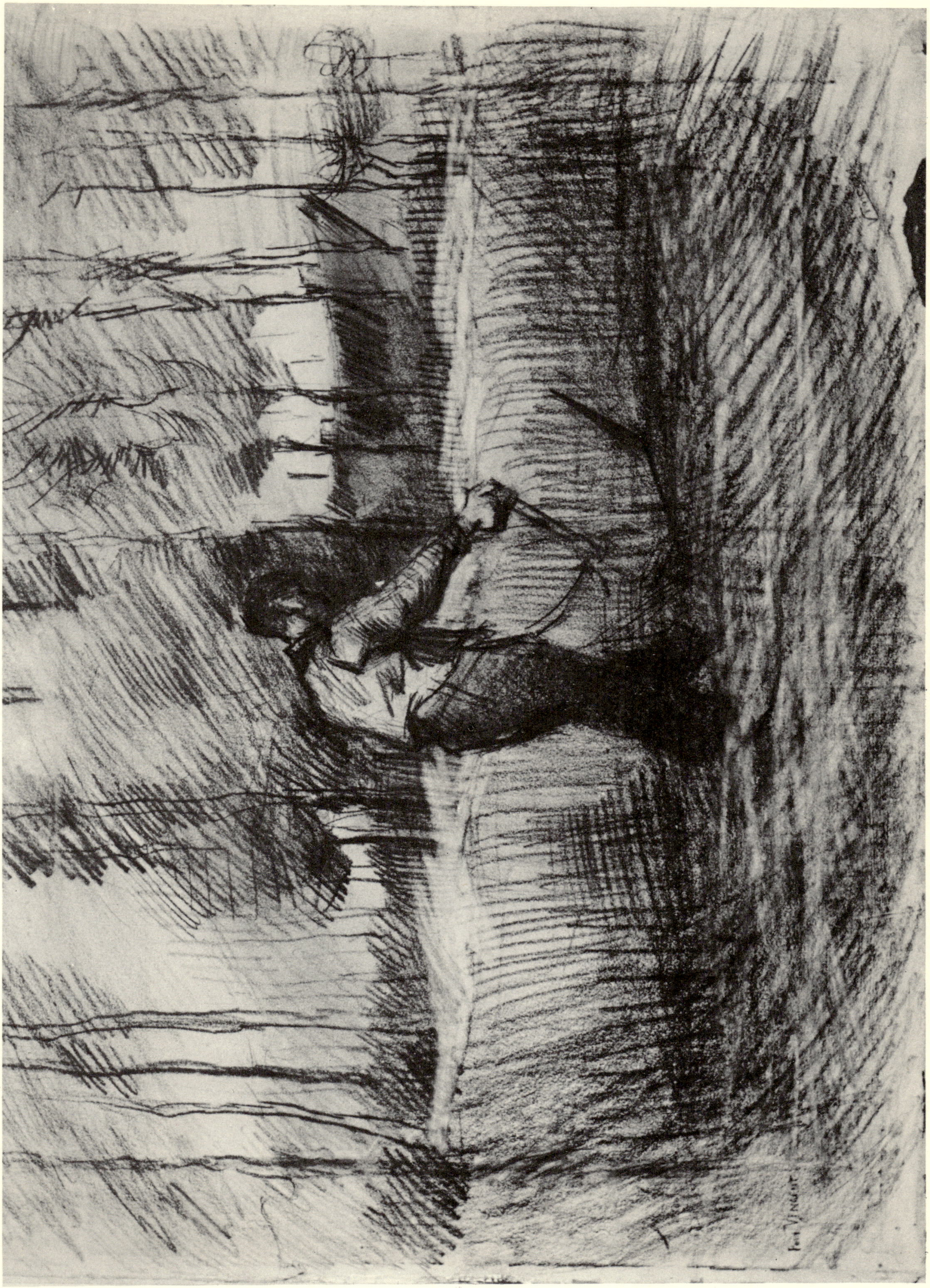

Plate 69

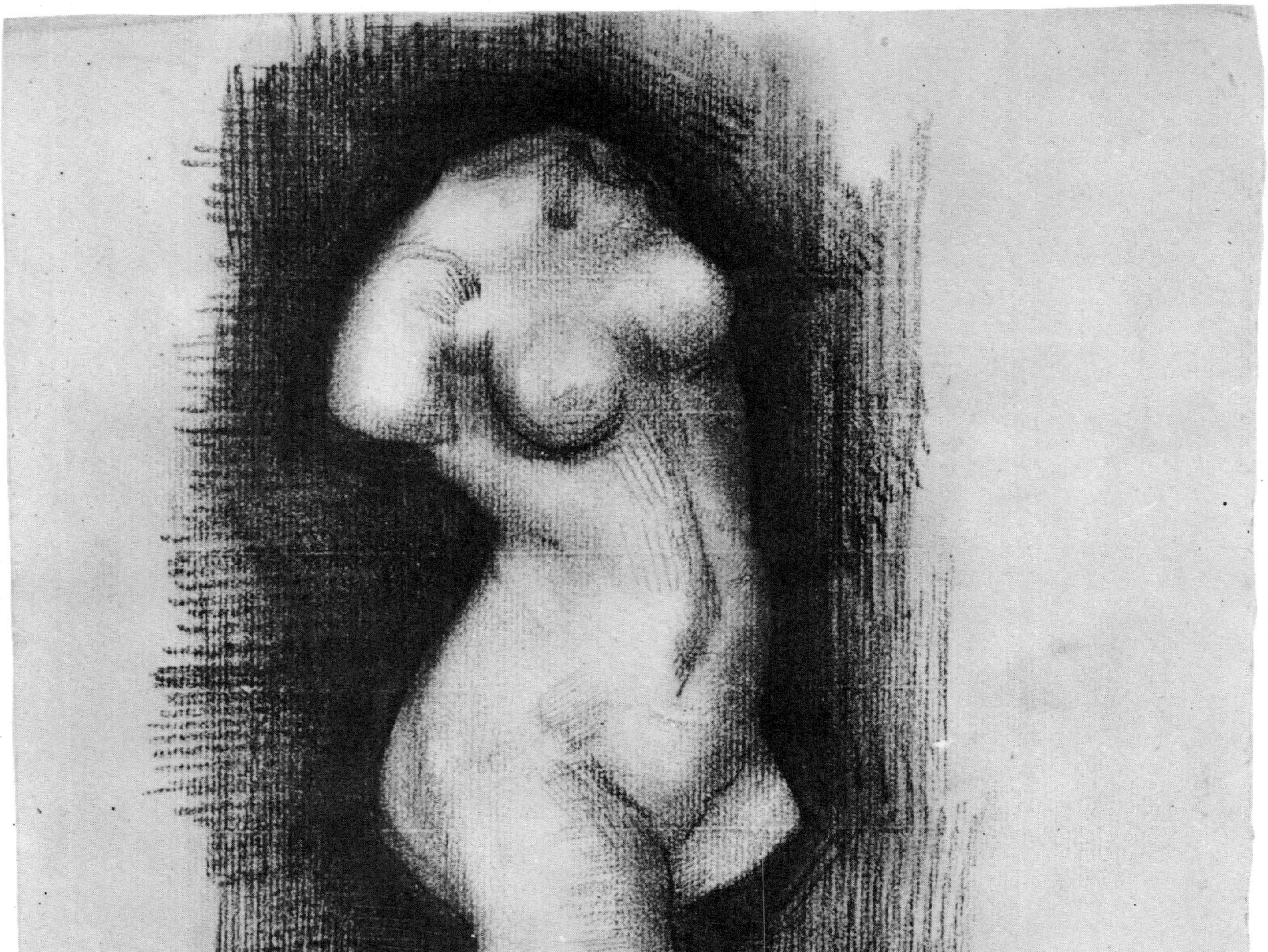

Plate 70

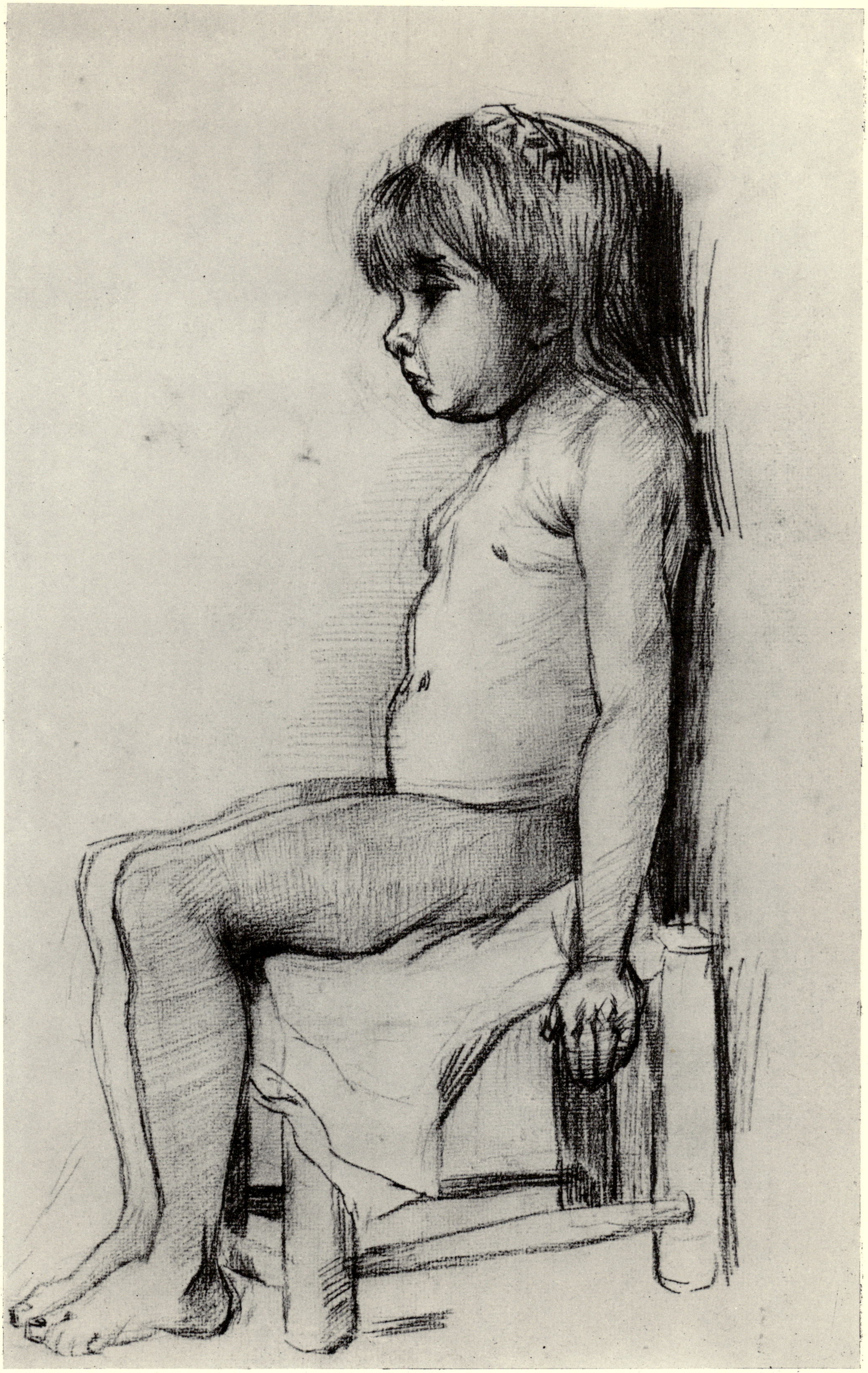

Plate 71

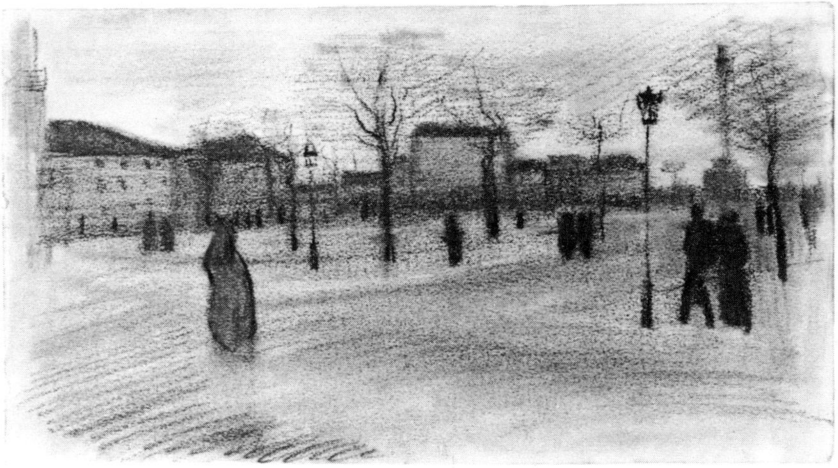

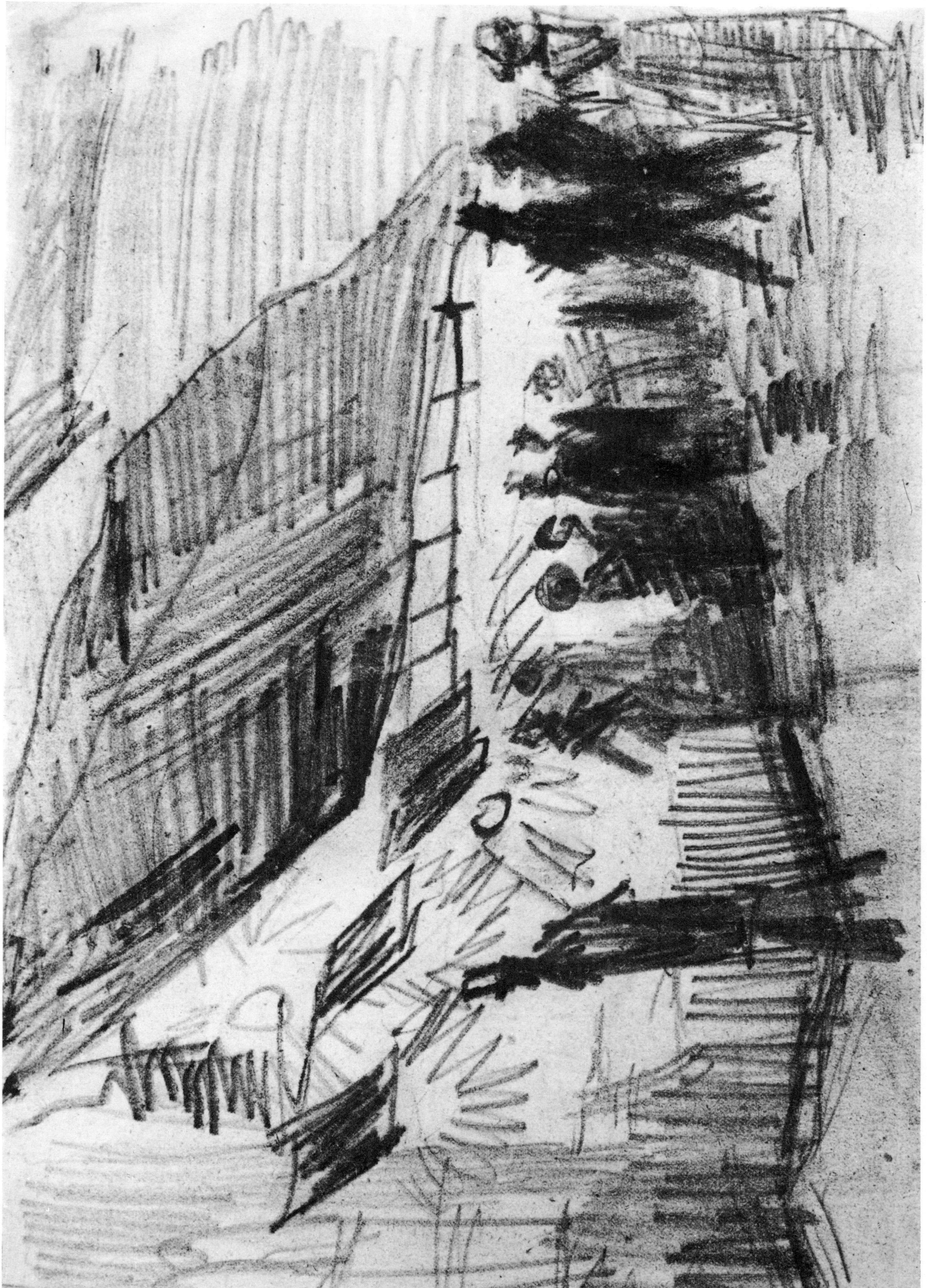

Plate 73

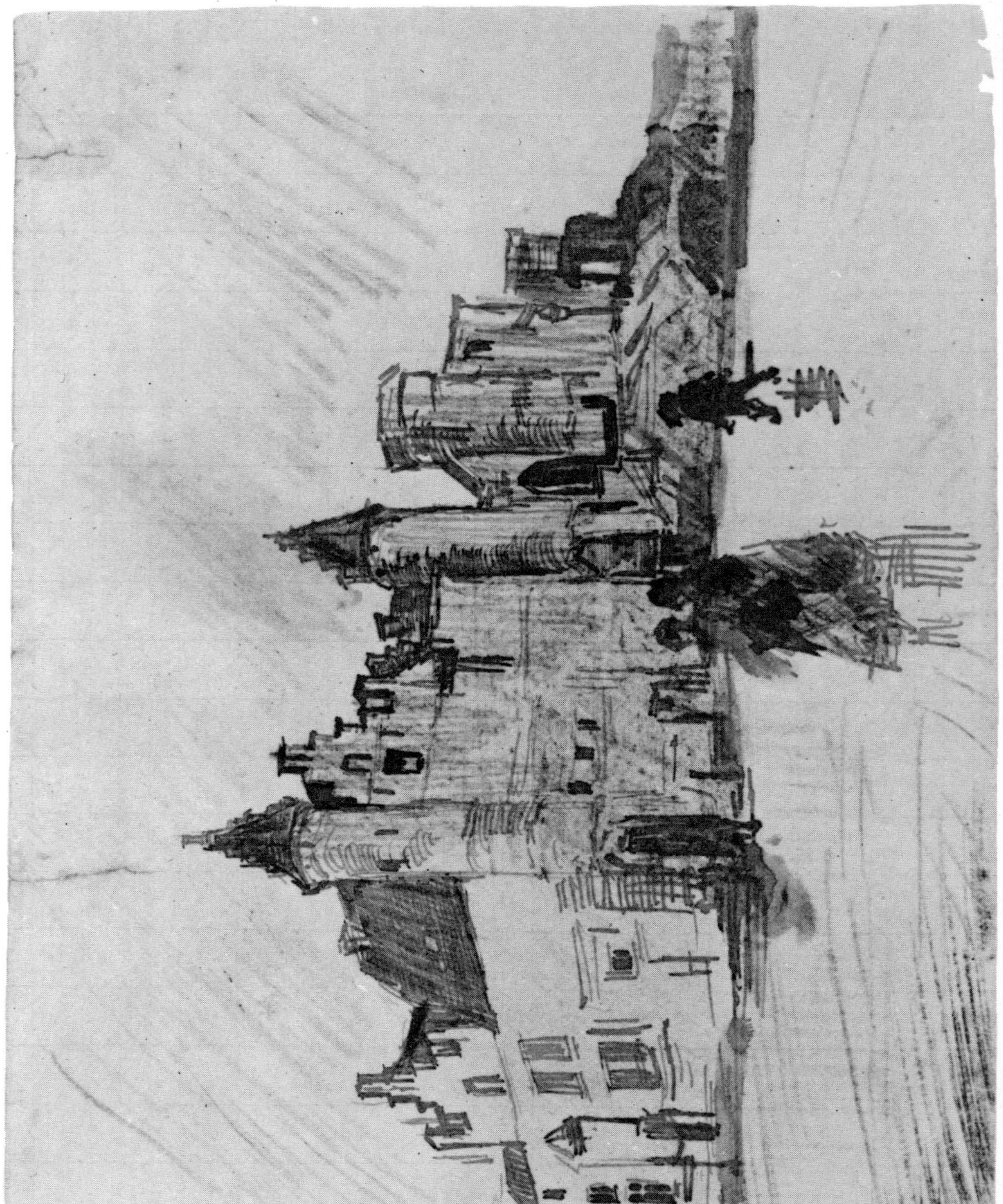

Plate 74

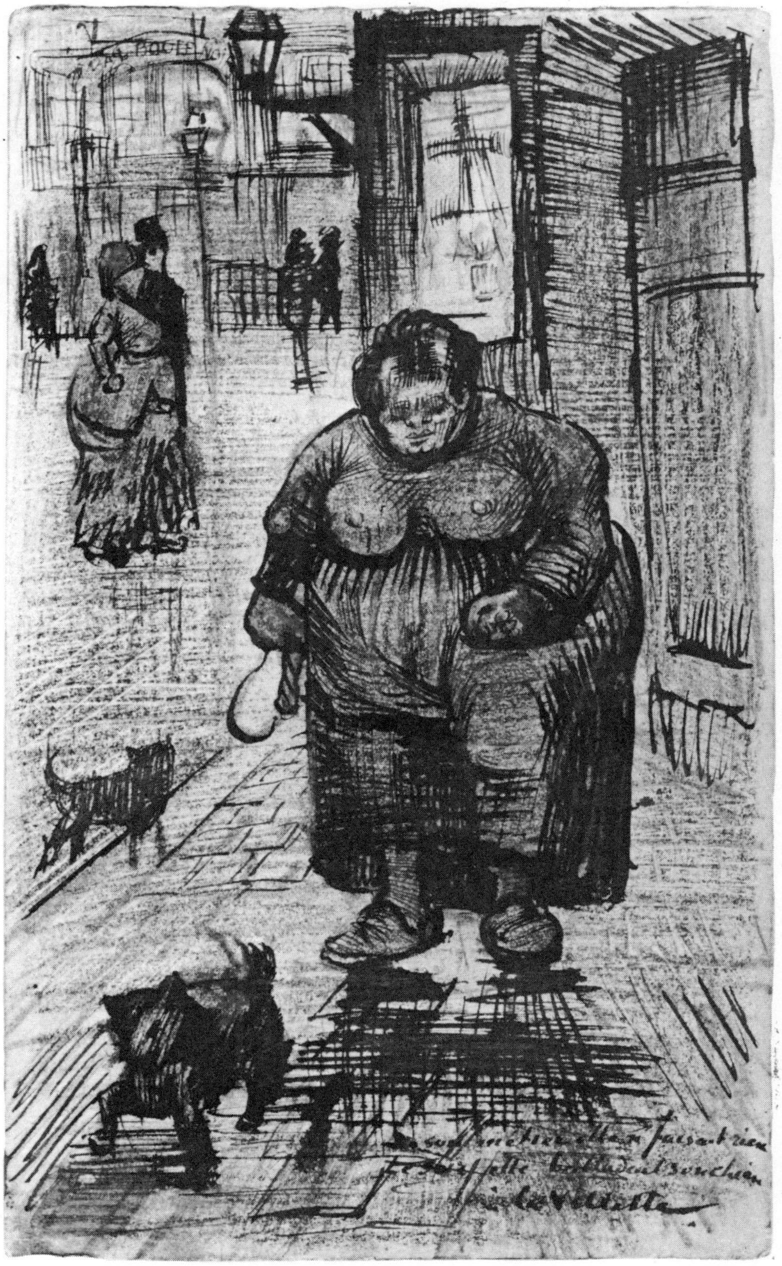

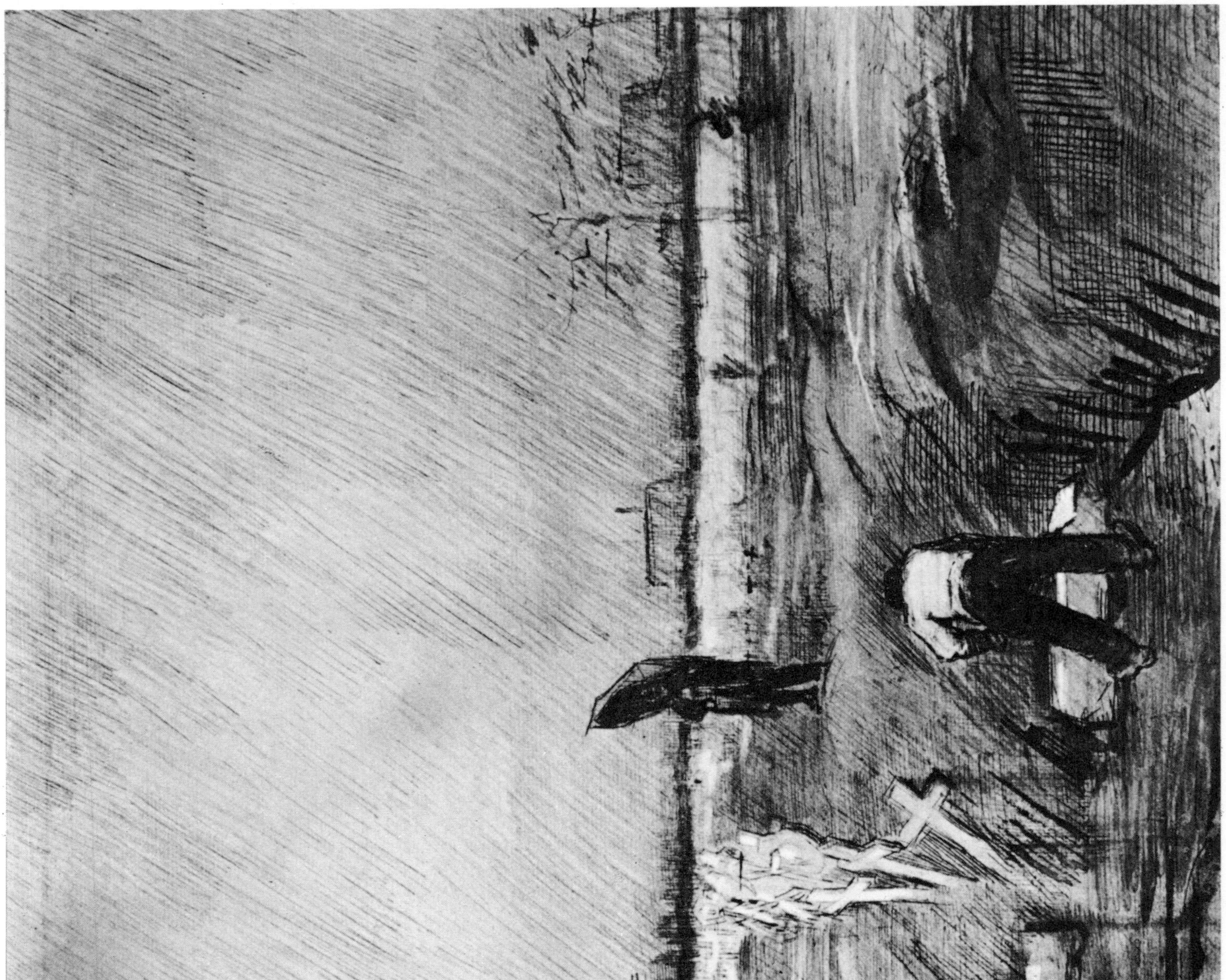

Plate 76

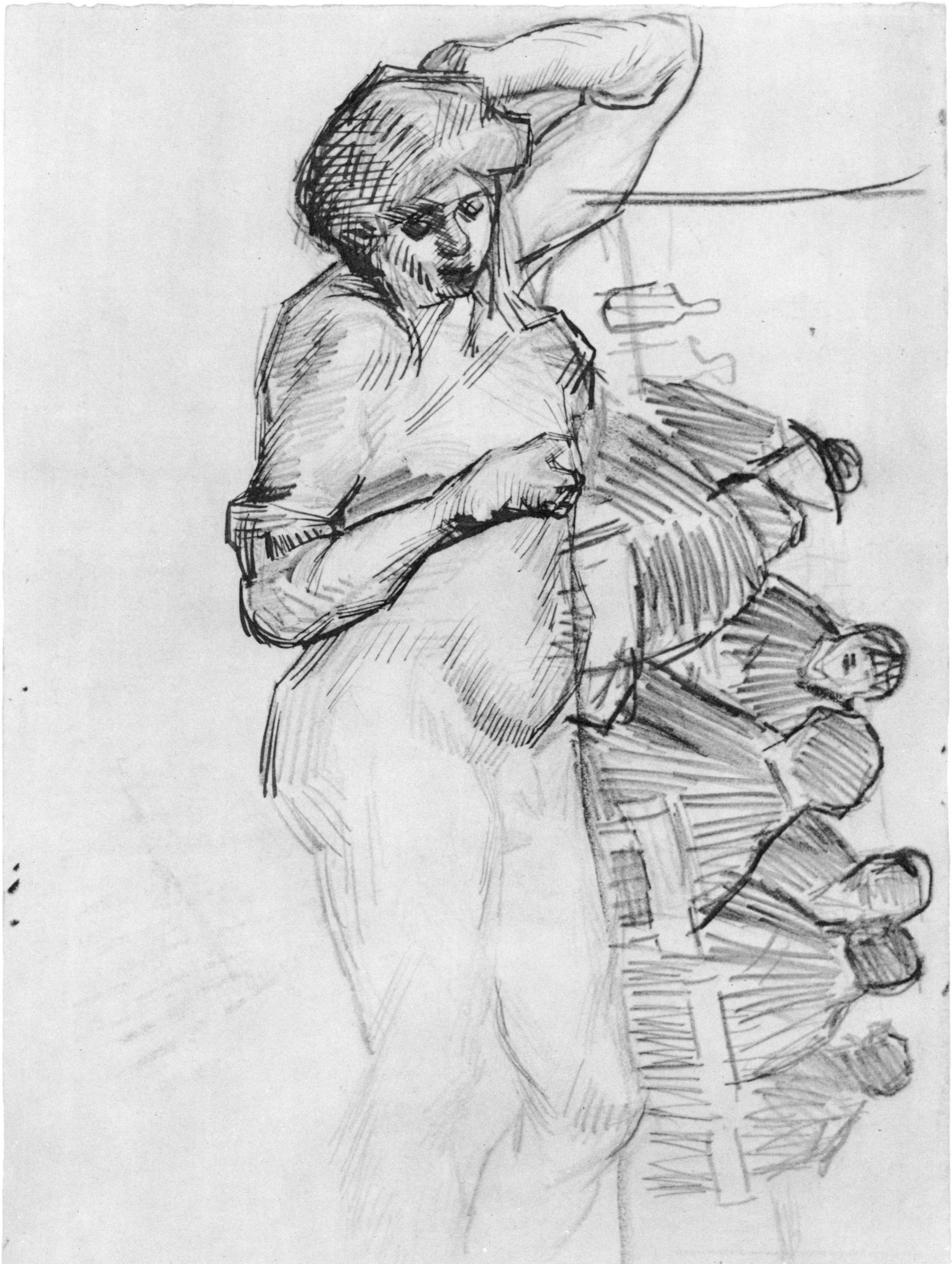

Plate 77

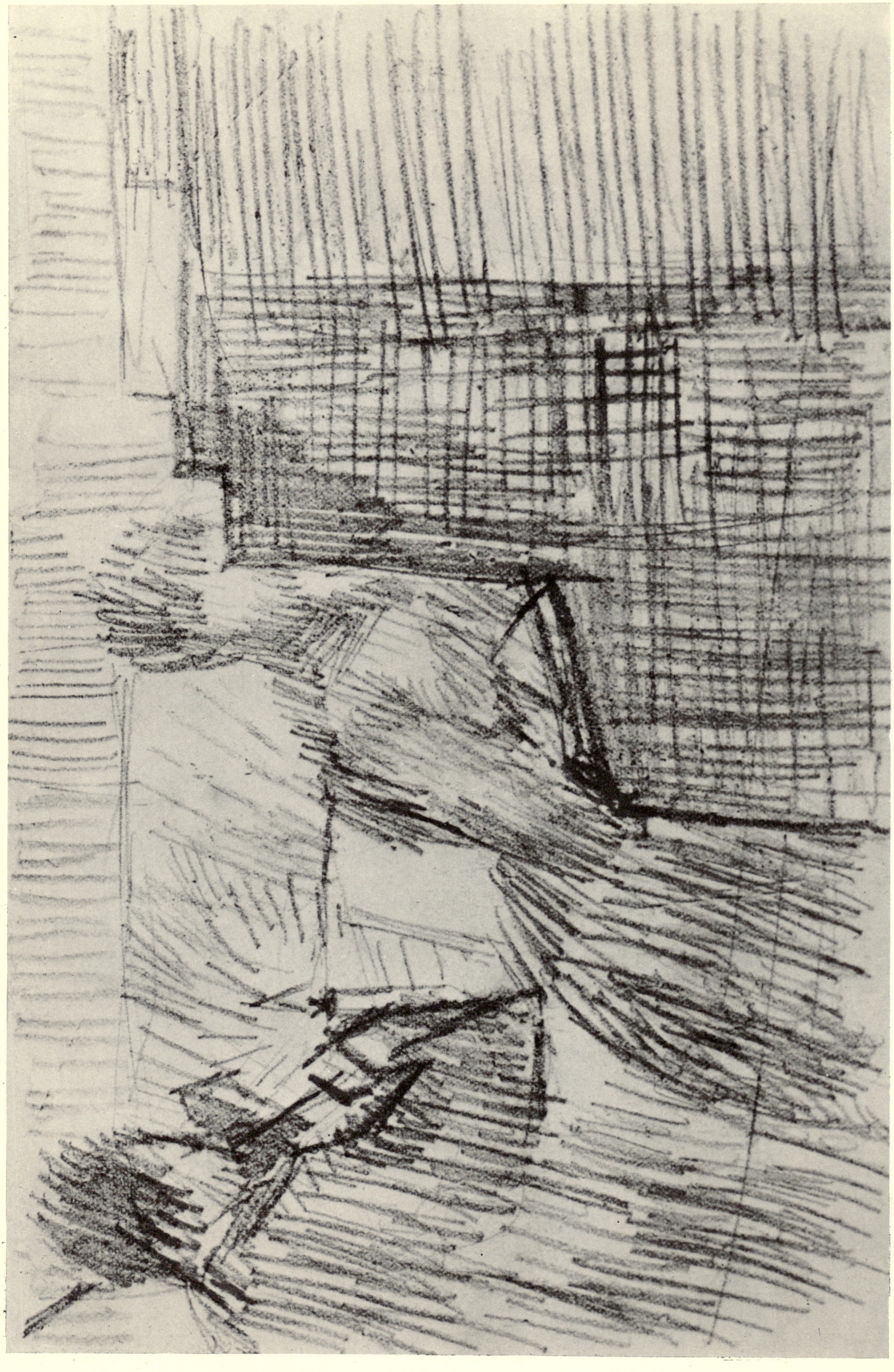

Plate 78

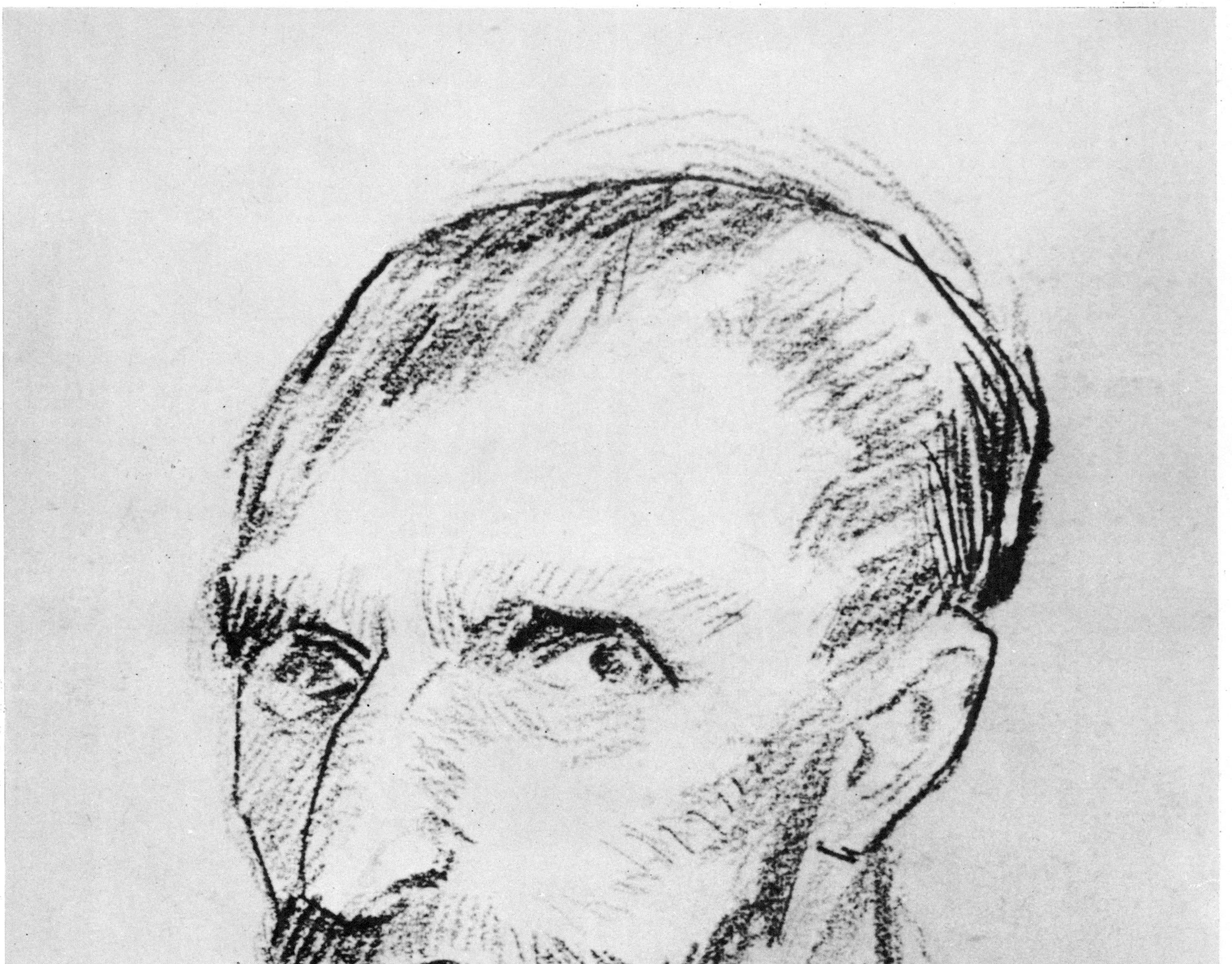

Plate 79

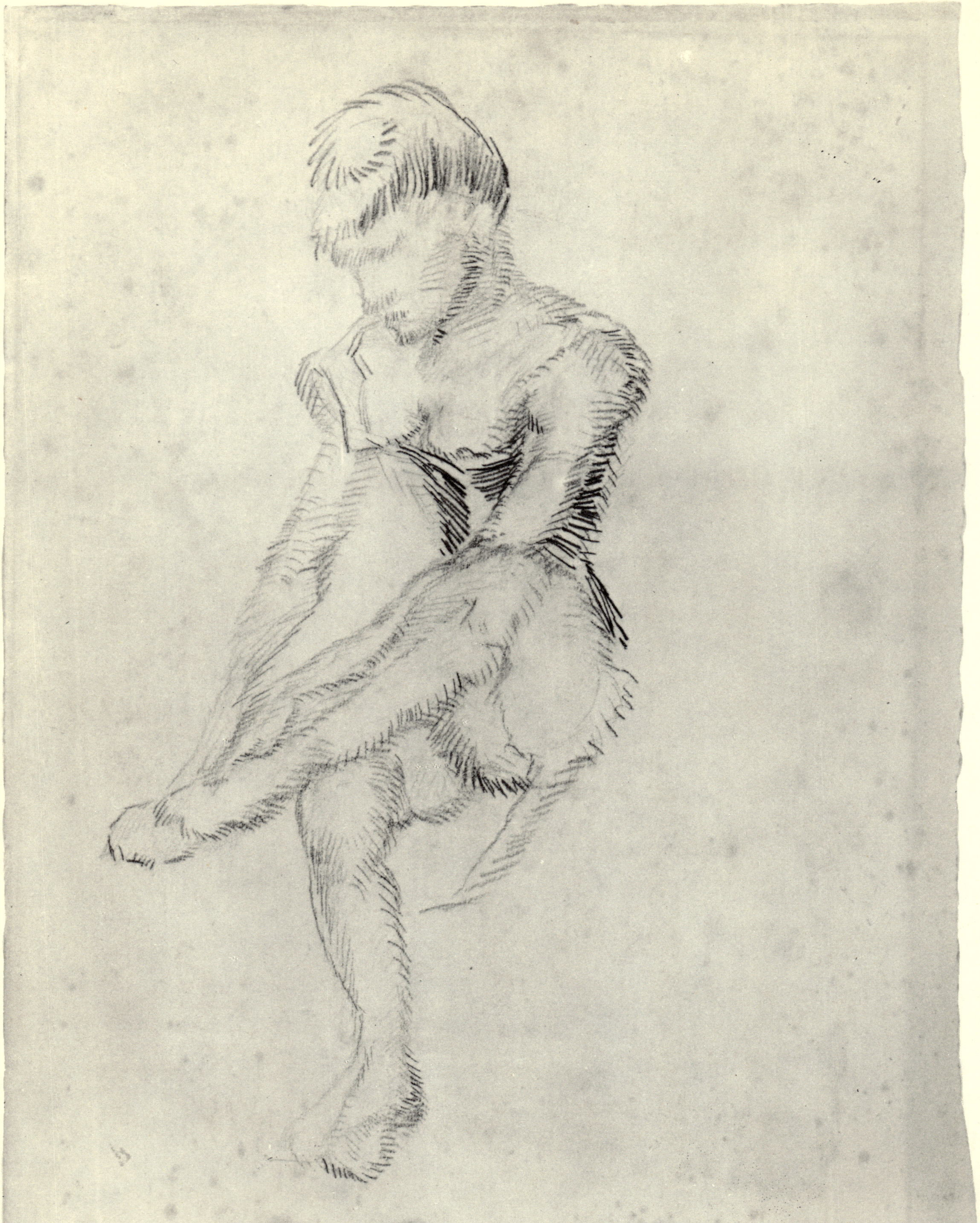

Plate 80

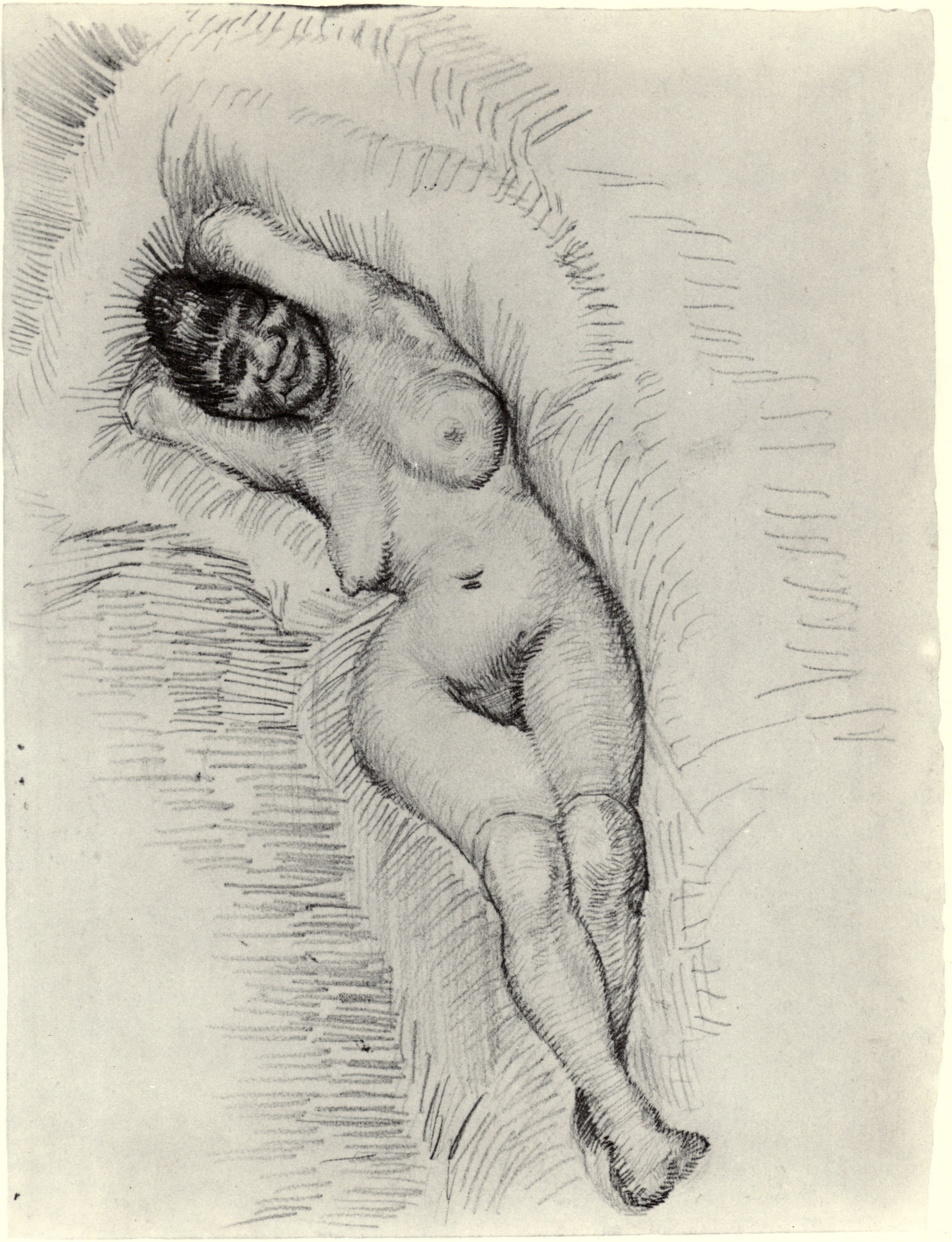

Plate 81

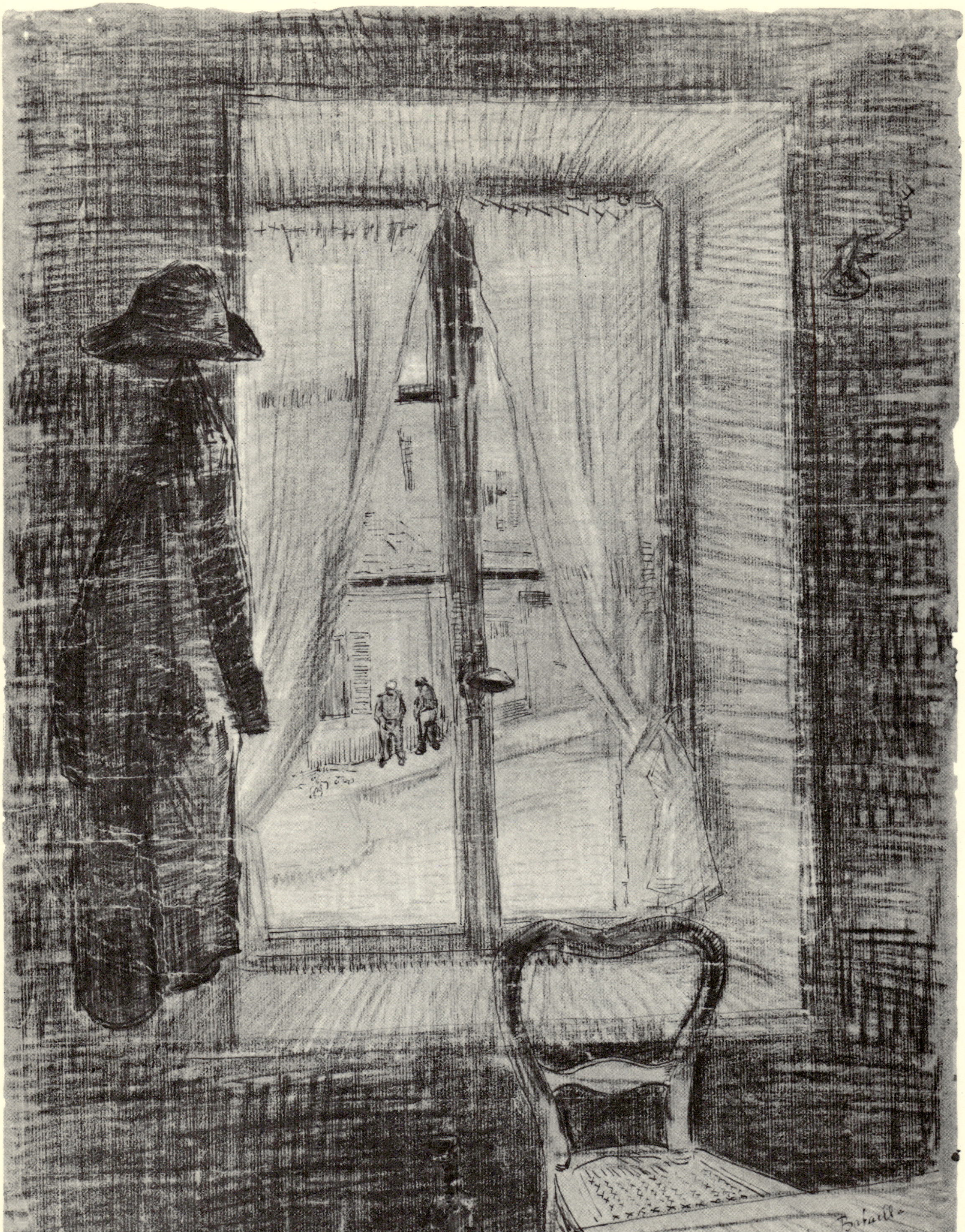

Plate 82

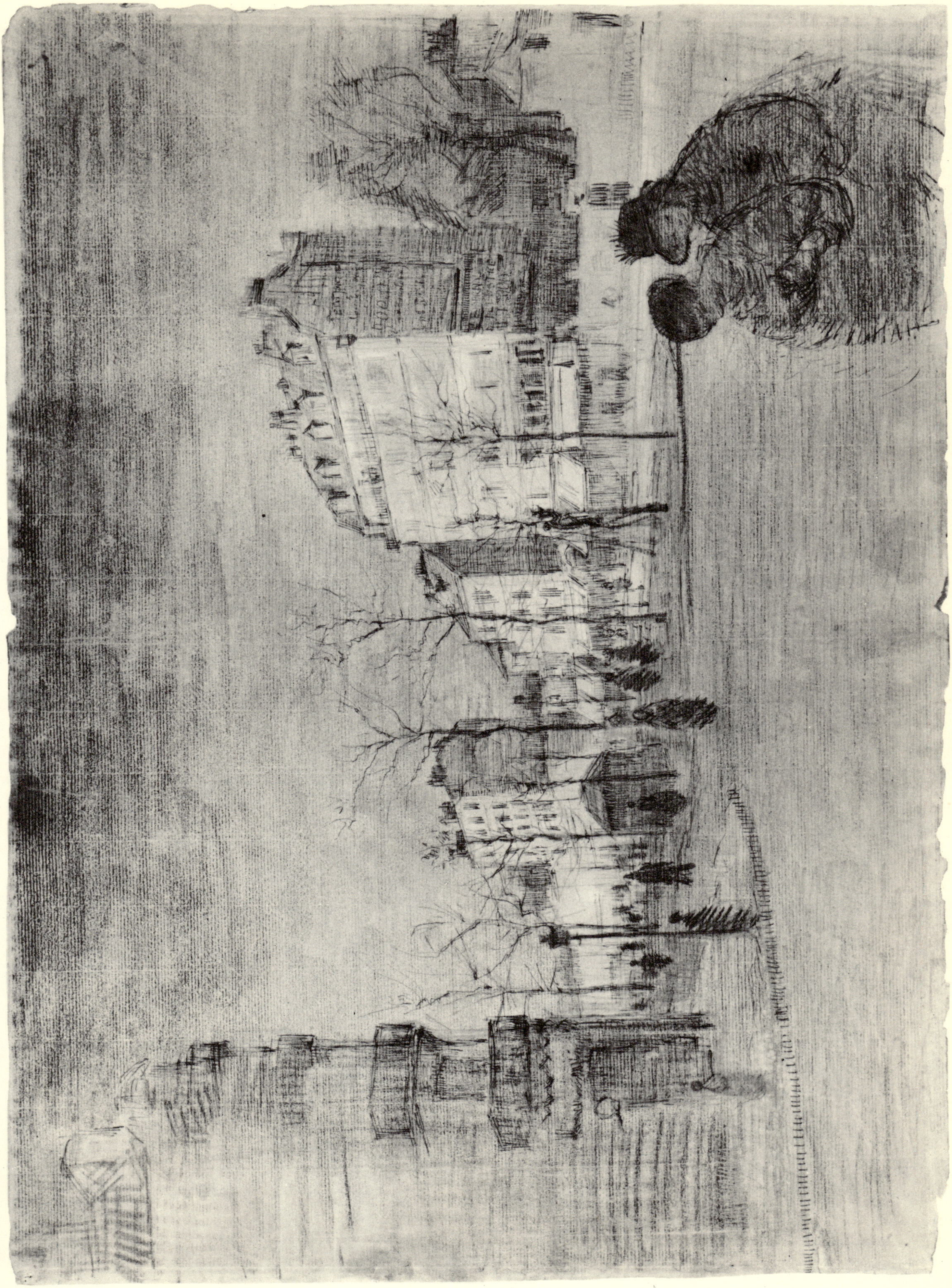

Plate 83

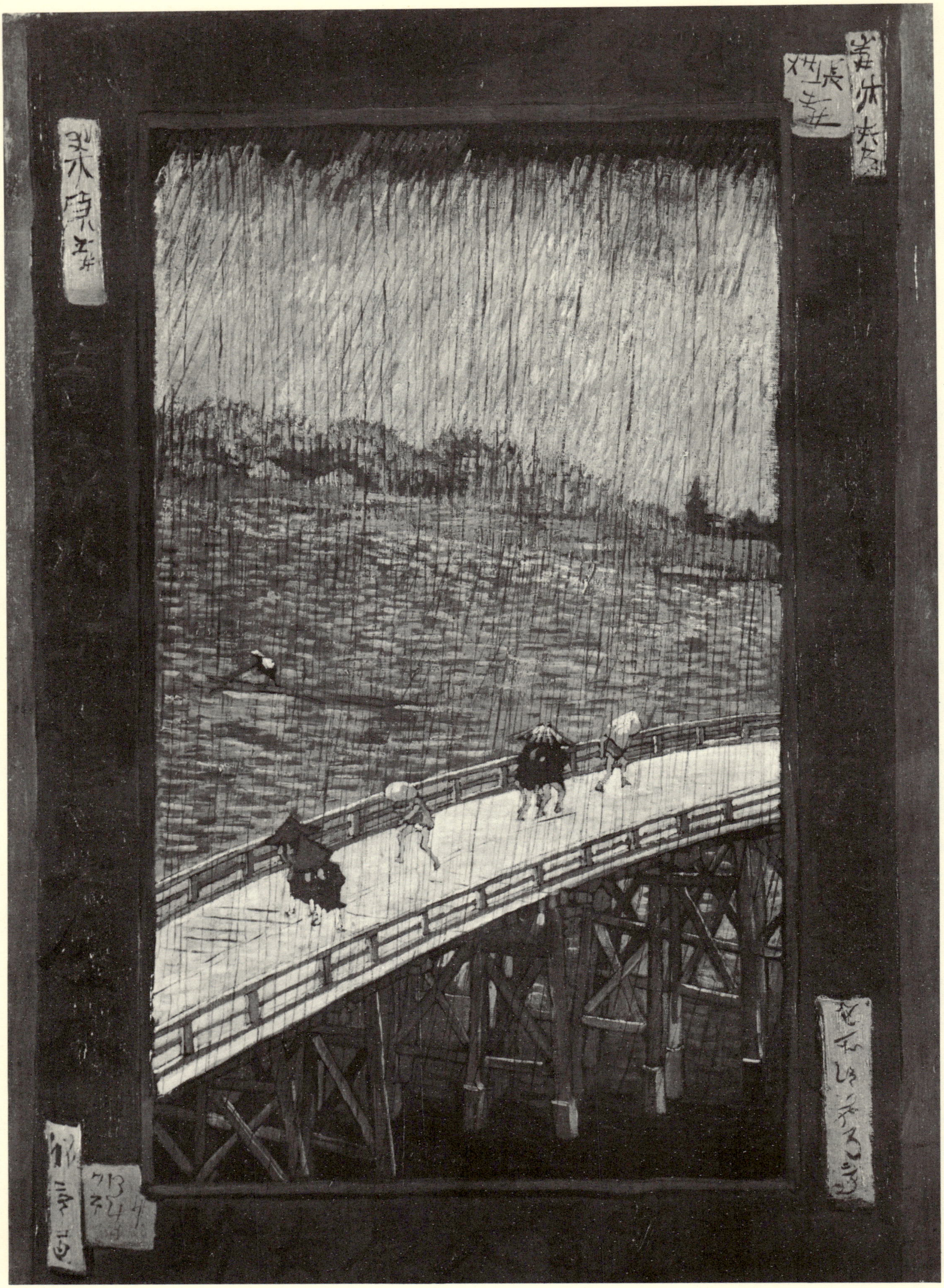

Plate 84

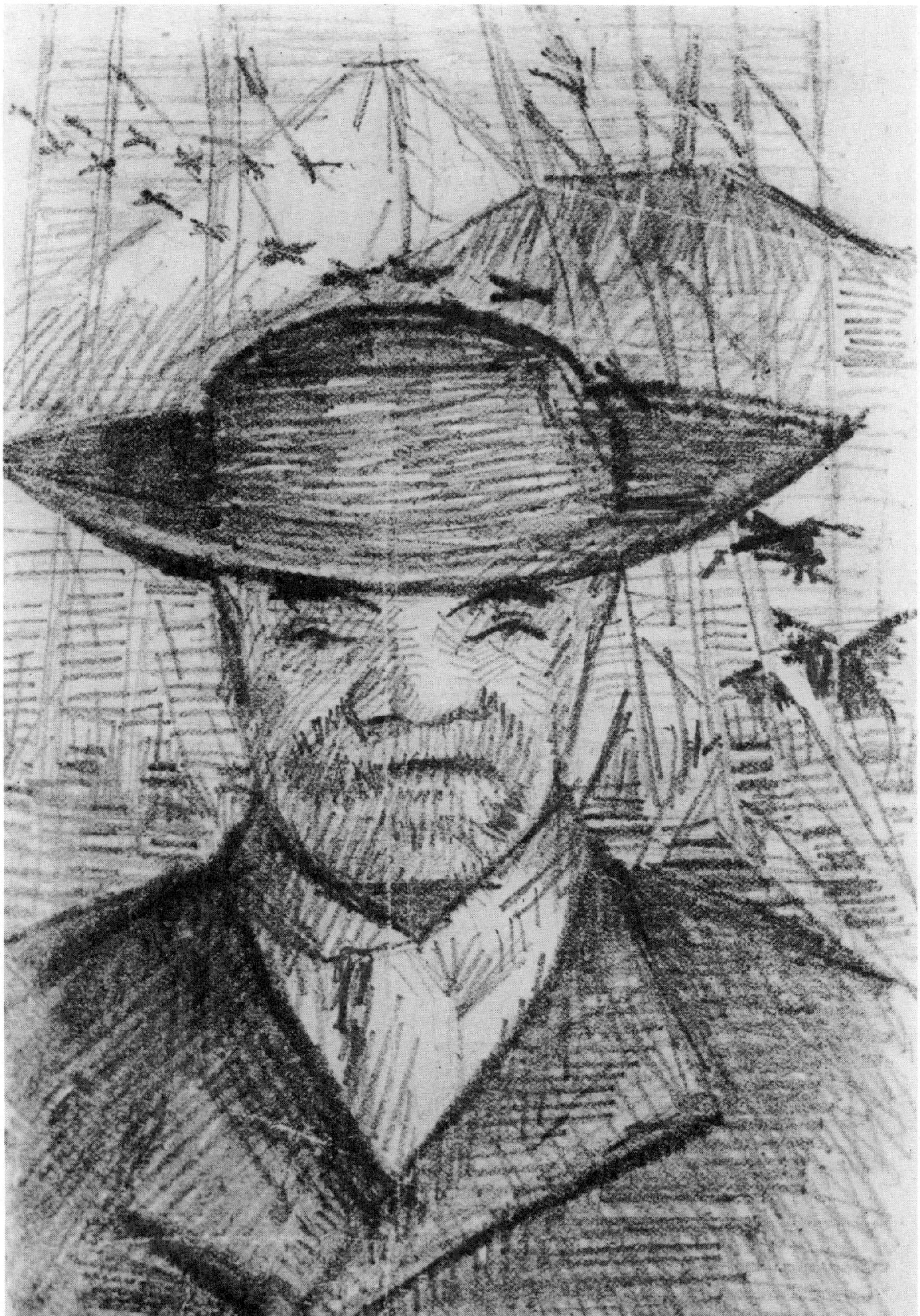

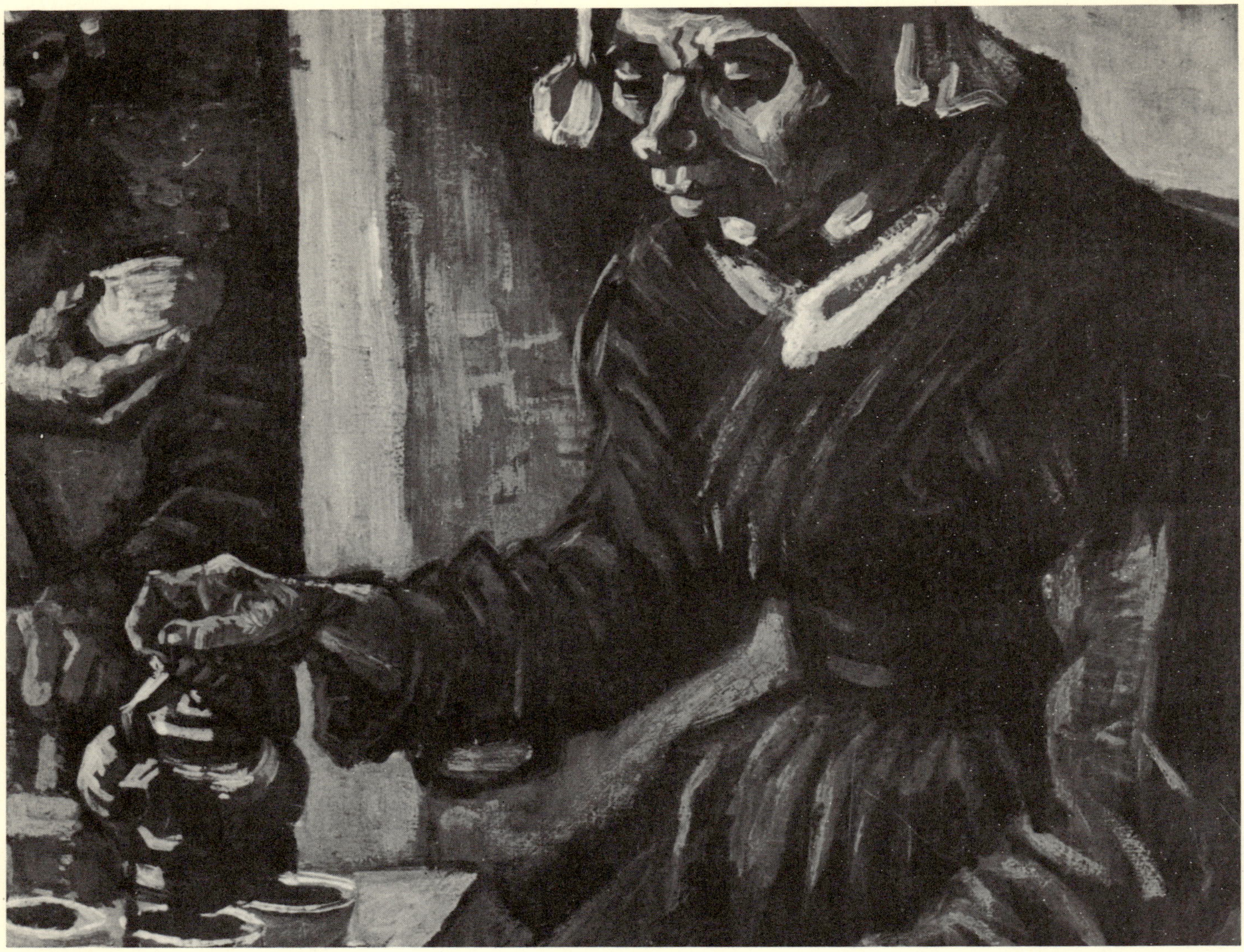

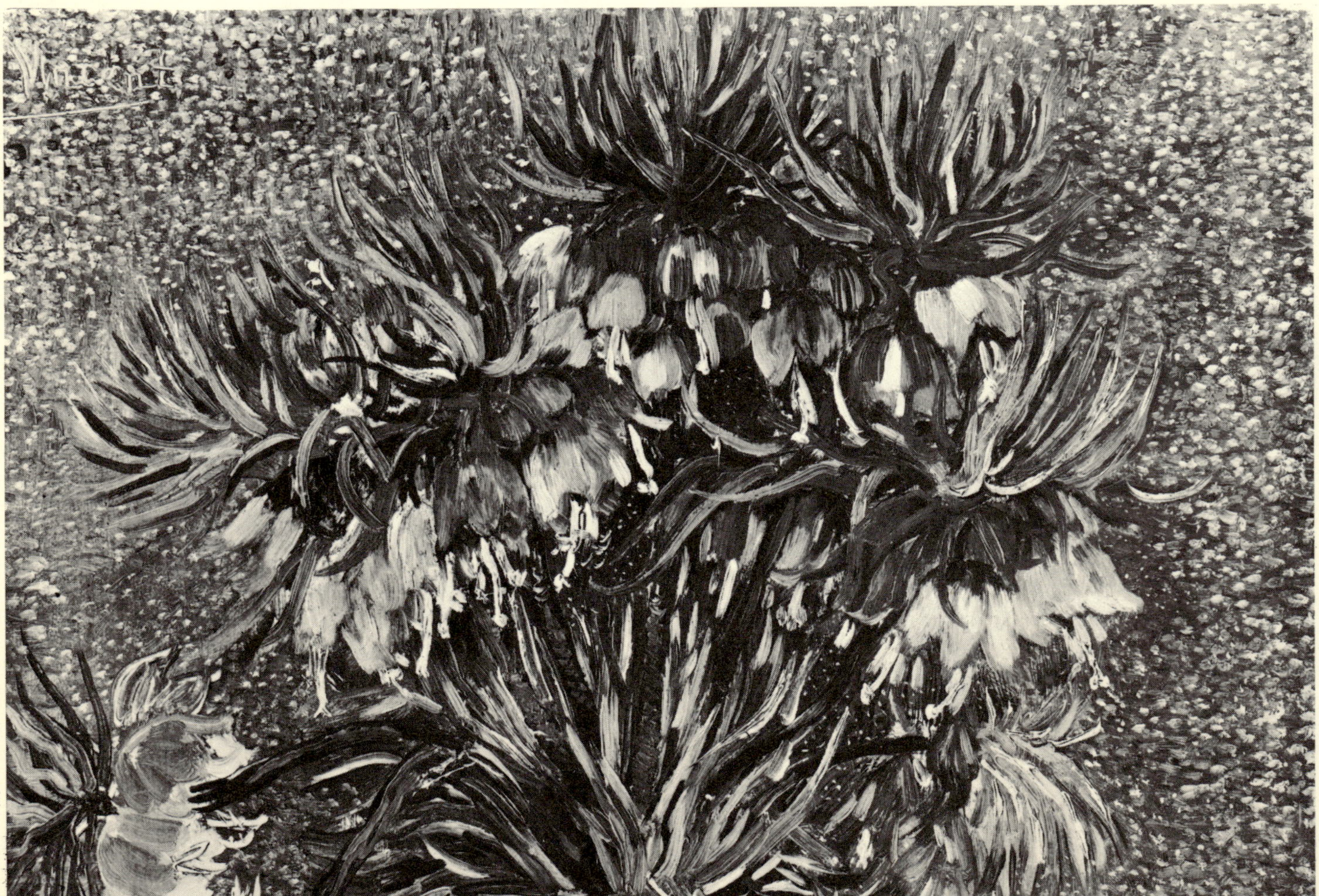

Plate 86a, Plate 86b

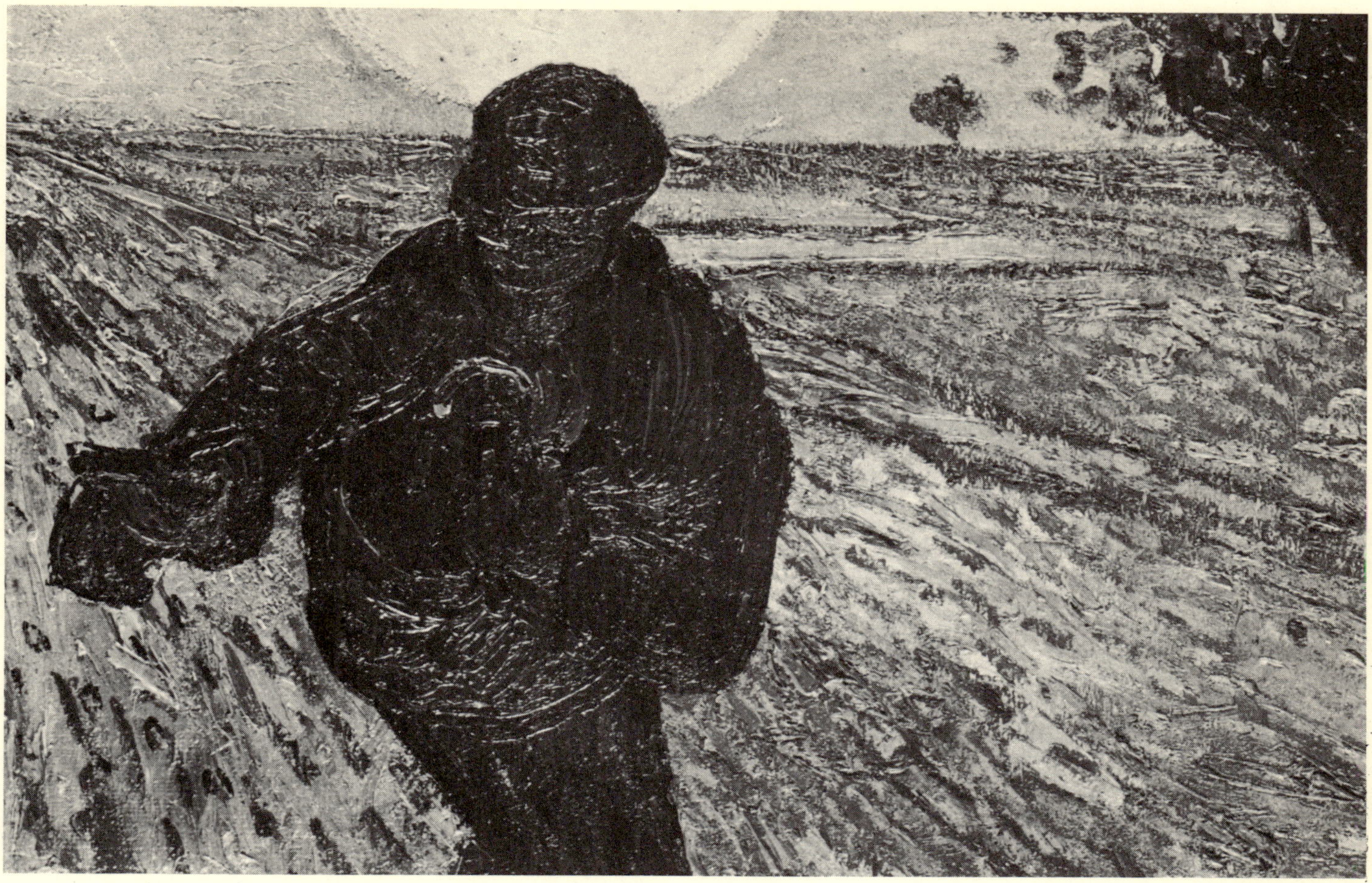

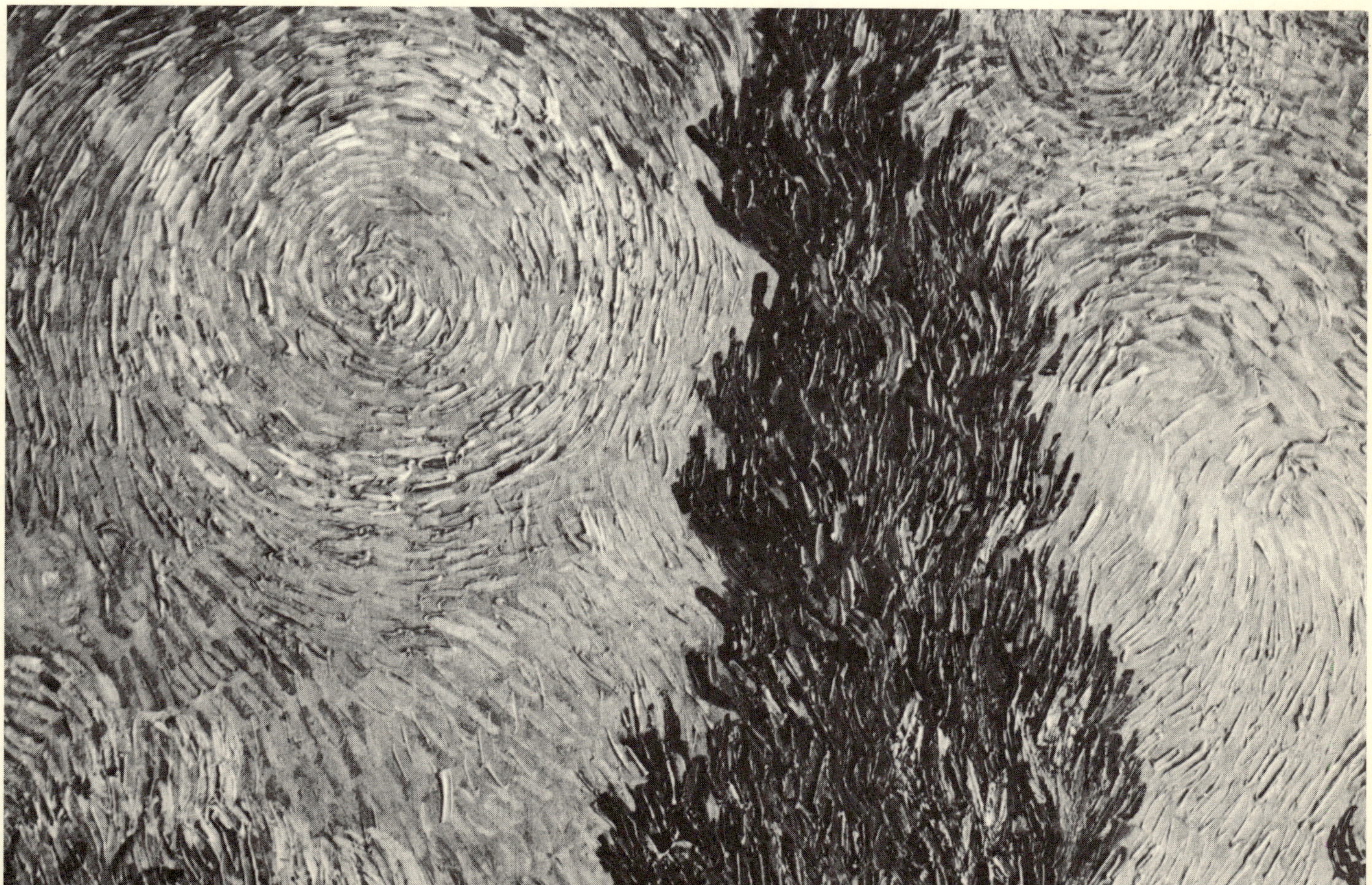

Plate 87a, Plate 87b

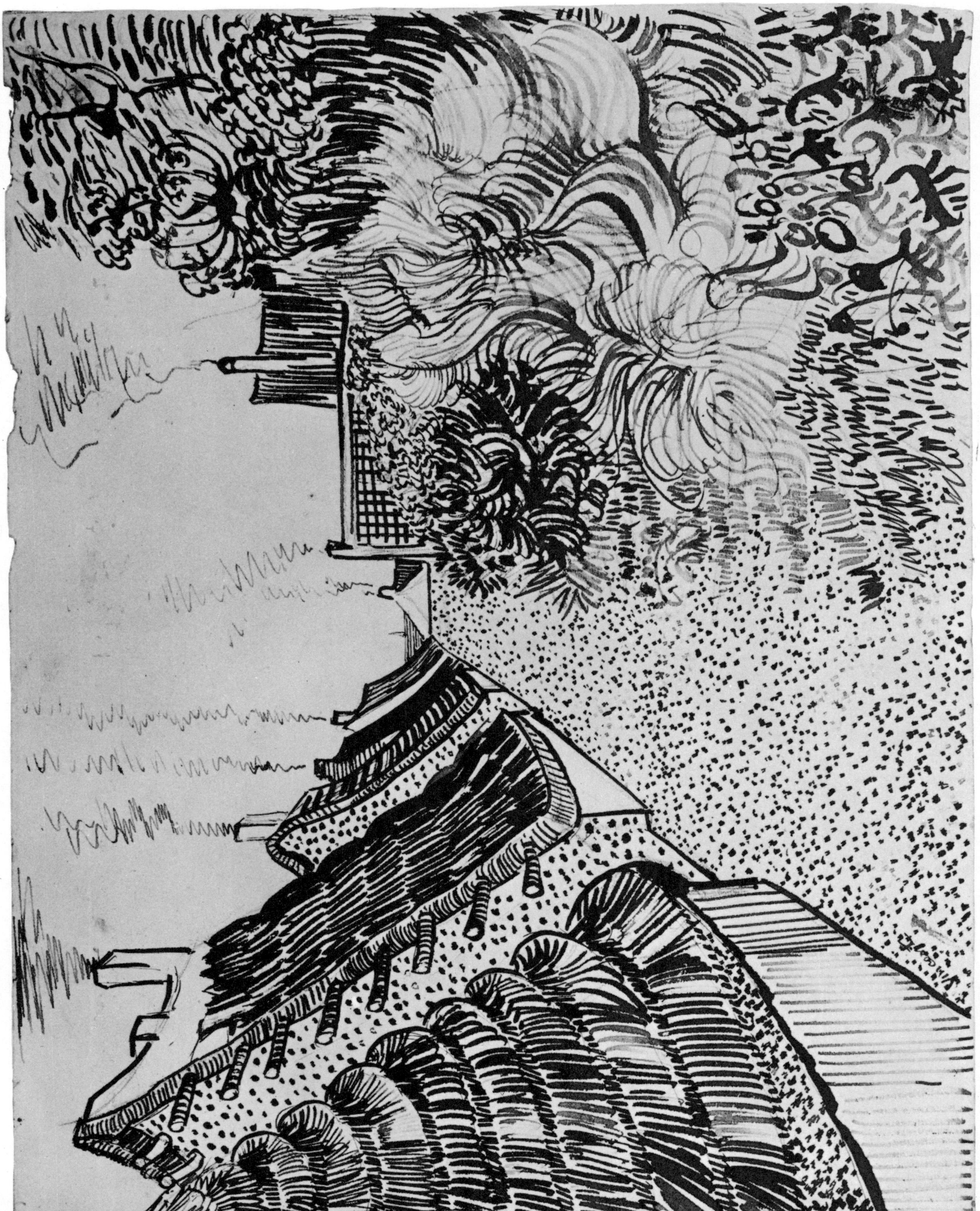

Plate 88

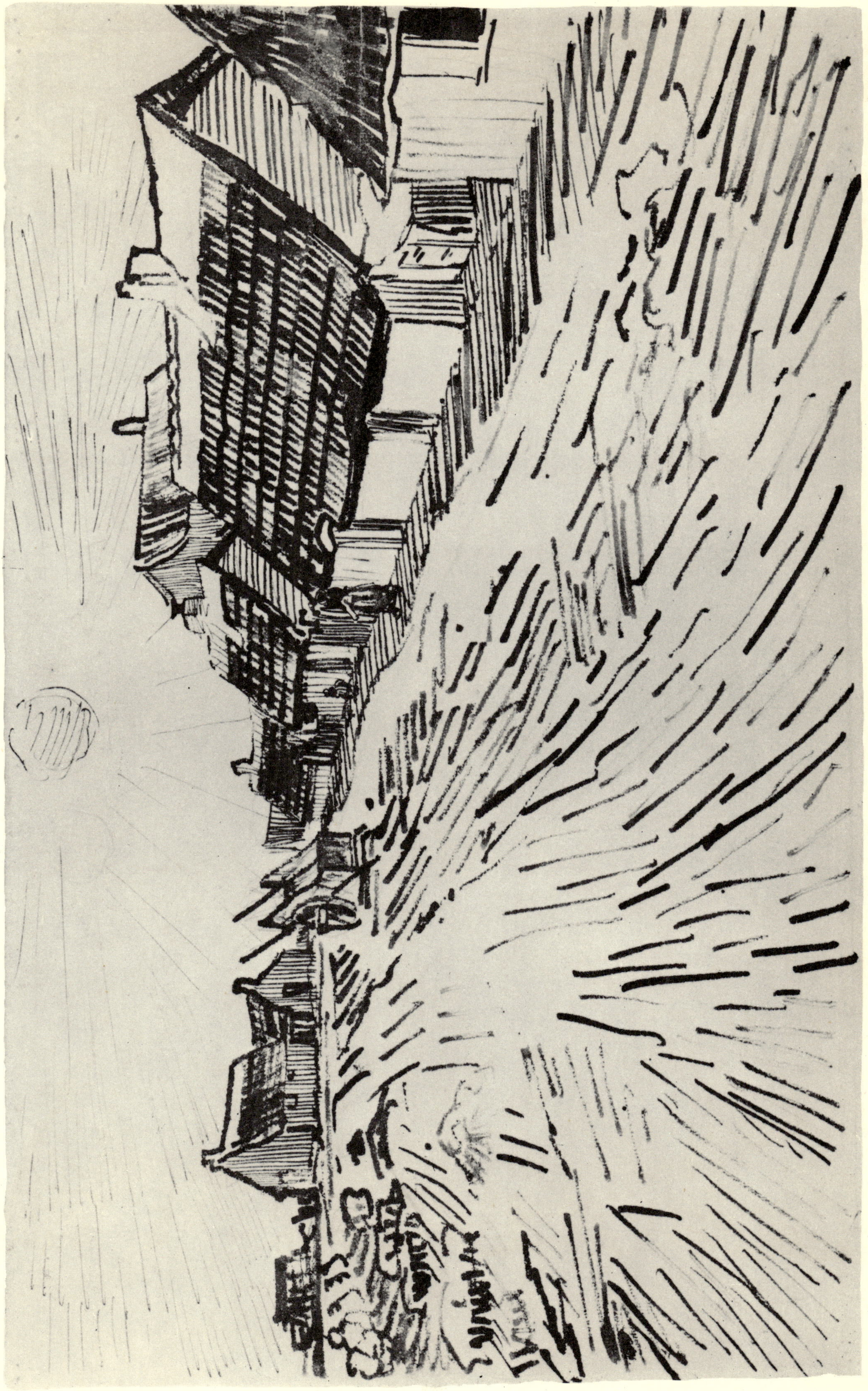

Plate 89

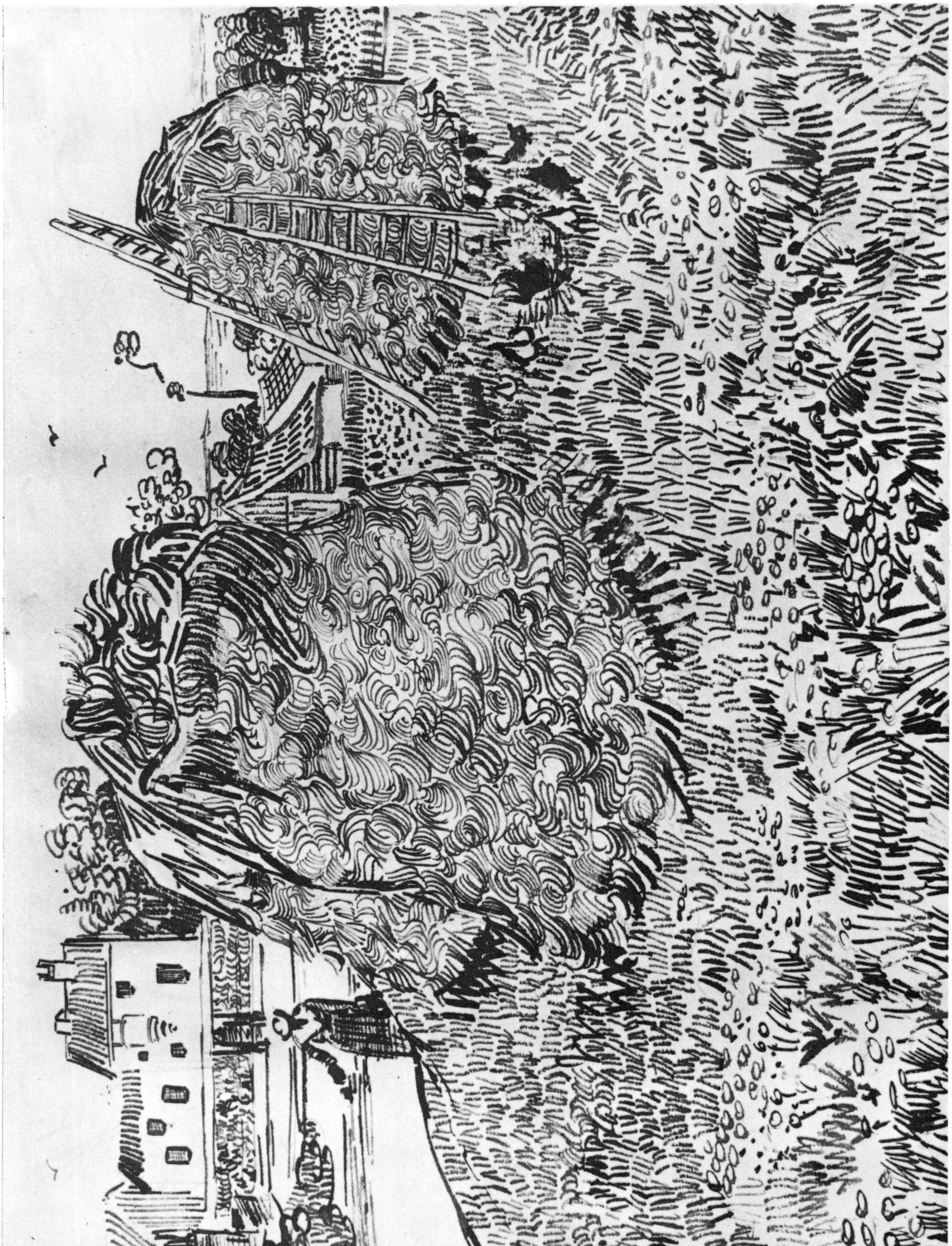

Plate 90

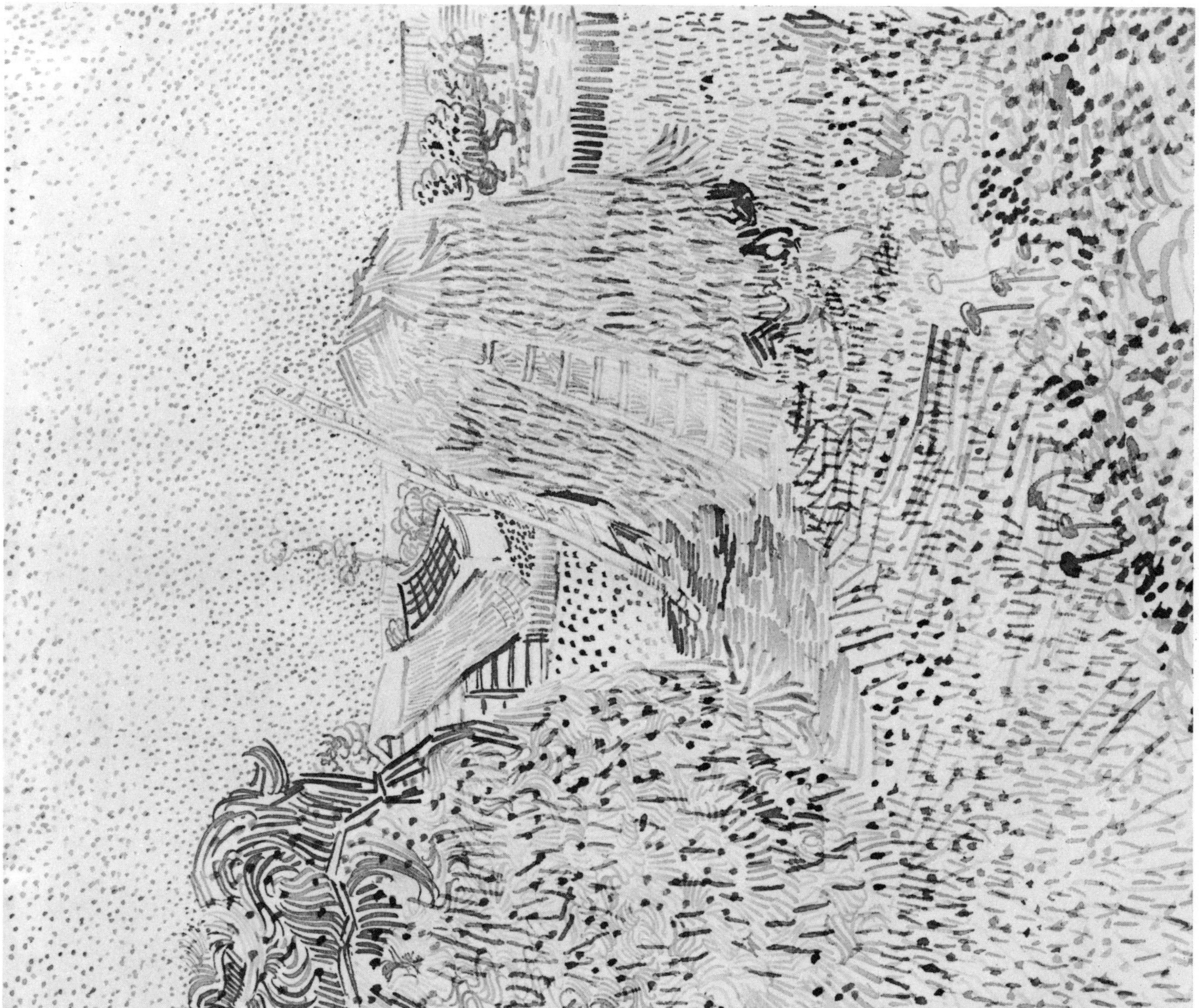

Plate 91

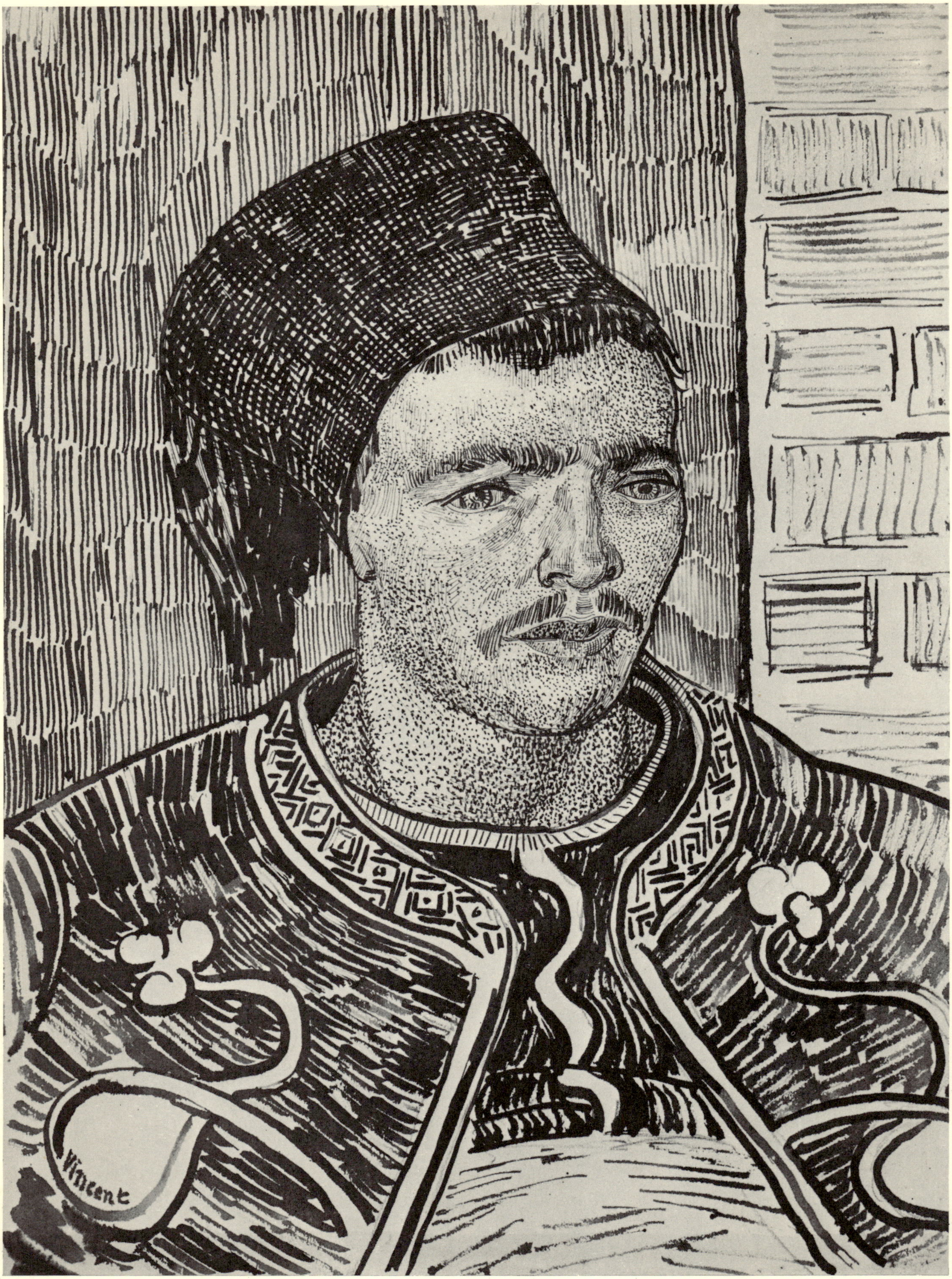
Vincent

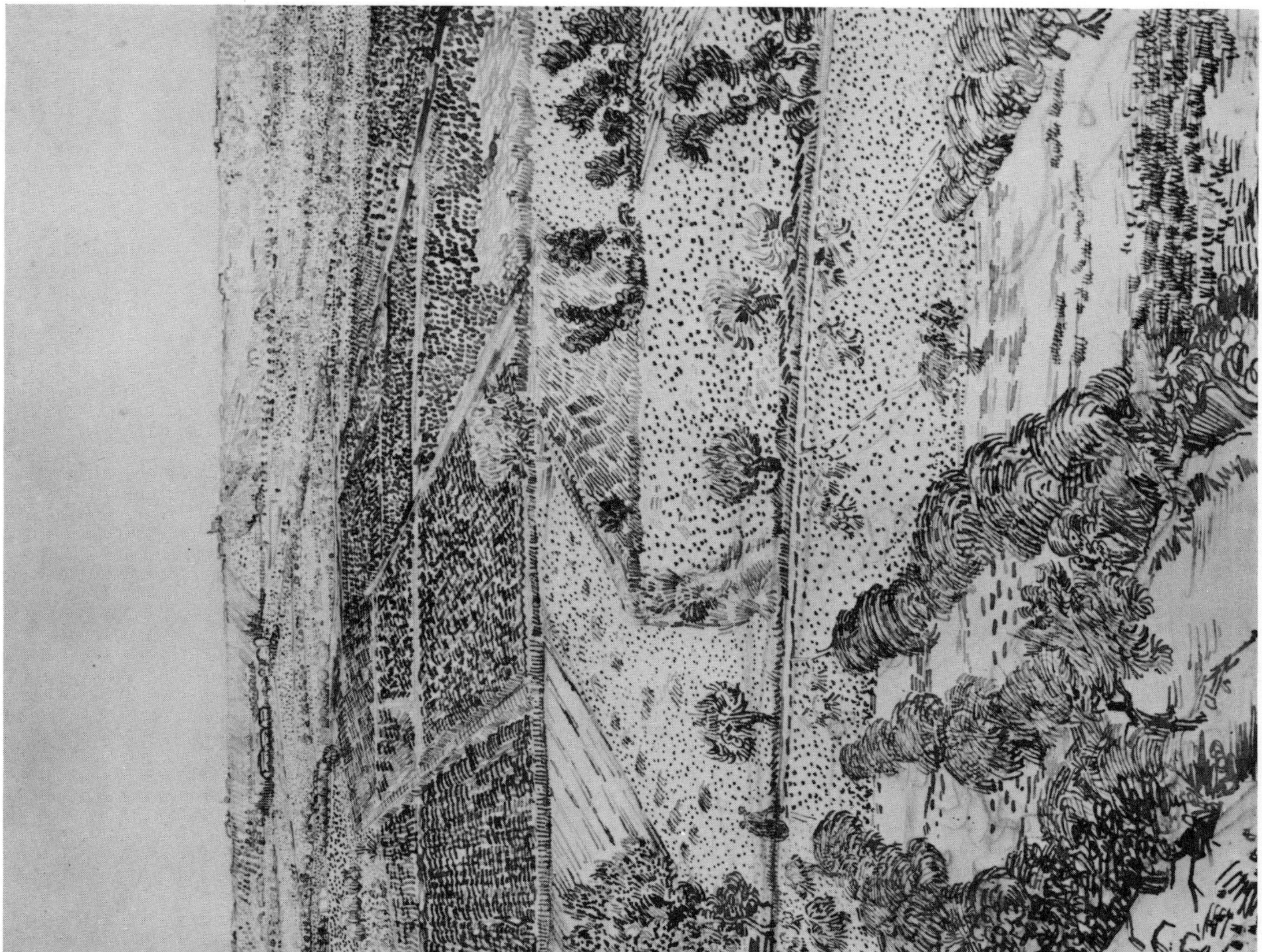
Vincent
La Crau
Vue prise à Mont majour

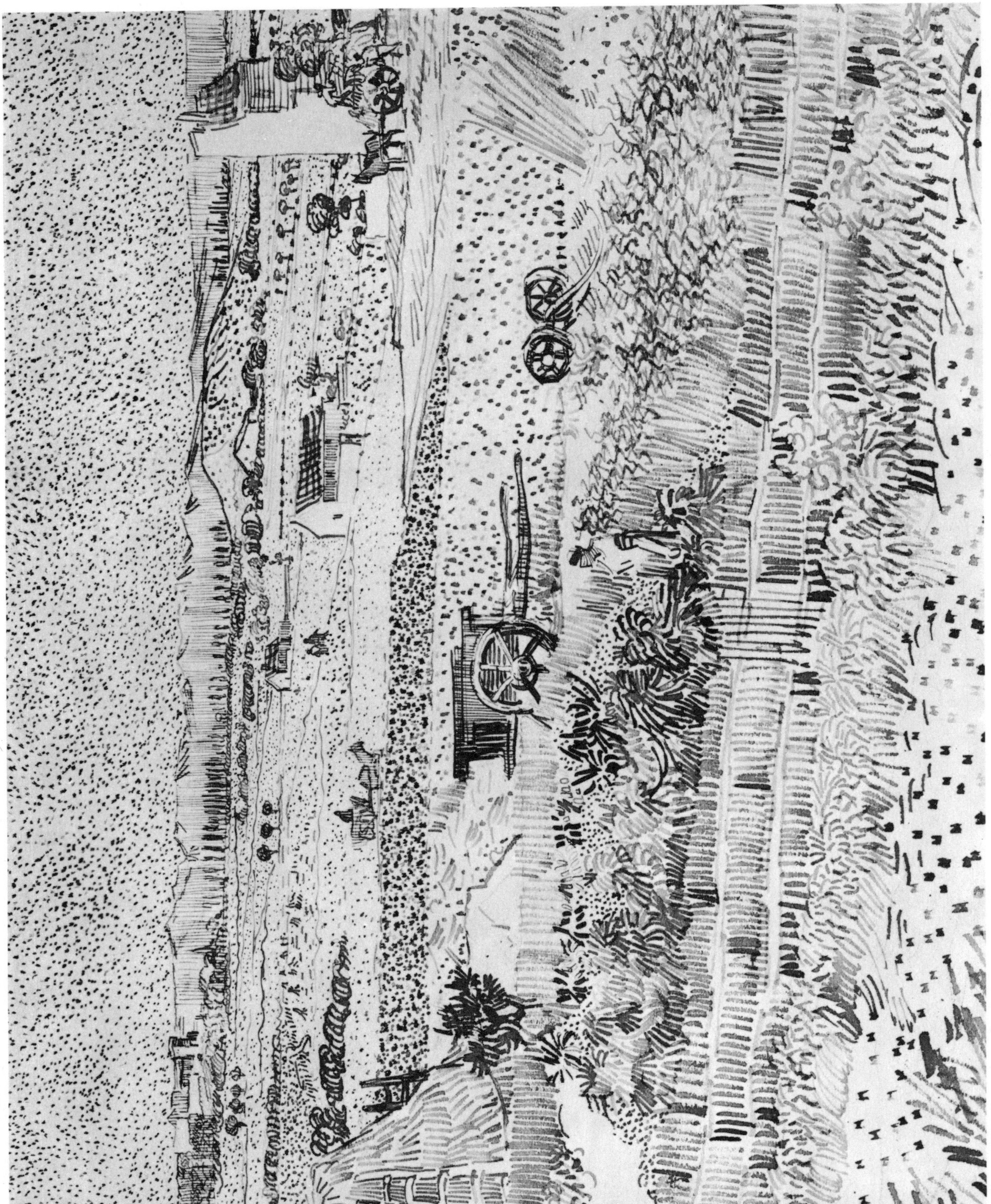

Plate 94

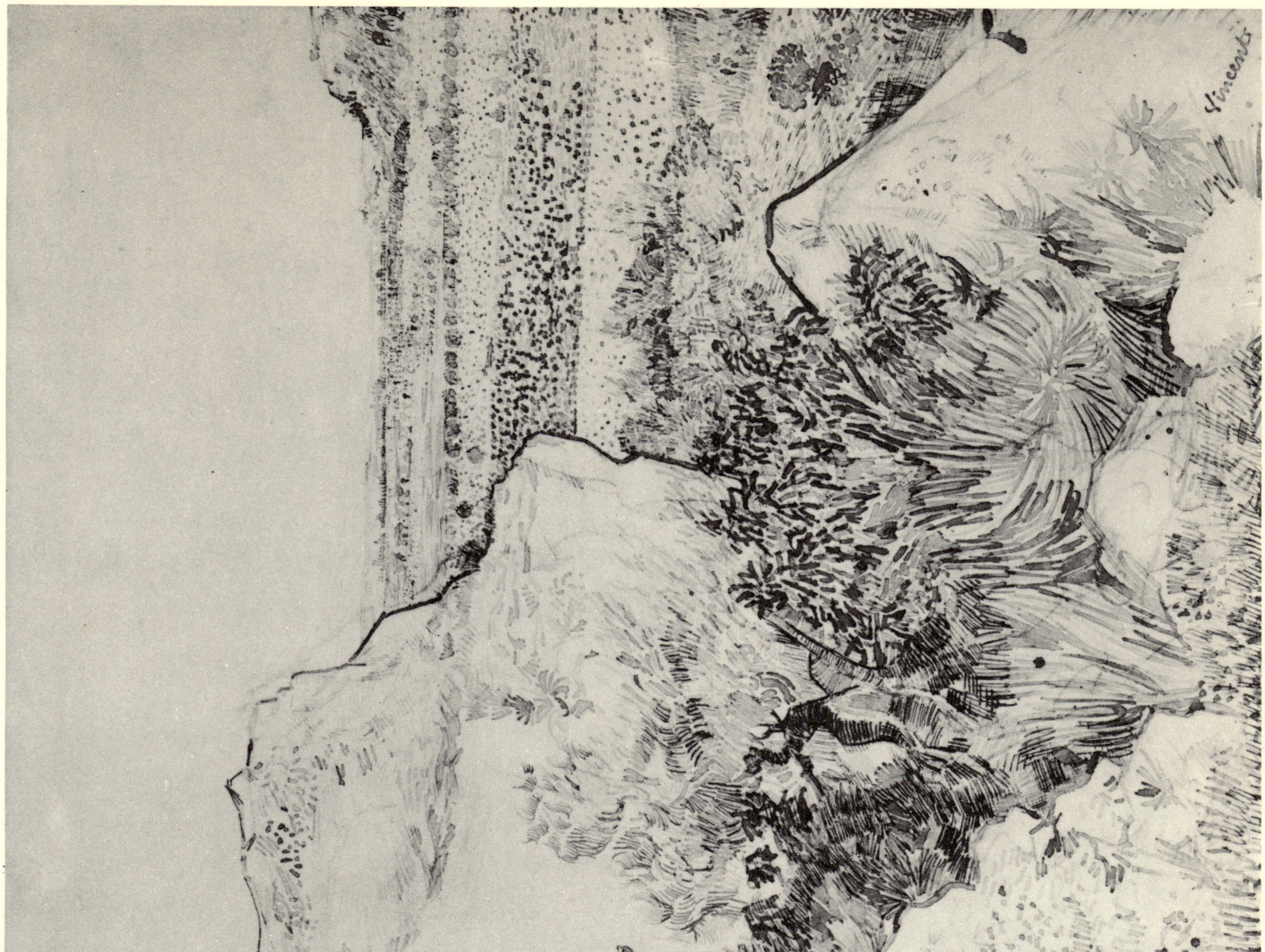

Plate 95

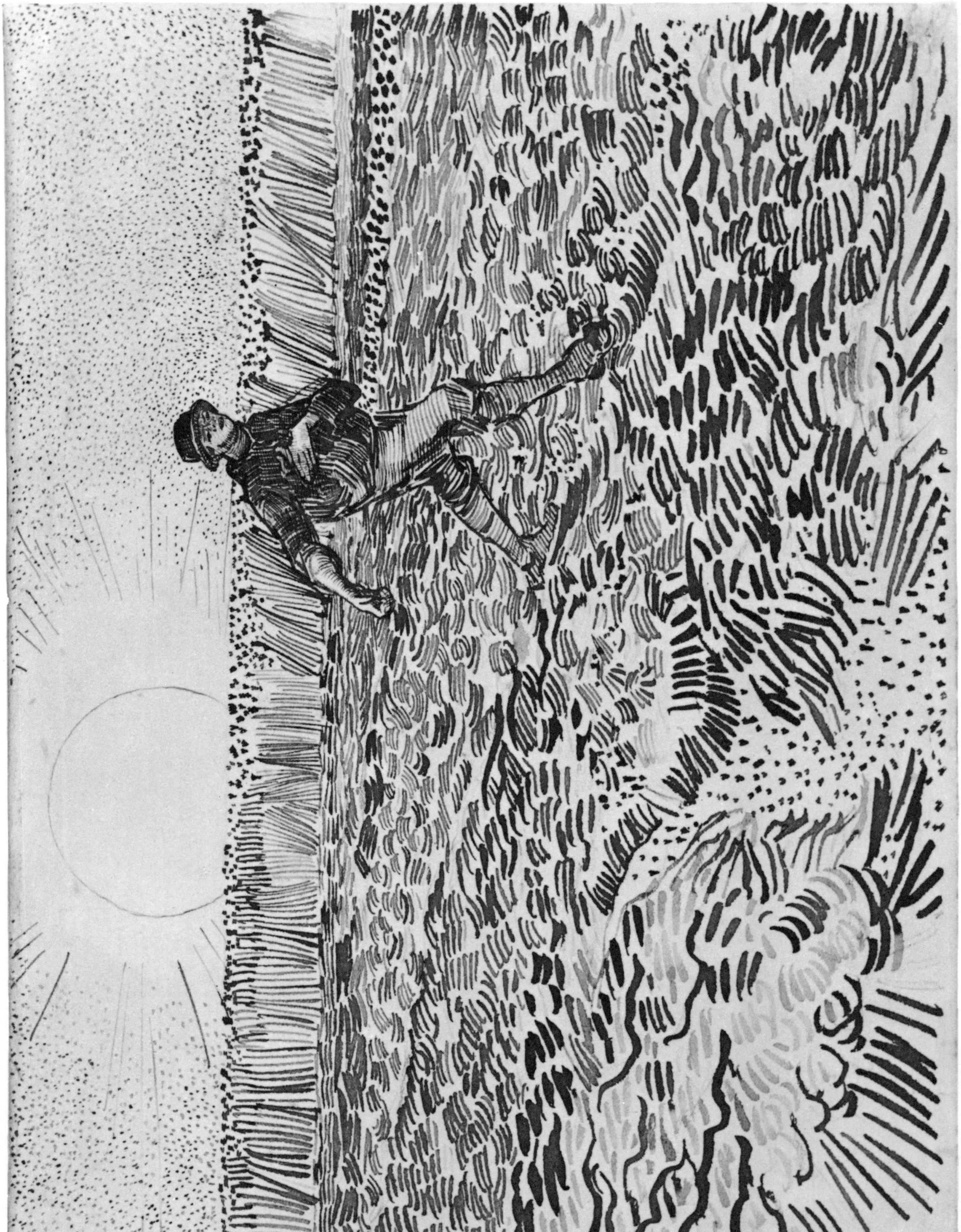

Plate 96

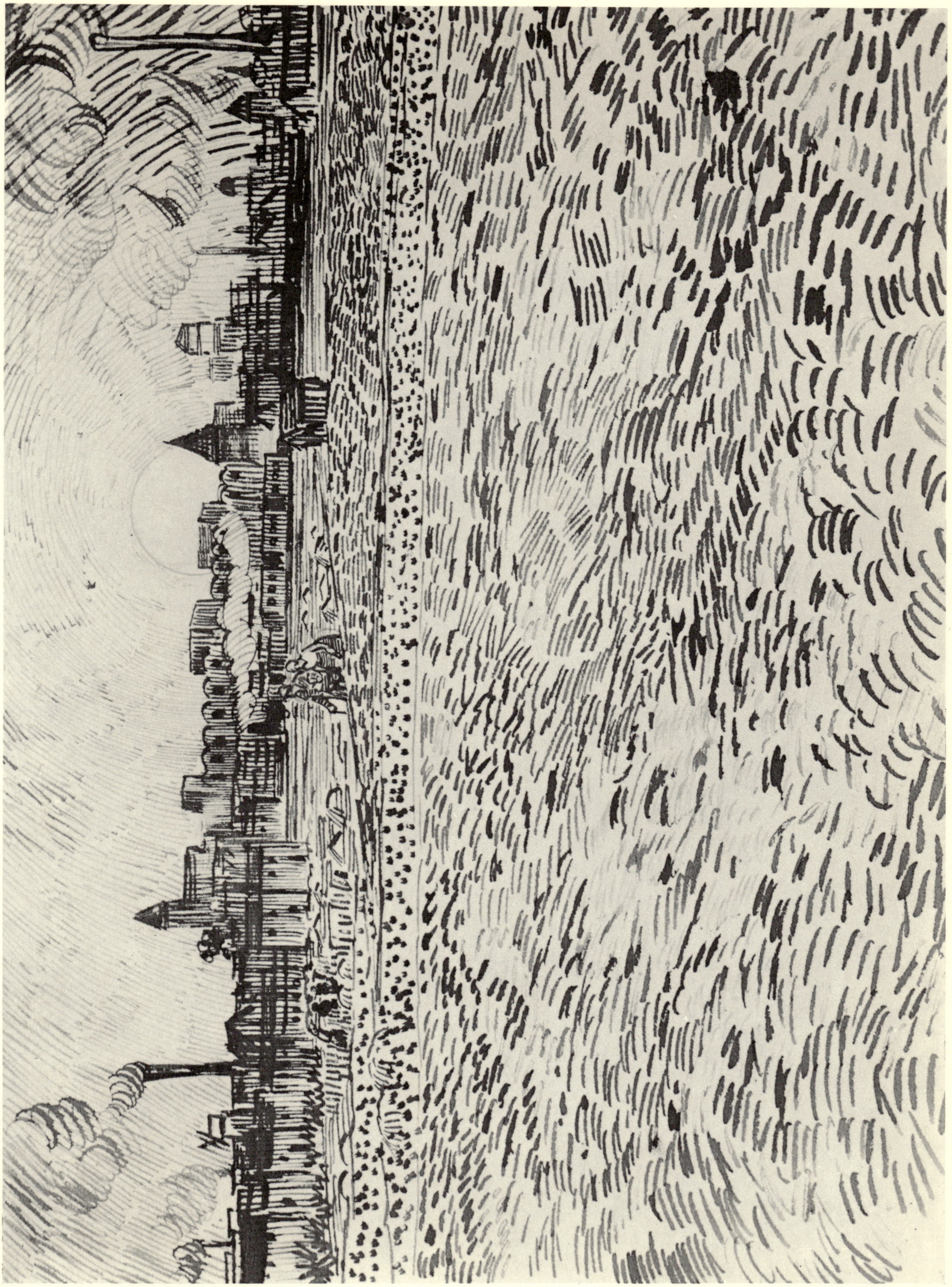

Plate 97

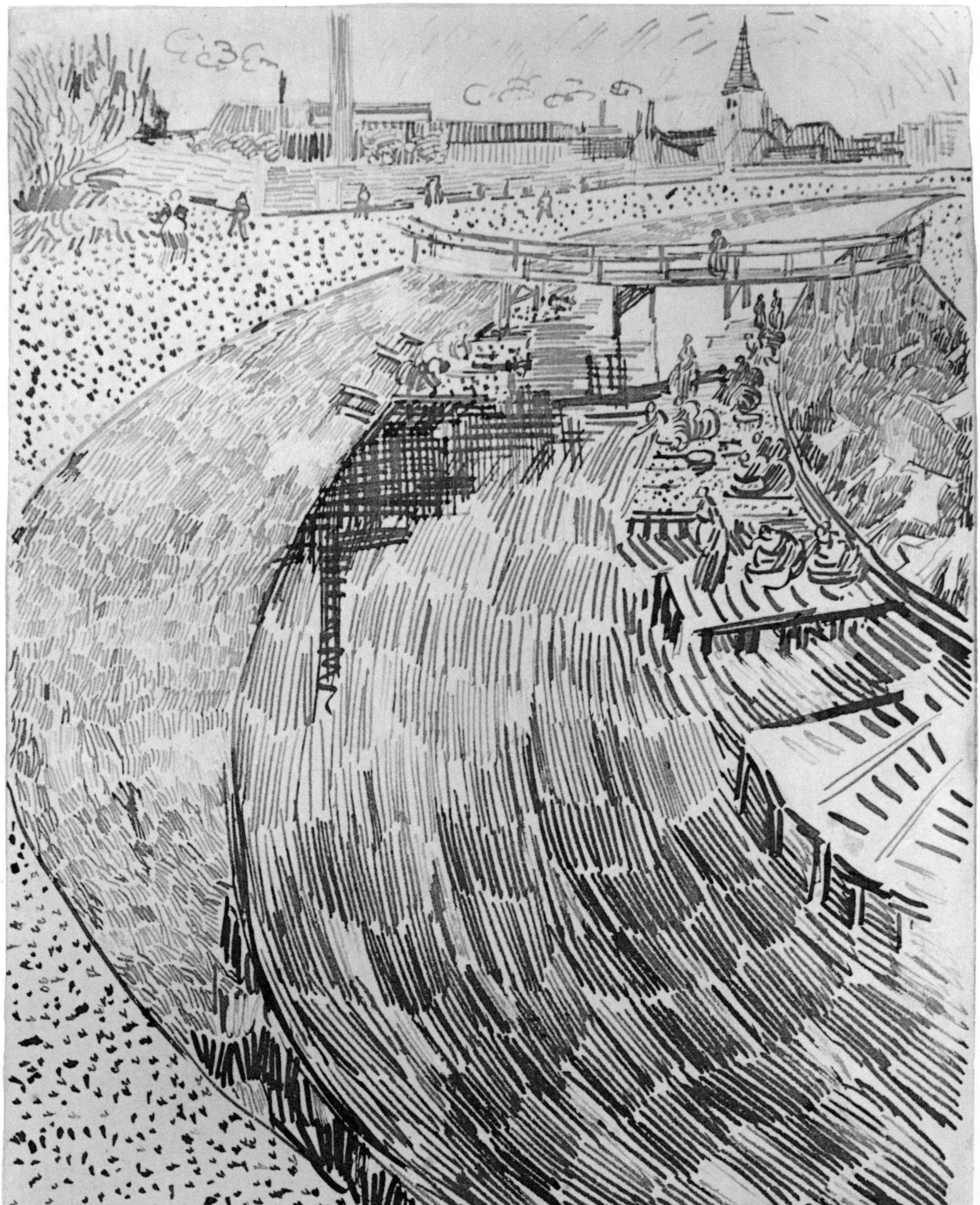

Plate 98

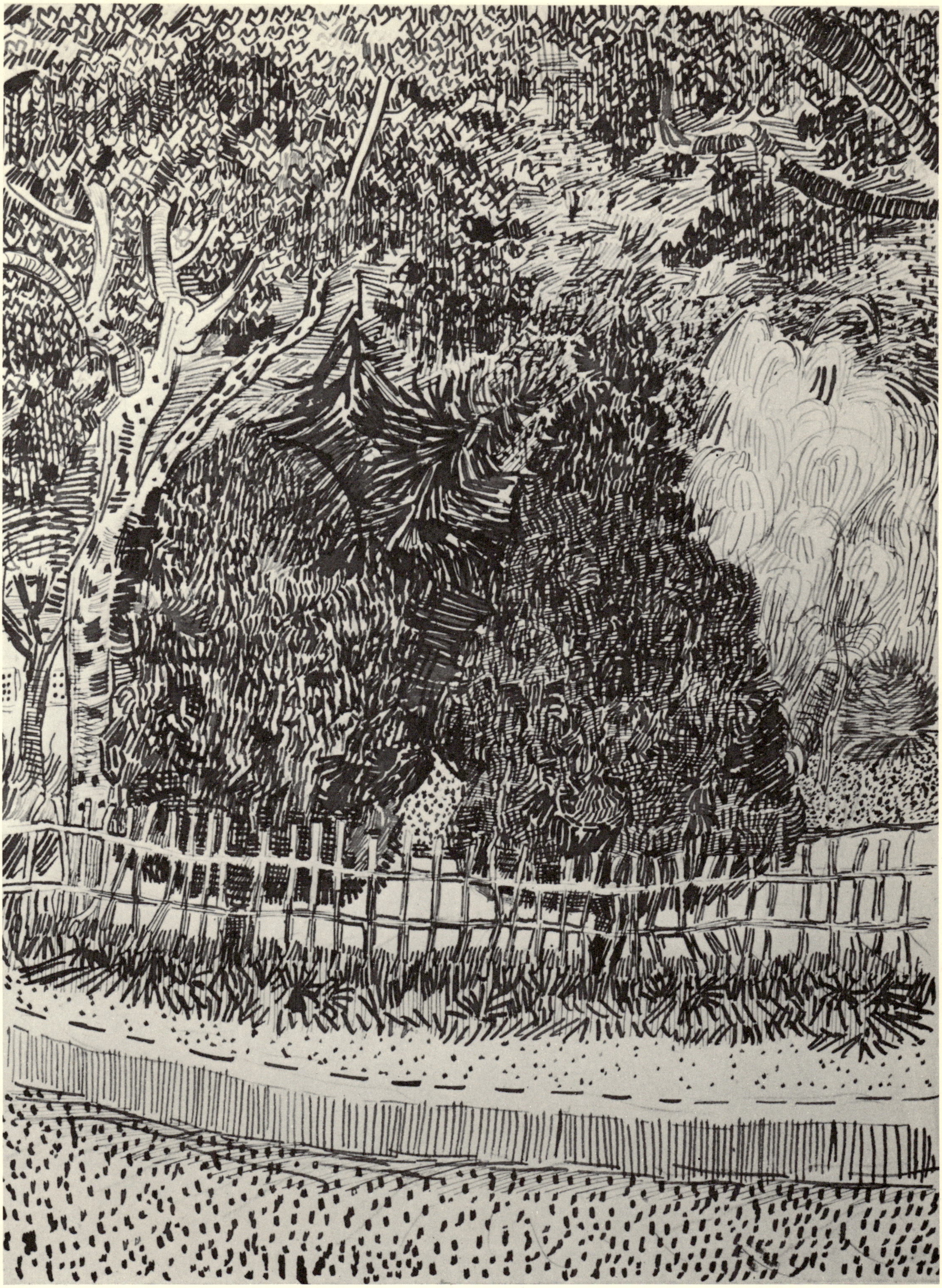

Plate 99

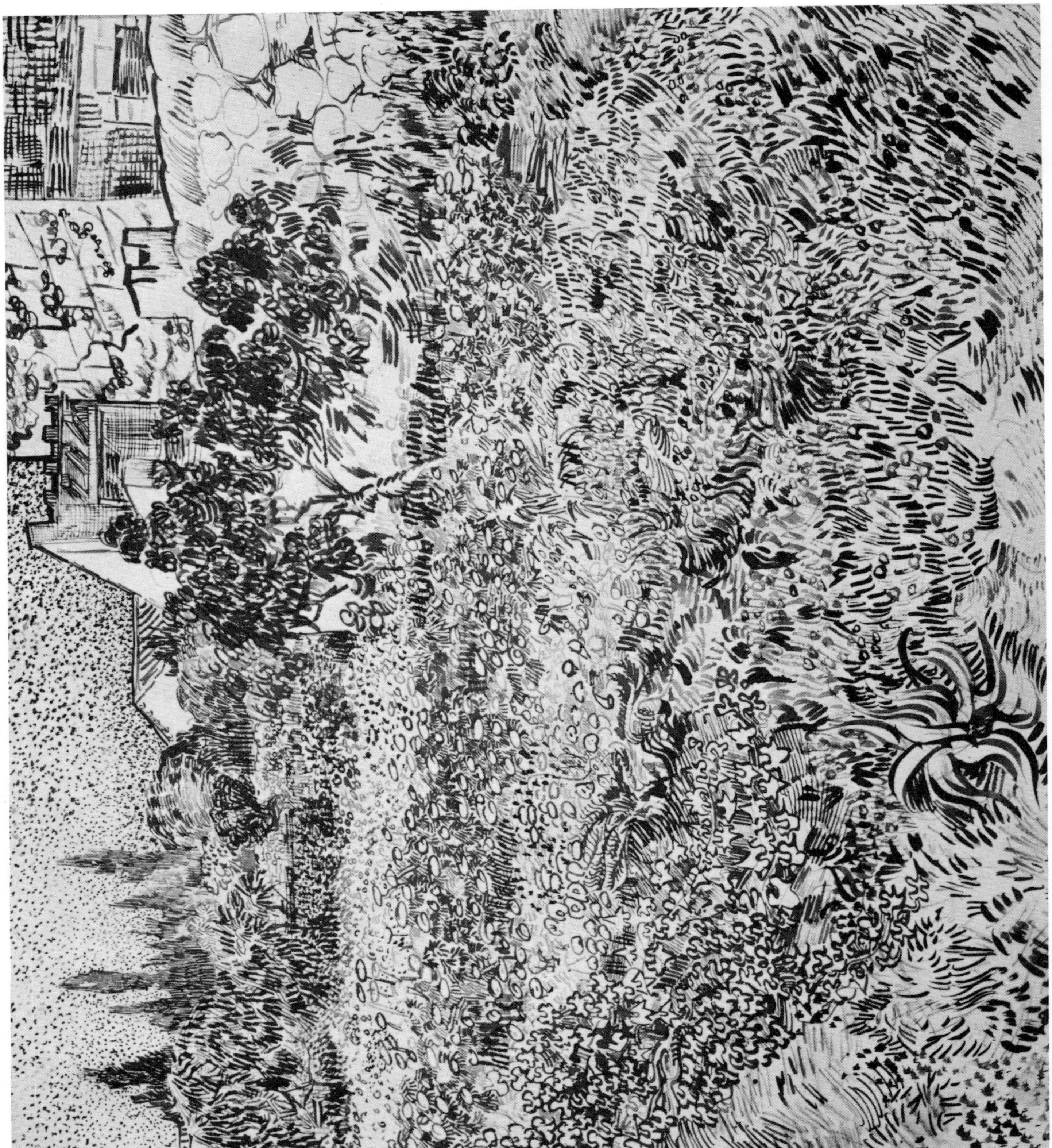

Plate 100

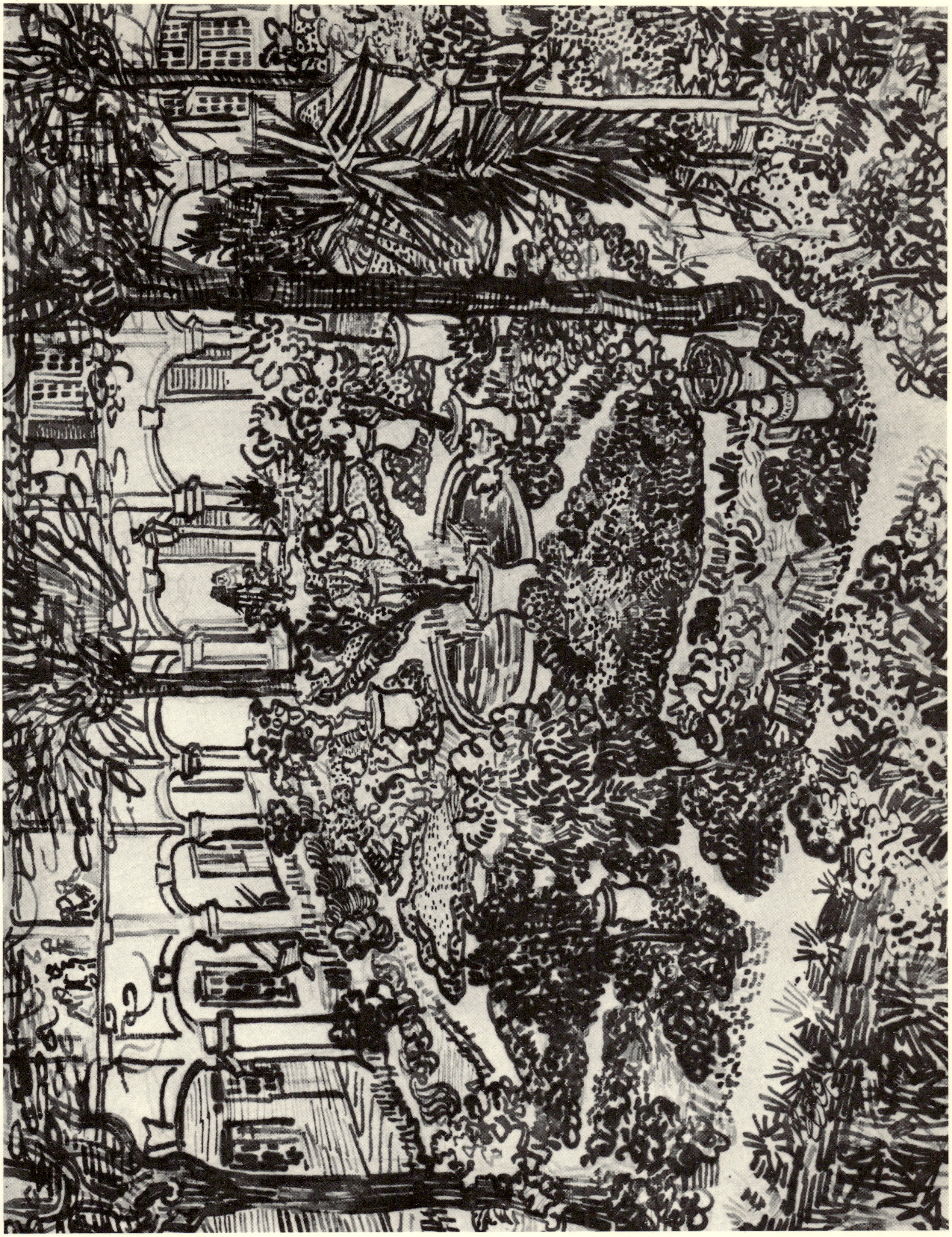

Plate 101

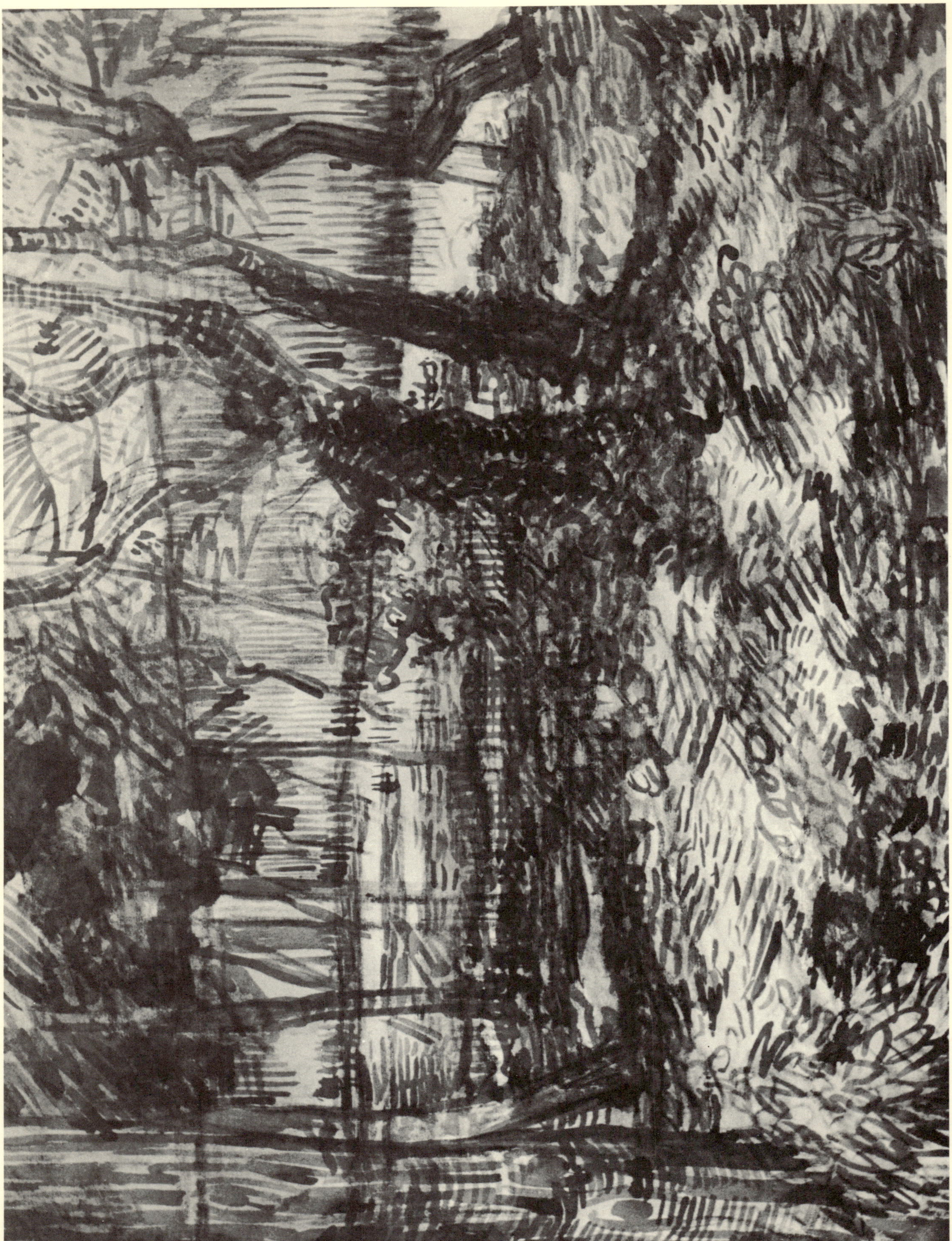

Plate 102

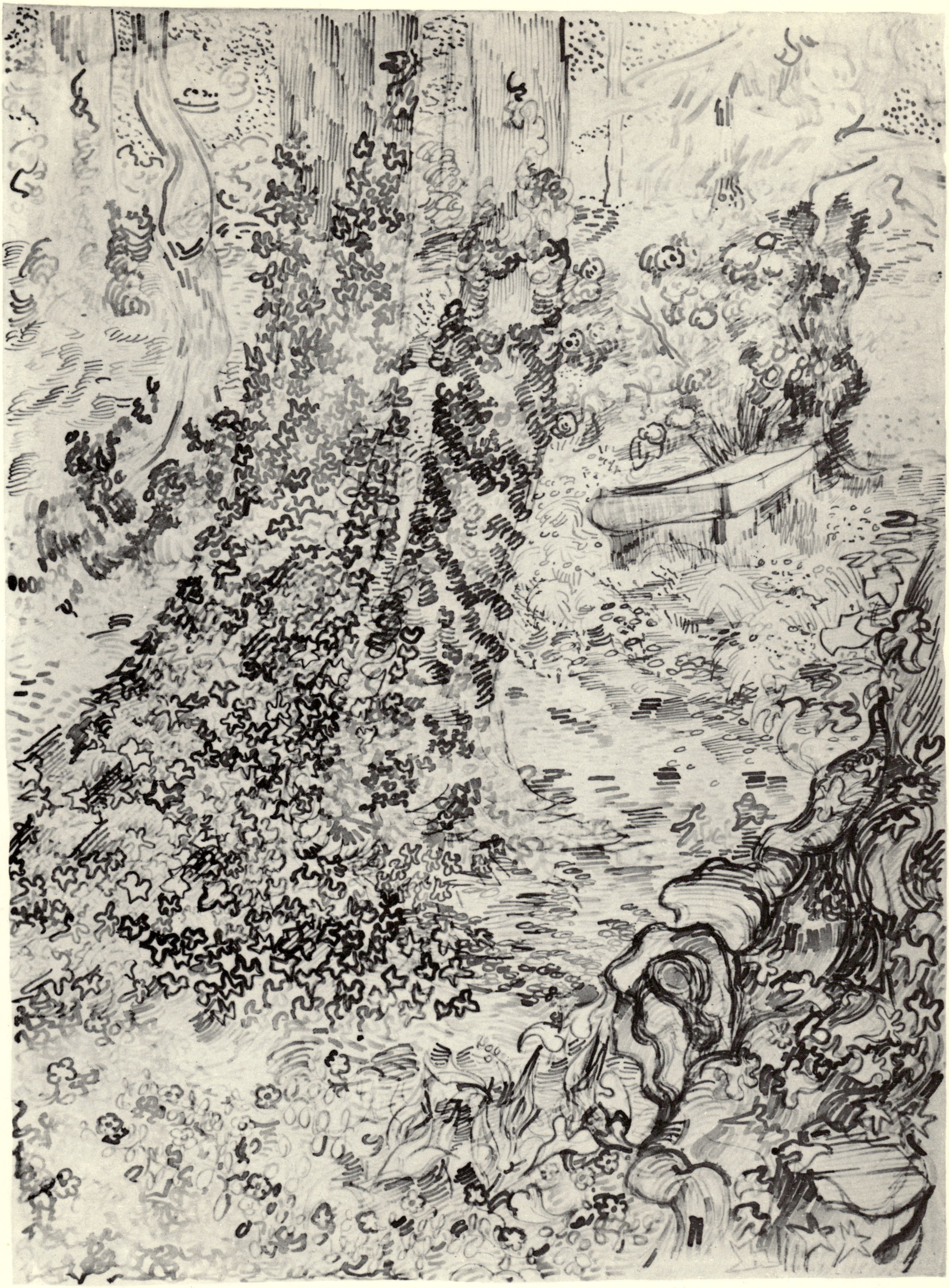

Plate 103

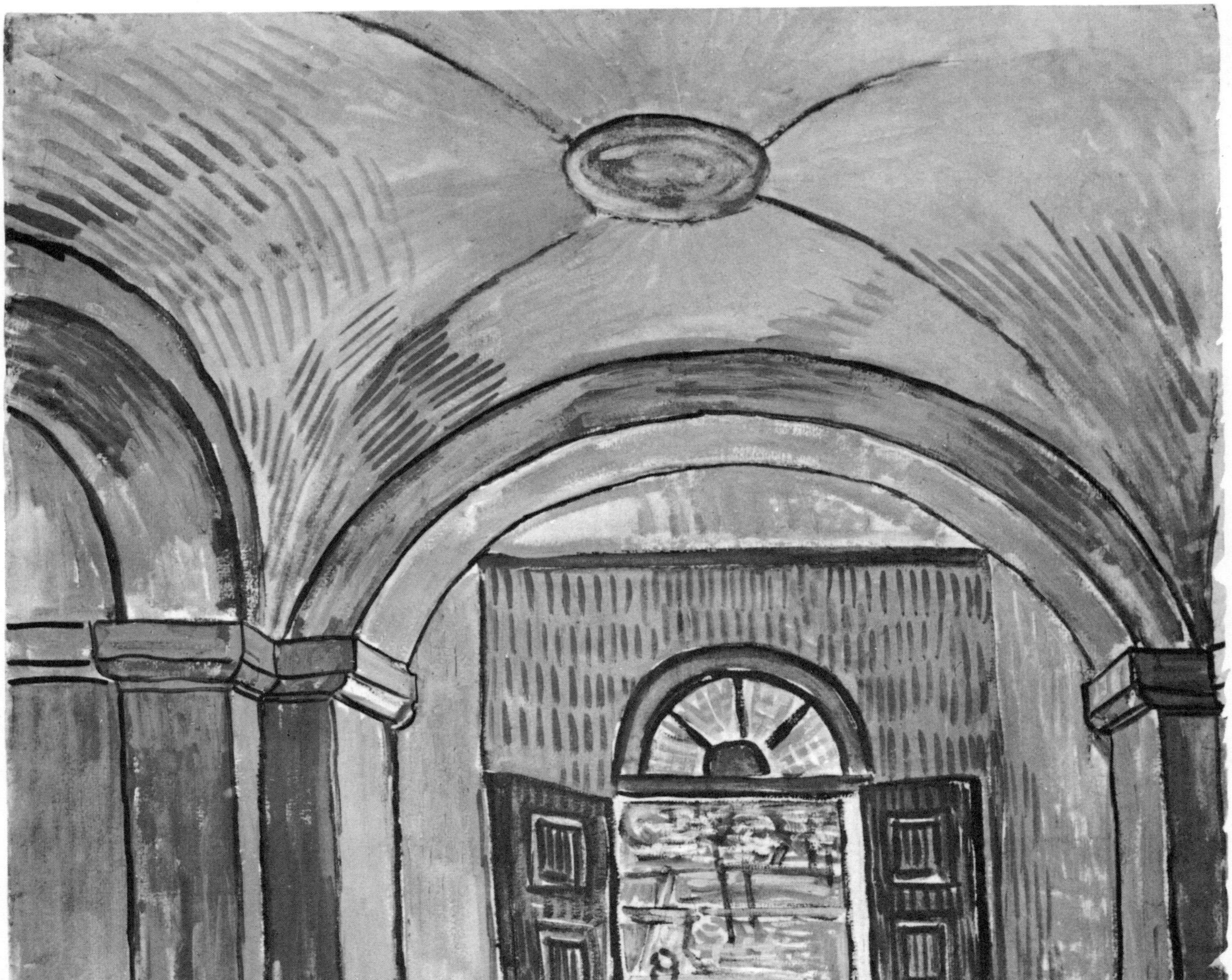

Plate 104

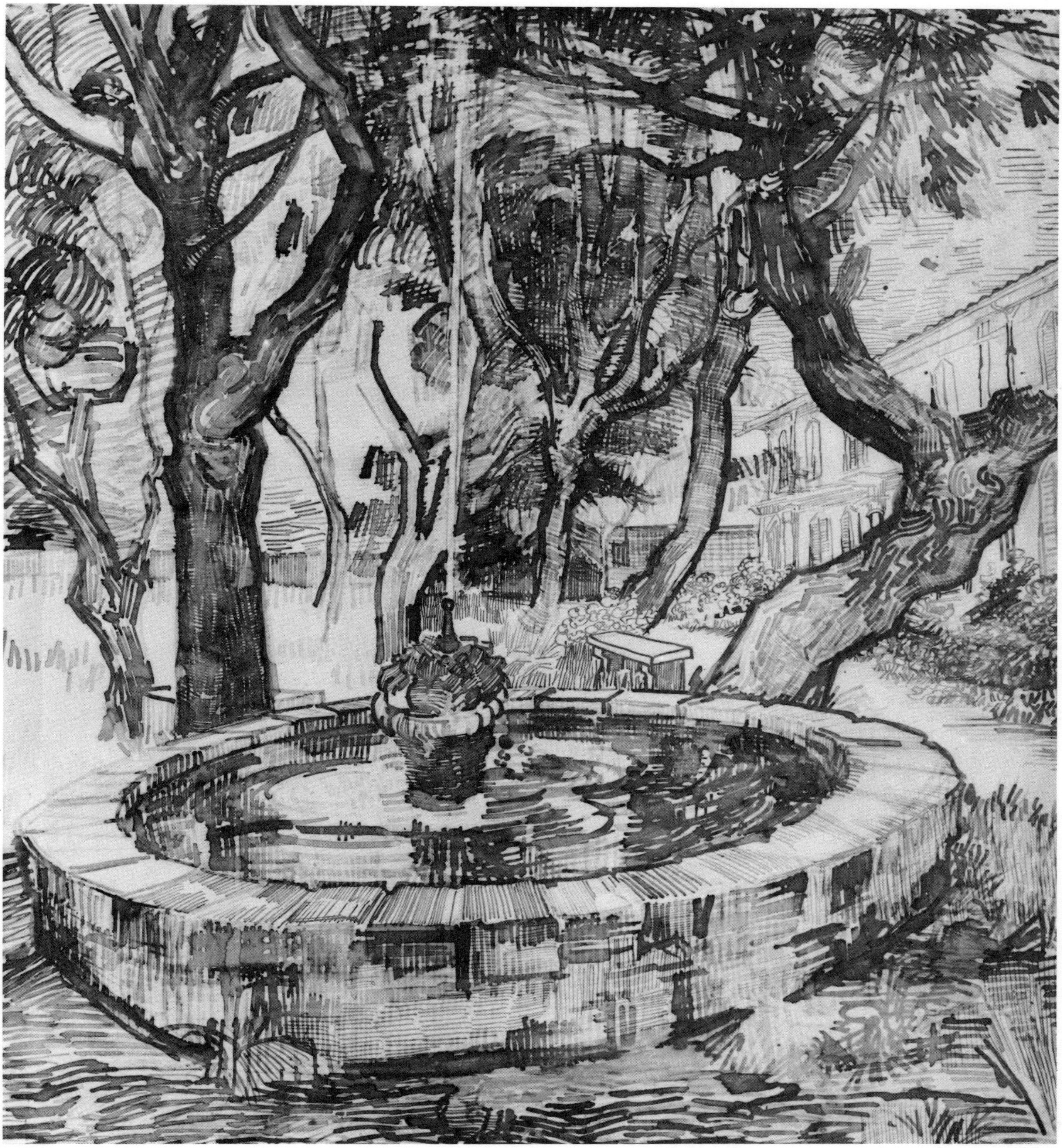

Plate 105

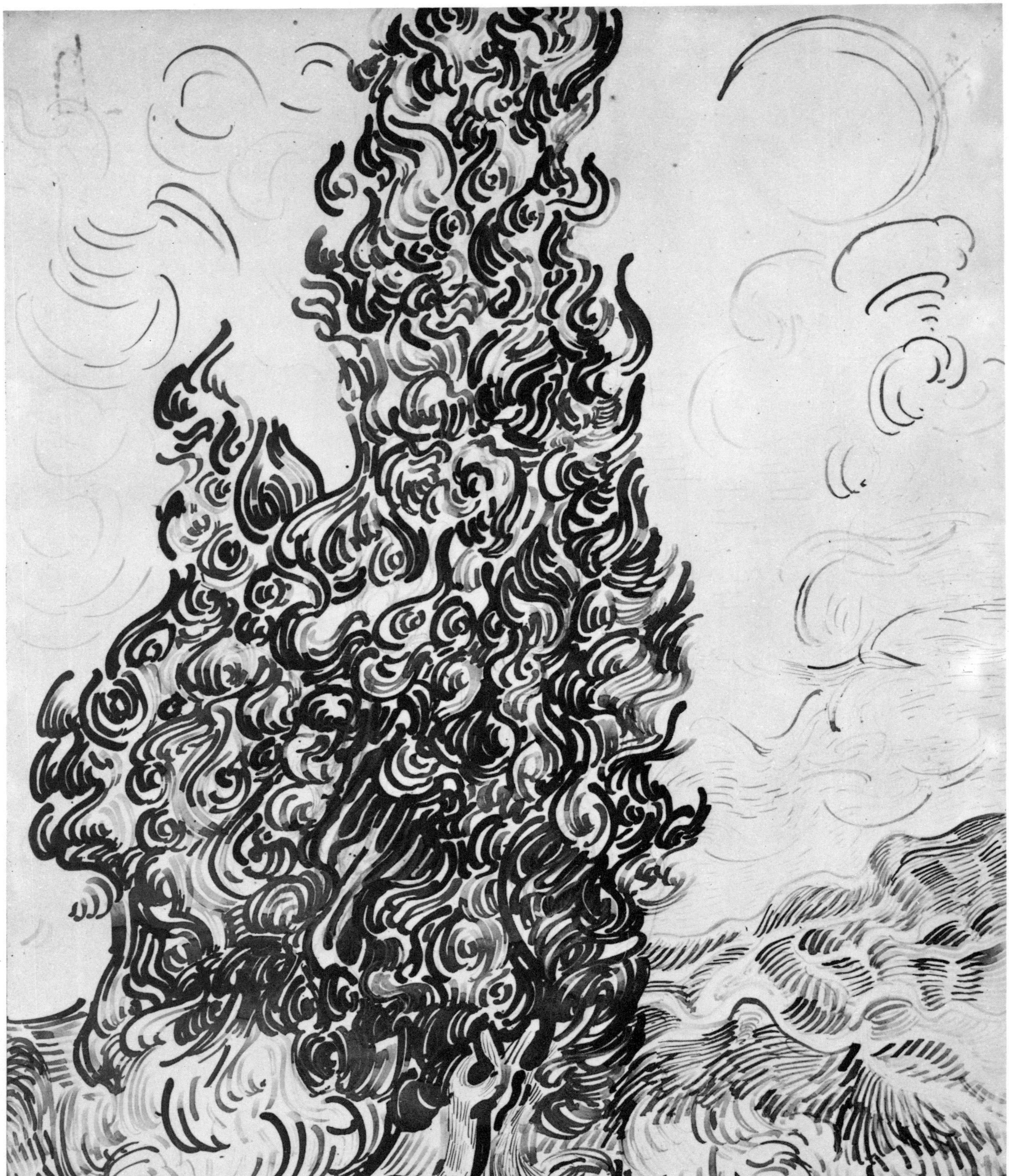

Plate 106

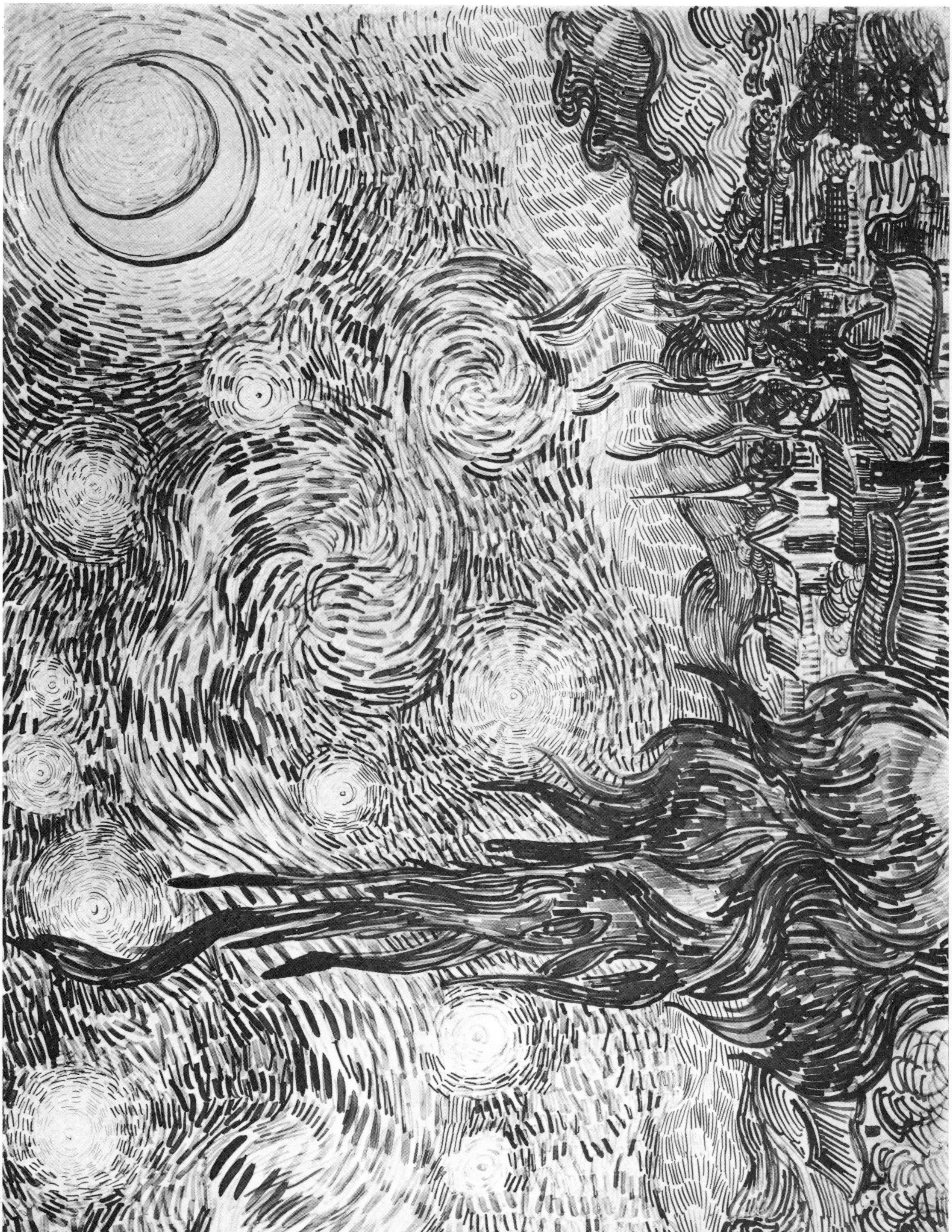

Plate 107

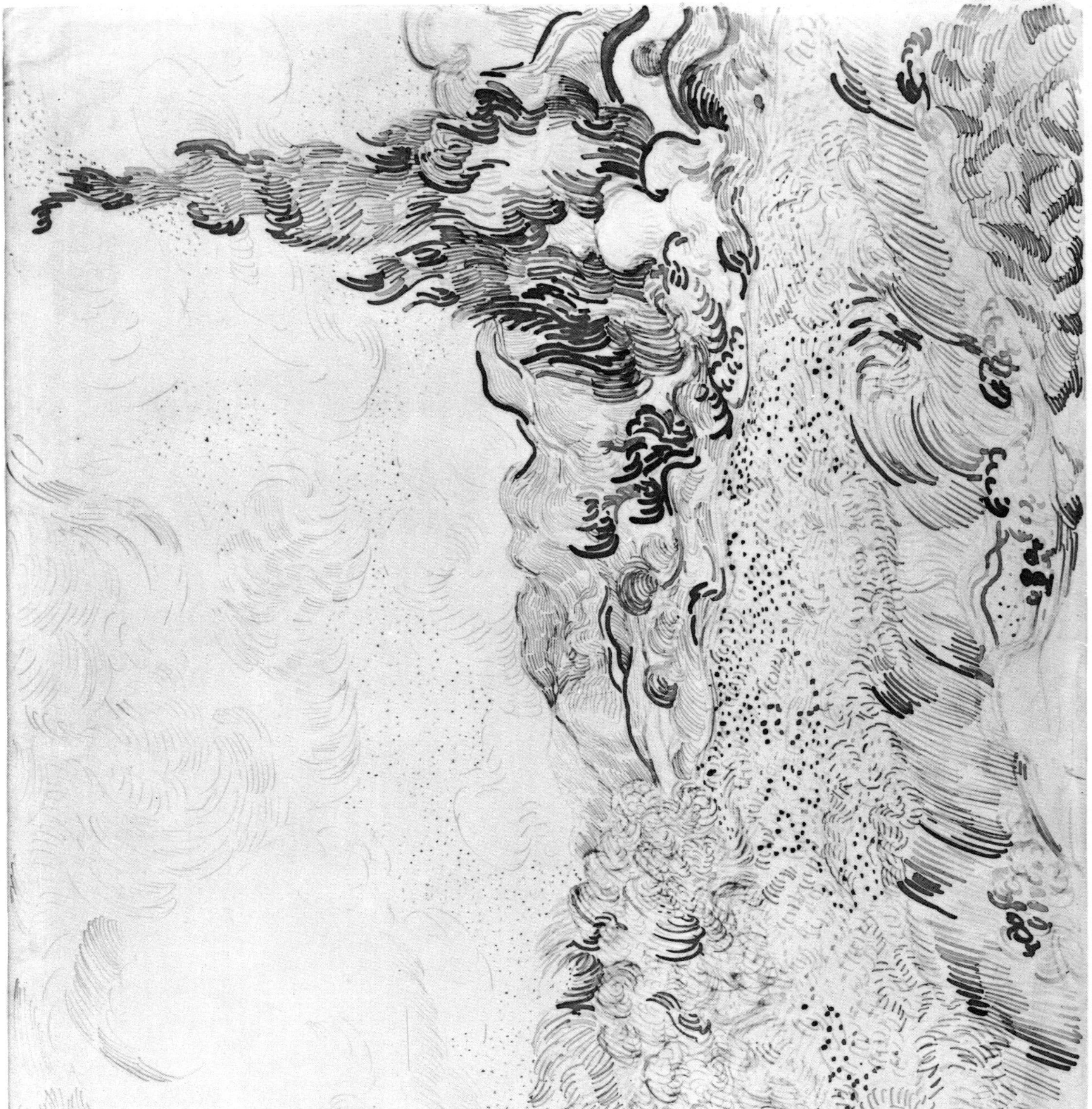

Plate 108

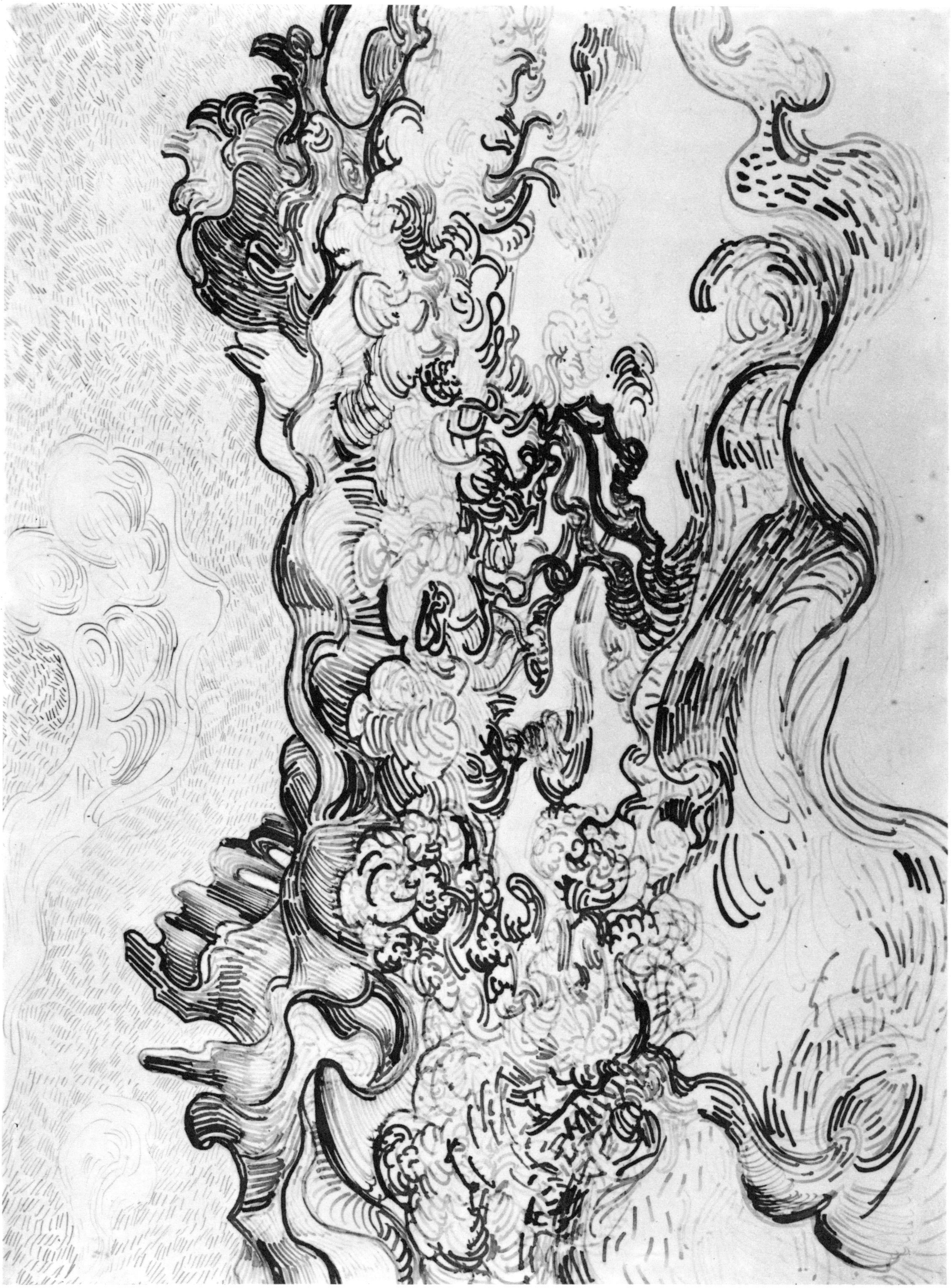

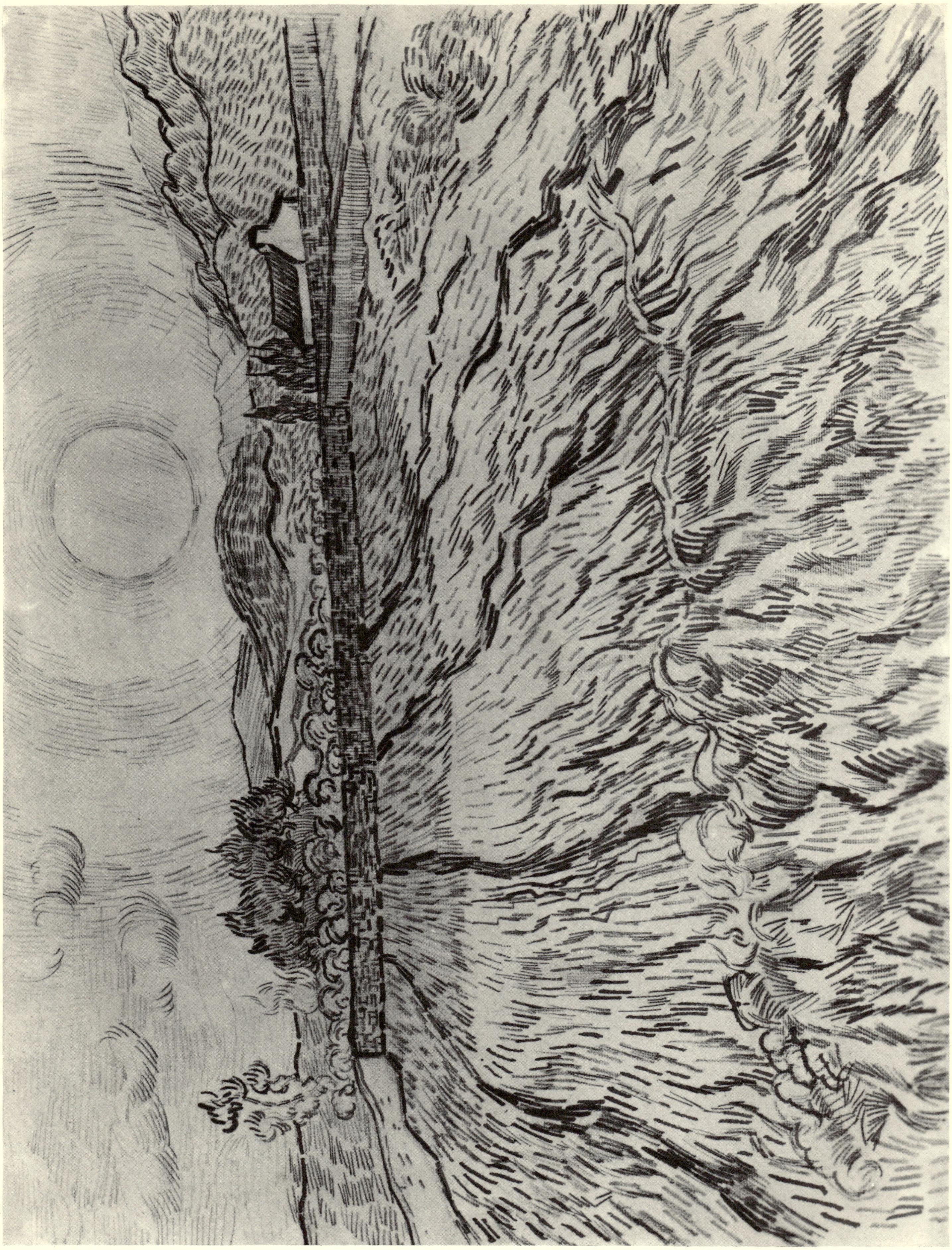

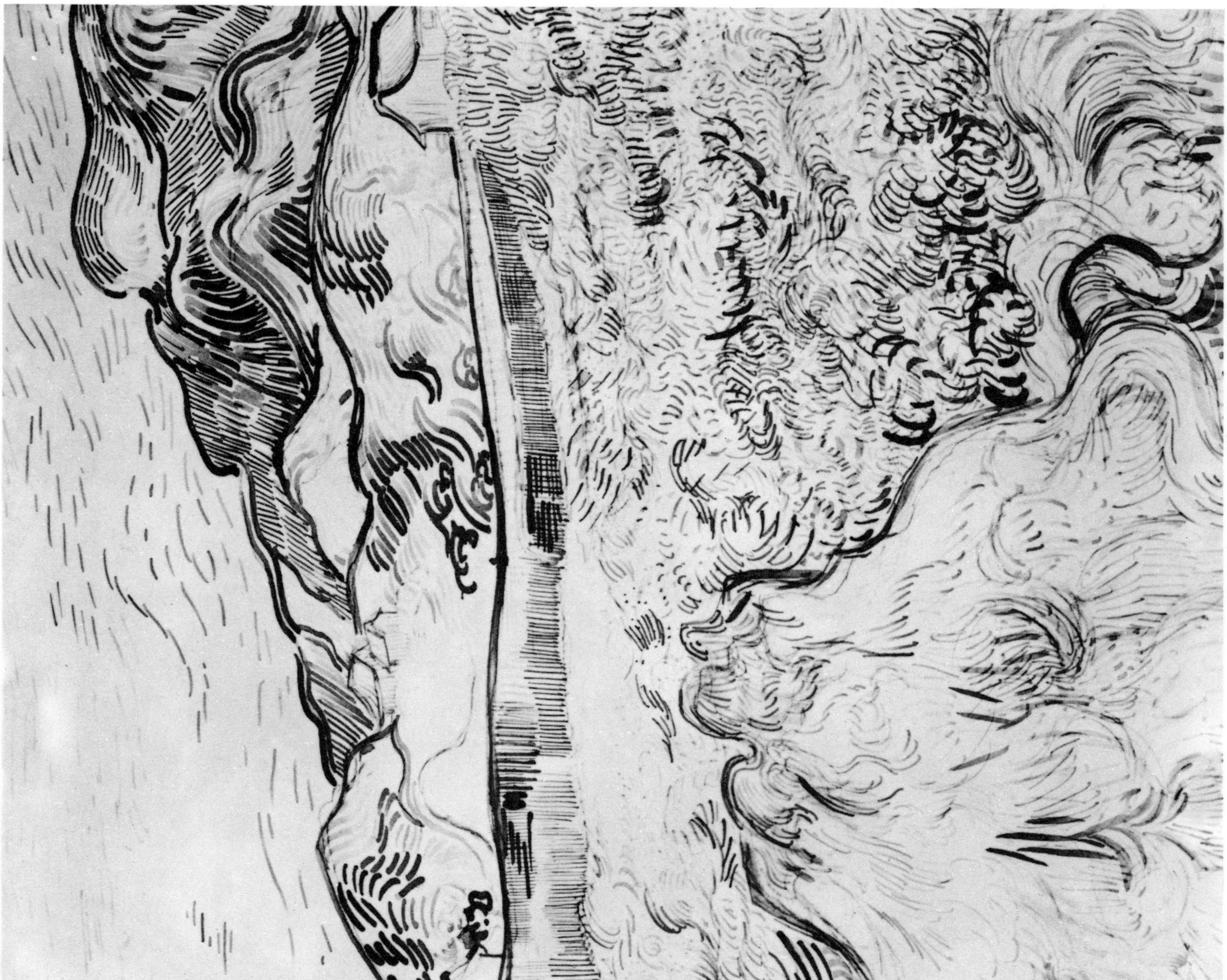

Plate 111

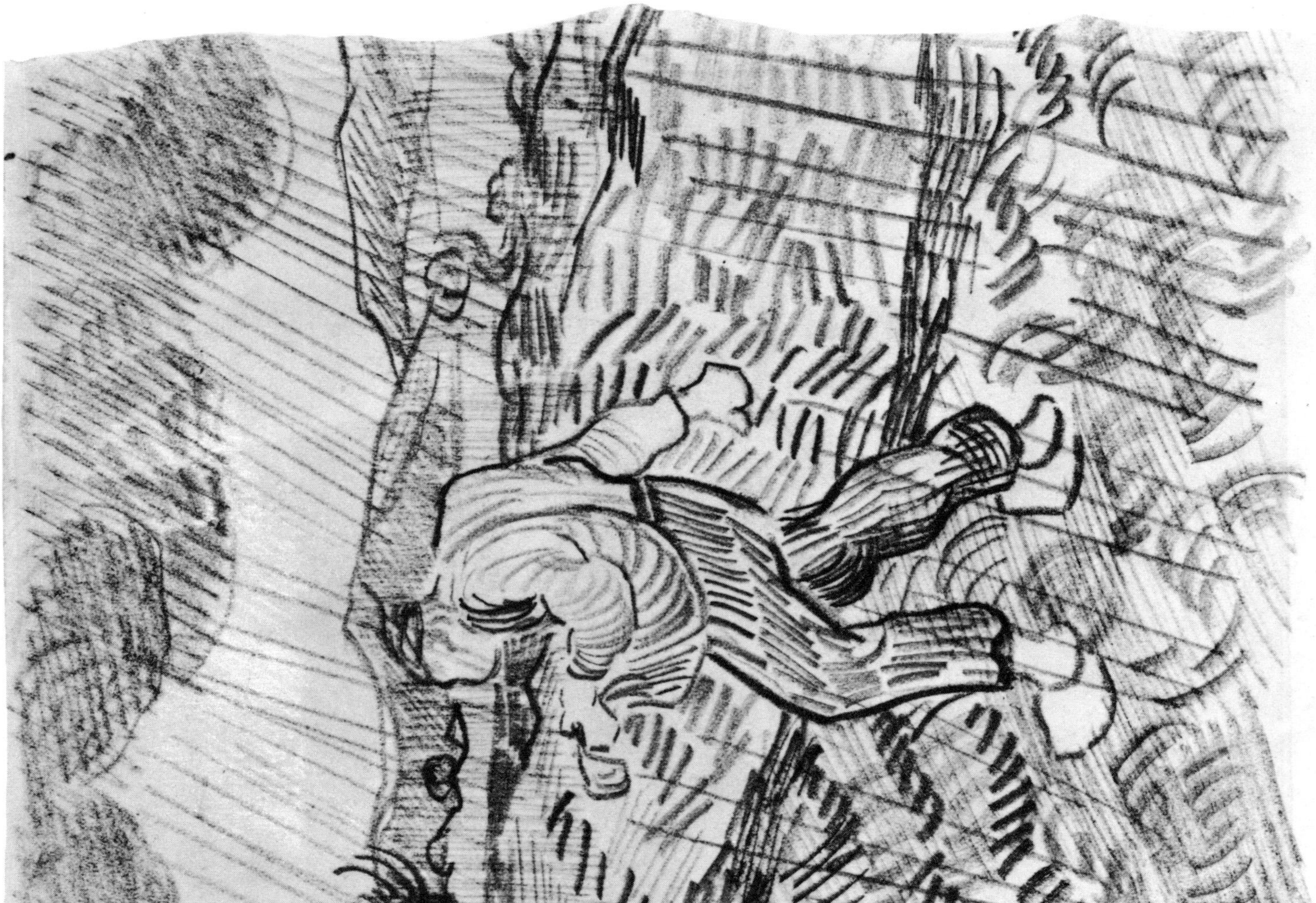

Plate 112

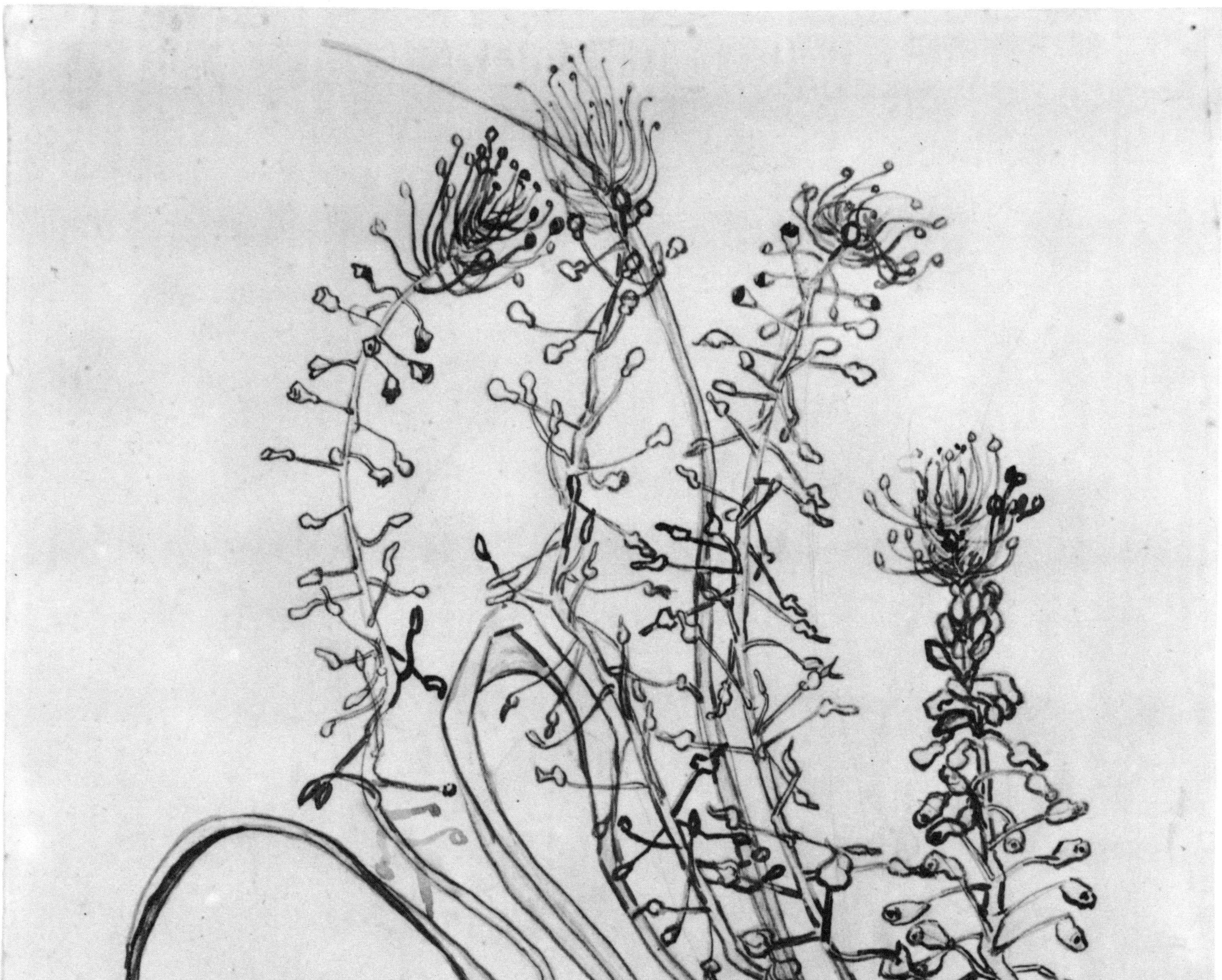

Plate 113

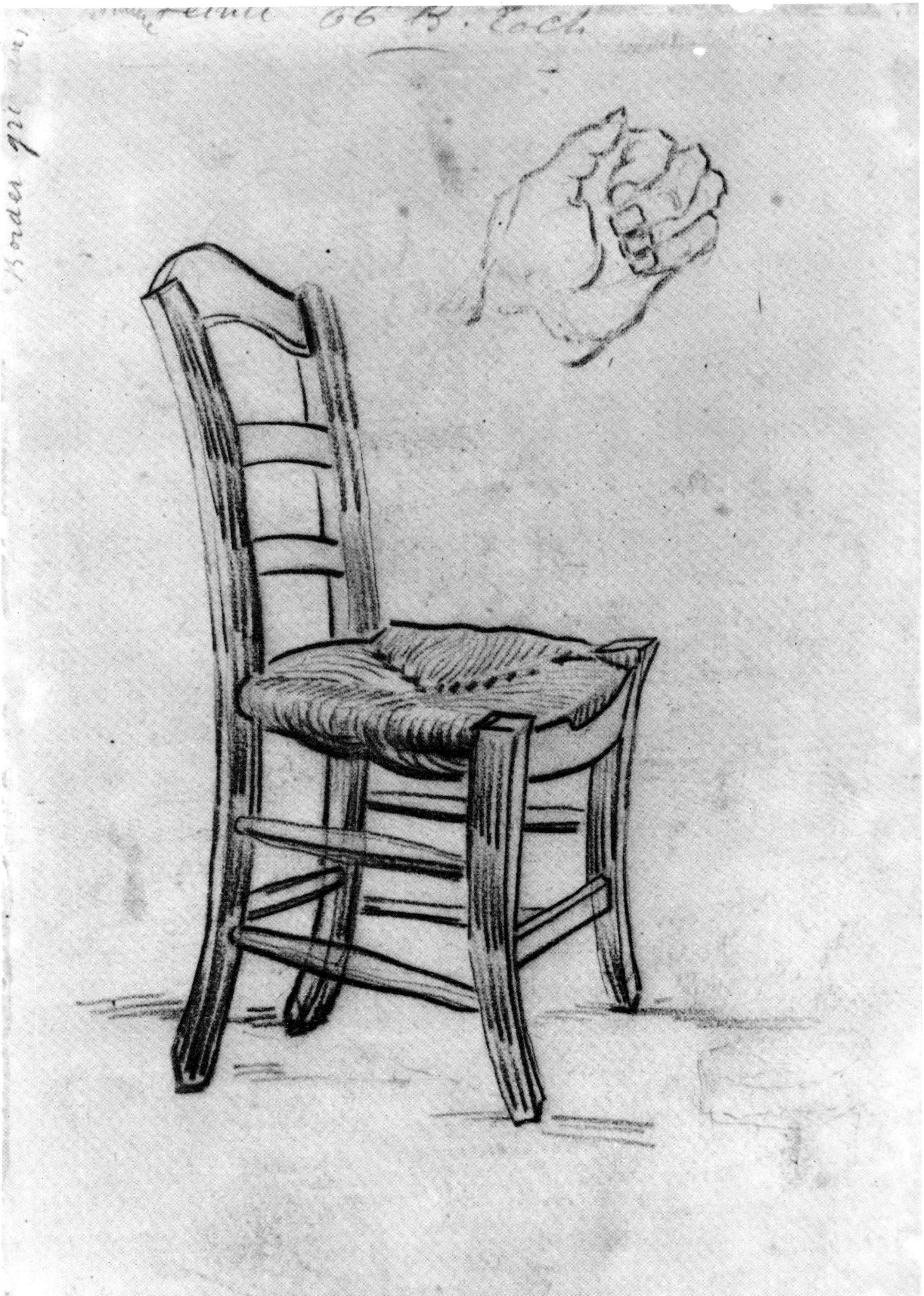

Plate 114

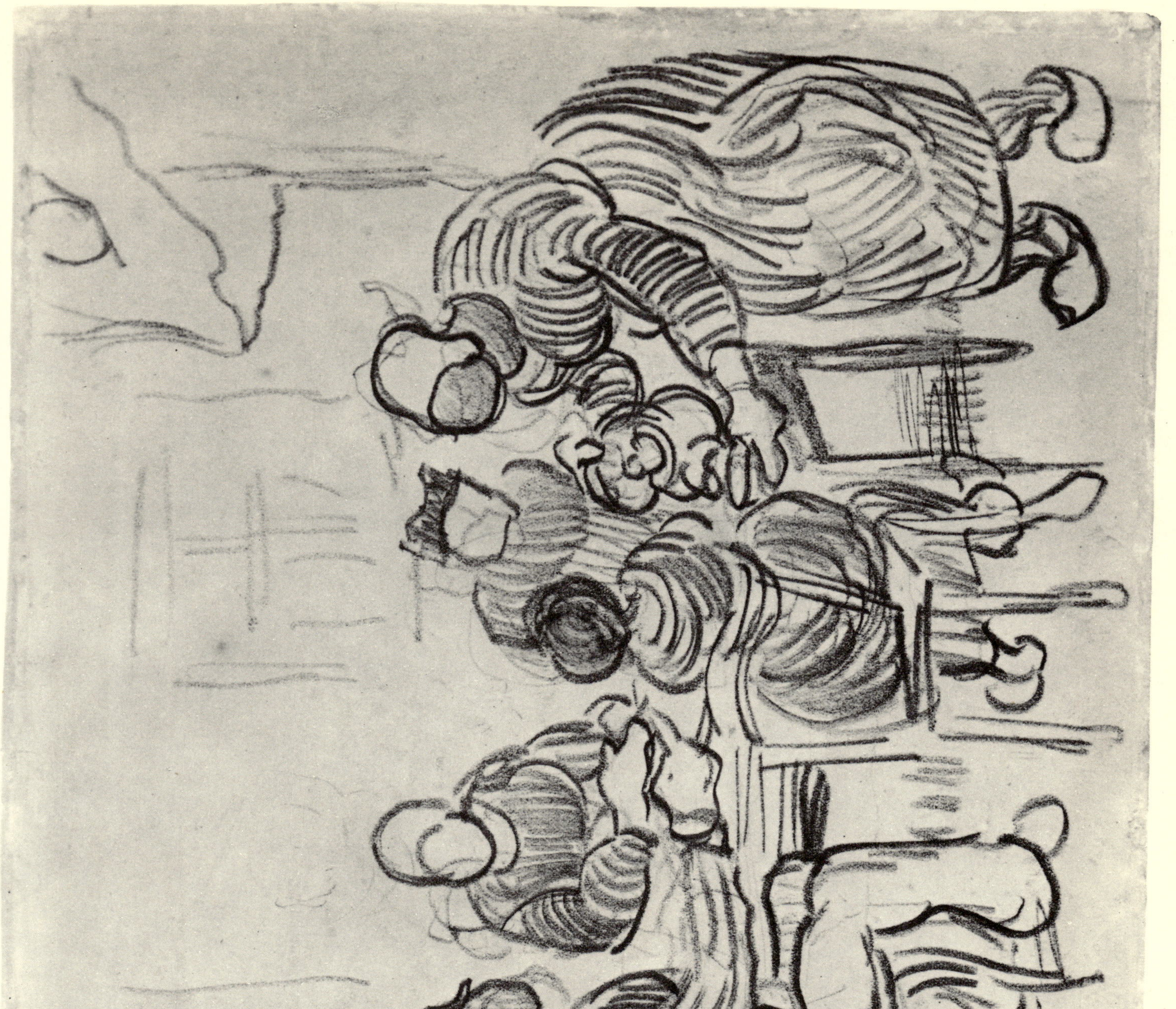

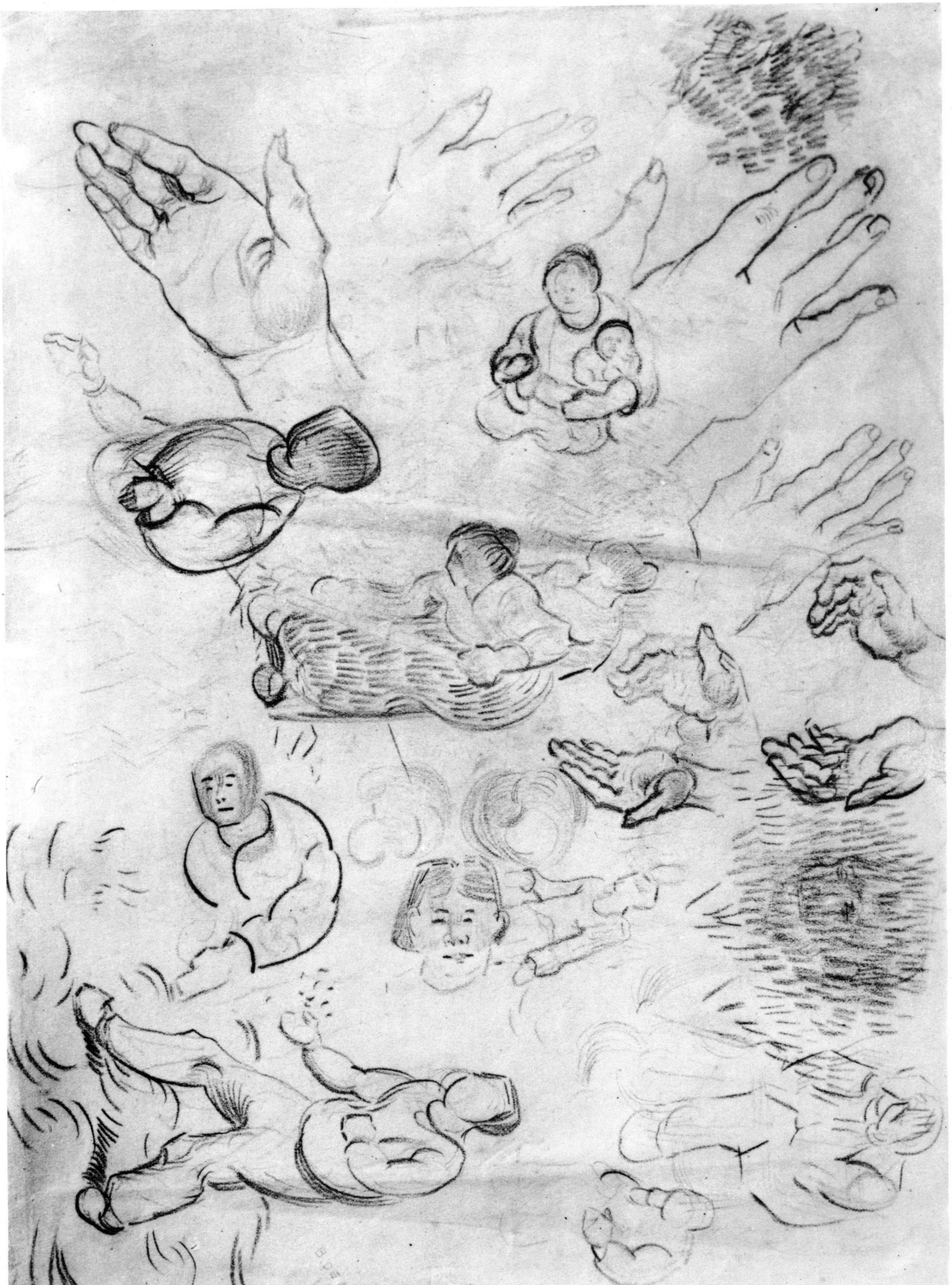

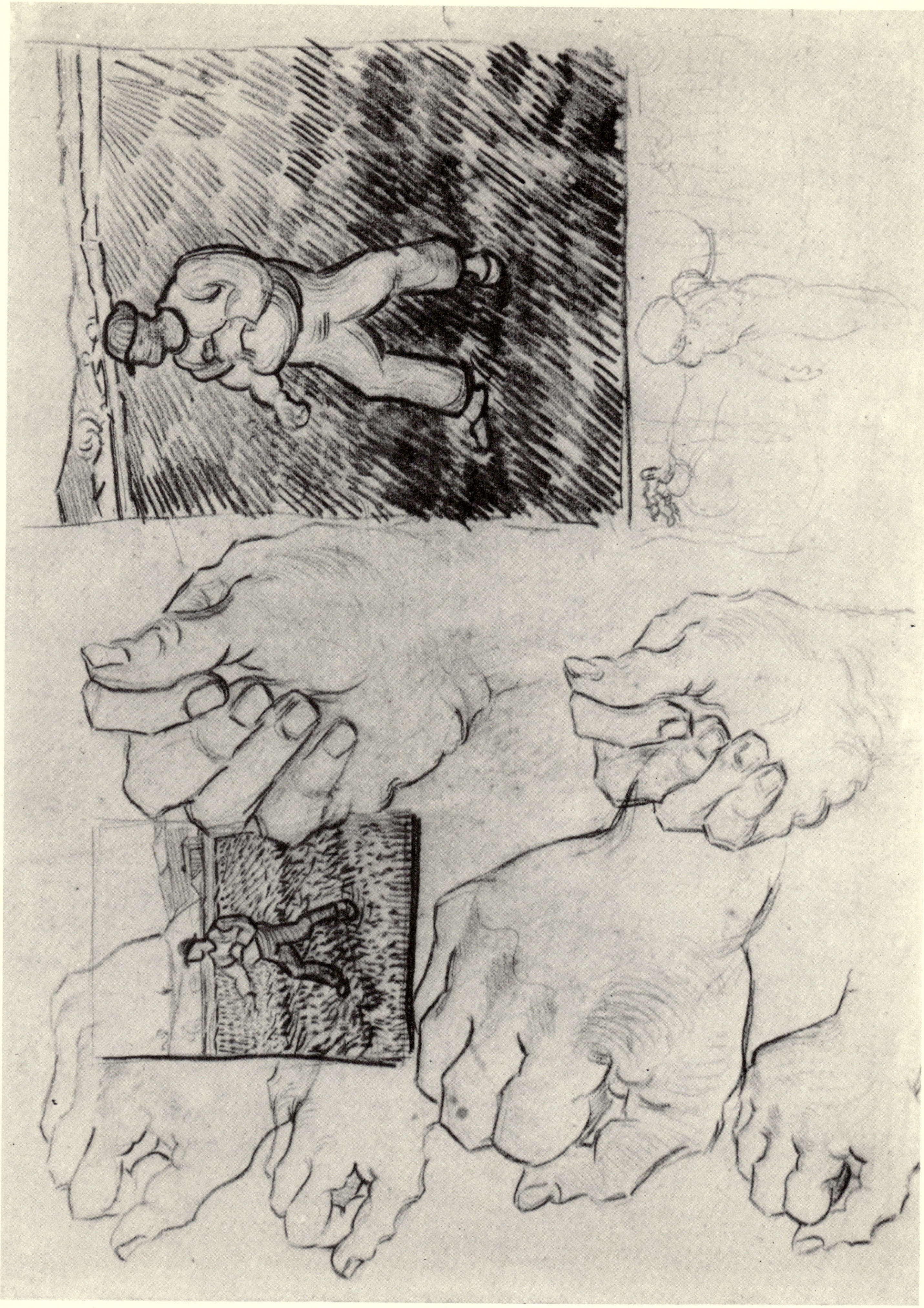

Plate 117

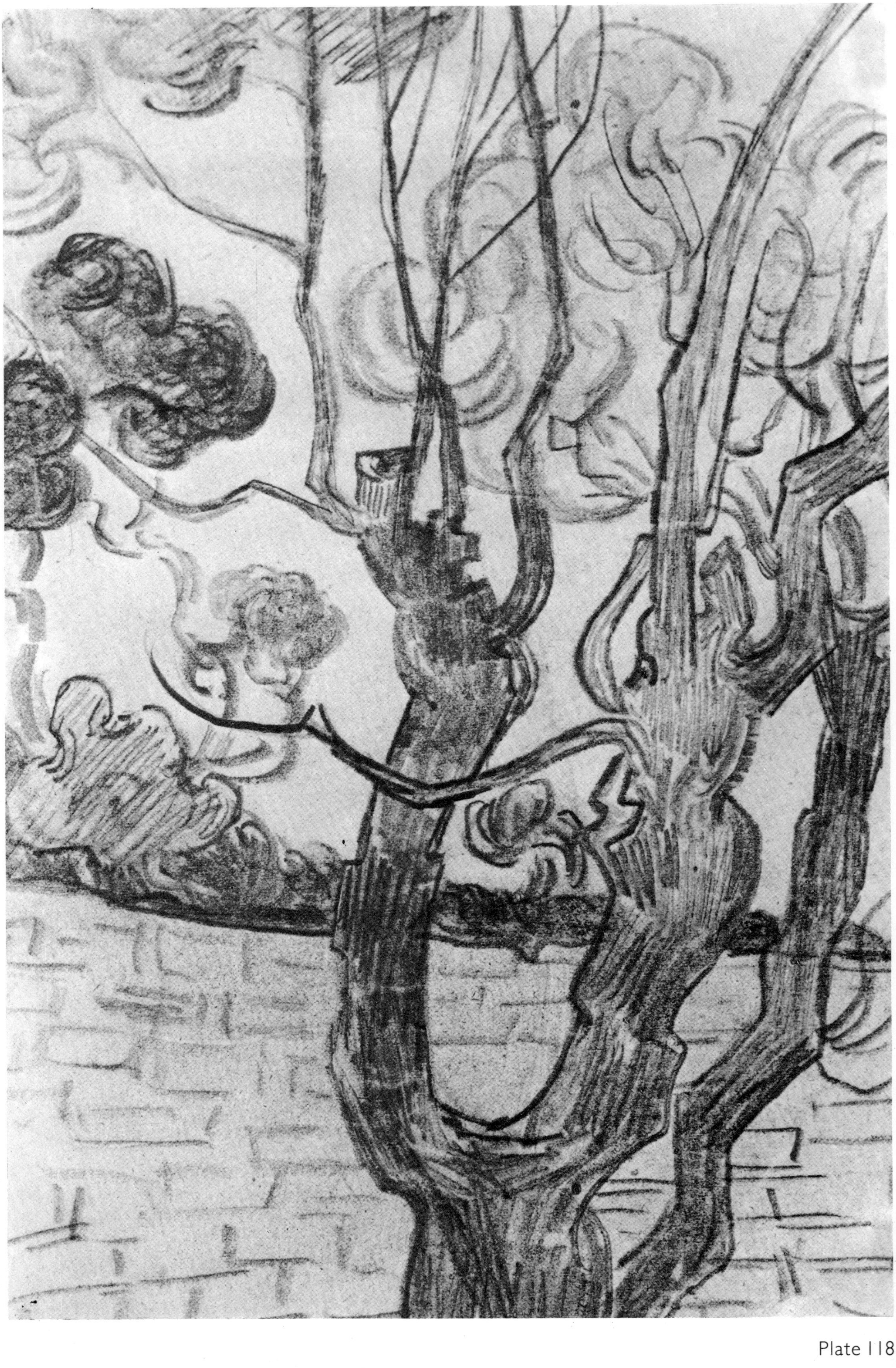

Plate 118

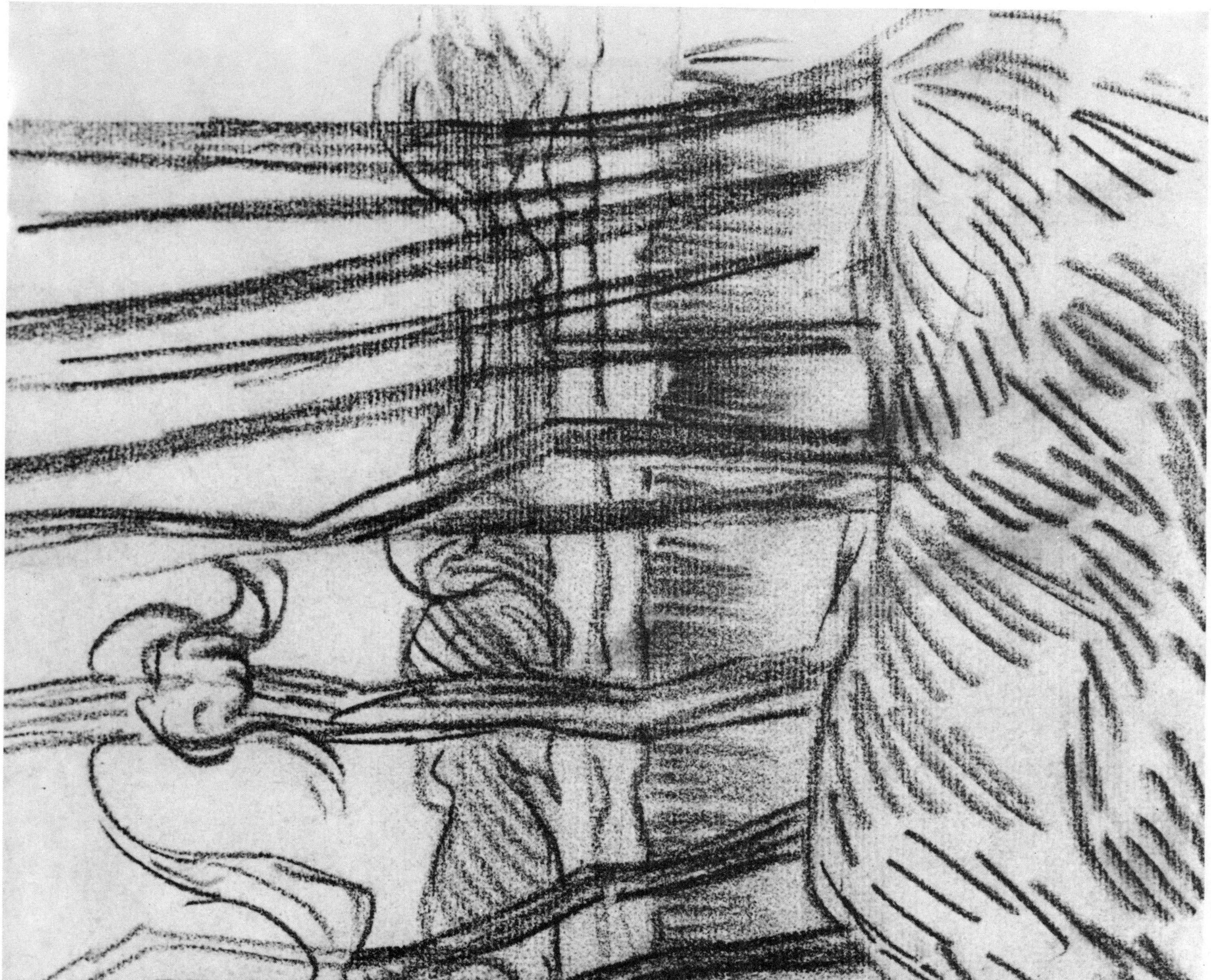

Plate 119

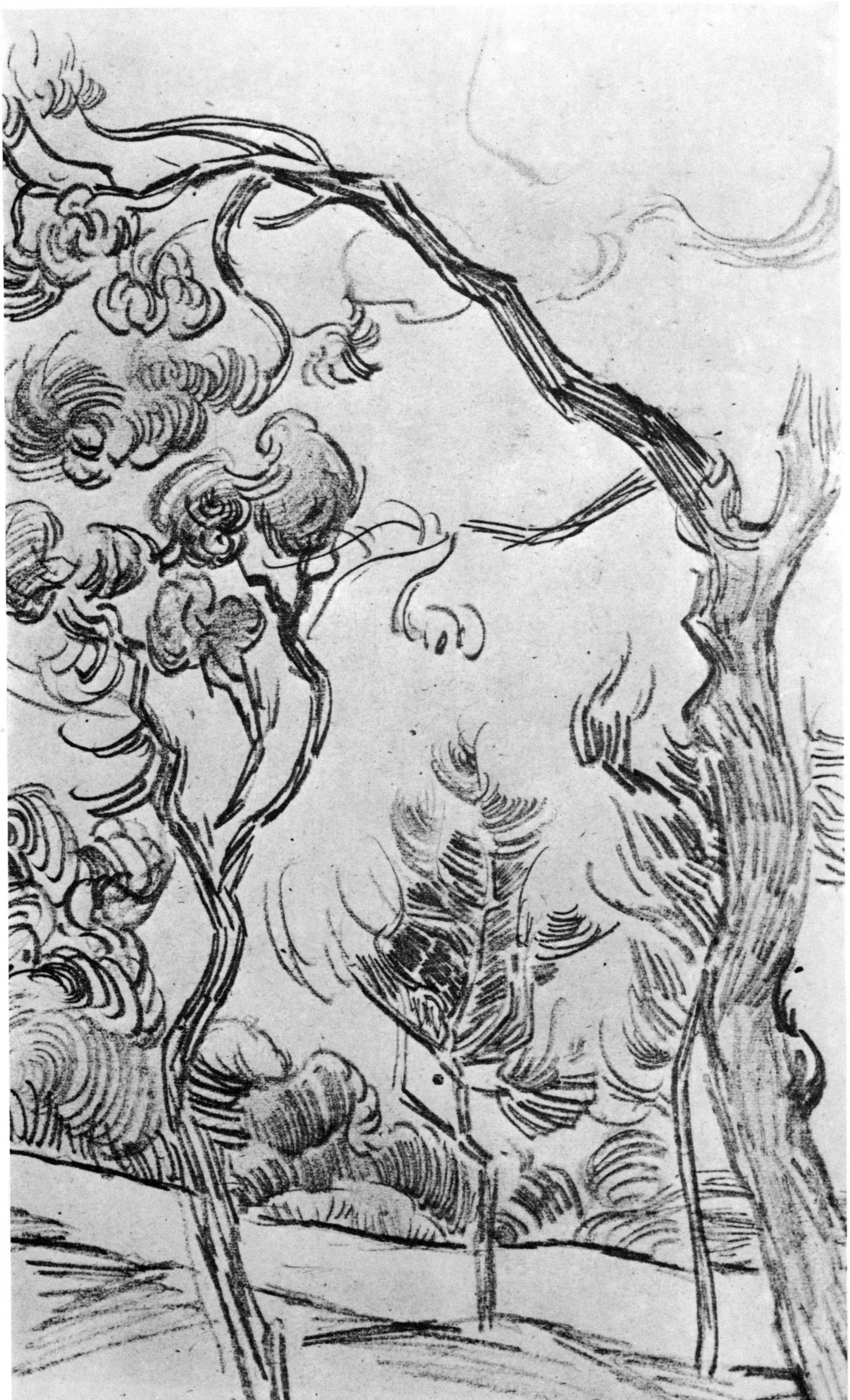

Plate 120

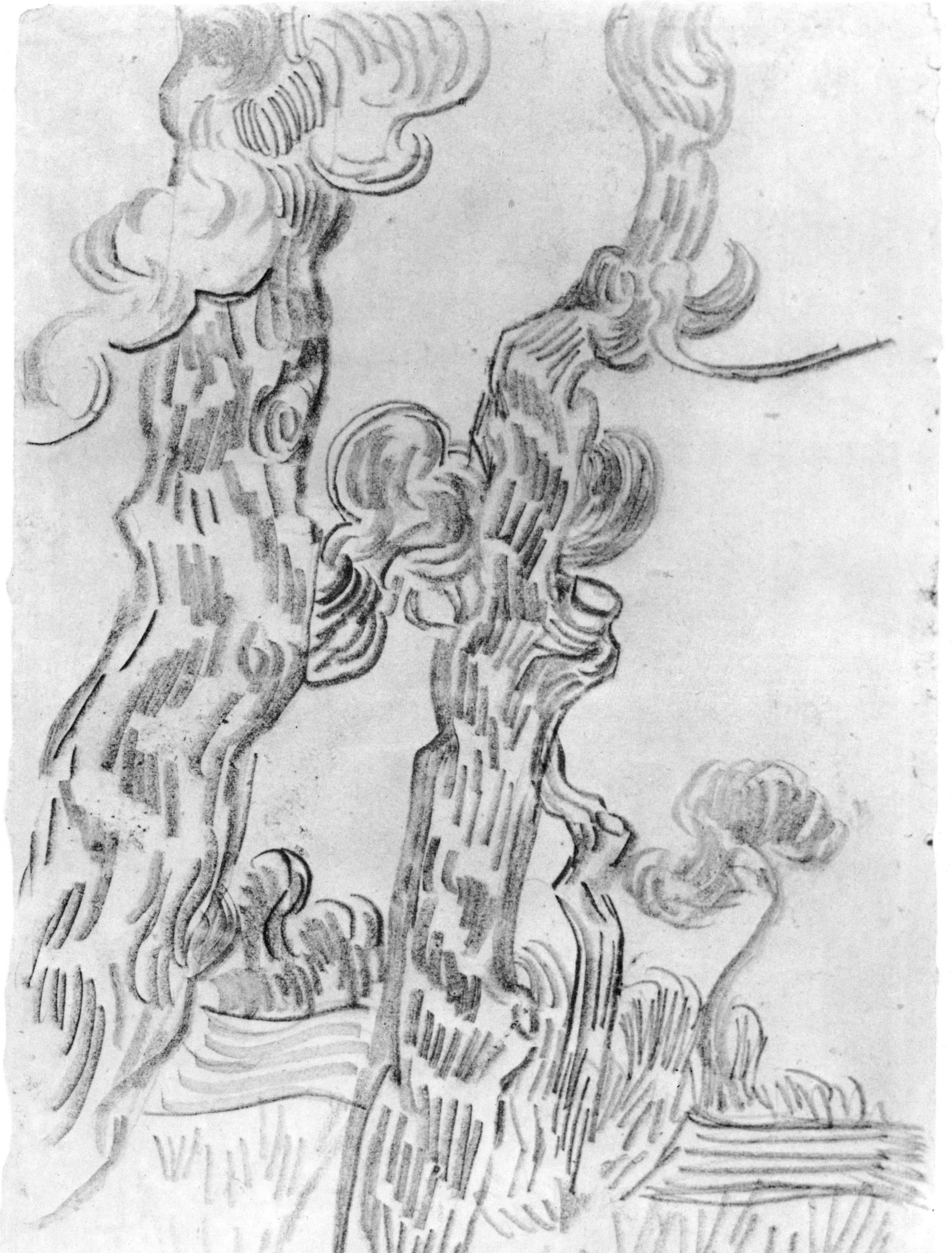

Plate 121

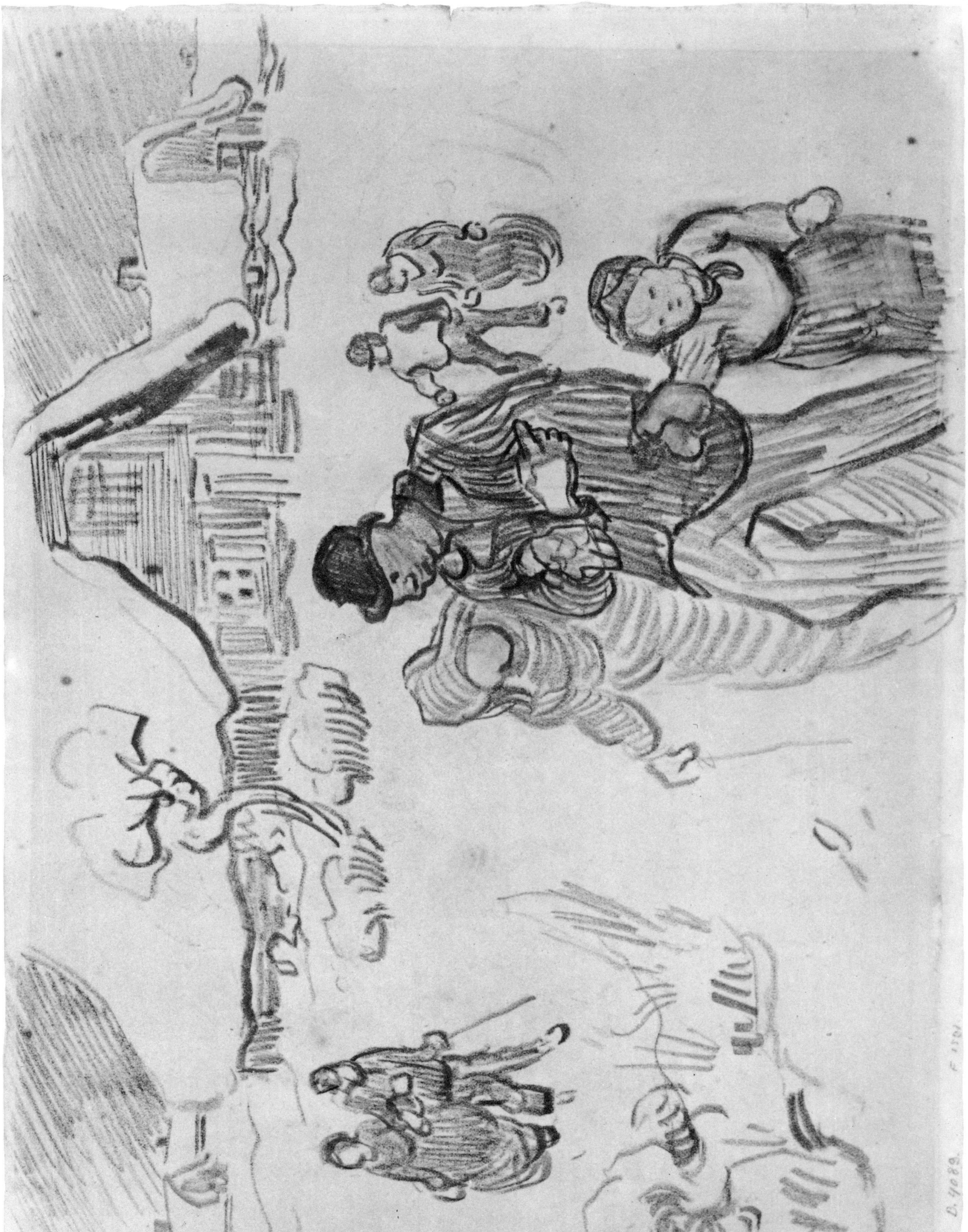

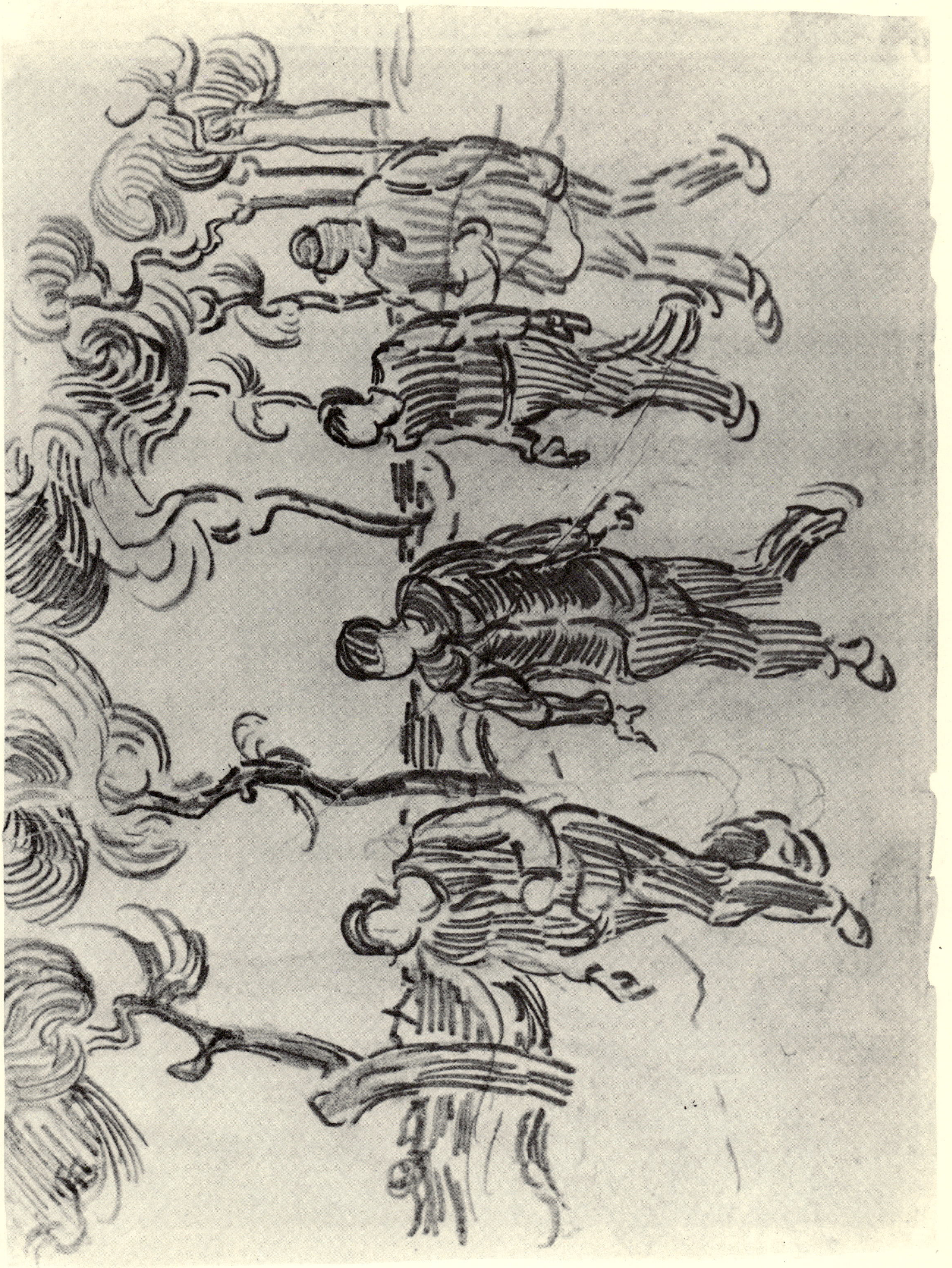

Plate 123

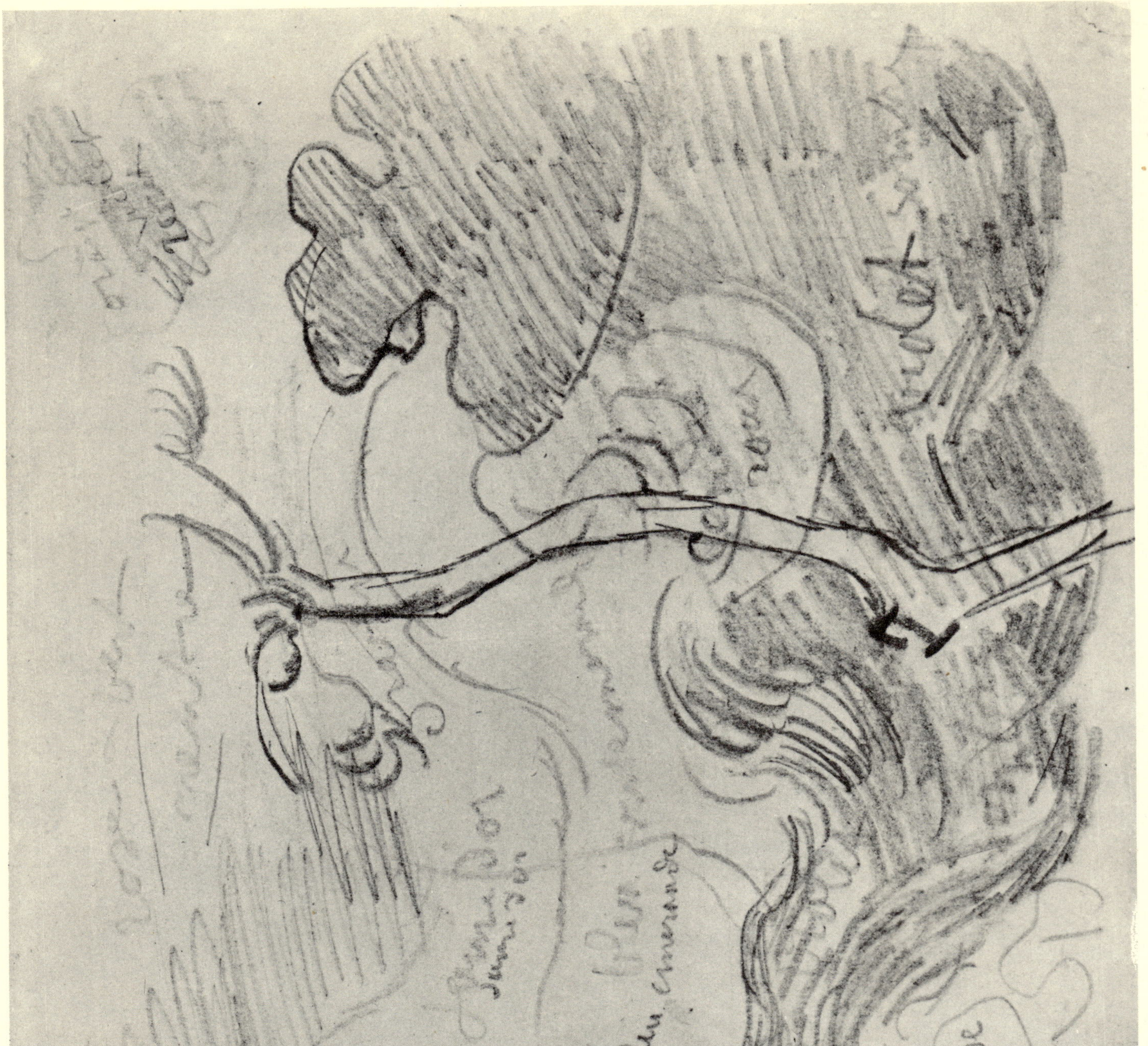

Plate 124

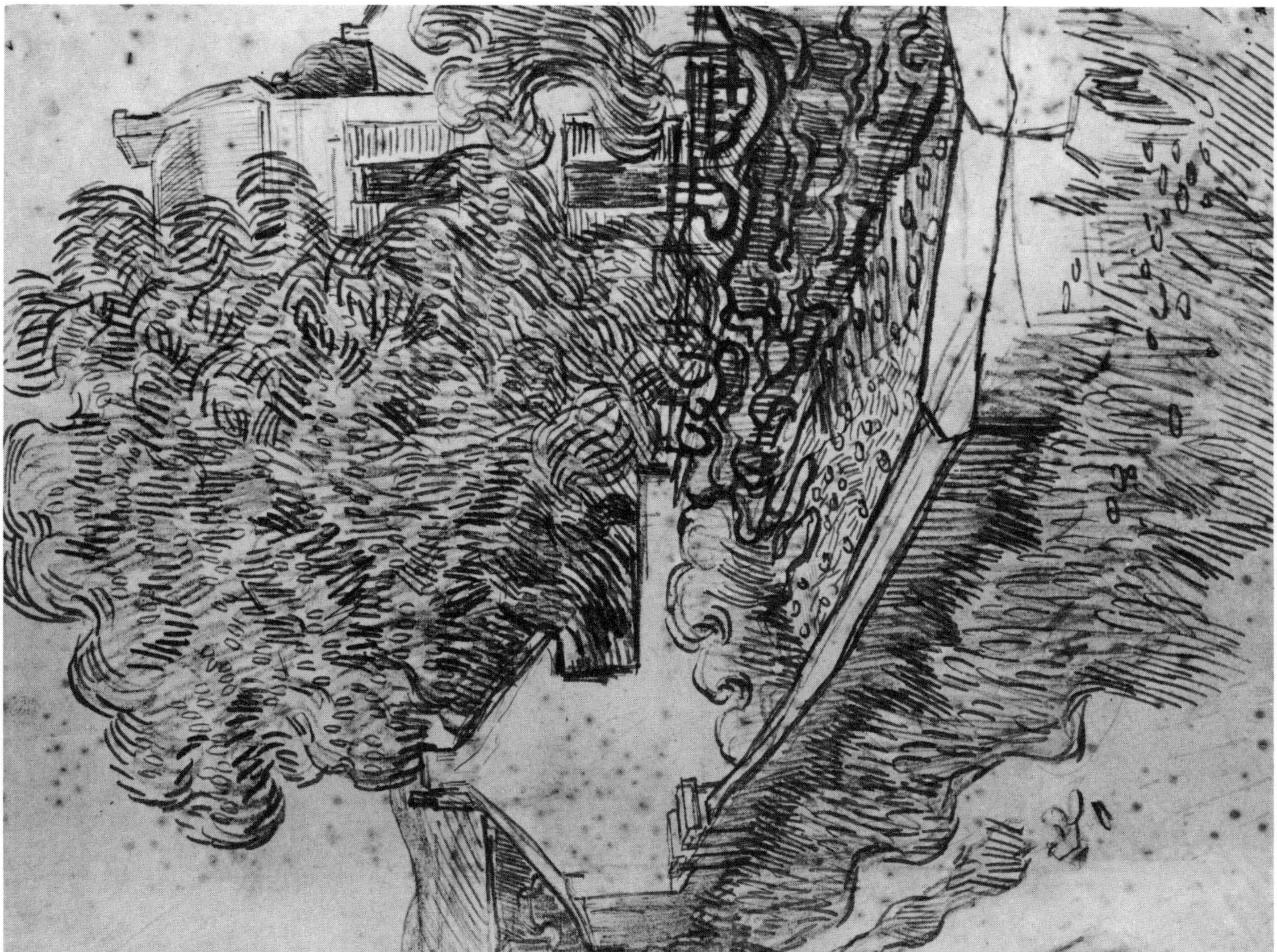

Plate 125

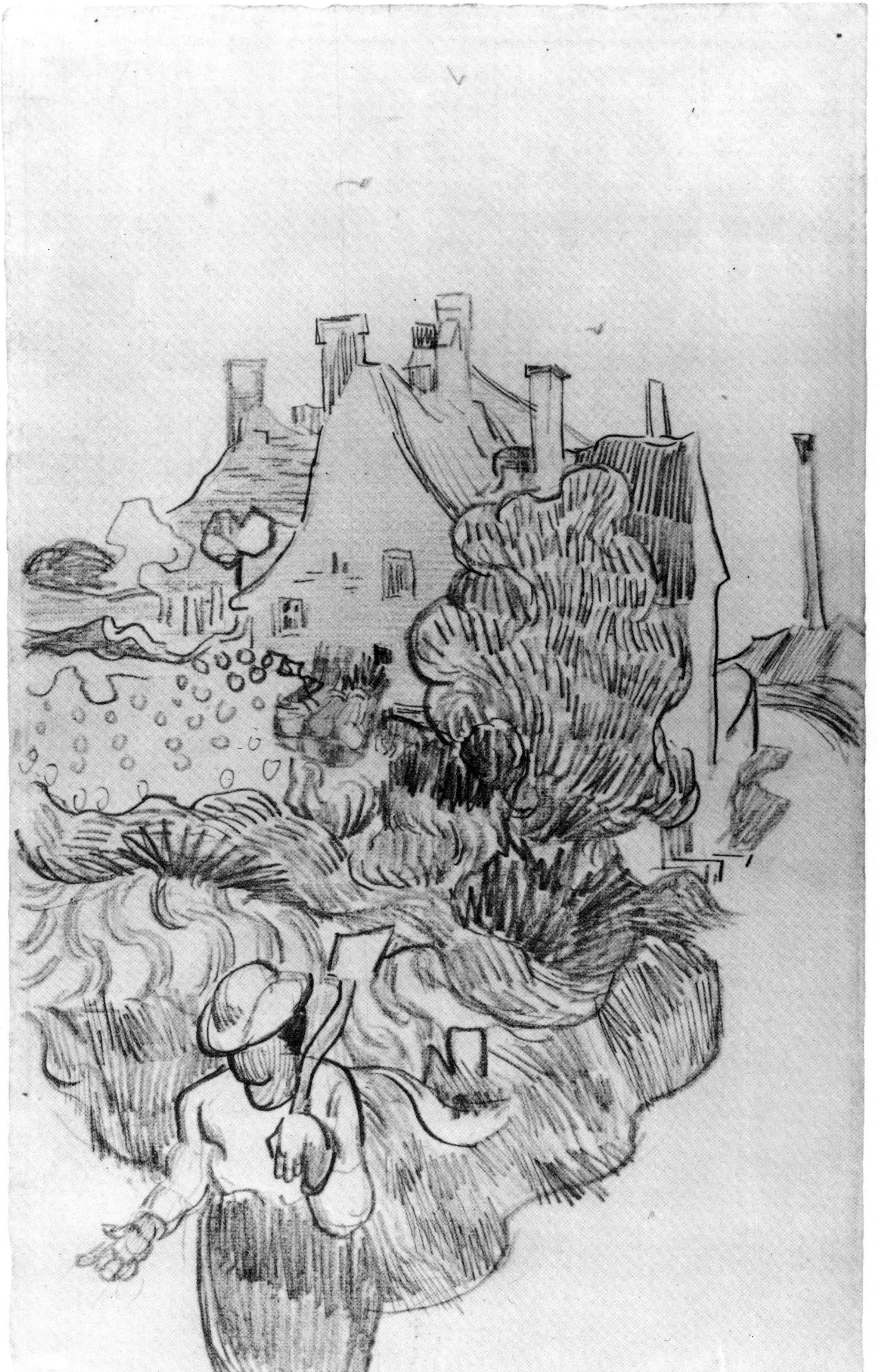

Plate 126

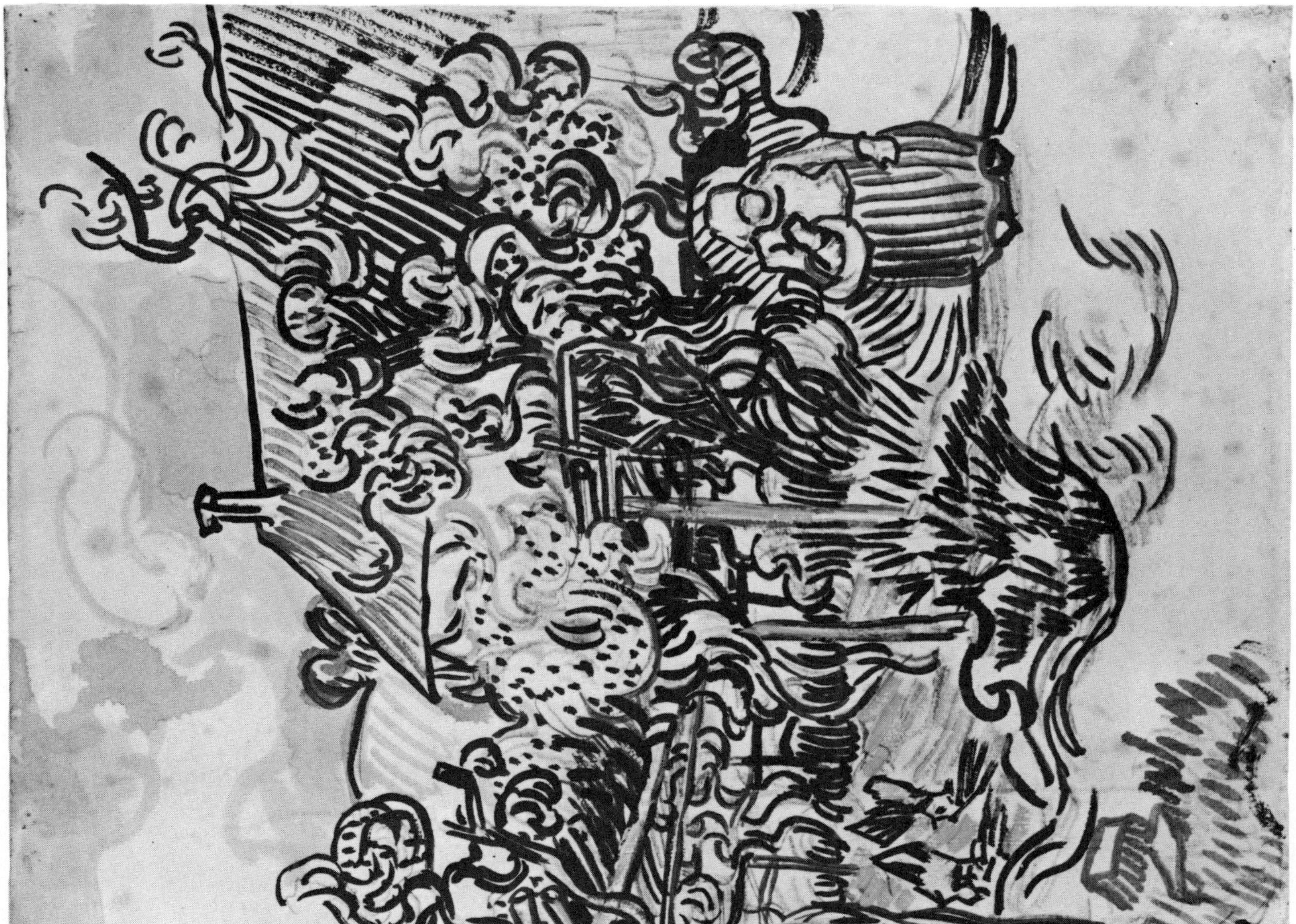

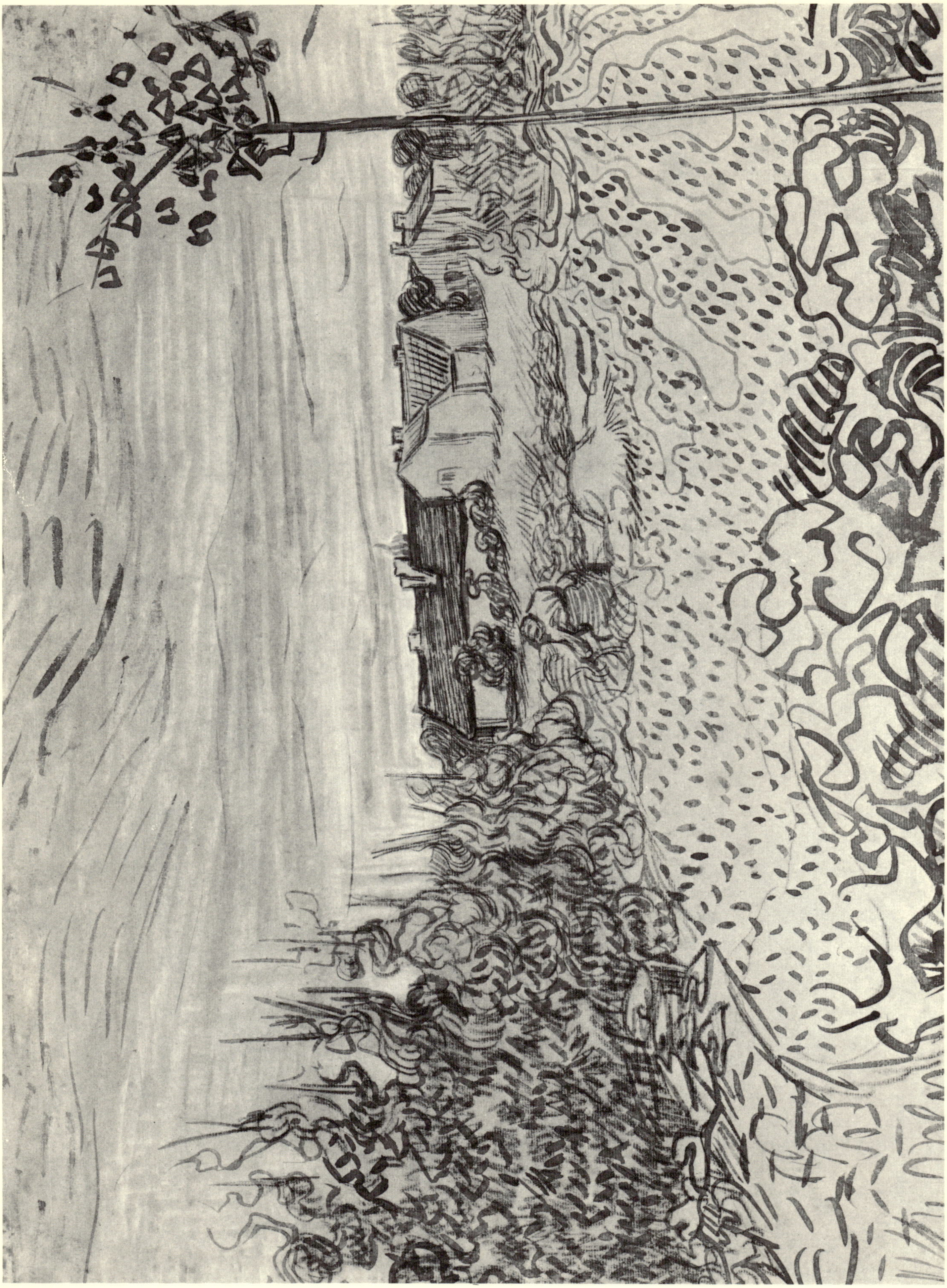

Plate 128

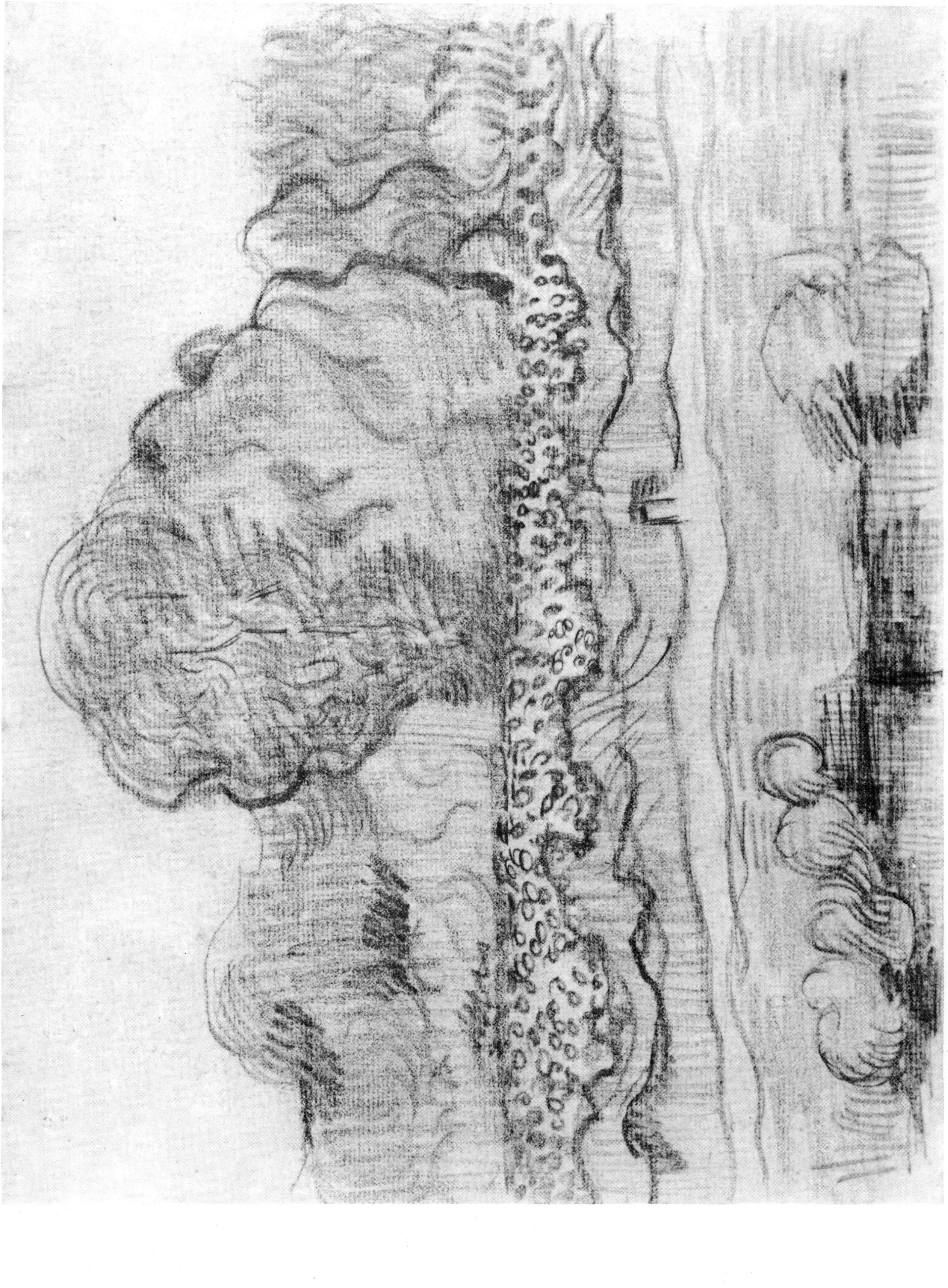

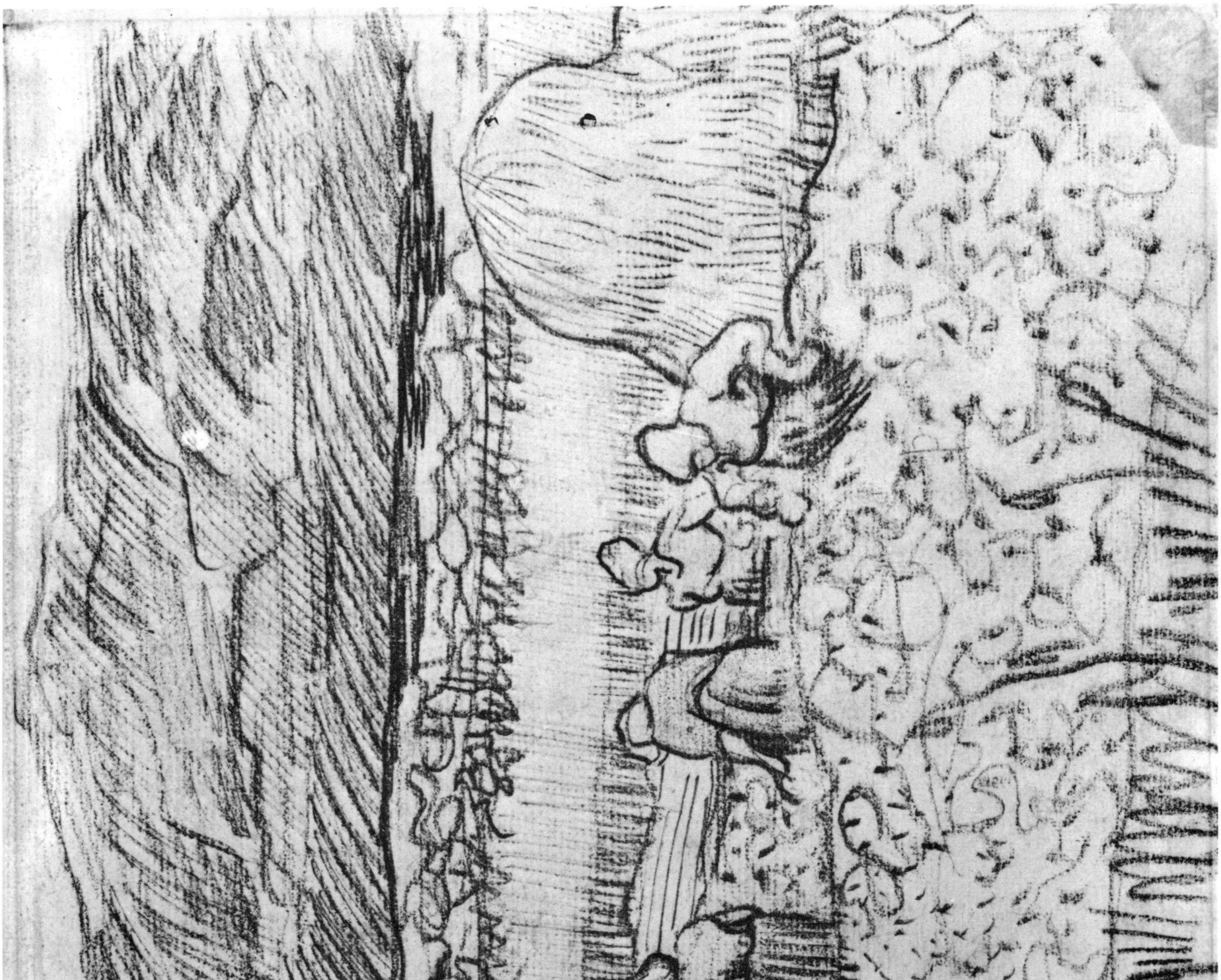

Plate 130

Plate 131

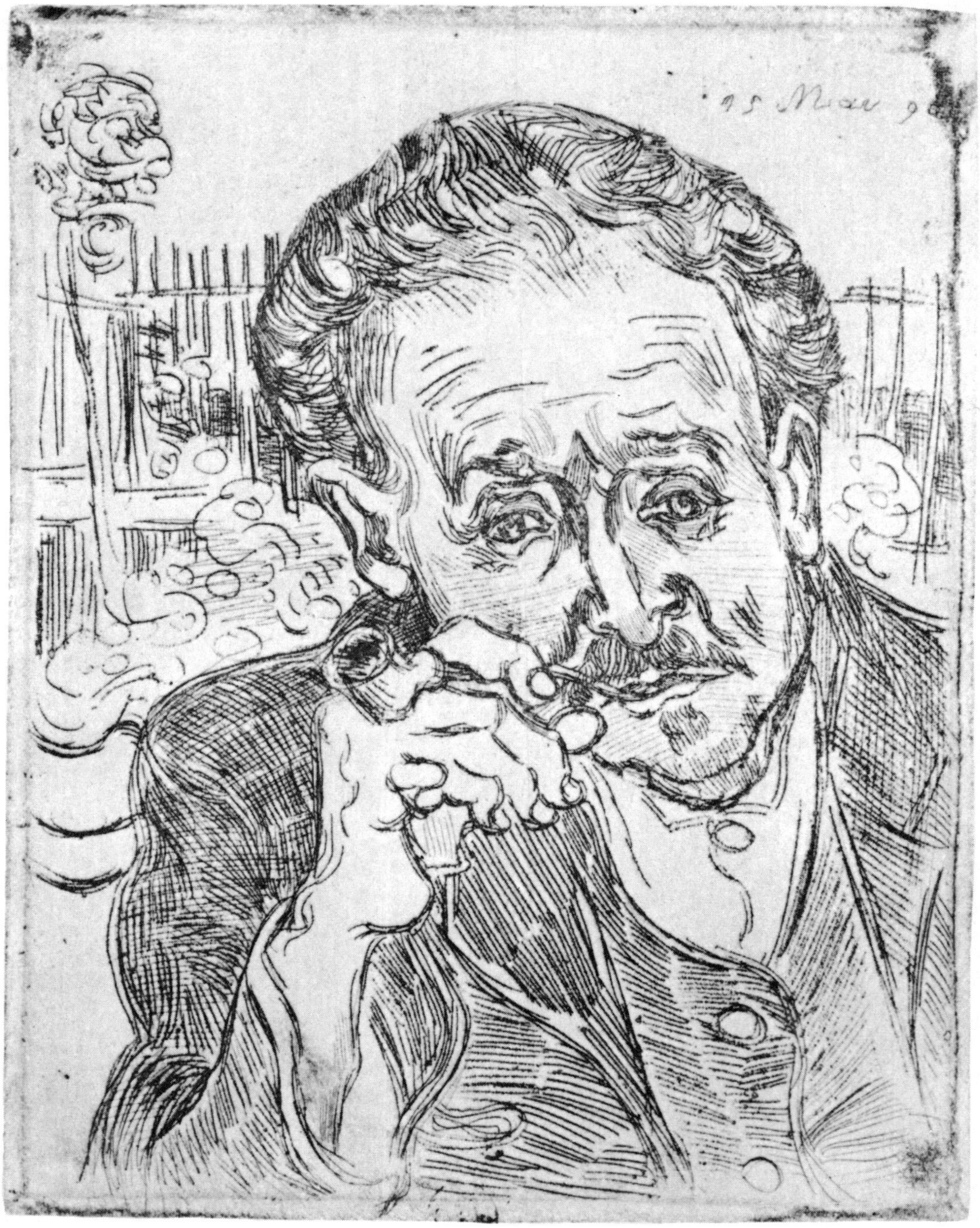